FABIO
CAPELLO

**THE MAN
THE DREAM
THE INSIDE STORY**

FABIO CAPELLO

THE MAN
THE DREAM
THE INSIDE STORY

MARK RYAN

BOOKS

First published in Great Britain in 2008 by
JR Books, 10 Greenland Street, London NW1 0ND
www.jrbooks.com

A catalogue record for this book is available from the British Library.

ISBN 978-1-906217-78-5

1 3 5 7 9 10 8 6 4 2

Typeset by SX Composing DTP, Rayleigh, Essex
Printed by MPG Books, Bodmin, Cornwall

Photography: Page 6, top; page 7, top; page 8/9 bottom left and right; and pages 10-16 © PA Photos

CONTENTS

For my four-year-old son Luca – even though he thinks that animals and dinosaurs are more interesting than football.

ACKNOWLEDGEMENTS

WHEN I FIRST THOUGHT ABOUT WRITING THIS BOOK IN March 2008 I had no idea of the adventures and challenges that lay ahead. I was only able to complete the story so swiftly, in order that one of football's most intriguing characters can be celebrated in a colourful yet objective way, because of the help of various key people. Though this is by no means an official biography, I am extremely grateful to Fabio Capello and some of those close to him, including some members of his family, for the assistance they felt able to give me in order to paint what I hope is an accurate portrait of a fascinating England manager and his journey towards the top of world football. The idea that one can attempt to understand a man without examining his childhood and talking to his family is simply too absurd for words. The fact that Capello still took time to address many of my queries, even during an incredibly pressurised first year in England, says much about his character. The fact that he chose to do so, even after we had almost fallen out about a certain line of questioning I had taken, shows that Capello is more flexible and considerate than many of us had previously been led to believe. Again, I make no claim to be his official biographer, in any sense, or even his friend, but I feel he did pay attention to my needs when he could, and that warrants due acknowledgement here. I hope that he and those close to him will be pleased with the end result. I never sought to flatter him or avoid difficult issues in the telling of the inside story, and if I have earned some respect from him for that reason alone, it will be a bonus. He certainly has my respect for the way he rose from poverty and never forgot his roots; and for the way he handled a tricky first year in England and stuck to his guns.

Others have helped me, such as Marco Mataloni in the archives of the Rome-based newspaper, *Corriere dello Sport*, and countless Italian journalists who have always remained supportive friends, ever since the days of Paul Gascoigne's eventful stay at Lazio. Even those I didn't previously know, such as Gianni Mura of *La Repubblica* and Sara Faillaci of *Vanity Fair*, have shown the wonderful Italian generosity of spirit that makes theirs one the world's greatest countries. Dealing with Italian journalists has made sports journalism so enjoyable over the years. Meanwhile Croatian reporter Sanjin Spanovic and photographer Bruno Konjevic deserve thanks for their assistance with some of the pictures included here.

At JR Books I must pay tribute to Jeremy Robson for backing the project through thick and thin, and for his impeccable guidance on structure and tone when the temptation was to try to be too clever. I hope and believe that his reward is a book on Capello that includes something for everyone, even those who are more interested in the make-up of successful people than football itself. Lesley Wilson, Senior Editor at JR Books, put up with my bad temper and approached problems with the sort of patience and cool professionalism that is a cornerstone in any publishing house. We got there in the end, Lesley, as we always knew we would. My copy editor Chris Stone also has much to do with that arrival.

At home my wife Victoria gave me the benefit of her technical expertise on many a tricky day, and my son Luca put up with his daddy spending too much time in front of the computer. As the dedication suggests, he would have been more enthusiastic about the project had I been writing a book about animals, but he has already vowed to do that himself one day.

Finally, I would like to thank two other people: Julian Brand for inviting me out for a proper kickaround of a football when I was eight years old and still marvelling at Pele and the Brazil team that had won the 1970 World Cup; and Bal Bahia for giving me a similar chance when I was forty-six . . . and still in awe of the Brazil team that won the 1970 World Cup. Fundamentally I still love football in the same way I did when I was a kid, even after decades reporting the game for newspapers. Perhaps Fabio Capello loves it in a different way, and that's part of what this book is about. Enjoy!

CHAPTER 1
A PRAYER FOR ENGLAND

PUT YOURSELF IN FABIO CAPELLO'S SHOES. YOU ARE supposed to lead England to World Cup glory in South Africa, 2010. By then it will be 44 years since England last won the biggest tournament in football. Forty-four years of hurt – that's what people keep reminding you. But in your first few months in charge, the team fails to play with any sparkle. Even before you begin your World Cup qualification campaign, you feel the media have turned against you. Partly due to their hostility, the pressure is reaching uncomfortable levels. The serious competitive action is about to begin and you know it is time to deliver or face derision. You could be forgiven for wondering whether any individual has ever shouldered so much sporting expectation.

But then it emerges that the priest in Capello's home village has already seen a man endure just such an ordeal and prevail. Yes, the priest lets slip to Fabio's mother that he used to have a World Cup-winning coach among his congregation. And how did that coach overcome his troubles to win football's biggest prize? He showed a stubborn streak after being written off as a profound disappointment. He believed in his players, defied the growing pressure and inspired a quality of football that not only silenced his critics but won them over. Trusting in his own judgement, this man brought his country World Cup glory – after 44 years of hurt.

1

It sounded unbelievable; but Don Pierpaolo Soranzo, priest to Capello's mother Evelina in Pieris, northeastern Italy, was real enough. And Don Paolo, as he was known locally, felt understandably proud of his World Cup record. 'I was priest to Enzo Bearzot,' he confided in the summer of 2008. 'Bearzot was Italy's coach when they won the World Cup in Spain in 1982. Now maybe I'll be the priest of a second world champion. That would be nice.'

It seemed unlikely when England hadn't even managed to qualify for Euro 2008, and spent much of the year demonstrating why. But Don Paolo didn't think England fans should feel too disheartened. 'You know, when Bearzot took Italy to that World Cup in Spain, people didn't think he had much chance. "Get back home," they shouted, because Italy didn't start so well. But little by little the team gained momentum, believing in their ability . . . and then they won the tournament.'

Anyone lucky enough to have been in Rome the night Italy won that World Cup in 1982 would never forget it. The ancient city rocked all night as people danced on moving cars and ran huge flags down narrow streets. The rhythm of horns and drums became more and more frenzied as the night went on; this was football fever at its best. Italy hadn't won the World Cup since 1938. But could Capello do that for London and the rest of England?

The amiable priest laughed long and loud at the suggestion that 44 might just be the magic number; that Bearzot had cracked it for Italy and therefore it was Fabio's turn to do the same for his adopted country. Similarly, if Don Paolo had prayed for Bearzot's Italy, perhaps he could also pray for Capello's England? 'You're putting me in a difficult position,' he chuckled. 'There is Fabio to consider, it is true, and I am keeping an eye on England's results; but then there is Italy to consider too. As for God, He doesn't take sides in sport. I will pray for a return to the old sporting values, so that people come before money in football. I will pray for joy, and for football's power to act as a unifying force.'

Although God does not take sides in sport, it soon became clear that Don Paolo, as a mere mortal, had remained an Italy fan. But it was equally clear, the longer we talked, that he was also supporting England in their bid to qualify for South Africa in 2010. That was a comfort in itself, given his record as a World Cup-winning priest; it appeared prudent to have Don Paolo on board. Even though you sometimes wondered whether Capello and England would get anywhere near South Africa in 2010, history had shown that anything could happen when the main event started. What if England made it to the tournament and defending champions Italy were knocked out early? Would the holy man with World Cup glory on his CV support England then? 'Yes,' Don Paolo confirmed happily. 'In that case I will support England and Fabio.'

It wasn't quite the same as the promise of a prayer, but then England's football team was quite used to not having a prayer. They needed all the help they could get, and the Almighty seemed to like Don Paolo's football managers. If Capello and England could stay together long enough, perhaps the 'Don Paolo-44' factor would kick in to write some new football history. It was about time from England's point of view. The events of 1966 seemed so long ago that they didn't just belong to another century – they belonged to another world. Fabio Capello's life had certainly been very different back then.

Capello was relaxing in his home town of Pieris on 30 July 1966 – the last time the Three Lions became the number one football force on the planet. Fabio remembers it well, although the sight of a toothless Nobby Stiles, England's tenacious midfielder, dancing round Wembley with the World Cup didn't spark wild celebrations in Capello's particular corner of Europe. You had to hand it to Fabio 42 years later, because in this spin-driven age he could have told me he had supported England all the way in that unforgettable final, as they eventually overcame West Germany 4-2. He could have claimed that the sheer drama of that sunny day created a burning ambition in his heart. He could have gone all teary-eyed and explained how, in that very moment, he had decided to follow in Sir Alf Ramsey's footsteps, and lead England to World Cup glory one day. But Fabio doesn't make PR noises just to please others. The reality back then was that he didn't even know he wanted to become a coach – and he wasn't even cheering for England.

In 1966 Fabio was already a promising midfielder with Spal Ferrara in Italy's top-flight, Serie A. It was high summer and he had time to visit his family in Pieris, not far from Venice. His parents still hadn't bought a television, so Capello went to the local bar to watch the World Cup Final live from Wembley stadium. Fabio didn't care which team won; he was just interested in the final as a sporting contest. As it turned out, the man who scored West Germany's opener, Helmut Haller, was destined to become a team-mate and friend at Juventus just four years later.

Capello watched enthusiastically enough as the game entered extra time; but since he was no England fan, bias could not persuade him that Geoff Hurst's controversial second, England's extra-time third, went over the line when it came down off the underside of the crossbar. As Wembley went wild, Fabio took it all in and decided that the officials had made a mistake.

As we all know by now, it was the definitive moment in England's football history, and Hurst's captain, Bobby Moore, went on to lift the trophy. But as London and the rest of the country celebrated, Capello felt no elation. Then, as now, he considered himself to be first and foremost an Italian. But Capello is also the consummate football professional, a man who goes where the most fascinating challenges take him; and later in life it wasn't Italy but England who asked him to be their national manager.

It was a curious turn of fate that a man who didn't even support England for that 1966 final could end up as the manager upon whom all English dreams depended. This would be a tough challenge, perhaps the toughest of all, because England certainly didn't have a Kaka or a Cristiano Ronaldo in their line-up. But when Capello's name was connected with the job following the sacking of Steve McClaren, he seemed to think that, by harnessing the potential England had always possessed, he could succeed where others had failed. Fabio declared, 'All coaches would like to coach England, above all to take on such a difficult challenge, seeing that England's national team has won nothing since 1966. With all the great players they have had, I still can't explain how they have only won one World Cup. A team comprised of all these great players in the past and present, only one World Cup, I don't understand it.'

Fabio was convinced he could break that disappointing England run. 'It would be really nice to finish my career with a World Cup win,' he explained. 'I've always had a winning mentality.' The Football Association liked what they heard, and wondered if he might just be able to inspire England to World Cup glory in the same way he had inspired AC Milan to the Champions League in 1994. Barcelona's cocky coach back then, Johan Cruyff, had written off Milan's players in a shocking display of arrogance before the final. Cruyff seemed to assume that his so-called Dream Team wouldn't just win the cup but thrash their Italian opposition. So Capello looked his men in the eye and virtually challenged their masculinity in the face of such disrespect.

'If you have balls,' Fabio told his players, 'you cannot lose this match.' AC Milan produced the performance of a lifetime and won 4-0 to make history.

Is coaching really that simple? Capello assured me it isn't. The trick to motivation, he explained, is to know the right time to speak. Sometimes you need to talk a lot, sometimes much less. That seems logical enough; but how do we know when to rant and rave, and when to come up with a classic one-liner? This seems to be a fundamental question, since the difference between a good and a bad coach depends on such timing. According to Capello, it all depends on what you see in the faces of the players. That's it. Look into the eyes.

England fans were waiting for Capello to issue the '*Coglioni* Challenge' (*coglioni* means 'balls' in Italian) to their stars too, preferably on the afternoon of a World Cup final. You could almost picture it: Brazil the overwhelming favourites; Rooney, Ferdinand and the boys written off as hopeless also-rans. With the Samba beat thumping through the dressing room walls, Fabio walks in, eyeballs his players and says: 'If you have balls, if you are real men, you cannot lose this match.' Rooney, Rio and the lads go out and give the Brazilians a masterclass; they thrash the South Americans 4-0 and lift England's second World Cup.

It may have been no more than a fanciful dream, but England

seemed to need all the motivation they could get if they were to reach that 2010 World Cup. The friendly matches before qualification started had been dreadful, and it was clear that England lacked a top quality goalkeeper and striker during that worrying phase. However, as Fabio knew only too well, he would not have been given the chance to manage the team if England's strikers and goalkeepers had performed well enough to help their country qualify for Euro 2008 under Steve McClaren. The problems had created his opportunity, and now they required a solution. Unfortunately, as the summer of 2008 drew to a close, it began to look as though it would take a magician rather than a coach to turn England into world-beaters. Still, such fantasies are what sustain football fans; and just occasionally a strange momentum takes over to make those dreams a delicious reality.

The FA was dreaming almost as wildly as the fans when they appointed Capello. Within a few months of Fabio's arrival they had made it clear that they had extremely high expectations. Brian Barwick, still England's powerful chief executive back then, certainly talked a good game.

'England's qualification for major tournaments is a must,' he said in April 2008. 'And our objective is to reach at least the semi-finals. That means we are then in the mix at the sharp end of tournaments, with a real chance of winning them.'

Easy to say, wasn't it? Capello was the man who had to deliver. But then Fabio had once looked me in the eye with a steely kind of stare and told me that fear simply wasn't an emotion with which he was familiar. So we could safely assume that he wasn't going to get spooked by Barwick and his soundbites.

'I don't feel any pressure,' he said calmly. 'I am here with the intention of doing good things. You need to improve from one time to the next, with a view to achieving the important target we have set.'

He had almost nailed the classic English football cliché already – one game at a time. If England fans had seen genuine improvement from one game to the next in the early Capello days, they could have lived with the cliché. But through the friendlies in 2008, there was no evidence of any improvement at all. Understandably, the fans became uneasy. The World Cup dream had to be driven by a reasonable level of football, especially if supporters were to retain any kind of belief in their new messiah. Worried, the fans began to ask whether Capello was really the right man for the England job. Who was the man behind the tough-guy persona?

CHAPTER 2
CREATING CAPELLO

WHEN FABIO WAS BORN ON 18 JUNE 1946, IT MEANT yet another mouth to feed in the already crowded Capello household. As a youngster, life was a little cramped for Fabio in his family's modest apartment in Pieris. Although he claims that there was always enough food to eat, it must have been a pretty close-run thing. Capello told me that he was one of six people living in that small apartment, and they were all surviving on one man's weekly wage. Fabio, his grandfather and grandmother, his mother and sister were all dependent on his father, Guerrino's modest earnings as a schoolteacher. Fabio's mother Evelina told me she found ways to chip in too sometimes, though occasional odd jobs would hardly have eased the constant pressure.

Much of the Gorizia region of northeastern Italy was stricken by poverty. Yet the Capello family still had reason to be thankful, because it was a miracle that Guerrino was with them at all. Indeed, given the hardships his father had been through, it was truly miraculous that Fabio Capello was ever born.

As he pointed out later, 'My father conceived me after having been imprisoned in Nazi concentration camps. He was taken to six different camps in all. He was so devastated by them that he never wanted to talk about that experience, not with me or my mother.' Guerrino Capello might easily have died in one of those Nazi concentration camps at any time during the last two years of the Second World War.

In a way it was a cruel irony that he should have suffered so much at the hands of Adolf Hitler's Nazis. Fabio's sister Bianca Soprano explained: 'My father was a great Italian patriot, but his side of the family were from Hungary.' The country had historical links with the Germans, but that wasn't all. Hitler had learned so many of his fascist techniques by watching Benito Mussolini thrive in Italy. And like many Italians, Guerrino had begun the war on the side of Mussolini's Fascists.

Capello's sister admitted her father's wartime loyalty to a man condemned by history. She told me: 'At the time my father was for Mussolini. In time my father recognised all the errors Mussolini had made. And of course when someone loses, the natural reaction is that everyone runs to the other side. But when the war started my father wasn't much more than 20 years old, and they didn't have all the different things that young people have to occupy their minds now. There were things about Mussolini which seemed attractive at the time. In life there isn't just one side that is completely right and the other that is completely wrong.'

Mussolini represented strength, order, discipline and a brighter future, or so Guerrino thought. In addition, the dictator represented something even more fundamental – Italy herself – and Guerrino loved Italy. Living in the village of Pieris, an hour or two northeast of Venice, there was a feeling that the communists across the border in Yugoslavia, as it was then, might want to claim this part of Italy for themselves.

As Fabio Capello explained later, 'From when I was almost a baby I can remember people saying that there was a risk that the border with Yugoslavia might be moved onto the nearby Isonzo River, which would mean that our territory and Pieris would have been handed over to Yugoslavia. We were always ready to evacuate, to move in order to stay Italian.'

So it was understandable that a young Guerrino, doubtless ignorant of the worst consequences of fascism, would favour a man like Mussolini, who could eliminate the perceived threat from over the border and bring back Italy's sense of pride. And long before

Fabio came along, Guerrino's love of Italy had manifested itself in his own village. He had a keen sense of responsibility to his own little community, and he was already an energetic young teacher at the local primary school. On the football field, meanwhile, he had helped inspire tiny AC Pieris to punch way above its weight in Serie C, the third tier of Italian national football. With just a few hundred inhabitants at the time, Pieris had found its way onto the national sporting map as the tiniest place ever to have a team in Serie C. It seems incredible now that such a small population could sustain a club in a division just two below the Italian equivalent of the Premier League.

Even when war came to Europe, Guerrino continued to play a proud part in the AC Pieris Serie C team. A picture of the 1940–41 side is included in this book. Perhaps Guerrino senior could have risen to even greater heights as a footballer, had the war not changed everything. But soon he found himself part of a far deadlier game than football.

By the time he was called up to Mussolini's Royal Army for serious action he had already married Evelina, Fabio's mother, and conceived Bianca, their first baby. Evelina recalled, 'When the war started in 1939, he was here in Italy; then he went to Yugoslavia with his battalion because he was doing his military service there.'

Guerrino went into an artillery unit for the invasion of Yugoslavia by Italian forces in April 1941. But when Italy pulled out of the war suddenly on 8 September 1943, in what Italians call the 'armistice', Guerrino was stranded in what is now Croatia. He faced a race against time to get home to safety before he suffered the consequences of Mussolini's downfall. Unfortunately for Fabio's father, it was a race he lost. He was left very vulnerable as the Germans took revenge for the decision of their former ally.

Evelina explained, 'He departed on a train at five o'clock in the morning and he was in the town of Fiume (in what is now Croatia) when the Germans arrested him and took him prisoner. That was the start of two or three very hard years for him.' Along with many other Italian servicemen, he was sent to Germany for what would soon become an even bigger personal battle – for survival against starvation and Allied bombs. Evelina added, 'He was near the border with Holland a lot; they were always transferring him. And when they (the Allies) bombed Nuremberg he was a prisoner there, and he said they dropped so many bombs that I don't know how to explain it to you.'

Fabio wouldn't have been born if those bombs had hit the Italian prisoners, or for that matter Evelina back in Pieris. Bianca recalled, 'Some bombs dropped near us too; I think they were trying to hit the railway bridge which went over the nearby river. I remember my mother taking me to safety in her arms.'

For Guerrino, starvation was the more consistent threat to his dream of returning home to his wife and young daughter. In some ways the situation was just as painful for his wife, who knew how much he was suffering because the occasional letter would find a way through.

Bianca explained, 'My father wrote to my mother and said: "Please send me anything to eat that you can, even if it is just scraps of whatever you are having, such as polenta crusts." But all the systems in Italy had broken down and we were very, very poor; we had very little.'

Despite the chaos, Fabio's mother did all she could. Evelina explained, 'I wrote to him every week, and sent him baskets of food, but I don't think he received much. Sometimes he managed to write and ask for cigarettes.'

But cigarettes could not keep Guerrino alive and his body began to waste away. To compound his agony, he could see others being treated so well in certain camps that it was almost as though they were on holiday. Bianca explained, 'The Americans were being protected and sustained by the Red Cross, and some of them were even playing tennis.'

So Guerrino learned to help himself, and others. He had nothing to feed his body, but he could still feed his mind. Bianca spoke movingly about how Fabio's father overcame adversity. She said, 'He used to dream with his eyes open while he was suffering in the concentration camps. He would say, "Ah, I'm back home in Pieris, and everything is fine." He was an optimist, as we all are in our family, and his positive thinking helped to keep others alive too. I know this, because three years after the war was over, when I was eight, a package arrived with some *Torroncini* (pieces of nougat) and *liquori* (liquors). With them came a letter from a man who had been with Guerrino in Germany and he wrote: "This is to say thank you because without your positive spirit I don't think I would have stayed alive." '

At the time, there was considerable doubt whether any of the prisoners could stay alive long enough to return home. While his mind and spirit triumphed, Guerrino's body turned on itself. Just a little more war would have killed him, just as it killed 60,000 of his fellow countrymen in the German concentration camps alone.

Fabio's mother revealed, 'He went down to just 40 kilos (about 6 stone). The Americans saved him in the end. So many of the starving prisoners died after their liberation, because they went rushing out into the fields to eat potatoes or anything they could, and their bodies couldn't take so much food so suddenly. But when the Americans reached my husband in April 1945 they saved him by persuading him not to eat too much. He didn't want to come home in the state he was in and he realised that his recovery had to be gradual, so even though he was free in April he didn't actually get back to Pieris until September.'

His emotional ties to the village had sustained Guerrino. The buildings were simple and functional rather than beautiful like so much Italian architecture. The land was agricultural and pleasant enough, and some of the wines its fertile soil helped to create, such as the famed Sagrado, were heavenly. On a fine day the white, jagged peaks of the Dolomites could be seen tearing through the haze on the blue horizon. Venice was a couple of hours' drive along the coast, though in truth it belonged to another world. The location of the village gave rise to the inhabitants' nickname, *bisiachi*, which meant 'between two waters'. The place had a dour feel to it, and the people were neither country peasants nor dynamic city dwellers. Pieris' people were used to making sacrifices to maintain their everyday existence, and it gave them a profound balance without necessarily adding much flamboyance. Their character owed as much to Slav influences as it did to the fiery Latin temperament for which Italians are better known.

But there was no holding back when Guerrino saw Evelina again after all those years in captivity. Evelina recalled bashfully, 'Guerrino came back in September and in June Fabio was born!'

The young Capello was exposed to English influences from the start, because the region was under Anglo-American rule. The local English servicemen played a bit of football too, and Guerrino liked their style. By now it was 1946, Guerrino's strength had returned, and he was already back playing for his beloved AC Pieris in Italy's third division. But the local Italian footballers weren't just anxious to prove their sporting prowess against each other, they also had in their sights the occupying forces of Britain's Eighth Army, who had fought to liberate Italy from the Nazis in the preceding years. The match, played on 19 March 1946, would give Guerrino, and then, in time, Fabio, a lasting love of English football.

The AC Pieris football team was a hardy but skilful outfit full of canny characters. These young men were determined to express themselves and make their mark – to excel beyond the limitations of their surroundings; perhaps that is why Fabio Capello was able to reflect proudly, 'This little place of 1,200 inhabitants has given 15 players to Serie A.' Mario Tortul, Fabio's uncle, was one of them. He even played for Italy's B team.

The memorable match against 'the English' was actually a friendly between AC Pieris and the 'Gazelles', of nearby Villa Vicentina, where the Eighth Army had its barracks. In 2008, 83-year-old Bepi Fabris, who featured in that game for AC Pieris alongside Guerrino, told me, 'When we played that day, they said there were two players in the other team who had played for Arsenal before the war. There were a few more English in that Gazelles side too.'

The match had the feel of an unofficial Italy v England international, and AC Pieris upset the odds by winning 2-1. But it was the way the game was played, in a spirit best described as 'hard but fair', that everyone loved. 'The events of that day were one of the reasons why Fabio's father admired English football,' said Fabris. 'He had an affection for the people who had taught the world such a beautiful sport.' He passed that affection on to Fabio, whose England advisor Franco Baldini was quoted as saying,

'Capello thinks about England as the mother of the game and the teacher of football.'

Bianca has very clear memories of Guerrino talking enthusiastically about English football, and is in no doubt that young Fabio's love for the England national team originated in postwar conversations around the family table. She told me, 'England was the father of football, and for my father England was always an example to others. As he was a teacher, and also taught others to play football, he taught with England as the shining example. The English knew how to fight and play the game in a manly way. He loved the physical strength and discipline of their game; it was his ideal. He was still very patriotic for Italy, but I remember a speech by Winston Churchill about giving blood and tears for the cause, and this was the sort of thing that appealed to my father; it was an example for him, because he admired loyalty and sacrifice when the going got tough.

'I remember one time he split his head open during a match and needed to be bandaged up to prevent more blood loss, and yet he just played on. He was a hard man. Another time he had a badly swollen knee and there was less than a week to get him ready for the next match. You didn't have all the modern-day anti-inflammatory medicines in those days, so my mother used salt water and vinegar solutions, homemade concoctions based on what we did have. Sure enough, by the end of the week he was always ready to go out and play again.

'So he didn't just admire the English approach to sport, he showed that respect in the way he approached sport too. And when he said these things about how he loved the English way of playing, he said it in front of the family, because I remember it. So if I heard it then Fabio heard it too. For Fabio it was an education which may have gelled into an admiration later.'

At the turn of the millennium, admiration turned into ambition. Fabris, who has known the England manager since he was a boy, explained, 'People say that Fabio is the best coach around when it comes to discipline, serious work, responsibility and so on. Therefore for him to go and coach England, the country that gave football to the world, it is the Mount Olympus for him. It is the perfect end to his career. It will suit him, because he is the Field Marshal Montgomery of Football.'

The process which turned Fabio into a granite-faced commander of football's battlefields began painfully young. Guerrino appears to have been determined to ensure that, like himself, his son became a tough guy. One way was to make the future England manager hurl himself off cliffs and into the sea, beneath an English-held castle in a fairytale coastal resort.

It may not quite be Acapulco in Mexico, but the cliff-divers of Duino take themselves pretty seriously just the same, and rightly so. When Fabio joined them at the age of four, it was an early test of his courage. And the spectacular setting of Duino, below a castle in the province of Trieste, was a world away from the comparatively grim surroundings he was used to in Pieris, even though it was only a long cycle ride away.

Capello has talked of this, one of his most vivid childhood memories, something that helped to form the steely character we know today. In a superb in-depth interview with Gianni Mura of the quality Italian daily *La Repubblica* Fabio revealed, 'I remember when I was four years old we went on a trip to Duino, and he (Guerrino) helped me to climb up onto the rock and then he went down into the water and told me to throw myself in. It must have been 10 metres (30ft) up and I threw myself in, even though I was a bit of a reject as a swimmer.'

Fabio's mother recalled, 'They used to go to Duino, in the direction of Trieste, on bicycles. They went onto the rocks under the castle. There was a ledge on the rocks there, from which they could dive down into the sea. Bianca used to go too. Fabio was so small, only four, but he jumped down from 10 metres up. My husband carried him up and then went down first to wait for Fabio. He said it was character-building and I suppose it was, but I didn't want to watch.'

You can just imagine what he must have gone through before making his first jump from a height that would terrify most adults, let alone a tiny child who could barely swim. The fear, the adrenalin, and the conquering of his demons by following his father's iron will, must have been both traumatic and exhilarating moments for a four-year-old. But once he had leapt through that fear, Fabio must have felt practically indestructible, a feeling he seems to have carried with him into his football career.

Bianca remembers those days when her little brother was invited to summon the courage of an adult almost as though they were yesterday. For her, the memories are still amusing and beautiful, and once Fabio had taken the plunge a few times their father didn't even need to be on hand every time to save him in the sea.

'Duino is a magnificent place and I am lucky enough to have a little house there even now', she says. 'As children we went on bikes, with friends, and Fabio didn't know how to swim. You used to be able to climb down the rocks from near the castle at the top, down to the point where you could dive off. I don't know whether it was 10 metres because that is very high but it was 8 metres (24ft) for sure, and my friends and I would be waiting for Fabio when he came down and disappeared under the water.

'We weren't too worried that he couldn't swim, because he was like one of those babies who are somehow able to breathe when they are put under water; they don't choke and neither did Fabio. My friends and I would be waiting in the water to bring him back up to the surface in an instant just in case, or otherwise my father was there. First I think Fabio used to go feet first, but it was head first later.'

Down by Duino's picturesque little harbour, 85-year-old Giuseppe Boidi, a local cliff-diving expert, explained how anything could be achieved once fear was overcome on those cliffs.

'My friend Angelo, who was national diving champion of Yugoslavia three years running, goes from 20 metres (60ft) up, climbing from the beach until he is almost halfway up to the castle. He does a double somersault with half twist before entering the water. I was the champion from around here but I only used to do one somersault. So maybe Fabio threw himself down feet first as a four-year-old from that height of 10 metres, why not? That's the height of that tree there,' he added, pointing to a very tall tree by the quayside. 'But it can be done.'

By the age of nine, Capello had conquered similar dizzy heights again, this time headfirst. It was all too much for his mother

Evelina, who said, 'I didn't go to Duino on these trips because I was scared Fabio would smash his head open on the rocks. It wasn't just feet first, it was headfirst too when he dived into the sea.'

But the cliffs of Duino were not the only natural challenge Fabio accepted, despite the dangers. Most children are warned to stay away from fast-flowing rivers when they are young. Fabio decided instead to become an underwater spear fisherman in his local river. At first, his fishing expeditions on the fast-flowing Isonzo River followed more traditional techniques. A neighbour, Clara Ridolfi, remembered, 'Fabio and his father Guerrino used to go down the river in a little boat, fishing all the way to the mouth of the river, where it meets the sea.'

But that wasn't adventurous enough for little Fabio in the long run. In his interview with *La Repubblica's* Gianni Mura, the England manager recalled, 'We used to go hunting like scuba divers in the river, my friend Berto and I, with sharpened umbrella sticks attached to our wrists with bits of elastic. We'd pull up a few *cadevano* fish but we used to call them sharks.'

Clara explained, 'He might well have used an umbrella stick because he might not have been able to afford fancy equipment. We were all extremely poor if the truth be told. But the fish were there for the taking whether you had money or not. These *cadevano* were like trout, they could be small or up to a kilo or even a kilo and a half. The river water was so clear in the old days that you could drink it.'

But Fabio's sister said, 'It was very dangerous, fishing under the water like that, because the water was very cold. Still, children have no sense of fear, and we all learned to swim in the river, we were taught to do it.'

Fabio's mother recalls this time fondly. She explained, 'Fabio went spear fishing with another friend too, called Niccolino. One day they came back with a whole load of fish, big like trout, all attached to a line, which was slung over their shoulders. It was quite a sight, I can tell you.'

Even as a child, Fabio was turning into an excellent provider. With six mouths to feed in his household, his hunting skills would have been much appreciated. As for the underwater skills he was developing against the odds, they served him well in a lifetime of scuba diving all over the world with his wife Laura. By then he was a multi-millionaire and could afford some decent equipment.

Childhood strength was also challenged by an even more fearsome natural phenomenon – the 'Bora'. Clara Ridolfi, the Capellos' neighbour, explained, 'The Bora is a terrible wind and when it comes it blows at around 130 kilometres (80 miles) per hour. In Trieste, the sea port near here, you had to walk attached to each other with ropes when that wind came.' It used to hit Pieris too; indeed Fabio explained, 'For me, Pieris represents the memory of the Bora, which blew especially hard in February.'

Evelina remembered how her husband and son were determined to play football, whatever the conditions. 'The Bora was such a strong wind that for most of us it meant that we wouldn't even go out. But Fabio and Guerrino still used to play football in that wind, they were strong. The ball would blow around everywhere but they would adapt and it didn't matter.' Nothing got in the way of practice. Fabio explained, 'My father ... was a primary school teacher but he also taught football and I remember the routine. Stop, shoot. Stop, shoot.'

Fabio still chuckles at the memory of battling the Bora, and the way the ball used to boomerang back to him when he kicked it into the wind. That awesome adversary may even have helped him to improve his power and technique. If you didn't keep the ball down on the ground and deliver short, sharp passes to your father or friends, you were inviting a world of trouble. What a pity some of England's footballers didn't grow up with the Bora for company. Fabio recalled that it was difficult to play against the Bora, but he got used to it and mastered the art. Pretty soon mere mortals were an easy opposition by comparison.

Clara Ridolfi remembered, 'Fabio's father would come home from teaching at the primary school and in the afternoon he would take him to the local football field and they would practise for hours. I tell you one thing, every bit of success Fabio has had at football he deserves, because he worked so hard at it from the start.'

Elisa Cosolo, who was later taught by Guerrino at the school, said, 'Fabio's father always wanted him to have a diploma first, before becoming a footballer. He pushed him hard, as he pushed himself.'

But Fabio's mother said, 'You couldn't call Guerrino a pushy football dad because Fabio used to want to play anyway, and he would go out into the courtyard here or even out on the street with the other kids from the age of three or four. The football pitch here in Pieris used to be right by the house in those days, before they moved it, so he was out there all the time too.'

Football dominated the lives of father and son, however the village team was doing. Guerrino's AC Pieris were relegated from the Serie C to the regional Division One for the 1947–48 season. A restructuring of the Italian leagues meant that their return to national standing was blocked. Even though they bounced back as champions, AC Pieris were placed in a newly created division, which fell short of Serie C's national football status. They fought hard just the same, and by the time Guerrino began to disappear from the photographs of the AC Pieris line-up at the start of the 1950s, he could look back proudly on a career as a player.

By 1954–55 Guerrino Capello was back – as coach of the *Ragazzi*, the AC Pieris Boys. And in 1956–57 a family dream came true, as father and son joined forces. Guerrino was in charge of the younger *Giovanili* (youth) of AC Pieris, and a picture of the team shows one boy who looked considerably smaller in stature than the others – Fabio Capello. The photograph included here shows father and son, coach and player, at opposite ends of the line-up, after Fabio's team had beaten Aquileia 5-1 in April 1957. A smiling Fabio was almost eleven by then, but he doesn't look much more than seven. His physical strength would come in time. Mentally he was already strong, bolstered by what he told me was a very special feeling, playing for a very special kind of coach.

As for Guerrino, he may no longer have been a formidable player, but he was determined to lead his local club into the future just the same, and coaching his son was just part of his wider vision. His old team-mate, Bepe Fabris, told me, 'He had come home from the war, and played plenty of football. Then I was with him one day when he said, "We must have a new football pitch near the school." He was a schoolmaster and a coach, and he had a great passion for both.'

Guerrino was one of life's givers, but he also had a stubborn streak, as Evelina explained: 'He used to make the sign of the cross before lessons and the children did the same, but later on, when the authorities told him he couldn't do that for political reasons, he stopped teaching. He was a good man, a righteous man; he never said a bad word about anyone.'

Even when he was teaching, money was extremely tight, and Evelina remembers how she had to help her husband financially so that the respect he commanded at the local football club wasn't undermined, especially while he was organising the construction of its new home. She explained, 'Here they were building a new football field, but there was no money. I had to give Guerrino five lire (a few old pennies) every Sunday so that he could afford a cup of tea or something after a match. He was coach, president, everything for the boys' team, but he didn't even have enough money to pay for a cup of tea – nothing. He spent everything he could on football. If he wasn't here with me, he was overseeing the new football field being built, or travelling around for football.'

The club's vice-president, Franco Stefano, said, 'I can remember Fabio's father when he was coach of the men's team, and youth team, and also the groundsman. He sowed the seeds when the pitch was just mud and turned it into grass.'

And now that Fabio was in the team, as a tough and perceptive midfielder, there was an extra motivation for all that hard work. But whether Fabio was playing at home or away, the rules were always the same for his mother. Evelina recalled, 'I wasn't allowed to go and see him play, because Fabio didn't want me to go. He was a big mummy's boy in many ways, but not when it came to football. I don't know why, he was just like that, perhaps he was ashamed of the idea of having his mother there watching him. The fathers used to go, the women didn't. To tell the truth I didn't mind not being invited all that much, because I didn't want to act like the pushy mum, shouting for him on the touchline and all that.

'But one time when he was playing in Pieris Guerrino said, "Come on, come and watch, see him play." He was so happy that

Fabio was turning into such a good footballer and he wanted me to see for myself. So I watched through a little hole in a screen, which was supposed to stop people from seeing the matches from outside. He was always good at football, even when he was little, and as he grew he became even better.'

Meanwhile, on the world stage England were still regarded as one of the great teams in the 1950s. The exploits of Stanley Matthews captivated Fabio and his father. Matthews had written his name into football history when Fabio was only a toddler, starring in England's 4-0 demolition of Italy in Turin in 1948. He had also played in England's 10-0 win over Portugal in Lisbon. Although 'The Wizard of the Dribble' was no longer at his peak when Capello was growing up, he was already regarded as a living legend. Matthews won the first ever European Footballer of the Year award in 1956, when Capello was 10. Incredibly, the Englishman was already 41, and continued to wear the England shirt until the following year. Even in 2008, Stanley Matthews is the name that most readily comes to Capello's lips when he talks about how he first fell in love with the English game. Teetotal, vegetarian and superbly disciplined, Matthews 'The Magician' was able to play until he was 55. To Capello, who was brought up to value self-discipline above all, he was the perfect example.

By early 1961, Fabio Capello was a strong young 14-year-old who had almost outgrown AC Pieris, even though the club's new stadium was finally ready to take the team into a new era, and he was still being photographed with the *Ragazzi* team. Bigger clubs had come calling, and Fabio was about to leave home. Pieris had been a tough training ground. Now he was ready to test his mettle elsewhere.

CHAPTER 3
LOVE AND MARRIAGE, ROME AND SWINDON

FOOTBALL MAY BE MOSTLY ABOUT MONEY THESE DAYS, BUT Fabio Capello's father Guerrino didn't see it that way. Fabio told Gianni Mura of *La Repubblica* just what Guerrino had sacrificed in order to stay true to himself.

Capello junior explained, 'I left home at 14 to join Spal 1907 in the city of Ferrara. They were in Serie A at the time. It wasn't the best weather change, from the wind to thick fog and heat without a breath of fresh air. There were other requests for my signature, one from a team called Marzotto in Serie B, trained by Cestmir Vycpalek (Fabio's future coach at Juventus). And after my father had already given his word to Paolo Mazza, the president of Spal, AC Milan came calling in the person of Gipo Viani. This man Viani said I had a compass instead of feet because my passing was so accurate, and he offered double what Spal had agreed to pay. But in those times it was figured that someone's word was his bond (or *parola e parola* in Italian). And as far as I was concerned, whatever my father decided was OK by me.'

His mother seemed proud of her late husband's stand back in 1961 – even if they could have done with the knock-on benefits of a bigger deal for Fabio with a bigger club. Evelina revealed later, 'That has always stuck in my mind. Milan wanted Fabio at all costs, they were prepared to give more money to my husband if only he would leave Fabio to them, but Guerrino said, "No, I have given my word." *Parola e parola.'*

Viani, who had helped to turn AC Milan into the European force they remain to this day, simply couldn't believe that Fabio's father was potentially risking the boy's future at the highest level for the sake of a promise he had made just a few days earlier. 'Do something,' he urged Guerrino. 'Tell Mazza that you were confused the day you promised Fabio to Spal, that you weren't feeling yourself. Invent an excuse; say you were drunk. You certainly weren't in possession of all your mental faculties when you made that agreement. I guarantee you money in the bank for your son and for the family if he comes to Milan.'

Guerrino just kept replying the same way, his arms outstretched as though further conversation was futile. 'I gave my word, and that's it,' he explained. Mazza, who had been part of Italy's technical team at the 1962 World Cup in Chile, had secured his young star for a bargain price. AC Pieris are reported to have received less than a thousand pounds in the deal.

As it turned out, the transfer to Spal could be said to have represented the right move for Capello junior, both morally and personally. There were advantages to starting off at the smaller club. One of the greatest of those advantages in Capello's case was that he soon found himself being coached in the Spal youth team by a man twenty years his senior, called Giovan Battista Fabbri. 'He was a very important coach in my career,' confirmed Fabio later.

'Gibi' Fabbri could even be said to have invented 'Total Football' long before the Dutch had ever thought of such a concept. He once set out his philosophy by saying, 'Every player in my team is involved in every move; no one wastes the ball. When we attack, we all attack and it starts with the goalkeeper. When we defend, we all defend and it starts with the striker. Each outfield player should be covering the same amount of ground, and if the sweeper drives forward then the midfielder becomes the sweeper.' Dutch coaches later became famous for promoting the ability of each member of their teams to be able to play in any position. Fabbri already seemed to be thinking along those lines several years earlier, and he would go on to influence Enzo Bearzot, Italy's 1982 World Cup winning coach, when they worked together at Torino.

Capello was also captivated by Fabbri, who allowed him to express his natural strength of character. An early colleague in the youth team, Gigi Pasetti, remembered Fabio like this: 'He was already a coach on the field, definite and commanding in his ways, not too fast but always anticipating where the ball would come and always able to send it where he wanted to. Off the field he was witty, kind and good company. He used to go out with the young lads from his part of Italy and enjoy a sandwich and a glass of wine.'

Already a leader among his peers, Capello nevertheless completely idolised one of the senior professionals at his club, a player called Oscar Massei. An Argentine 12 years Fabio's senior, Massei may well have been one of the big reasons behind the haughty Capello demeanour still in evidence today. Having already played for Inter Milan and Triestina, Massei acted as though he knew it all, and he probably did.

Capello recalled, 'He was out of this world and he played as I intended to. He taught me everything about football. I watched him in training, I really scrutinised everything about him, and I learned. My father also said, "Now that is what I call a player." He taught me everything I knew. Perhaps he was excessively proud, but I have always had pride.'

With men like Massei to learn from, Fabio knew he was in the right place; but life still wasn't easy. Capello explained, 'That was a traumatic passage from one chapter of my life to another, because in the first year I was in some lodgings organised by Spal, and there was no telephone in the house, and I used to write two letters a week to my family because I was homesick. When my father understood that I was down, he came to see me.' He was young to be living away from home, and he learned to dig in and appreciate what he had. Life improved somewhat when he moved into new lodgings. He explained, 'I moved into a house belonging to two old spinsters whose cooking was divine. And in these first years I struck up a great friendship with my Spal team-mate, Edy Reja, which has lasted the best part of half a century.'

Since the young Fabio had shown himself to be an intelligent boy at school in Pieris, with Maths one of his stronger subjects, he continued to study at Ferrara, aiming to use his geometry skills to qualify as a surveyor. He took bus rides to class and that was how something wonderful happened. Fabio remembered, 'Ferrara is a beautiful city, and I am not just saying that because of whom I met there.' He wasn't talking about his friend Reja, but about his girlfriend. His mother Evelina recalled the life-changing development, and how she heard about it second-hand. 'My daughter Bianca told me the news one day, because Fabio told her first, not me. She said, "Mamma, Fabio has found a *fidanzata*" (a serious girlfriend).'

Bianca confirmed, 'I had just come back from Germany and went to see Fabio in Ferrara, and he told me about this beautiful blonde girl he had met. He was so happy.' Fabio also remembered this period with joy, and said simply, 'Ferrara is where I met my wife Laura. We took the same bus. She was studying to become a teacher one day; I was studying to be a surveyor.'

When Laura Ghisi, from a village outside Bologna, fell into a conversation with Capello on that number five bus, she could hardly have known that she was talking to a man with whom she was destined to spend the next 40 years or more. Though it sounds romantic, Capello insists that it wasn't a case of love at first sight at all. There have even been suggestions down the years that Laura initially considered Fabio to be rather too surly and silent. But he must have found the right words and warmth to touch her soul somewhere along the line, because friendship turned to romance eventually, even though Capello told me that it took a good few months to win Laura's heart. The secrets of courtship are personal, though we can safely assume that Fabio didn't woo his future wife by wearing ankle socks – one of his pet hates. 'I can't stand them,' he once said gravely. 'When a man crosses his legs and the trouser leg rides up to show hairy shins, it offends my eyes.'

Whatever Laura thought of Fabio's shins, when he finally exposed them to her, they don't seem to have put her off, hairy or otherwise. Romance, when it came, had an enduring depth to it. 'Laura is my life, my mirror,' Fabio once said in a rare show of emotion.

Capello was turning into a man, although that long process had probably started on the cliffs of Duino when he was only four. To make his happiness complete, there was progress on the football field too. His patience and hard work paid off on 29 March 1964, when he made his Serie A debut as a 17-year-old against Sampdoria in Genoa. Not that his big day, or even the climax to the season, really followed the script. Fabio recalled, 'We were winning 1-0 and then they did us with three goals, one more stupid than the other. But I didn't play badly.' After that 3-1 defeat, however, he only played three more games in his first campaign. Unfortunately Spal were relegated to Serie B at the end of his debut season. But Fabio had made a personal breakthrough, and he had learned how to survive as a growing teenager in a man's world.

Gianfranco Bozzao, a tough and experienced team-mate, recalled, 'Capello was a good lad, very educated and religious, and he was respectful towards everyone. He wasn't that durable physically back then, he would go strong for 20 minutes and then fade. The oldies like me had to step in to help manage the situation then, but we did it willingly because he was likeable and Mazza was definite about using him.'

Though relegation hurt Capello, he was gradually learning how to leave football disappointment behind, and besides the good times would return to Spal soon enough. First Capello had an operation to solve a cartilage problem he had in a nagging left knee. Meanwhile Mazza, a terrific wheeler-dealer, strengthened his squad and ensured that they bounced straight back up the following season, with Fabio fit and on fire.

By the 1965–66 campaign, Spal were making a big impact on Italian football again, with Capello playing a starring role in midfield and his pal Reja almost as impressive. When Spal beat Roma 2-0, that midfield was packed with young men who were barely 20. The boys from Ferrara turned it on around the country, showing how much promise they had. Transfer dealers at the bigger clubs would remember Fabio's displays a year later. Life for Fabio was exciting, and the future couldn't come soon enough. In February 1966 Capello attended his sister Bianca's wedding. Since he was already in love and remained religious, he could have been forgiven for wondering whether his own wedding day might not be all that far away, even though he wasn't yet 20. Professional objectives were more pressing, however, and the immediate target was to keep Spal in Serie A. This time Fabio helped his team to do just that with the decisive game against Brescia ending in a nail-biting 2-2 draw in Ferrara on the last, tension-filled day of the season.

On 30 July, England won the World Cup. The Italians had suffered the humiliation of being knocked out at the early group stage having lost to North Korea. But Fabio wasn't looking for another country to support instead of Italy, even if he did respect players like Bobby Charlton and warm to England's fighting mentality.

He did know that he wanted to play in a World Cup one day though. England had set the standard to which Italy and Fabio, if ever he made it onto the full international stage, had to aspire. His promise had already been recognised in the form of appearances for Italy's under-23 team, and he was also picked to represent the Italian League side. Such honours would amount to some 26 appearances in all for junior Italy teams.

But it would take a big leap to break into the senior Italy team, and he was still a long way from making that dream come true. Indeed the 1966–67 season was a tricky one for Capello, who suffered another knee injury which sidelined him for half the season. Although he required another operation, he bounced back and did enough to help Spal stay in Serie A. However, it proved to have been his last campaign on behalf of his first professional club.

His 47 Serie A appearances for Spal brought him only three goals; but then scoring wasn't his job anyway, and he would learn that craft better in years to come. Already his reading of the game, his eye for an incisive pass and the stabilising influence he brought to midfield had attracted the biggest talent-spotters in the Italian game. Internazionale of Milan – better known as 'Inter' – wanted to sign him. But Roma wanted Capello even more, and Spal did a deal to transfer their star youngster south to the capital for 250 million lire – around £100,000 – in the summer of 1967.

Fabio and Laura were confident their romance would survive his rising stardom and his glamorous move to the Italian capital. The relationship never had been based on the glitzy, superficial trappings of professional football. Laura didn't love Fabio just because he was a footballer. She wasn't even a great fan of the game. Meanwhile Fabio loved Laura for her mind as much as her beauty. He described her like this: 'She is an intelligent woman, very intelligent, it is a really important virtue and not very widespread.'

Laura was no shallow football groupie – and she was certainly no gold-digger. Fabio wasn't even earning big money yet anyway, though he was doing well enough for a 21-year-old. But Laura was too classy to be excessively materialistic, and the hero worship players received didn't seduce her. She saw through it all and she remained herself. Later, as a coach, Capello would tell his players to find a similar sort of woman for themselves if they could, rather than succumb to a more superficial type of admirer. He recognised that potential distractions were even greater in the modern game than they had been when he was a player.

Fabio once revealed, 'I tell my players that girls hang around them because modern-day footballers already have millions in their bank accounts by the age of 25. Before such girls used to hang around film stars or television celebrities, now it is the turn of footballers, who are also robustly built and this helps them a lot. These girls are all the same, all part of a set. Adjusted here, puffed up there. They are all interchangeable and all false. I like classy women, such as Virna Lisi and Catherine Deneuve.'

And above all, back in the 1960s, he liked Laura Ghisi; but what was he going to do about it? They weren't going to live together out of wedlock; Fabio was a traditional Catholic and he didn't want that. He knew what he wanted for them, and it was only a matter of time.

Laura travelled down to see him whenever she could, and this new chapter in the love affair could hardly have been played out against the backdrop of a more romantic city. But Capello was captivated by the Italian capital for other reasons too. He had always possessed an ability to apply his intellect beyond the boundaries of football, and Rome had plenty of ways to stimulate the mind. His last days as a single man were still vivid in his memory many years later. It wasn't that he felt any desire to chase other women. The eternal city of Rome herself would be his second love.

'Dazzling,' said Capello looking back. 'That's the only way to describe Rome at that time.' No wonder. The 1960s was the era of *La Dolce Vita*, the glamorous Roman lifestyle immortalised by Federico Fellini. There was simply no better time in modern history to be in one of the world's greatest cities.

Capello explained, 'I went all around Rome on foot, guided as I walked by a friend called Rubens Ricci, who wasn't actually Roman but was in love with the place. How could you not fall in love with Rome at that time? Trastevere (the old, Bohemian sector) was still a real place at that time, not for tourists. We used to go to restaurants there such as *da Brozzi*, or *alla Balduina*, places where you would find the most splendid people. And in that period I began to become passionate about politics.'

But it was virtually impossible to live in Rome at that time and be consumed by politics alone. Sophisticated Fabio also developed a love for films, especially the art-house work of the great Fellini and Luchino Visconti. You could add to that heady mix the best of English music, for even the Roman airwaves were vibrating to the sound of the Rolling Stones and The Beatles. But again, Capello showed more refined musical tastes too. He loved the jazz of Ella Fitzgerald and the classical genius of Mozart and Bach.

In this explosion of intellectual stimulation, with politics, art, music and film rushing around in his head on a daily basis, it was a wonder that Fabio found time to concentrate on football at all. In fact under his first coach at Roma, Oronzo Pugliese, Capello's maiden season was interrupted by more physical problems. He only played 11 times and the club finished 11th in the table.

Fabio was determined that life on the pitch would improve, and he was helped by the arrival during the summer of 1968 of a new coach, Helenio Herrera, who had already won the European Cup twice with Inter. Nicknamed 'The Magician', French–Argentine Herrera was the father of the famous *catenaccio* (meaning door-bolt) system whereby Italian teams would suck the opposition in and then hit them on the counterattack. He had great faith in

Capello and made him a pivotal player in midfield, so that much of Roma's flowing play revolved around the dynamic youngster with the vision of a veteran. If England prove to be successful under Capello, then Herrera is one of a select list of mentors the nation will have to thank for the treasure-trove of football knowledge he passed on to the current England manager. Fabio recalled later, 'As a footballer I owe much to Herrera. He believed in me, he taught me many things and he made sure I matured tactically. I think he was the greatest coach ever to come to Italy, the one who ensured that our football reached maturity.'

With his football back on track by the end of the summer, there was a very important personal matter to attend to – Fabio asked Laura to be his wife. Don't bother trying to picture Fabio going down on one knee to pop the vital question to his fiancée, because Capello assured me that he didn't. In Italy, the proposal isn't as important as becoming *fidanzato* and *fidanzata* – steady boyfriend and girlfriend – in the first place. After that significant step, there is almost an assumption after a certain period of time that marriage will follow sooner or later. One look at our picture of a young Fabio and Laura together in Rome gives an indication of just how spectacularly in love they were. As Capello remembered later, Laura never doubted that he was the right man for her, but simply had natural concerns about how young they still were to be thinking of tying the knot. Those worries didn't stop her from agreeing to be his wife, though.

Bianca wasn't surprised when he and Laura broke the news that they had decided to get married. She explained, 'I think it was a natural progression because when they met, Fabio was 17 if I'm not mistaken, and he was 23 when they married, so they had already been together for six years or so.' It wasn't time for the wedding day in Ferrara just yet though, because Fabio was still establishing himself at AS Roma.

Largely thanks to Herrera, Capello's form for Roma was so impressive that people began to talk about him as a future prospect for the Italian national team. The club only finished eighth in Serie A, a full 15 points behind champions Fiorentina, but Fabio finished as Roma's second highest scorer with six goals. At the same time, there was glory to be found in the Italian Cup, the equivalent of England's FA Cup. The young Capello played a starring role. He fired the all-important first goal in the quarter-final second leg against Brescia, as Roma erased a 0-1 first leg deficit with a resounding 3-0 triumph.

The last four teams left in the competition fought one another in a round-robin group format in order to see who deserved to lift the cup. Fabio netted again in Roma's 3-0 win over Foggia at home. Two draws with Torino sandwiched a victory at Cagliari, leaving Capello and the Roma boys one step from glory. The final hurdle was an away trip to Foggia, where Fabio played one of his best matches. He scored twice in a 3-1 romp to spark wild celebrations back in the Eternal City. June had turned to July before the party subsided. But for Fabio the party was to continue, because he had something far more profound to celebrate than his first major football trophy. A week later, on 5 July, 1969, he married his beloved Laura in a little church in Ferrara.

Capello's mother Evelina was hilarious as she recalled the occasion. 'I'll always remember that day they got married, Fabio and Laura, it was a horrible day.' Listening to this, I didn't know whether I had understood her correctly. 'Yes,' she confirmed, 'it was July 5, a tremendous heat, 40 degrees centigrade, humid and misty.' A nice day all the same, I suggested hopefully. 'Yes,' she admitted, 'a nice day all the same, but I will always remember the heat.' Still, Laura seems to have been a good daughter-in-law. 'She is ever such a nice girl,' said Evelina happily.

Fabio's sister paints a rather more romantic picture. 'They married in this church in Ferrara, a really lovely building. And there was Laura, this beautiful young blonde woman in a classic dress. It really was a classic wedding, and our father Guerrino was so proud.'

Bianca believes her brother chose well and explained, 'I think he needed what most men need, and that was to be married to someone who wasn't going to get on his nerves. Laura is intelligent, has a good sense of humour when she tells a story and she has various interests of her own. I don't claim to know her all that well, because we do our own thing as a family and go our own separate ways in life. But Laura and I do share a great love for plants, and she calls me sometimes to talk about a certain plant she has bought.'

Laura probably loves plants and classical music more than she loves football. It is understood that she does watch football matches when she has a personal interest, for example if her husband's team is playing, or someone they know within the game is involved. But she is not like Evelina, Fabio's mother, who told me she liked to watch sport on TV for pleasure, whether she had a personal connection with the protagonists or not. If Laura has a sporting passion, I am told it is for golf, the game Fabio began to play some afternoons, especially later in life when he became Roma's coach. His wife enjoys the social aspect, the exercise and the skilful nature of the game. She is pretty good, too, though I understand she has not been tempted to enter tournaments.

Since her husband was a footballer, Laura learned to live with soccer, as she had from the start. But she didn't have to love the game; indeed it was probably fortunate for her that she didn't. The last thing Fabio wanted to do when he came home was talk about football. Win or lose he preferred to keep home life separate. Laura provided that important stability a young man needs beyond the crazy world of football, and she would always be at Fabio's side when he needed her, no matter where his career took him. He revealed later, 'I've never spent more than a week alone. Hotels make me sad, I need a home. Our problem is all the moves we have had to make, too many.'

However, Fabio and Laura have spent a lifetime travelling to far-flung corners of the world, where hotels are sometimes a necessary part of the experience. They have shared a passion for scuba diving, and together they have explored the most amazing underwater worlds the planet has to offer. They have also sought out the ruins of ancient civilisations, from places like Cambodia and Tibet in the Far East to Mexico and Peru in Central and South America. They delight in learning all they can about the way intelligent communities lived in times gone by. Fabio and Laura have always married intellect with action, stability with exploration; and they seem to have always been able to find a new form of stimulation each year. No wonder their marriage has survived so well down the decades.

Italo Galbiati, Capello's longstanding assistant, once gave a snapshot of what life could be like on the road with Fabio. 'Golf matches, photographic safaris, bullfights, diving expeditions, whatever. Try to keep up with him and he'll exhaust you. He has two personalities, the serious Fabio at work and the fun Fabio away from work.' Laura Capello kept up well with the fun Fabio; and in 2008 they still looked like the perfect couple.

Back in 1969, Fabio already had reason to believe that his success in football would be the key if the world was to be their oyster. So he was determined to produce performances worthy of his big new sporting stage in the Italian capital.

Roma's players were treated like superstars for the rest of the summer, and it must have been hard even for the level-headed Capello to keep his feet on the ground during such an extraordinarily happy time of his life on both a personal and professional level.

Then, in late August, mighty Roma played an unknown English side, Swindon Town, in a new competition known as the Anglo-Italian League Cup. This inaugural tournament was contested between the winners of England's League Cup and the Italian Cup. Swindon, who weren't even in the English First Division, as the top flight was known then, had qualified for this showdown because of an unexpected triumph at Wembley. A player called Don Rogers had scored twice to see off Arsenal 3-1 in the League Cup final. Now everyone expected the upstarts from England's West Country to be put firmly in their place when they travelled to the daunting cauldron of Rome's Stadio Olimpico. Some 50,000 fanatical supporters greeted Capello and Roma as they marched out to put Swindon to the sword. It was supposed to be an entertaining welcome to the new campaign, a chance for Roma's goal-getters to find their destructive rhythm against vastly inferior opposition. The first game didn't turn out to be quite as one-sided as everyone had expected.

Clive King's excellent match report for the *Swindon Advertiser* began, 'Amid the terrific din of fireworks, bugles and claxon horns,

Swindon Town put up a terrific fight before they had to admit defeat at the Olympic Stadium in Rome last night. Finishing only one goal in arrears (1-2), the Town must be in with a great chance of becoming the first winners of the new trophy when Roma visit the County Ground for the second leg on 10 September.'

The report goes on to describe how Swindon goalkeeper Peter Downsborough, Swindon's hero of the night, 'threw himself to his right to finger-tip a shot from inside-left Capello to safety.' And Downsborough later recalled, 'Capello stood out. He was quite tall and a good ball player. Roma were always well organised and Capello seemed to be at the heart of their organisation, which is how teams like AC Milan and Real Madrid played when he became their manager.'

But the little English club fancied their chances in the return match in the less spectacular surroundings of the County Ground because of their team spirit. As Swindon keeper Downsborough later observed, 'We played for one another, always covering for each other.' Fewer than 12,000 supporters turned up to see the Roman superstars strut their stuff, and Fabio was one of a small hardcore of Roma players who seemed prepared to meet the challenge of such an alien environment. He was quick to force a diving save from Downsborough and later brought more heroics from the man between the sticks. By the time his old adversary became England manager, Downsborough was a school caretaker in Halifax. Football didn't always ensure its heroes a glamorous future. Back in that late summer of 1969, however, Downsborough was the hero, not the Roma midfielder. The underdogs were rampant and Arthur Horsfield scored a hat-trick, as Roma were routed 4-0 and 5-2 on aggregate. Don Rogers scored Swindon's other goal and the Romans were run ragged. The more Capello and his colleagues tried to attack, the more they were punished at the other end.

Herrera admitted sportingly, 'My team were punished for moments of distraction ... We had plenty of opportunities, but Swindon showed us how to shoot.'

It wasn't quite the start to the 1969–70 season that Capello had anticipated; neither could he have foreseen how that campaign would end. Behind the scenes in March 1970, Italo Allodi, the Juventus general manager, was closing a deal that would take Fabio and his Roma team-mates, Luciano Spinosi and Fausto Landini, to Juventus. The transfers would be kept secret for months before they were announced, because everyone knew the defections would cause outrage among fans in the Italian capital. Capello would later insist that even he didn't know he was leaving until the summer.

Roma's march towards glory in the European Cup Winners' Cup provided a welcome diversion, and by April they could almost touch the trophy. Only a strong Polish side, Gornik Zabrze, stood between Fabio and the final, but the marathon that evolved at the penultimate stage became the stuff of legend. The semi-final first leg saw the Poles battle hard for a 1-1 draw in front of Roma's fans. In Katowice, however, Fabio was given the chance to put Roma ahead from the penalty spot. The freezing cold and screaming, vodka-fuelled crowd would have chilled the soul and tested the resolve of any man. Capello struck his shot firmly with his right foot and saw it brilliantly saved. Holding his nerve and keeping his balance, he drilled home the rebound with his left foot. He shook his head as he accepted the congratulations of his team-mates, clearly unhappy that he had failed to convert the original spot kick, yet relieved that he had reacted so well. That might have been enough to send the Italians through to the final, had Wlodek Lubanski not come up with an equaliser to force extra time. The same Polish genius then scored again to send Gornik fans into raptures, but Roma weren't finished and equalised six minutes from the final whistle through Francesco Scaratti's powerful drive.

Believing that last away goal to have been decisive, RAI television broadcaster Nando Martellini told the nation that Roma were through to the European Cup Winners' Cup final. There were all-night celebrations in the piazzas of the capital, and it was only the following morning that the truth sank in: the away goal in extra time hadn't counted double and it would be necessary to play a third match at a neutral venue to determine English club Manchester City's opponents in that keenly-anticipated final. The last showdown in the trilogy between Roma and Gornik was scheduled for the Stade de la Meina in Strasbourg on 22 April;

one way or another the marathon semi-final would be decided that night.

A fine piece of writing by Massimo Lo Jacono in *Corriere dello Sport* described how the yelling and the fear in Katowice had motivated Capello and the Romans, whereas in Strasbourg the strange sound of a paramilitary marching band, strutting around rather comically as it welcomed the players out onto the pitch, gave the occasion a surreal atmosphere. He wrote, 'Fear and enthusiasm in Poland, nervousness in France. A less vibrant yet more dangerous build-up, players smiling because they didn't know how to react. We knew that Capello was afraid in the dressing room, and we hoped that something would happen now to shake Roma so that they would remember the importance of the match. We had lost that sense of value, perhaps because hope had already corroded fear.'

The sort of fear the reporter had recalled from Poland was a positive fear. Capello later pointed out that he had not shrunk from the challenge there; neither would he do so in Strasbourg. The fear, he explained, was that natural anxiety any team feels the longer a tie drifts on unresolved; and in this case it was the fear of not succeeding after three games. Something didn't feel right in Strasbourg, and the surreal feel to the evening only increased when the floodlights failed twice in the opening 10 minutes. There was a 20-minute delay the second time around, and play could only resume at around the moment the first half was meant to have been finishing. Along with his fellow midfielders, Fabio was described as having tiredness in his legs, because Roma had fought hard to achieve a draw against Juventus in Turin a few days earlier. And he was said to be too preoccupied with defending in Strasbourg, along with the entire midfield unit, instead of organising their offensive game.

There was no evidence of defending at all in the 42nd minute, however, when the ever-threatening Lubanski carved a path straight through that Roma midfield and unleashed an unstoppable shot to claim a superb individual goal. But the tie was on a knife-edge when Sergio Perelli was body-checked by Stefan Florenski and Roma were awarded a penalty. Fabio Capello, whose job it was to take that penalty, was forced to wait an eternity as the Poles employed some deliberate delaying tactics. Even photographers ran the length of the pitch to put themselves in a better position behind the Gornik goal. Fabio took his usual long run-up from the edge of the area. According to *Corriere dello Sport*, he admitted to 'a certain palpitation in the heart.' Capello took up the story later that night. 'Then I calmly decided to change my mind and not hit it to the right of the goalkeeper, as I usually do, but on the other side of him, hard and skimming the grass.' The keeper, Hubert Kostka, guessed correctly. Fortunately for Capello he had put plenty of power behind his effort, and the ball flew under his adversary's body. Once again, Roma were dreaming of glory.

Two hours of football were played out in Strasbourg, yet the scores remained level. It was becoming ridiculous. After a total of 330 minutes in three different stadia, nothing could split the teams. Penalty shoot-outs hadn't been adopted yet, and the players had reached the end of the road. There was only one thing for it – the dreaded toss of the coin. A little crowd formed on the pitch, tense with anticipation; and in the middle of that chaotic gathering referee Machin could be seen throwing the coin up in the air. Joaquin Peiro, the Roma captain, chose heads.

Francesco Scaratti, a Roma goalscorer from the previous match who had been substituted at half-time, saw a white-sleeved arm go up in triumph. Since Roma had played in white, Scaratti began to celebrate wildly. It was a cruel visual trick, because Gornik's darker tops had also been designed with white sleeves. Peiro had chosen incorrectly, the coin nestled in the grass with tails looking back up at the desperate Italians. It was Gornik Zabrze that had made it through to the final and the Poles began to jump for joy. Capello could be seen trudging manfully towards the dressing room, but inside he was as devastated as anyone. Capello was asked to talk about his penalty, and concluded, 'It went well. Unfortunately the night didn't finish well, when it was really essential.'

To add insult to injury, the Poles had demanded that the Italians be tested for any signs of drug abuse. Roma's president, Alvaro Marchini, reflected his players' indignation when he hit back, 'We are offended. What do they think, that we have something to hide?'

As soon as they had won, Gornik withdrew their request for the dope-test.

Manchester City were waiting for Gornik in the final, and their manager Joe Mercer expressed sympathy for Roma. He said, 'I've never been a fan of tossing a coin to decide a match. I don't know whether we'll be facing the best football team or the best at heads or tails. I know it would have been a great game if we had faced Roma.' Mercer's City beat the Poles 2-1 to lift the European Cup Winners' Cup.

But Capello's semi-final farce was considered too gut wrenching and unfair for professional footballers to go through again in the future. It is curious to think that penalty shoot-outs, England's nightmare in a succession of big tournaments, were born partially because of Fabio's suffering. When the point was put to Capello in 2008, he admitted that he had never made the connection, but on reflection he felt there was some truth in this. He even apologised, showing the same sort of grim humour England fans have adopted. The reason Fabio jokingly wished to say sorry for the Strasbourg deadlock was because the very next season UEFA adopted penalty shoot-outs as the way to decide drawn ties in both the European Cup and European Cup Winners' Cup.

No one can tell Fabio that penalty shoot-outs are excessively cruel and too much of a lottery. He knows what cruelty in football really feels like, and he wants England's players to see penalties as a marvellous opportunity in big competitions – one he was denied when so close to glory. Back in 1970, football's level playing field had taken Capello through five and a half hours of evenly matched football against Gornik, and seen him score goals when it mattered. After all his efforts he had been denied glory by the unfaithful flight of a coin – supposedly in the name of fair play. If anything was going to make a player cynical about professional football, this bitter moment was it.

Later, as a coach, he would partially attribute his success in derby matches to a sharp, analytical brain primed by 'my 40 years spent in football from the time I was a player, the coldness, the experience, the disenchantment.' Those words might have described the overriding feeling the night Roma's European dream died. But in 2008 Capello insisted that the Strasbourg experience hadn't turned him into a cynic, but simply left him with a profound sense of disappointment.

Shattered by the knife-twisting drama of Strasbourg, Roma faced trips to England in May 1970 for Anglo-Italian Cup matches in Middlesbrough and West Bromwich. Unsurprisingly, since the first game took place just 10 days after Gornik's victory, Roma looked jaded on Teeside and lost 1-0. They collapsed completely at West Bromwich, crushed 4-0. A promising season fizzled out as Roma finished 11th in the league. Capello was about to move on.

First the planet's great and diverse football community watched in awe as the 1970 World Cup was played out in Mexico. It was, quite simply, the greatest tournament of them all. Italy reached the final, beaten by the best Brazil side in history, packed with magicians such as Pele, Jairzinho, Rivelino and Tostao – the most spectacular team football has ever seen. This was the big time, the greatest stage the game had to offer, and the next World Cup had to be Capello's goal. To play for one's country was everything, and you increased your chances if you were at one of the very best clubs in that country.

Before very long, Allodi's secret deal to take Capello to Juventus was made public. Fabio insisted later that he had known nothing about his transfer away from Roma until that summer of 1970. Spinosi and Landini were to head north too, meaning that the so-called 'Three Jewels of Rome' were about to be well and truly plundered. And what was the artful Allodi giving Roma in return? Luis Del Sol, a player of Real Madrid pedigree who was nevertheless 35 years old; and two inconsistent goal-poachers called Gianfranco Zigoni and Roberto Vieri, father of the latter-day Italy striker Christian. In addition, an undisclosed sum of money passed from Juventus to Roma – thought to be less than £1 million but far more than the £100,000 Capello had cost Roma from Spal. Fabio later claimed that he was never told what he had cost Juventus, due to the complicated nature of the deal. But if it felt like a good deal to Roma's president, Alvaro Marchini, it didn't to the fans.

Violent demonstrations greeted the triple transfer. Passionate fans burned Roma flags on the streets of the Italian capital, season tickets were torn up, and at one stage it looked as though fans would storm the club offices as they chanted threats aimed at Marchini in particular. *Corriere dello Sport* ran one such threat as a headline: 'If you sell the jewels we will shoot at you from the rooftops.' As it turned out, Marchini didn't lose his life but he did lose his job within a year, his position having become untenable.

On a personal level it must have been gratifying for Capello to realise that the outrage over his departure was essentially commensurate to the outstanding contribution he had made at the club. In terms of his family life, it would have been wonderful for Fabio to stay where he was in Rome, particularly since Laura had just given birth to their first son Pierfilippo, on 12 June 1970. But clubs had the big say in transfers in those days, not players. Besides, Fabio had always been ambitious, and now that he was a father he had an added reason to achieve even greater things. Turin and Juventus beckoned.

Fabio played 62 games in Serie A for Roma and 11 in the Italian Cup, a trophy he had helped them to win. He had only captained the team once, though that was still good going for a player in his early twenties. The extraordinary statistic, for a natural leader with such a forceful, imposing character, was that Capello would never captain a team again, not for the remainder of his playing career. There were always more senior players in each club he joined, those who had been there longer, though that didn't necessarily mean they were finer leaders.

Even without the captain's armband Capello had shown great leadership and nerve already, especially while playing for Roma in Europe. He had made eight battling appearances in the European Cup Winners' Cup, an adventure callously wiped away by that infernal toss of the coin. Now, at the age of 24, he was joining Juventus. Behind the scenes and unbeknown to the Juve players, certain shady characters would try not to leave the Turin club's big European nights to chance if they could help it.

CHAPTER 4
ATTEMPTED SUICIDE, PREMATURE DEATH

FABIO CAPELLO DIDN'T LIKE TURIN, HOME OF JUVENTUS, very much when he first moved there. The city seemed to have precious few of the charms and intellectual stimulations of the Italian capital. He explained: 'Moving from Rome to Turin was like passing from a colour film into a black and white film. There weren't many attractions. When I left Rome to go to Juventus in 1970 I just couldn't get used to my new surroundings in Turin. So "The Lawyer" (Gianni) Agnelli (the owner of the club) told me, "We pay Capello and he thinks of Rome." Turin was a dark city, a gloomy city, but luckily I found friends there too, bonds which would endure all the way through until when I was next there much later in my career as a coach. Back in the early 1970s the Ilio restaurant was a refuge. And the Juventus General Manager, Italo Allodi, was passionate about art, and I caught the bug from him. He takes the credit.' Allodi lived up the road from Capello on Turin's prestigious Strada degli Alberoni, so no wonder the bug spread easily. Inspired by Italo's extensive knowledge of the subject, Fabio was soon hooked.

Although Capello later insisted that he had never seen Allodi as a father figure, he did admit that they enjoyed a very good relationship in Turin, and remained friends even after they had both left Juventus. There was nothing wrong in that, particularly given their shared love for art. Indeed many prominent people in Italian football still talk with great affection about their innovative friend Italo, so Fabio certainly wasn't alone in his apparent admiration for the man. But a leading Turin journalist, Gian Paolo Ormezzano, had another view of Allodi: 'He is not just corrupt – he is a corruptor.' The highly respected British journalist and sports writer, Brian Glanville, described Allodi as 'the quintessence, the incarnation of corruption.'

Fabio Capello always played hard and fair, whatever the circumstances, because that was all part of his highly competitive nature. But others in Italian football may have been more vulnerable over the years. Allodi's world was often ruled by unspoken agreements. Sometimes suggestible footballers or officials from opposing teams knew the score and one glance might confirm a mutual understanding: if you don't try too hard in this match, since it is more important to us, we won't try too hard in the next one, when the result might be more important to you. Even Luciano Moggi, his protégé, admitted that it was perfectly acceptable in Allodi's world for one club to pretty much throw in the towel before a game had started if the result meant more to the other side. Was bribery also thought of as oiling the wheels of business, getting a team where it needed to be?

Treat a referee right, reasoned Allodi, and the result would probably turn out right for his club too. Intriguingly, Allodi once asserted with undeniable subtlety, 'You don't buy a referee. You make it possible for him to do his duty, without being accused of bias. For me (Cassius) Clay (later Muhammad Ali) is the greatest boxer in the world: if I face him I'll lose, even if my father is the referee. If I face Joe Louis and my father is referee, no one would find it scandalous if Louis won.'

Though he was talking in riddles, the underlying meaning was clear enough. Juventus were expected to win most of their matches anyway, because they were one of the best teams around. That was the beauty of Allodi's position. A little effort on his part to 'make it possible for (the referee) to do his duty, without being accused of bias' could guarantee what was already the anticipated outcome. If a referee acted rather more generously towards Allodi's team than their opponents, it would hardly be noticed. And it was only human nature that referees often acted that way, given how generously Allodi used to treat match officials.

In the late 1960s and much of the 1970s Allodi was one of the most powerful men in Italian football. Inter president Angelo Moratti, the late father of more recent owner Massimo, made Allodi secretary at his club in 1960. Brian Glanville takes up the story in his fascinating book, *Champions of Europe: The history, romance and intrigue of the European Cup*. He writes, 'Wheeling, dealing and manipulating in the transfer market, Allodi became very rich. He acquired a splendid collection of paintings, which he often conferred in the shape of gifts. Gifts, indeed, were his stock in trade, from his early days in Mantua. He believed in liberally oiling the wheels, not least when it came to journalists and referees.'

Glanville alleged that Allodi played a part in fixing matches for Inter's European Cup triumphs of 1964 and 1965. Liverpool were allegedly the victims in the second of those campaigns. In the semi-final the men from Merseyside won 3-1 in the first leg at Anfield.

Glanville wrote, 'In later years, Bill Shankly would tell me that afterwards he had met a large Italian journalist who shook his head and told him, sadly, "You will never be allowed to win." Nor was he. The return leg in Milan was lost 3-0, with a couple of really strange goals. For one of them, (Joaquin) Peiro ... ran back from behind Tommy Lawrence, the Liverpool keeper, who was preparing to kick the ball, kicked it out of his hands, and put it in the net. (Mario) Corso scored an equally contentious goal. A free kick was given to Inter, on the edge of the box. With his famous left foot, Corso struck it straight home. Though the referee, the Spaniard Ortiz de Mendibil, had clearly indicated that the free kick was indirect, he allowed the goal.'

Triumphant, the artful Allodi then switched to Juventus as general manager in 1970, where he signed Capello. There was nothing particularly artistic about the newcomer's midfield game, however. Initially the new young Juventus coach, 35-year-old Armando Picchi, had appeared to be in agreement with his bosses about Fabio's game. They had all thought that Capello was special precisely because of his football simplicity, supported by his sharp tactical intelligence. The combination suggested that Capello could develop the sort of pivotal midfield role he had enjoyed at Roma, with everything built around him. That was the idea, anyway.

Fausto Landini, who was transferred from Roma to Juventus along with Capello and international defender Luciano Spinosi, said of Fabio, 'He was like an accountant in midfield, processing everything. He had perfect feet and a strong character, and you could see straight away that he was a leader, not withstanding his relatively young age. He always went onto the pitch with one thought in his head, to win, and in order to stimulate his team-mates he wouldn't hesitate to make his feelings known during a match if he felt the need. Off the pitch, naturally, he turned back into the calmest young man in the world.'

While most of the time it was true that he was calm off the pitch, events in that first year in Turin were to push Capello to the limit. On the face of it there should have been no reason for a crisis to develop. At Juventus, Capello had magnificent players around him, and he could learn from them as well as make his own opinions known. Some of the very best, future legends such as Roberto 'Bobby-gol' Bettega from Varese, and Franco 'The Baron' Causio from Palermo, arrived at around the same time, to bring spice and excitement to the Juventus line-up.

The 1970–71 season didn't get off to the best of starts, however, when Juve were eliminated from the Italian Cup in the very first round. But league form held steady, and Capello found himself at the centre of yet another gripping European adventure. The forerunner to the UEFA Cup, the Inter-Cities Fairs Cup, was played for the last time that year; after thumping US Rumelange of Luxembourg 11-0 on aggregate in the first round, Juventus faced a formidable second-round obstacle in Barcelona. They overcame the Catalans by winning both matches 2-1, Capello scoring a vital goal to help his club progress. Hungary's Pecsi MFC were the *Bianconeri's* (black-and-white's) less glamorous third round opponents, and Juventus were rarely in trouble as they cruised to a 3-0 aggregate win. The Italians were due to face FC Twente of Holland in the quarter-final, although the tie would be decided only after Fabio Capello had caused one of the greatest controversies of his career.

At his Turin home on 12 February 1971, Capello gave an explosive interview to *Corriere dello Sport*'s Alberto Marchesi, who set the scene nicely. 'Strada degli Alberoni, 11/9. On the slopes of the hill where the well-off Turin people live, Fabio Capello has chosen his residence. Fifty metres away is the Haller family. Up the road is Italo Allodi, the man who in the month of March 1970 had closed the big deal with Roma. The Italian capital learned only three months later that Capello, Spinosi and Landini had been sold to Juventus. And, you will remember, the news was greeted like the end of the world . . .'

Marchesi described entering 'the ultra-modern apartment block that houses the Capello family,' how Fabio was waiting for him at the lift, and how the visitor met 'his young and delightful wife, Laura, who struggled to keep their very vivacious heir in her arms. Pierfilippo, "Roman of Rome," will be eight months old tomorrow . . .'

The writer then recalled the one-hour-and-twenty-minute Juventus training session they had just witnessed, with gymnastics, ball work, individual technique and mini-games played across the field, during which Capello had looked at him 'with a sullen air' and seemed 'like a man whose morale has been shot to pieces.' One line is particularly poignant. 'Armando Picchi was on the field but in a poor physical condition, due to the pain between his ribs that is destroying him.'

In fact Picchi, Capello's coach, was suffering from a cancerous tumour on his spine, a condition that would kill him before very long. No one was aware of this at the time, and it was Capello's mood that drew the main focus. Marchesi explained that the previous Sunday Fabio had 'suffered an affront, an insult that demoralised him terribly.' The coach, Picchi, had hauled him off twenty minutes from time against Bologna, just as he had done against Inter in Milan during a previous big match. This, the journalist wrote, constituted 'a genuine shock for a chap like Fabio Capello, who can point to a brilliant past and left Roma for Turin with so much hope ... He is mortally offended, to put it bluntly.

In seven years of service in Serie A (Spal, Roma, Juventus), it has never happened to him before.' Marchesi put what followed down to 'an unmistakeable sign of his pride – the pride of a serious professional footballer.' But it left Capello's career hanging by a thread. This is how an angry Fabio described his predicament at the time.

'I've been a cretin, I should have understood from the first sign that things weren't going well for me. I was used to playing in a zonal system at Roma. Last Sunday Bologna held back a lot and perhaps that put us in a bit of difficulty. But in future, after this bitter lesson, I'll sort myself out better. Now I understand how you have to play. I'll look after number one and I won't care about the others. Everyone dribbles like mad here at Juventus, while I break free from my marker asking for the return ball. I get the ball back maybe four times in twenty. I, on the other hand, never dribble. I'm simple; I don't like doing that kind of 'number'. It means that from today I will adjust to the circumstances.'

When asked if he was sure he had found the right position on the field at Juventus, Fabio raised his shoulders in discomfort. 'I have, yes. It is a position I've occupied on the field for 10 years already. The others I don't know. But by playing zonally, I'm often forced to confront three opponents, mine and the ones the others don't look after. That way I'm killing myself with exhaustion and I remedy a load of mistakes that would otherwise make people look stupid. They have even arrived at the point whereby they are saying that I – yes I, really – am slowing up the game! But if I never dribble?! In any case the ones who slow up the game are the ones who indulge in damaging dribbling, resulting in the sort of show that only an incompetent orchestra would put on. Really incredible! The truth is that at Roma there was real team spirit. More than team-mates we were friends, brothers. Here, on the other hand, it is rather different. Each man for himself. So I will take the same line from now on, as I've said. I'll only take care of my opponent and the others can arrange themselves accordingly. I've spoken honestly to the boss man to man. Basically I've told him that if he is only playing me because I cost a lot, that's no good for me. I only want to play if he has faith in my ways and my technique. If it's not like that, all the better. I'll sever my ties from the team completely, and goodnight to the musicians! I couldn't bear a third scene like the ones against Inter and Bologna. Potentially, Juventus is a great team. In order to ignite that explosive potential it would be enough to have better collaboration between ourselves. Mr Picchi has told me in every way that he has taken me off because he needed a real striker.'

As if this extraordinary attack on his own team was not sensational enough, reporter Marchesi further stoked the fire by drawing Capello's attention to some adverse comments made by a team-mate Fabio had respected more than most – Helmut Haller, the man he had watched scoring a goal for West Germany in the 1966 World Cup final against England. 'A Milanese weekly,' he explained, 'reported quite gaudily some declarations from Haller about you. The German said you will never be a (Gigi) Rivera and that the main man in the Juve team could be (Franco) Causio in the future and not you. What do you think about that?'

Capello replied, 'It seems to me impossible that Haller, with whom I am close friends, could have said this. However, he has made a wonderful discovery, saying that Rivera is better than me. What a phenomenon! Rivera is one of the greatest players in the world. Anyway it would be good if Haller minded his own business.'

Drawing Capello into further potentially damaging remarks, Rome-based Marchesi explained how Fabio's strengths were being squandered in Turin. He wrote that Capello was 'an excellent midfielder who, if placed within a well formed, functioning midfield, can play to a high level. He can send a ball where he wants with his forehead. He can kick hard with either foot, though his best is his right, with which he can launch long passes; but that doesn't work so well at Juve where, instead of breaking free from their markers and running ahead, they turn back and look for the ball. Many these days reproach him for using precisely this, his speciality.'

Fabio took the bait in order to defend himself. 'The long pass? Well if my team-mates don't release themselves to receive the ball that way, who am I supposed to give the ball to, the opposing sweeper?'

Capello asked to be judged at the end of the season, at which point he would also judge Juventus. He explained, 'There are still 13 games to go and Juventus have to meet all the best teams. It will be here that we will see if I know what to do or whether, as someone here says, I'm a "bluff". Football is like boxing, where the last rounds are the ones that really count. However, I would be glad to return to Roma where I still have so many good memories. I would only be sorry to leave Juventus without having demonstrated my true worth. Here I haven't been able to show it in full yet. I've only been able to release around sixty per cent of my potential.'

To say that this public attack was explosive and ill-timed would be an understatement. By 14 February, newspapers had announced that Picchi had gone to hospital for a series of exploratory tests on the back problem that had caused him discomfort for 40 days or more. That happened between the two matches against FC Twente, so Juventus required a replacement. Cestmir Vycpalek, the Czech tactician who had been looking after the Juventus youngsters since the previous summer, took over as caretaker coach.

But before Picchi's illness began to overwhelm him that spring, he left hospital temporarily and in considerable pain to become part of the three-man tribunal which would decide Capello's punishment for talking to the media about his ailing coach and team-mates with such apparent disrespect. The other two judges were the Juventus president, Giampiero Boniperti and Allodi, an indication that the matter could hardly have been treated more seriously by the high-powered Juventus hierarchy. Fabio knew he could easily be kicked off the team for having spoken out of turn. Much depended upon how the target of Capello's criticisms, Picchi himself, felt, since it was the coach who determined the style of play that Fabio so abhorred.

Capello still remembers how gravely ill Picchi looked at the hearing as he justified the interview. To the player it had seemed as though he had been chatting to a friend about his frustrations. If he had seemed excessively critical, he had always spoken with the team's best interests at heart.

To his eternal credit, the dying Picchi took pity on Capello. Instead of ruining the young man's career, Picchi argued that a heavy fine would be sufficient, while Boniperti and Allodi were reluctant to argue against the verdict of the man who had been most wronged. By the skin of his teeth, Capello therefore got away with one of the most withering outbursts a player has ever made against his team-mates. Picchi had saved Fabio Capello, one of the last significant footballing acts of his life. By keeping Capello at the top of the game, he helped to lay the foundations for the excellence that would eventually attract England. The air was cleared, Fabio had made his point, and he later told me that the bust-up had been the turning point in his time at Juventus, because after that he settled down and made the best of his situation.

It was against this extraordinary backdrop that the Juventus campaign for European glory continued. Capello had warned that FC Twente would be 'dangerous', and he was right. Juve's 2-0 first leg advantage was wiped away during normal time in the return match. Only in extra time of a tense quarter-final did Capello's team finally triumph with two goals when it mattered. Juve went through by an aggregate of 4-2 to meet FC Koln in the semi-final.

A 1-1 draw in Koln, Germany, was followed up with a very professional 2-0 victory in Turin. Capello had known for some time that his team would face English opposition in the final if they prevailed, because Liverpool and Leeds had contested the other semi-final. As it turned out, the Yorkshiremen won their match by the only goal in 180 minutes of football.

Now Fabio had the chance to erase the memory of his previous defeats against the English, and ease the pain of that excruciating exit to Gornik Zabrze in his last big European campaign. But Don Revie's Leeds were by far the best English team Fabio had faced so far, packed full of stars such as their little midfield general, Billy Bremner and the more artistic Johnny Giles. The spectacular Peter Lorimer was always unpredictable, and at the back Norman Hunter and Jack Charlton struck fear into opponents with their fierce tackling.

Capello could consider himself extremely lucky to be able to prepare himself for that final against Leeds. Tragically, Picchi died of the tumour on his spine just hours before the first leg kicked off, but none of the players were aware of what had happened. Roberto Bettega confirmed to me, 'We played the first time in Turin without knowing about Picchi. It was thanks to him, and the faith he showed in me, that I was still in the Juventus team. I had gone 12 weeks without scoring at one stage and that is a lot for any striker. He didn't drop me and I repaid him by scoring 12 goals in the last 15 games.'

Bettega didn't have time to improve on his record on this occasion, because the game was abandoned due to a waterlogged pitch just six minutes into the second half with the scores still goalless. By the time they were ready to try again two days later, the sad news about Picchi had come out. Italian football was still reeling from the shock on 28 May when an emotional 45,000 fans watched the first leg of the final against Leeds played to a dramatic conclusion. Bettega recalled, 'It was an emotional occasion for all of us. But I was still a young player and I was being marked by Jackie Charlton. He was too big!'

That didn't stop the agile Bettega from putting Juventus ahead after 27 minutes in Turin, a fitting tribute to his late coach and mentor; but the elegant Paul Madeley equalised just after half time. Then Fabio took control and reduced the fearsome Leeds defensive pairing of Charlton and Hunter to spectators, rifling the home side's second on 55 minutes. That, undoubtedly, was for Picchi too, and Capello's team-mates showed their appreciation in the emotional way they congratulated him.

Bettega was still in awe of Capello then, and no one was surprised that Fabio had found his way onto the scoresheet on the big occasion. Roberto recalled, 'He was already an expert compared to me; we younger ones looked at him as a master of the game.' It seemed as though Fabio's strike would hand Juventus a slender advantage to take to Elland Road, but Revie sent on his substitute striker Mick Bates, and within five minutes he had scored the English club's second equaliser. That never-say-die English attitude had struck again, and Juve knew they had it all to do as they travelled to Yorkshire for the second leg, by which time May had turned to June.

Bettega explained, 'We were just a young team back then and still growing, while Leeds were a very good side, at their peak.' Picchi's successor, Cestmir Vycpalek, had his work cut out. Capello later described Vycpalek as 'a great psychologist', but the sense of responsibility on his shoulders during those moving weeks must have been immense. With so much going on behind the scenes, the second match in England had the feel of 'mission impossible', especially when Allan 'Sniffer' Clarke fired through a crowded penalty area to give Revie's men a 12th-minute lead. Pietro Anastasi soon offered Juve new hope when he equalised to leave the match on a knife-edge.

Sadly for Capello, however, there was to be no more scoring; the two Leeds goals in Turin had proved decisive, and 42,483 fans cheered the home team to the finishing wire. Yet again European competition had kicked Capello in the teeth, and the victory he had so wanted to secure in honour of Picchi's generosity of spirit had eluded him. When he had done his grieving, he might also have started to wonder when he would get his hands on more silverware. As it turned out, he didn't have to wait very long.

CHAPTER 5
TAKING THE
MICOREN

FOR A MAN WHO WAS BORN TO WIN, FABIO CAPELLO LOST ON an awful lot of English football grounds as a player. In 1972 Juventus had reached the quarter-final of the UEFA Cup, but once again English opposition – this time in the shape of Wolverhampton Wanderers – threatened his dream of European glory. After 1-1 draw in Turin, Wolves smelt blood.

Some 40,000 fans went to Molineux, the club stadium, to see if the Midlanders could finish the job against one of Europe's most respected sides. Danny Hegan conjured a brilliant chip to put the men in gold ahead; then Northern Ireland legend Derek Dougan clinched a memorable 2-1 triumph. Wolves went all the way to the final, only to lose to Tottenham Hotspur. Capello, meanwhile, must have been wondering whether there was anything he could do to overcome the English fighting spirit. Fortunately there wasn't much time for dejection because, after returning home to lick their wounds, Juventus quickly had to concentrate on domestic matters.

The 1971–72 Italian league title race turned into an inter-city battle between the two Milan clubs, AC and Inter, and the two Turin clubs, Juventus and Torino. The Turin derby took place on 5 December, and Juventus were 2-1 winners. By Christmas, Capello and his team-mates had begun to feel that their title dreams could become a reality. Fabio had already played a huge part in creating the momentum; his perceptive passing and midfield organisation providing the ideal platform for the killer instincts of Roberto Bettega. 'Fabio was a very intelligent midfielder,' emphasised a grateful Bettega when he looked back later.

But early in the New Year Bettega went down with what proved to be the first signs of tuberculosis, and Juventus were up against it. They dug in, showing the sort of team spirit that Fabio had demanded all along; and in April Causio's hat-trick at Inter put them right back in contention.

Fabio was winning rave reviews for his outstanding work in Juve's engine room, and an international call-up seemed imminent. But he was nearly 26 and if it didn't happen soon it might not happen at all. Capello let his boots do the talking and hoped he could still make the breakthrough. His proud moment came in the quarter-final, second leg of the European Nations Cup – what we might now term 'Euro '72'. In Brussels on 13 May of that year, Italy coach Ferruccio Valcareggi placed Capello on the bench for a crunch match against Belgium. The Italians had only drawn the first leg a fortnight earlier in Milan 0-0. Fancied for the Euro title alongside England and West Germany, the players were therefore under big pressure to come up with a decisive result away from home.

At the Constant Vanden Stock stadium in Belgium the early exchanges didn't go according to plan. Wilfried Van Moer put the home team ahead after 23 minutes, and a helpless Capello was still an anxious spectator among the substitutes. At half-time, Fabio was given his big chance to try to turn around the fortunes of his country. However, events didn't follow the script he must have dreamed of since he was a boy. When Paul Van Himst added a second in the 71st minute, the writing was on the wall. Even though the legendary Luigi 'Gigi' Riva pulled one back to give Italy frantic hope just four minutes from time, the clock beat the revival bid and Italy had been dumped out of the tournament.

Capello soon had to put that bitter taste of international defeat behind him, because Juve's battle against their Serie A rivals was reaching its climax that very month. Gianni Agnelli, the Juventus owner and car tycoon, would choose such key moments in a season to turn up for a flying pep-talk. Nicknamed '*L'Avvocato*' – the lawyer – his economy with words left a deep impression on Capello. When it was eventually his turn to manage other men, Fabio would sometimes adopt the same technique, though he would never become as flamboyant or as dramatic with his entrances and exits as Agnelli.

Fabio explained, 'I remember he (Agnelli) would come and see the players at Villar Perosa (the Juventus training ground) and give us two or three blazing and witty remarks, then leave again in a helicopter. It didn't take him half an hour to explain something to you; he was direct and concise, just as I like to be.'

Though Juventus president Giampiero Boniperti may not always have appreciated Agnelli's legendary 6.00am phone calls quite so much, those flying visits never did any harm. But Juventus had another 'tonic' to help them, the effects of which were rather more debatable. It was a respiratory stimulant called Micoren, which allegedly helped to oxygenate the blood. In an interview with *L'Espresso* magazine in 2004, Capello admitted that he and other players took Micoren regularly. 'We regularly took it,' he claimed, although his team-mate of the day, Roberto Bettega, later insisted to me that he had never even heard of the stuff. Capello added, 'I took it even when I played for the national team. At the time it was not illegal, it only became banned afterwards.'

Micoren contained prethcamide, and was later alleged to have dangerous side effects. Nello Saltutti, a former Milan, Sampdoria and Fiorentina player, revealed that Juventus weren't the only Italian club exploring its possible benefits. He explained, 'Micoren was taken off the market in 1985, because it was found to be harmful. However, we took it for 20 years without any doctors telling us that it was wrong, or with any side effects after the match. The anti-doping controls were a joke.' Saltutti died aged 56 in 2003, prompting questions about whether his use of Micoren might have taken its toll. Unlike Bettega, Dino Zoff, the legendary Italian goalkeeper, remembered Micoren well, and explained how commonplace it was. 'It was a mild cardio-tonic,' he said. 'It was allowed and it was taken like people take aspirin now.'

It was a time for cool heads and a ruthless focus. If Juventus won at Vicenza, it wouldn't matter if AC Milan did the same at Catanzaro or if Torino saw off Bologna. Sure enough, Juve clinched the Italian championship with a 2-0 victory. They had pipped Milan and their own city rivals Torino by a point, so the triumph could hardly have been sweeter.

Capello had played a leading role that season and even finished as the club's second-highest scorer in the league, with nine goals in 29 matches. Now Fabio had Italian league and cup winners' medals to his name, as well as that precious first international cap. Importantly, he had done well enough against Belgium to be given another chance.

In June he played his part in a 3-3 draw against Romania in Bucharest, and a 1-1 draw against Bulgaria in Sofia. After three international matches for one of the world's best sides, Fabio was still looking for his first win; but from a personal point of view, these were magical moments. At 26 he had established himself in Italy's starting line-up just in time to embark on the first stage of a World Cup adventure.

September 1972 saw the final international friendly of the summer, before the serious business began of trying to qualify for the 1974 World Cup in West Germany. Italy hosted Yugoslavia in Turin; so the stadium was packed with fans who knew and loved Fabio Capello already. It was a happy occasion for the 'local' favourite; he experienced a winning feeling in the *Azzurri* (Blues) shirt for the first time, even though he was substituted 18 minutes from the end of a 3-1 win.

On 7 October 1972, Fabio experienced the thrill of scoring for his country for the first time. It didn't matter that Luxembourg was the lowly opposition. Neither was his joy diminished by the fact that Giorgio Chinaglia had opened the scoring as early as the third minute, and Riva had added two more before half-time. When Capello netted his country's fourth goal after 62 minutes, he had rounded off a rout in a World Cup qualifier and he was on cloud nine. By the following spring, Italy and Capello were well on the way to booking their ticket for West Germany. Now he could concentrate on his biggest matches to date in a Juventus shirt.

On and off the pitch, Fabio displayed a natural authority that even his friends didn't tend to question. Dino Zoff had arrived at Juventus that summer and struck up a friendship with the mid-fielder that would last a lifetime. Describing Capello's influence within the players' group at Juventus rather well, Zoff told me 'Fabio was known as "*Geometra*" – "The Surveyor". He could see everything happening around him and he could really direct a game from midfield; he was the complete player in his position. You couldn't say he was a flare player; you are talking geometry not fantasy. But he had great influence over matches just the same; he was really very effective. Off the pitch, people didn't try to pull his leg because he was a forceful personality there too. He wasn't severe with people, but he was quite serious about what he was doing. He had enough friends but not too many.'

Italo Allodi, the Juventus executive whose enduring gift to Capello was his love for art, remained one of his most influential friends beyond the dressing room. Soon Capello wasn't just admiring pictures. He was buying them too. Fabio began by collecting works by a Greek-Italian futurist, Giorgio De Chirico, who was still alive when Fabio was a player. 'Capello started collecting in his late 20s when playing for Juventus,' explained the Italian-based general editorial director of *The Art Newspaper*, Anna Somers Cocks. 'The team's (general) manager, Italo Allodi, tipped him off that buying art was better than just splurging money.' In 2008 Fabio insisted that stories about him owning a painting by Marc Chagall were untrue, though I'm told his private collection would still impress any art expert.

Back in his Juventus days, abstract artists such as the Swiss genius Paul Klee and the Dutchman Piet Mondrian captivated Capello completely. Later he was happy to explain why that is still the case: 'Figurative art has been done since forever, and what interested me more were those who were looking for another way, another language.'

But what interested Fabio most in the early 1970s, was the pursuit of honours. And as the 1972–73 season built to a climax, there was every chance he would add to his medals, because Juventus were still in contention at home and in Europe. After beating Marseilles 3-1 on aggregate over two legs and Magdeburg

2-0, Juventus scraped through their European Cup quarter-final against the Hungarians of Ujpest on away goals. Suddenly all that stood between Capello and the European Cup final were the relative unknowns of England, Derby County. Brian Clough's team had shocked English football by stylishly winning a domestic title the previous year. They showed they were also a European force to be reckoned with by crushing Benfica 3-0 in their quarter-final first leg, which proved decisive.

Allodi was determined that Juventus would not suffer the same fate as the Portuguese club. Behind the scenes he went to work. By the time Juve's European Cup semi-final first leg against Derby County came around, the English side may no longer have been facing fair odds. The referee in Turin, German Gerhard Schulenburg, seemed to give a considerable amount of leeway to the Juventus right-half Giuseppe Furino and his ferocious tackling. Then Peter Taylor, Brian Clough's assistant, claimed to have seen Schulenburg 'talking earnestly in German' with the Juventus substitute, Helmut Haller, as they walked down the tunnel at half-time.

Haller, Capello's former friend and neighbour, had risen from the bench to engage the official in conversation. Brian Glanville explained, 'Taylor followed them and, he says, "tried to intercept them" to show he knew what might be afoot, but his way was blocked, apparently on Haller's instructions, "by a group of tough-looking Italians" and a scuffle ensued. Taylor had already been warned before the game, he said, by the old Juventus favourite, John Charles, that "Haller was in with the referee again."'

In the second half Schulenburg booked key Derby players Roy McFarland and Archie Gemmill, thus ensuring they would miss the second leg because they had already been booked earlier in the tournament. Even 25 years later, Clough was still claiming, 'Haller had suggested the right bookings.' His accusation at the time was slightly more general as he stated, 'The Italians were in the referee's dressing room before the match and during the interval.'

Schulenburg and Haller have always denied that they did anything wrong or had been having anything more than a casual chat as fellow West Germans. There is no evidence that anything underhand was going on. 'Nothing can ever be proved', said Taylor. However, McFarland in particular appeared to have been booked for no reason that was immediately evident.

Capello later argued that Derby wouldn't have complained had they won the tie. The Juventus players, Fabio explained, had been thinking about the match and nothing else, while Roberto Bettega insisted that Derby were no match for the Italians anyway. 'Derby were not on the same level as that Leeds team we had faced a couple of years earlier. Derby were less famous, less important, less strong than Leeds. We were a bit more mature by then too. The first game in Turin should be remembered for what (Jose) Altafini did.'

After 28 minutes Altafini, by then a veteran striker who had played for both Brazil and Italy, met Anastasi's cross with perfect timing to open the scoring. But Clough's men showed typical grit and more than a little skill to hit back quickly. Kevin Hector played a one-two with John O'Hare and maintained his momentum to score a glorious equaliser. Then came the half-time controversy, and Derby found themselves under massive pressure after the interval. Not only were Clough's men unsettled by the bookings of their key players, but also Juventus, with Capello in the engine room, worked up a fearsome head of steam. Causio kept a powerful shot admirably low to register the Italian club's second, and then the rampant Altafini beat three Derby defenders, including England international McFarland, to lash Juve's third into the roof of the net.

In the closing stages Derby, who had only been promoted to England's top-flight in 1969, were nearly overrun completely. Causio struck a post and Francesco Morini's header was cleared off the line. But the final scoreline of 3-1 gave Derby a realistic chance of turning the tie back in their favour with a couple of goals at their ground, known as the Baseball Ground – or at least it would have done if McFarland and Gemmill hadn't been eliminated by their bookings. So it was understandable that Clough was more than a little emotional at the end of that draining first match, although his comments were controversial and inflammatory even by his standards. Apart from calling the Italians 'cheating bastards', he went on to question Italy's courage and conduct in the Second

World War, not an attack that would have greatly impressed Fabio Capello, given the brave way his own father had born his suffering in captivity. But the controversy was far from over.

When Allodi had switched allegiance from Inter to Juventus, he had brought with him a 'fixer' called Deszo Solti. Juventus later claimed that Solti was acting independently when he tried to bribe the Portuguese referee called Francisco Marques Lobo just before the official was due to take charge of the second match in Derby. A few days before the return leg, Solti travelled to Lisbon in secret to try to persuade the referee to accept gifts and hospitality. Somehow Solti knew who the referee was going to be before Lobo did. His problem, it emerged, was that Lobo remained honest.

Lobo later swore that Solti claimed to have made travel arrangements for him prior to the second match. Had Lobo accepted the invitation, he would have flown from Lisbon to Madrid and thence to Milan, his ultimate destination Turin. 'You will stay at my house there,' promised Solti, according to Lobo, 'and I want you to meet the president of Juventus and other officials.'

In *Champions of Europe*, Glanville wrote, 'Solti then made one of those gestures common in his career, at once flamboyant and insidious. He reached into his pocket, produced a car key, and dangled it in front of Lobo. "The implication was," said Lobo to my colleague Keith Botsford, "that when I left Italy, I would not have to fly back, but would have a car of my own to drive back in."'

Lobo had tipped off the Portuguese Referees' Association as soon as he had known the meeting was to take place, so he stayed silent. Solti thought he had an agreement. The referee remembered Solti's words well. 'Look, Lobo,' he now said. 'My friends and I are very interested in the return match. It's really nothing for me. I have to pay the players anyway. There's no problem. I already have to carry 19 on my list, and it isn't difficult to put down 20. Anyway, I have a free hand to do what I want for the club. If I put down 20 instead of 19, nobody is going to say anything. The price is about $5,000, and I can do this without any trouble.'

As Lobo later pointed out, $5,000 and a car was four years' work for him, but in the end he made his excuses and didn't accept the invitation. Still Solti persisted, this time by phone, because there was enough time to tip the odds even further in favour of Juventus before the second match against Derby. On this occasion Lobo recorded the conversation. Here is an abridged version of that exchange:

LOBO: 'I have received the notification to do the return match between Derby and Juventus, but I cannot go to Turin . . .'

SOLTI: 'Can you come through Paris? . . .'

LOBO: '. . . Ah, I see. We will make the arrangements in Paris.'

SOLTI: 'Yes.'

LOBO: 'The arrangement we talked about at the Ritz Hotel was $5,000, wasn't it?'

SOLTI: 'Yes.'

LOBO: 'Well, I haven't got anything more.'

SOLTI: 'I think we will discuss it personally.'

In the end Italo Allodi's attempt through Solti to ensure an uneven playing field for the second match failed. Francisco Marques Lobo turned down the bribe, informed the authorities about what had happened and was allowed to referee the second leg. Fabio played in that second match, just as he had played in the first. Lobo's impartiality was underlined when he awarded Derby a second-leg penalty, although Alan Hinton fired his 57th-minute spot-kick wide. In the closing stages, Roger Davies was rightly sent off for retaliation. Davies had been provoked by some dreadful Italian tackling, but when the Derby striker head-butted Morini, the Rams' challenge was finally over. 'It was the missed penalty that I remember as being decisive,' said Bettega pointedly about a match that ended 0-0.

Finally Fabio had been on the winning side against an English club and he had reached the European Cup final. What had been attempted in order to ensure victory for the Italian club, however, will stain the semi-final result forever in the minds of some football-lovers.

After an inquiry by UEFA in Zurich, no disciplinary action was taken against Juventus. Brian Glanville confronted the Juventus president, Giampiero Boniperti, about Solti's exploits soon after the scandal was uncovered. 'Brian, if there are these madmen going about!' Boniperti replied, as though Juventus could do nothing to stop misguided individuals. Boniperti got rid of Allodi soon afterwards.

Four years later Glanville uncovered a letter in Holland that Solti had signed in 1971 on behalf of Juventus, showing that there had indeed been a link between this shady individual and the Italian club.

Glanville concluded, 'That Solti, notorious for years as a fixer for Internazionale of Milan in their European heyday, had offered Lobo a bribe, I was convinced. Just as I was sure that Lobo had sturdily refused it. That Solti had been "run" by the general manager of Juventus, the notorious Italo Allodi, who for years had used him while Secretary of Inter, I was equally sure.'

Brian Clough thought he knew the score. He said later, 'In any other industry there would have been a full-scale enquiry into Juventus, but UEFA just looked the other way.' Dino Zoff told me in 2008, 'Brian Clough had problems with Allodi. But in the end it came to nothing.'

As for Allodi, he put the campaign against him down to jealousy. 'I have enemies; envious people, those who can't explain my fortune, if not with corruption and subterfuge. Instead I live on public relations. These are a gift, an instinct. Those who don't have it can't get it. Then I pay the price for having interests outside football. I know the difference between Chopin and Schopenhauer. I manage to speak about things which aren't football and I am not forgiven for this.'

Juve, meanwhile, always argued that that they couldn't possibly bear any responsibility for events beyond their control. Meanwhile UEFA, who didn't want to believe that one of their top clubs could go to such lengths to try to secure victory, went through the motions of holding a tribunal in Zurich, but didn't dig too deep. Perhaps to cover their own backs against the threat of a counter-action from Juventus, UEFA soon cleared the Italian giants and thanked them for their cooperation with the so-called investigation. There were never any UEFA sanctions against Juventus for the scandal. So Fabio Capello and his team-mates were left to prepare for the 1973 European Cup final against Ajax of

Amsterdam in relative peace, though by then the story of the scandal had broken over their club.

Eventually, of course, there was a well-conducted enquiry into Juventus; but that was in 2006 and focused above all on the 2004–05 season. It didn't relate to the Derby semi-final of 1973. There was a link between the two eras, however. The alleged perpetrator of corrupt deeds in the new millennium was Luciano Moggi – the protégé of the arch-corrupter in the 1973 scandal, Italo Allodi. When Allodi was sent packing by Juventus at the end of that 1972–73 season, Moggi stayed – and was promoted within the club until the 2006 scandal finally brought him down.

Thankfully Juventus post-2006 bears no relation to the club of 1973, since the staff was entirely different. Juve's reputation as a clean club that does things the right way off the field as well as on it has been restored in recent years. There are those who still deny that Allodi was ever involved in any foul play behind the scenes at Juventus in the early 1970s. Some of the biggest names in the history of Italian football continue to sing his praises. Roberto Bettega, the former Juventus vice-president who left the club in 2006 is still an admirer of Allodi. Asked what kind of man Allodi was, Bettega replied, 'He was a great man, a true professional, a person way ahead of his time, who belonged more in the year 2000 and beyond. He was so intelligent, he saw so far ahead.' Dino Zoff, another living legend of Italian football who played at Juventus under the Allodi regime, told me, 'Italo Allodi was the greatest manager of his time, the best in Italy for sure.' And Arrigo Sacchi, the legendary Milan and Italy coach, echoed, 'Allodi was a great director, a cultured man, and I prefer to speak about the man I knew than pay any attention to gossip about him.'

The ammunition available to Allodi's detractors was more than gossip. There is no doubt that he had a brilliant brain; it was how he sometimes used it that invited less praise. However, the likes of Roberto Bettega, Dino Zoff and Arrigo Sacchi would point to the way Allodi helped to revolutionise the transfer market by bringing in foreign stars and changed the way in which players were handled, so that virtually every aspect of their lives was taken care of. It is also worth mentioning that Allodi gave Sacchi his first big break coaching the youngsters at Fiorentina. He also set up *Coverciano*, Italian football's brilliant centre of coaching excellence and tactical education, a spiritual home for Italian managers and in time for the national team too. Fabio Capello wants an English equivalent of Allodi's concept and that is why he has supported the development of a National Football Centre at Burton. The late Italo Allodi, it is fair to say, had his fans. The problem is that he fixed a lot of football matches too.

Fabio Capello, Dino Zoff, Arrigo Sacchi or Roberto Bettega were not complicit in any wrongdoing by Allodi, but they admired the man's energy and intellect. Allodi always defended himself in typically articulate fashion when faced with any accusations of corruption, and continued to do so until his death in 1999. When his critics once suggested that the *Coverciano* centre was just another Allodi power base, the charming Italo is alleged to have smiled and said, 'Power in football is measured by the friends one has. I have so many of them.'

Meanwhile with a showpiece European Cup final against the mighty Ajax of Amsterdam looming, Juventus attempted to secure the domestic half of what they hoped would become a remarkable double. Sealing the *Scudetto* (Italian league championship) looked as formidable a challenge as overcoming the Dutch, however, when it came to the last day of the Serie A season. Both Juventus and Lazio were a point behind AC Milan at the start of a dramatic final round of matches. Capello and company travelled to his old club Roma knowing that only a win would do. They achieved it with the help of a penalty three minutes from time, scored by Antonello Cuccureddu. Milan and Lazio, meanwhile, crumbled under the pressure on that last, decisive day. It meant that Juventus had made more history, Capello had bagged another championship winners' medal, and his career was moving from strength to strength. He was in a team packed with winners – back-to-back titles had proved it.

Just how good Juventus were in European terms was about to become clear too. The much-anticipated final against the Dutch masters of Ajax, led by the incomparable Johan Cruyff, was about to begin. Ajax had already won two European Cups with their

'Total Football' – whereby every player was capable of doing the job of any outfielder, whatever the position, and the team attacked and defended as one. The stage was set when 93,500 fans packed into the Stadion Crvena Zvezda in Belgrade on a balmy night at the end of May. It was the 1000th tie in the glorious history of the European Cup; unfortunately for Fabio Capello and Juve, no team had begun a final with more panache than Ajax of Amsterdam did in the Yugoslav capital.

The imperious Cruyff hit a post after only three minutes, but Dino Zoff was soon picking the ball out of the back of the net. Johnny Rep was the only Ajax player who hadn't appeared in a European final before, but he made the biggest impact after just four minutes. Horst Blankenburg crossed, Rep rose above Gianpietro Marchetti, and Zoff couldn't stop his header.

Capello and fellow midfielder Franco Causio were rated among the best in Europe by now, but they were unable to do much more than watch an exhibition that bordered on football perfection. The only thing missing was the number of goals that Ajax deserved for their genius. Cruyff set up Arnold Muhren but somehow he missed; Barry Hulshoff headed against the crossbar when it looked easier to score, but the course of the match was never going to be diverted. The result should have been more like 4-0, such was the one-sided nature of the fight; but Repp's match-winner was enough to confirm Ajax's place in history as one of the greatest teams ever to play the game. Only Real Madrid from the Di Stefano and Puskas era of the late 1950s and early 1960s might have been able to give the Dutch, with their technical ease and unpredictable flare, a serious test.

With the possible exception of the goalkeeper, Zoff, the Juventus players trudged off the field that night knowing they were good – but not that good. Even someone as proud as Fabio, told me a quarter of a century later that Ajax had been on a completely different level, so good that there had been nothing Juventus could do. Ajax had raised the bar for everybody, and Juventus weren't the first or last team to struggle with the seemingly impossible question of how to deal with Johan Cruyff's extraordinary football brain.

Twenty-one years later Fabio and Cruyff would meet for

another European Cup final, this time as coaches. Back in 1973, however, Capello was left to reflect upon the endless succession of painful blows that European football had dealt him. Whether it was the toss of the coin or the realisation that, just when your fingertips were nearly touching the biggest club prize of all, a footballing genius spirited it away; this fascinating game had various dastardly ways of bringing a hard man crashing back down to earth.

'Two finals, two defeats, that was disappointing,' acknowledged Bettega, reflecting back on the UEFA Cup and European Cup reverses. Then he added with a touch of pathos, 'but we were younger then.' For Capello there was more than a consolation prize waiting for him back home in Turin, because he knew Laura would soon give birth to his second child. Sure enough Fabio's younger son Edoardo arrived on 1 August 1973.

In the years that followed it became obvious that, in his own way, Fabio loved both his children as much as he loved his wife. But he wasn't someone who could sit at home day after day and hope fatherhood would lead him to forget the blows to his professional pride. Pierfilippo later said of both Fabio and Laura, 'They weren't affectionate in their gestures (as parents). They were not into hugs and kisses.'

Fabio would leave most of the parenting to Laura. Of his dealings with his boys, he admitted, 'As a father I didn't nag or pester them. Laura followed them around more.' And Capello was never slow to point out that his wife made a very good job of being a mother. He said, 'She is a very peaceful woman, a teacher, and she dedicated herself to the mission of being a housewife and bringing up the children. She did it with joy and she did it very well.' Meanwhile Fabio was a superb provider for the children and still very ambitious; so ambitious, in fact, that he must have realised that his career as a footballer was heading towards a critical moment.

CHAPTER 6
HEAVEN AND HELL, WEMBLEY AND WEST GERMANY

THERE WAS ONE PRIZE IN FOOTBALL THAT WAS VALUED EVEN more highly than any European trophy, and could wipe away all the heartache. That prize was the World Cup, and Fabio still dreamed of winning it with Italy. He would not allow his spirit to be beaten, whatever Holland's best club had just done to him. He would learn from the defeat, he would come back stronger and even better. He would inspire his country and send out a warning to the rest of the world that Italy were a force to be reckoned with when it came to the World Cup. The countdown to West Germany, 1974, had begun.

As part of the celebrations for the 75th anniversary of the Italian FA, June friendly matches were arranged at home to Brazil and England, the countries who had won the previous two World Cups. Fabio Capello could scarcely have dared to dream about the leading role he was to play in both those fixtures. But as he later recalled, he had started to develop a knack of timing his runs forward to perfection, so that he was in exactly the right place at the right moment to score crucial goals. When I compared him to England's former captain, Bryan Robson, a great midfield hero of the 1980s, Capello enthusiastically agreed that he had been just that kind of player.

On 9 June 1973 Italy prepared to take on the Brazilians, the opposition every team dreamed about beating. But no team had defeated Brazil for some three-and-a-half years. The aura of invincibility had stretched across an amazing 36 matches, and the Samba Boys had earned themselves a reputation as one of the great teams of all time. However, Pele had recently hung up his international boots; and although the wonderfully talented Jairzinho and Rivelino were still going strong, there was a feeling in Italy that football's finest nation might just be there for the taking at last. Revenge was in the air as the teams prepared to step out in Rome's Stadio Olimpico, as the Brazilians had shattered Italy's World Cup hopes in Mexico in 1970 with a 4-1 victory in the final. Fabio Capello hadn't played in that famous match; at the time he hadn't even been a full international. Now he was ready to make his mark like never before.

Gigi Riva put the Italians ahead after just 16 minutes, but the magical backlash from the South Americans wasn't long in coming. That's when Fabio, straight-backed and tough as ever, made sure that the hosts were not completely overrun. He took a bad knock to his knee, but bravely he battled on. The Italian tennis legend Nicola Pietrangeli, who was a spectator in the stadium, later commented, 'Capello fought like a lion.' Even so, Brazil were unlucky not to be awarded a penalty when Inter's defender, Mauro Bellugi, appeared to foul Leivinha in the area. And the South Amercians were still seething when, against the run of play, Capello added Italy's second in the 76th minute to send the crowd wild.

Looking back, Fabio was less than convinced that his strike had crossed the line all those years ago. At the time, however, *Corierre dello Sport* wrote that Capello had celebrated 'too quickly and instinctively' to suggest otherwise, and that he had been 'in the perfect position to see where he had kicked the ball, having sent it over the diving goalkeeper.' The referee pointed to the centre circle without hesitation to award the goal, while Brazilians urged him to consult his linesman; but the assistant only agreed with his boss.

As with Geoff Hurst's controversial goal in the World Cup final of 1966, all that mattered was that it had been given. 'Phantom goal' or not, Capello still recalled the thrill many years later of being responsible for the eruption of that 1973 Rome crowd, as everyone realised Italy had humbled the world champions and brought Brazil's incredible sequence of results to a dramatic end. Although Capello had never been short of confidence, he could now consign the recent memory of having been outclassed by Ajax to the past. A 2-0 victory over Brazil makes any team feel on top of the world, and this would be seen as the moment when Fabio reinforced his reputation as one of the finest international midfielders in the game. He hadn't finished impressing the world that month, though. *Corriere dello Sport*'s headline on their Brazil match report was mindful that this was very much a question of one team down, one to go. 'And now down with the English' screamed the newspaper's front page in a fit of nationalistic fervour. On that same front page, Capello was named as one of the four very best players on the pitch. In a match against Brazil, that was some accolade.

Five days later England were Italy's guests in Turin. Incredible as it seems today, Italy had never once beaten England. Fabio described what it felt like to be Italian in that era. He said, 'In the 1970s Italy wasn't a world force but a poor country. Italians abroad didn't have respect or great importance. There was an inferiority complex and then some. On a sports field there was a feeling of physical inferiority. We had a complex that we ran less too. From the moment in 1934 when Italy had lost 3-2 to England, we had lost a total of four times and drawn four against England.'

But striker Pietro Anastasi began to rid the Italians of any inferiority complex in the 37th minute when he opened the scoring against Sir Alf Ramsey's men. And Capello, also on his 'home' ground, was determined to make a similar impact. First he completely cancelled out the threat of England's World Cup winner, Martin Peters, while covering every blade of grass necessary to turn defence into attack. Then after half time he became even more deadly. A second goal for his country in the space of a week seemed too much to ask for, but he managed that notable feat in the 51st minute when he pounced instinctively to lash a left-footed strike beyond the English defence. This time there was no doubt about whether or not the ball had crossed the line; England's hopes had been dealt a mortal blow. The Capello goal prompted the home fans to sing 'Juventus 2, England 0', and the party in Turin could begin early. Looking back, Fabio's pride lay in the fact that his strike had again been the one to seal victory.

Mario Gismondi of *Corriere dello Sport* led the plaudits after the win over England when he wrote, 'Today Capello surpassed in tactical acumen and impact even the Capello of the Olimpico in Rome against Brazil, and that can be said without even taking into account his two goals in the two games. Seeing him play, it just reinforces the feeling of regret over not having had him in Mexico in place of De Sisti ... he adds an element of order, of calm.' The remark was tantamount to suggesting that, with Capello in midfield, Italy could have downed mighty Brazil in 1970 and won the World Cup.

The newspaper's headline proclaimed, 'Myth Shattered by Masters, Not Pupils ... the English were not invincible after all.'

Capello had become a symbol of Italy's triumph over its own inferiority complex; he was an icon in the country's rise from humble origins to become a force capable of conquering the giants of the game. Neither was there an excessive amount of respect evident in some of Capello's post-match remarks about the opposition. Fabio's verdict on England was controversial because he even appeared to criticise the second-half tactics of England's World Cup-winning coach, Sir Alf Ramsey. With what was described as 'an imperturbable air about him,' Capello damned England with faint praise before focusing on the most respected manager in English football history. Fabio told *Corriere dello Sport*, 'It is not that easy to play against these English, even though our opponents today showed themselves to be inferior to the expectations we had of them. We played cautiously for the first 25 minutes. Then, little by little, we took up the reins in midfield. After the interval Ramsey released (Emlyn) Hughes into a more fluid role, and (Bobby) Moore went over to cover the right-hand area of defence. That allowed our strikers to create more space for themselves and we had more chances to score another goal.'

So Capello, the future England manager, was picking holes in the tactics of the greatest England manager of them all. And he was even more stinging in the remarks he made to journalist, Brian

Glanville, in the aftermath of Italy's victory in Turin. Fabio told Glanville, 'Your play is predictable and perhaps monotonous. In my view, you lack a player like Bobby Charlton, to switch the ball about. On the crosses, you take too much time to get there and make them. You miss (Terry) Cooper a lot, he was a real winger (sic), he didn't just come forward, he actually beat defenders.' Later Capello reflected on his playing days by saying, 'Always when I played against an English team they ran a lot and were very strong but not good technically.'

Ironically, after England's friendly matches under Capello in 2008, people were saying much the same thing about the static, predictable and technically poor nature of the football on show.

Back in 1973, however, Fabio was given an early taste of the sort of penalty shoot-out agony that would become a familiar theme of England's adventures in big tournaments, before Capello's arrival as manager. The occasion for Fabio's first shoot-out heartbreak was the *Coppa Italia* or Italian Cup final against AC Milan at the Stadio Olimpico in Rome, less than a month after his great triumph against Brazil in the same arena. There was deadlock after Romeo Benetti's penalty just after the break cancelled out Roberto Bettega's opener for Juventus. The penalty shoot-out was still a relatively new concept, but preferable at least to the heartbreak of the coin-toss. Capello's own experiences against the Polish had been the catalyst for the introduction of the new solution. But within a few minutes of the final whistle of extra time in that Coppa Italia final, Fabio wouldn't have felt much better than he did in Strasbourg.

It wasn't the ever-reliable Capello who failed from the penalty spot when it really mattered, because he had been forced off after just a few minutes of the showpiece with a recurrence of that troublesome knee injury. No, Italy internationals Pietro Anastasi, Roberto Bettega and Luciano Spinosi were the culprits, while Milan surprisingly out-foxed the formidable Dino Zoff each time. Juventus were therefore well beaten in the acid test by 5-2. Capello had been a victim of cruel fate yet again as he missed out on another winner's medal. His consolation that summer was the knowledge that he had climbed to the very top of football and shown that he could not just survive while rubbing shoulders with the greats of the international game, but he could also become the star of the show.

While Capello and Italy were growing stronger on the international stage, England were struggling. The great Bobby Moore was a fading force and his World Cup-winning manager, Alf Ramsey, seemed beyond his best tactically. In an unforgettably frustrating 1-1 draw with Poland that autumn, goalkeeper Jan Tomaszewski, who was branded 'a clown' by guest television pundit Brian Clough, constantly denied England's strikers on the night. Clown or not, Tomaszewski's saves effectively knocked England out of the World Cup, because they had needed to win that final qualifier in order to reach the tournament proper.

Italy had faired much better. Capello had inspired the side to a 2-0 victory over Sweden on 29 September in Milan; and then the Italians had swept aside Switzerland by the same scoreline in their final World Cup qualifier in Rome on 20 October. They had won their last four matches 2-0, and the one before that, against Luxembourg, 5-0. So there was really no reason to feel inferior when Italy travelled to Wembley for a friendly on 14 November 1973, even though such feelings, in sport as in life, can sometimes remain longer than logic demands. The Italians may have beaten England 2-0 in Turin and broken a lamentable run, but one victory hadn't wiped away history. After decades of feeling second best, Italy would have to prove that their change in fortunes hadn't been a fluke. To do that, they would need to overcome their nerves in the intimidating atmosphere inside Wembley Stadium.

Capello explained, 'There are places in which you feel the breath of history itself. There are very few stadiums like that in the world. The Maracana in Brazil, Anfield or Old Trafford, the San Siro or the Bernabeu. And then English stadia had something more – there were no fences separating the players from the crowd. We Italians appreciate it immediately – you enter, and breathe in the tradition and respect.'

If Capello and his team-mates were inspired by the magnitude of the stage, Alf Ramsey was finding it tough to see beyond one Italian danger man. Asked to name the four best Italian players in a pre-match press conference, Ramsey replied quite seriously, 'Rivera,

Rivera, Rivera and Rivera.' But the match wouldn't be remembered for the player singled out by the England manager – rather for the player who became England manager.

England were desperate to restore some pride to their national football team after their failure to qualify for the World Cup the previous month. Although the home team wasn't quite the threat it had once been, they still had enough talent to bombard Dino Zoff's goal with ominous regularity. But Capello's friend was in the middle of a run of international clean sheets that would see him play 1,142 minutes of football for Italy without conceding a goal. With four minutes to go on that cold Wednesday evening, the match-winner struck. Fabio Capello set the attack in motion, threading a pass to Giorgio Chinaglia under pressure. The Swansea-born Chinaglia drew Bobby Moore out to meet him as he advanced down the right; then he tricked the England captain with a sudden burst of pace.

England's goalkeeper, Peter Shilton, seemed surprised by Chinaglia's early shot, which was delivered with ferocity from an angle. It was all Shilton could do to parry the ball into the path of any predators who might be arriving in his six-yard area. Moore's central-defensive partner, Roy McFarland, had drifted too close to his goalkeeper, perhaps hoping to protect him as Shilton tried to gather the ball into his arms. So Fabio, who had run half the length of the pitch to end the move he had started, found himself unmarked when the rebound fell his way. The problem for Capello was that he only had a split second in which to react. There was a danger the ball would become trapped under his feet, or that he would not have time to move his boot into the right position to direct his shot goalwards. Reacting with all the sharpness the situation demanded, Capello stuck out his foot in the nick of time; but he sent his shot perilously close to Shilton and for a moment it seemed as though the shot might not have the power to beat the goalkeeper.

Capello said of that moment, 'Chinaglia had done some dribbling and then shot hard so the goalkeeper didn't hold onto it. I arrived and had a job to slam on the brakes, but got some contact with the ball and pushed it slowly over the English goal line. I knew immediately it was the winning goal, in the interminable moments in which the ball bobbled slowly towards Shilton's goal. I thought immediately about the historic nature of the result, but mostly about all the Italians abroad. For them it was a sort of redemption. That is why that goal is still, even today, my calling card as a player.'

Fabio's celebration was as impassioned as any in his playing career. He roared as he was mobbed by his team-mates and there was clearly more than joy at work. '"That's a present for all the Italians in the world," I told myself. It's a response to all the inferiority complexes. We had won 2-0 in Turin, and we won again in the same year in London with my goal: a record – and what a stadium to do it in!' Fabio seemed to believe that Italians abroad were seen as waiters and little else. He had set about changing that perception almost single-handedly.

No wonder Zoff's achievements in keeping the likes of Allan Clarke, Peter Osgood, Tony Currie and Colin Bell at bay were all but forgotten. Dino recalled wistfully, 'I made some good saves but it was my friend Fabio Capello who scored the important goal. He was in the right place at the right time. The one who scores the goals gets the attention.'

Capello was the hero of the hour and rightly so. Even in 2008, Fabio's mother couldn't resist her own little tribute to that night. When asked what had been her favourite moment of her son's career, Evelina said mischievously, 'Fabio's goal against England in 1973.' Then she laughed, and made me swear to make it clear that she had been joking.

'Scoring the winning goal at Wembley was the highlight of my entire playing career,' Fabio said, 'the greatest feeling.' No wonder. Nothing could have given his father more pleasure than to see his son hand Italy such a definitive moment of national pride. Guerrino wasn't present at Wembley to see his son's glorious night; but luckily, Fabio told me, a telephone had been installed in the Capello family home back in Pieris by then. When Fabio called to share his joy, his parents were able to convey their own sense of pride from a different country. Such moments, taken for granted in the 21st century, were wondrous and deeply special back then.

Given his own fierce patriotism at that stage of his life, a patriotism that he assured me he had retained even after taking the England job, it must have been hard for Fabio to say what he did when he reached England. 'Italy will now be an adversary? Yes, certainly, because we want to do really well.'

Back in 1973 he had done well for his native country. Not only had Fabio beaten England twice in a matter of months, he had scored twice. He was the Italian hero. You could have forgiven Capello at that moment in time for thinking that he was almost indestructible – unbeatable. Football, however, has a funny way of bringing its heroes crashing back down to earth.

Capello's next international challenge was Italy's prestigious friendly in February 1974 against West Germany, who would host the World Cup Finals later that year. This match was also played in the Stadio Olimpico, and the crowd was treated to a chess match with neither side too keen to show their hand. The meaningful action loomed too close on the horizon, so it finished goalless.

In such a massive year for his international career and those of so many of his club team-mates, perhaps it was predictable that Juventus missed out on more Serie A glory. Coached by ex-player Carlo Parola, they finished second in the championship. Disappointment at giving up their title was offset by the keen anticipation felt by Capello and the other top players as they prepared to face the biggest challenge of them all. There were, however, signs that the Italy squad was already tired as they went into the tournament. Just days before the World Cup in June, they played a friendly in Vienna against Austria; that one finished 0-0 too. This wasn't quite the way to strike fear into the hearts of their World Cup rivals, but they had had enough recent success as a group to believe the tournament would go well for them. After all, Italy went to the World Cup with an unbeaten run of 15 matches, a record largely inspired by Fabio. That sort of form made the Italians one of the favourites for the title, along with hosts Germany. Fabio was dreaming of World Cup glory, and why not when Italy had developed a winning blend of flare and organisation?

Then Italo Allodi was made General Manager of the Italy team for the finals and soon began to make his presence felt, encroaching into the football territory that was normally the domain of coaches alone. Preparations for the first match took place in an atmosphere of heightened tension. No longer was this the happy camp of champions-in-waiting. The degree to which the Italians had been distracted became apparent when, inexplicably, in the 46th minute of their first World Cup match, Haiti – the unlikeliest opposition – breached the Italian defences. Zoff's record, which still stands out as one of the greatest achievements in footballing history, was finally ended by an unknown player from a remote island – Emmanuel Sanon. He shocked the world with his opener for the underdogs, and although Italy stormed back to win 3-1, their reputation had been severely dented. Giorgio Chinaglia had been substituted in the second half and swore so loudly at the coach, Ferruccio Valcareggi, that the abuse was picked up by television microphones. He had therefore shocked the audience back home even before he reached the Italy dressing room, where he smashed several bottles of mineral water.

In their next match Italy drew with Argentina, who beat Haiti 4-1. This meant that Capello, Zoff and company had to draw with Poland in order to progress ahead of the South Americans. With so many clean sheets over the previous couple of years, Italy's progress was regarded as a foregone conclusion by most observers. They were masters at shutting out their opponents, and that was all they had to do in this case. But Poland had already qualified by beating both Argentina and Haiti, and two of their unheralded side had begun to distinguish themselves on the world stage. Jan Tomaszewski, the goalkeeper, clearly wasn't a clown after all, because he was showing a consistency to silence his critics. Poland's biggest star was Kazimierz Deyna, an attacking midfielder with an eye for goal to surpass even that of Capello.

Years later, Tomaszewski recalled, 'It was Deyna v Capello, two of the best midfielders in the world at the time. Deyna was an attacking midfielder and because Capello could be more defensive it was part of his job to stop him. If Deyna managed to score, that would not reflect well on Capello. We didn't have to win or even draw; it wasn't an important game for us because we had already qualified. So we were playing for pride and to make a name for ourselves.'

Free of all the pressure that Italian players now carried on their shoulders, the Poles struck first through Andrzej Szarmach, a beautiful strike that left Dino Zoff with no chance. Then the unthinkable happened, and Deyna added a second, shooting first time and beating Zoff just inside his left-hand post. Time was running out and the Italians were faced with the humiliating thought that they might have to go home early.

Tomaszewski remembered, 'Once Deyna scored, Capello, who was in my view one of the best midfielders in the world, went forward to start attacking. I think there were about 10 or 15 minutes to go when I noticed that he had switched with a team-mate. Until that point, Italy hadn't made much of an impression, but Capello changed all that. He was the first man to give Italy a genuine power in attack. With a few minutes left he began a beautiful move and raced through to finish it. He only had to beat me with his shot; it was one on one. I have to admit that he didn't even give me one chance in a hundred to save his shot. He fired it to my left-hand side. I went the correct way and did everything I could, but it was too late.

'Capello had scored and I remember him briefly putting his hands in the air, but there was no real time to celebrate. One of his team-mates picked the ball out of the back of the net and they all ran back to the halfway line. There were less than five minutes to go and they still needed one more goal to advance in the tournament. They did everything they could to make it 2-2, and I think Giacinto Facchetti had a chance in the last minute, but they just couldn't get their equaliser.'

Capello had tried hard to turn the game. He had starred for the Italians yet again, but the final whistle came like a death knell. His World Cup dream was over. Fabio recalled later, 'That remains one of the bitterest moments of my career. I hoped to win it, also to give joy to our immigrants in Germany. But a poor athletic condition and the sheer weight of expectation made us pitiful beyond reason.'

What made Capello's lifelong disappointment at those events in Germany harder to bear was the fact other Italy teams overcame problems and pressure to succeed at subsequent World Cups in 1982 and 2006. Although the patriotic Fabio was naturally delighted for those Italy teams, the successes only served to highlight the painful failure of the team of which he had been part. In 2008, Capello touched upon this when he said, 'I was part of the Italy team at the World Cup in 1974, when we didn't even get out of the group phase. But generally, the Italian players, when they face a problem, they close ranks, they connect, they always connect.'

The Italy of 1974 hadn't connected enough. At 28, Capello knew he was in his prime, but the Italians had simply burned themselves out when it really mattered. It was an experience he would try to turn to his advantage once he became England manager, so that similar mistakes were not made the next time England went to a major international tournament. But there was no more time for Capello to learn his World Cup lesson as a player. Fabio knew he would be 32 when the next World Cup came around in Argentina. To expect a footballer of such an advanced age to operate successfully in the searing heat of South America was probably unrealistic. So back in West Germany, in the moments after that defeat to Poland, Fabio was faced with the grim realisation that he would probably never be a World Cup winner as a player. It was a shattering blow.

Tomaszewski recalled, 'Every Italian player had the same expression on his face, the one you have just before crying. They had begun the game against us thinking it would be impossible to be knocked out. But it had happened, and they were shocked. I think only Dino Zoff, one of the greatest goalkeepers in history, was still in Italy's team eight years later when they won the World Cup in Spain. Capello wasn't, but he has learned from his own experience and tells his players that if there is one thing they must do, it is to avoid conceding a goal. His attitude is to do all he can to keep a clean sheet and then build on that defensive strength to go on and win the game. That's why I am convinced that if Capello had been coaching England when they faced Croatia at Wembley in that decisive qualifier for Euro 2008, they would have had a different mentality and they would have qualified. Maybe he can still win a World Cup. Who knows?'

CHAPTER 7
FROM PLAYER TO COACH

BOUNCING BACK FROM DISAPPOINTMENT WAS A FAMILIAR theme throughout Capello's playing career. The number of times he had to overcome painful setbacks contributed to the creation of the thick-skinned individual who arrived in London, seemingly so impervious to criticism, to coach England.

Not even the bitterness of World Cup disappointment back in 1974 could stop Fabio in his hunt for success. Sure enough, by the following spring, only the Dutch club, FC Twente, stood between Fabio's Juventus and the 1975 UEFA Cup final – with the Italians clear favourites to progress. But the tie didn't look so straightforward after Twente shocked the Italians with a 3-1 win in the first leg. Capello and company would always be chasing the game back in Turin, and their opponents knew it. The underdogs scored the only goal of the second leg as Juventus left themselves open at the back. To lose 4-1 on aggregate in a European semi-final to unfancied opposition was both painful and humiliating, particularly since their conquerors were thrashed 5-1 in the two-leg final by Borussia Monchengladbach.

Once again extracating themselves from the ruins of a European adventure gone wrong, it was to Fabio's and his club's credit that they managed to focus on their domestic championship in the 1974–75 season with sufficient determination and consistency to land the title. They had nearly always maintained the winning habit in Serie A, no matter what happened to them elsewhere. As a reward for his mental toughness, Capello now had three Italian *Scudetto* medals to his name, won in the space of just four seasons. It was an astonishing record of domestic success; and even as they celebrated, Juventus were already hoping to re-establish their credentials in the European Cup the following season. Instead Borussia Monchengladbach, fresh from their UEFA Cup triumph in 1975, derailed their campaign. Fabio was destined never to win a major European club trophy as a player.

Meanwhile, international glory for Italy was still Capello's dream, and June 1975 had seen Italy travel to Helsinki to play Finland in a qualifier for the European Championship of 1976. They won 1-0 and hopes were further raised in Rome in November when Capello played for Italy against Holland. It was the international showdown he might well have anticipated in Germany at the World Cup a year and a half earlier, had Italy lived up to expectations. Italy won this qualifier by the only goal of the match, scored by none other than Fabio. Understandably, looking back, Capello rated the moment as one of the most satisfying of his career, because Holland were such a strong team. In fact, as Fabio pointed out, many people regarded the Dutch as the best team in the world at the time, having taken over from a fading Brazil in terms of sheer quality, despite their 1974 World Cup final defeat at the hands of West Germany.

No wonder team-mates such as Zoff pointed to Fabio's extraordinary ability to score on some of the biggest occasions for club and country. Unfortunately that match-winning strike wasn't the definitive moment in Italy's bid to qualify for the following year's tournament in Yugoslavia. Fabio was injured for some of his country's other matches, and he was sorely missed. Italy only scored three goals in their entire qualifying campaign; and although they lost just once, three draws and two victories were not enough.

Dino Zoff explained, 'Poland and Holland were just too strong in that group in the end. Poland had just come from that marvellous World Cup they had in 1974; they were still very good, just like the Dutch.' Italy were edged out by a single point. Their failure to qualify meant that Capello would never win a major international tournament as a player either. As a meagre consolation, he did at least enjoy his country's last international of 1975. The day before New Year's Eve, the *Azzurri* won a spectacular friendly against Greece in Florence 3-2. They had ended another disappointing year on a high, and that was something.

Unfortunately, there was a further setback just around the corner for Fabio. The domestic season had been looking so promising for the *Vecchia Signora* ('old lady' as the club was known) when they had claimed 26 out of a possible 30 points in the first half of the season. But when 1976 started, the wheels fell off the Juventus chariot. To make matters worse it was their deadliest city rival, Torino (Turin), who wrested the title from their grasp.

Marco Tardelli, who would go on to win the World Cup with Italy in 1982 and later become an assistant coach with the Republic of Ireland, doesn't have pleasant memories of how the season fell apart. Tardelli – who had only recently arrived at Juve and had not yet begun his international playing career – revealed, 'That was an ugly year; we lost everything, there were problems within the club, problems with the players, and others were better. Our coach was (Carlo) Parola and we couldn't succeed.'

For all his experience and latent leadership qualities, Capello doesn't appear to have done much to improve the mood that year either, and he was struggling with injuries. 'I think I played more that year than he (Capello) did, even though I was a newcomer, because he had some physical problems,' recalled Tardelli, who didn't instantly warm to Fabio. 'Capello had a closed personality. He was a bit like Zoff, and perhaps this is a characteristic of northeastern Italy. I'm not saying you couldn't talk to him at all, because he was a professional team-mate. If you had an important question to ask you could ask it, and he would answer. He was respected, not feared. But as I say, he was quite closed overall.'

Even Capello and Zoff, good friends as they were, didn't manage to communicate about everything. Dino revealed, 'Perhaps strangely, given that we both became Serie A and international coaches later, we never talked about becoming coaches in all the

time we were playing together with Juventus and Italy. He had all
the characteristics to be a good coach even then, but we were too
busy playing.'

Tardelli may not have considered Capello to be the most
outgoing of team-mates, but he rated the older man's football brain
just the same. Quite independently of Zoff, he came up with the
same word the goalkeeping legend had used to describe Capello:
'*Geometra*' – 'The Surveyor'. He explained, 'Capello understood
where to put the ball, all the angles and diagonals. That's what
geometra means in the footballing sense.' So Marco wasn't surprised
to hear that Fabio had studied to be a surveyor at college and had
excelled at the subject. 'So did I,' laughed the former midfielder,
whose goal in the 1982 World Cup final became legendary for the
sheer joy of his celebration.

Later in life, Capello and Tardelli became friends. The younger
man explained, 'We both worked as sports commentators for the
Italian television channel RAI, and then an enjoyable situation
developed because we are both back in international football again,
not far away from each other. While Fabio joined England, I
became an assistant coach with the Republic of Ireland.'

Back in the late 1970s, however, there was just a suggestion that
Capello was struggling to come to terms with the fact that his
playing career might gradually be drawing to a close. That thought
wouldn't have made Fabio the most easy-going of companions.
And he hadn't been particularly amusing in his prime. Nevertheless, Fabio treasured every international appearance in 1976, the
last year he would represent his country. Already knowing they had
no part to play in the big European tournament that summer, Italy
travelled to the USA along with England, who had also failed to
qualify. Brazil and a 'Team USA' which was made up of players
earning their living in the States were the participating sides for the
Bicentennial Tournament, a one-off event held in May to celebrate
200 years of American independence. Italy thrashed the 'host
nation' 4-0 in Washington, although Team USA was actually
captained by England's World Cup winning skipper Bobby Moore
for that tournament. The English FA didn't even award caps,
though Italy's did. Capello was on target himself during his

country's rout of the American-based team, though he modestly admitted later that his goal, like the game itself, was nothing special.

Pretty soon, however, the Italians were leaking goals at an alarming rate themselves. Capello was involved in a five-goal thriller against England in the New York Yankees baseball stadium in the Bronx. 'We were 2-0 up,' recalled Zoff in 2008. 'But we were playing on a baseball field and at one end you could hardly see the football lines, only the baseball triangle. We were tired; it had been a long season.' England stormed back to win 3-2.

There was no cliffhanger at New Haven, Connecticut, on the last day of the month, against Brazil, although Capello scored for the Italians. Unfortunately, his niggling knee trouble forced his substitution in the 41st minute. Brazil seized their opportunity and took a jaded Italy apart later in the match to run out 4-1 winners. But with his first-half strike, Fabio had scored the second goal of his career against the magical South Americans. Brazil may not have been at their peak in the mid-seventies, but over the decades they have proved themselves to be the greatest footballing nation on earth. Not many midfielders could boast goals in separate internationals against the inimitable Samba Boys when the time came to look back on their careers. Capello could.

Fabio felt far from finished that summer, however. That is why he was so hurt that Juventus, the *Vecchia Signora*, were ready to bring down the curtain on his career in Turin. Very late in the process and without asking him first, Juventus simply informed Fabio that they intended to exhange him for another top midfielder, Romeo Benetti of AC Milan. This swap was perplexing, not least because Benetti, who had played alongside Fabio at the World Cup in 1974, was even a few months older than Capello. There have been claims that Fabio's haughty demeanour contributed to his downfall; but Fabio was furious that the club he had served so well were happy to trade him like a piece of meat, without even giving sufficient warning. It seemed that 239 games and 41 goals in the famous black and white shirt counted for little when it came to the crunch. Capello had shown extreme self-discipline during most of that time. He had only been sent off once, and even then he had been dismissed for quite under-standably lashing out with an elbow when an opposing defender had been tugging back his shirt. He needed all his self-discipline again now, in order to move on with dignity when it became clear that he was surplus to requirements. Giovanni Trapattoni had arrived as new coach for what would become a triumphant spell at Juventus. Naturally the club was keen to accommodate Trapattoni's every wish. So Benetti was in and Capello was out.

There wasn't much a player could do in those days to defy the will of a big employer. He was affronted more as a man than as a player. As it turned out, in making the switch in that summer of 1976, Fabio had reached the club that would ensure he stayed at the top of football for virtually the rest of his life. It could also be argued that AC Milan prolonged his playing career by a good number of years. But he wasn't to know that back then; and Juventus had been his life for a long time. Almost as if to twist the knife, the season after Capello's departure Juventus won their very first European trophy, the UEFA Cup. Marco Tardelli scored in the first game of a two-legged final against Athletic Bilbao, and Fabio's old team-mates eventually triumphed thanks to a Roberto Bettega away goal in the return match in Portugal. All the effort Capello had made to win European honours with Juve, all the controversy and heartbreak he had seen had come to nothing. Yet, as soon as he had walked away, his former colleagues had struck gold. It must have been tough to take, even for a hardened character like Fabio, who had seen it all. But then Capello was trying to engineer some success of his own in the twilight of his playing career. To help him achieve that, he immersed himself in his new surroundings with a passion.

'When I think about it,' he reflected later, 'Milan is the city I've lived in most, from 30 to 50 (years old) in general terms. I was worried by all the fog they had when I arrived though. I talked to a Neapolitan called Ciccio Cordova. He told me I'd be too happy in Milan to notice the fog. He was right. Milan is a splendid, open city, where you always find more of everything.' Why, then, did Capello choose to live north of Milan, up in Legnano? 'For con-venience,' Fabio explained, 'because by living there I was halfway between the city and Milanello, the club's training ground. But deep down I was living the Milan life, believe me. And I studied its history, which I always do wherever I go.'

Pierfilippo, Fabio's elder son, had lived in Rome, Turin and commuter-belt Milan already, and he was only six. None of his dad's clubs seemed to captivate him. 'Pierfilippo just used to read when he was taken to the stadium,' Capello revealed later. But Fabio would soon win over a new army of fans in Milan, who admired his attitude.

The new lease of life Fabio enjoyed in Milan may have extended his international career by a few games too. Fabio played a part in four Italian wins in three months. In September 1976, Italy edged out Denmark 1-0 in Copenhagen then gained revenge for the defeat in Yugoslavia two years earlier by destroying the same opposition 3-0 in Rome. They were only friendly matches, but the victories put Italy back in the right frame of mind for their World Cup qualifiers against Luxembourg and England in October and November. Predictably, Italy travelled to the Grand Duchy and won 4-1. Then it was time for Capello to clash with England's stars for the last time as a player. In front of a huge crowd in Rome, he helped his country to a 2-0 win over the country his father still respected so much. Playing in the England team that day and battling against Capello in central midfield was a young West Ham star called Trevor Brooking. Fabio didn't know too much about him back in 1976, though more than 30 years later they would apply their combined intelligence as FA colleagues to map out a blueprint for England's future. In 2008, Fabio admitted that, although he remembered the 1976 match, he didn't recall the part Brooking played in it, which might just be a fitting indicator of the way Italy's midfield prevailed on the day.

Back in the 1970s Fabio had done plenty to damage England's immediate future. He had played against the Three Lions four times in all. He had finished on the winning side three times, though his final victory was the only encounter that had meant something in terms of an international competition. It was Capello's penultimate appearance for Italy, and contributed in no small way to England's failure to qualify for the 1978 World Cup in Argentina. Fabio wouldn't be going either, even though Italy would. He put on the famous blue of Italy for the last time just three days before Christmas in 1976. The occasion was a friendly match against Portugal in Lisbon, and Capello was substituted in the 59th minute. He had no idea, as he trudged off and the home side won 2-1, that he would never be picked again. He could look back on some wonderful moments in an international career that had brought him 32 caps and eight goals. Some of those strikes had marked definitive moments in Italian football history, not least the winner at Wembley in 1973. But Capello would always remember his World Cup heartbreak as a player in Germany the following year, and he would always remain keen to taste glory in the biggest tournament of all when he became a coach.

Just because Italy didn't pick him any more didn't mean that Fabio was finished as a footballer. In his very first season at Milan, 1976–77, the club won the Italian Cup, though Capello didn't get to play in the 2-0 victory over arch-rivals Inter. The trophy nevertheless provided a bright climax to a turbulent campaign which saw one coach, Pippo Marchioro sacked as Milan flirted with relegation, leaving his replacement, the 74-year-old caretaker Nereo Rocco, to achieve league safety then cup glory. Better was to come for Capello as the next man took over in the hot seat that summer. It helped that he genuinely admired his new coach at AC Milan, the legendary Swede Nils Liedholm. Fabio revealed later, 'At 30 years of age I didn't think I could improve technically, but even in that area I improved with Liedholm. I learned a lot with him.' For his part, Liedholm looked back and said, 'I told Capello he would become a great coach. I made a mistake saying that. He has become the best.' The pair hit it off from the start, revealing to each other their love for art and their passion for collecting, while showing each other a professional respect that would be the catalyst for victories over their rivals. Indeed in 1978–79, AC Milan won the *Scudetto*, Capello's fourth. Playing in that team was a gritty little defender called Franco Baresi, who would later be Capello's AC Milan captain when he finally took charge in 1991. Baresi was certainly the best possible man to have on your side, full of running and defensive craft, capable of the toughest tackling when it was needed. For an aging midfielder like Capello whose legs were slowly starting to go, here was a man who could pick up the pieces, if ever the 'geometry' of Capello's game proved to be a few degrees out.

Fabio seemed as happy as ever in this winning Milan squad and was generous in sharing his know-how with the others. Perhaps he knew just how little time was left to enjoy the camaraderie between players – a precious part of a footballer's life that is missed more than anything when they are forced to retire. When assessing Fabio's contribution in the dressing room, Baresi did not have the same mixed memories as Tardelli had at Juventus. Indeed Franco recalled, 'I played the entire 1978–79 season and Fabio played some of the games, even though he was about 33 by then. He was very open in his dealings with the youngsters.'

To be precise, Capello played eight games in that brilliant title-winning season. Although restricted by injuries, he enjoyed every chance he had to be part of the well-oiled machine on the pitch. Milan's only serious setback came when they were knocked out of the UEFA Cup by Manchester City, thumped 3-0 at Maine Road after a 2-2 draw at the San Siro. Before long, however, Capello and Baresi would have the chance to scale the peaks of Europe in a new partnership. As team-mates, one *Scudetto* would have to do, because Fabio Capello was about to hang up his boots. The knee injuries were becoming less manageable, Liedholm's latest cycle as Milan coach was drawing to a close, and for Capello the writing was on the wall. In time for the start of the 1979–80 season, Liedholm handed the reins to Massimo Giacomini, who had coached Udinese. Fabio knew he would be lucky if he played a handful more games at the highest level.

It is hard enough to come to terms with the end of a playing career, when it is the only thing you have known for the best part of 20 years. It is even harder when journalists are taking cheap shots and virtually writing your obituary at the age of 33. One man who was being less than sensitive to Capello's nagging pain and loss of prowess on the field of play was a young journalist called Alberto Cerruti of *Gazzetta dello Sport*. A couple of weeks before Christmas, Fabio finally lost his temper and reacted to the provocation. He followed Cerruti into Milan's training ground car park and allegedly floored him. It is safe to say that by the time he stood up again, Cerruti had learned to think more before he wrote something, because he knew that one hurtful attack in a newspaper could potentially lead to another with a fist. It wasn't like Capello to snap in such a way, and it was a measure of how hard he was finding it to cope with such a fundamental change in his life.

Looking back with so much more experience under his belt, the amiable Cerruti said in 2008, 'We were both in the wrong, we both made a mistake and we also both apologised to each other for what had happened. Fabio is someone who recognises when he has made a mistake and he is prepared to say sorry. I am the same, and we realised that we had that in common. You could say that a friendship was born of that recognition.'

Nothing could prevent Capello's inevitable retirement, though. Fabio made his third AC Milan appearance of the term and the last of his career on 11 May 1980. It amounted to the final nine minutes of a 2-0 victory over Lazio in Rome's Stadio Olimpico. Fabio was almost 34, and he had been suffering from a troublesome knee for 13 years by then. It hadn't stopped him from hitting remarkable individual highs in the game; and although fate had decreed that European and international trophies had remained just beyond him, he had won everything that was worth winning in the Italian game. To mark the final curtain on Fabio the footballer, a delegation of players was formed, with the burning topic of Capello's future at the top of its agenda.

Giacomini recalled later, 'At the end of the match (Gigi) Rivera and Felice Colombo (Milan's president) came to ask me for my thoughts on a theory they had – that it would be a good idea to turn him (Capello) into a coach. Obviously I reacted favourably.'

Capello later confirmed to me that the first time he had thought seriously about coaching was when he finished as a player. Previously he had put all his energies into producing the goods out on the pitch. He had never considered it wise to start filling his head with thoughts of what he might do once his legs finally gave out. His new career would eventually make him even more famous than his first as a top midfielder.

Before Capello could make his mark, though, AC Milan was plunged into controversy in 1980. A betting scandal had rocked Italian football and Milan were implicated and relegated to Serie B as a punishment. Capello wasn't unduly affected as he began to coach Milan's youngsters and was not closely involved with first team affairs the following season. But naturally he was as pleased as anyone when Milan bounced straight back up to Serie A in 1981, with a young Mauro Tassotti showing promise in defence. The club was positively glittering with uncut diamonds by now, enough talent to make it a budding coach's paradise.

Meanwhile, Capello had more contact with the junior sides than the big stars. One of his jobs was to make sure the youngsters coming through showed the right level of personal discipline, while being allowed to enjoy their football enough to guarantee the necessary confidence and self expression. It was a tricky balance and the boys needed careful handling. In Capello they saw a character who oozed discipline and had done it all as a player. Here was someone they could respect, and he had that effect on everyone, young and old. He began to help out at a higher level too and his work ethic was a shining example to others. Joe Jordan, the Scotland international striker who was at AC Milan between 1981 and 1983, recalled, 'As a young coach at Milan Capello did everything. He assessed the opposition, he worked with young players, he worked one-on-one. Even then he had an aura about him. He was not a shouter but when he spoke everyone had a tendency to listen.'

It was a long apprenticeship, and Capello resents the well-worn argument that he was given the chance to manage Milan in Serie A without learning his trade the hard way at smaller clubs. 'I rose through the ranks just like anyone else,' he hit back. 'I did two years of teaching the *Allievi* (under-17s) and two years with the *Berretti* (juniors), and another two years with the *Primavera* (reserve/youth) side. I don't know if all my colleagues, my fellow managers can say as much. If they had, maybe they would teach more football and less tactics.'

The legendary defender Paolo Maldini admitted, 'Capello was my first, real teacher in the junior sides at Milan. He taught me how to handle myself out on the field and how to make a jump up in quality on the technical side. You could already have bet, back in those days, that he would become an exceptional coach.'

Fabio Capello was doing just what his father had done: teaching kids about football and inspiring them at the same time, when Guerrino Capello died in 1982. It was the year that Italy won the World Cup, their campaign masterminded by Enzo Bearzot, a thoroughly decent coach from the village of Aiello del Friuli, just down the road from Pieris. Guerrino lived to see his beloved Italy triumph, though Fabio was travelling the world on holiday and didn't get to watch the tournament with his father. Sadly, within months, the older man had passed away.

Guerrino's daughter Bianca recalled, 'He developed a tumour in his neck and only about 40 days later he died of it. I think that was quite merciful, given what some people are reduced to when they suffer from much longer terminal illnesses. He never complained once while he was dying, even though he was quite young by modern standards at 66. I know that Fabio's career in football had given him immense satisfaction.'

The biggest influence on Fabio's early football education had gone. No one was prouder of Capello junior than his father, who had been lucky enough to witness Fabio's rise to the top as a player. Guerrino didn't get to see his son become a truly great coach, though perhaps he suspected that Fabio had already taken the first important steps along that route. He had probably already guessed that the younger man would become an even greater coach than he had been.

Guerrino Capello wouldn't have wanted it any other way. 'How proud he would be of Fabio's coaching career,' said Evelina. But that career was nearly over before it had really begun.

CHAPTER 8
LEARNING TO BE UNBEATABLE

FOR MOST OF THE 1980s FABIO LEARNED HIS NEW TRADE behind the scenes at the Milanello, Milan's training ground near Lake Maggiore. But during the 1983-84 season he achieved his basic coaching qualification at Coverciano, the Italian academy near Florence that had been the brainchild of Italo Allodi. They taught everything at Coverciano, from coaching techniques to sports science; but one thing they didn't need to teach Fabio was how to handle his own diet, now that he was no longer a player. 'From the moment I hung up by boots, I made sure my calorie intake was only a third of what it had been,' he claimed later. You would never see any flab on Fabio, even when he was pictured on a beach in 2007, already aged 61, with his wife Laura. That's why the lack of dietary discipline on show among some England players when Fabio first took over was something he was determined to tackle over time.

Back at Coverciano in the early 1980s, important coaches regularly came to lecture the students, and Fabio soaked up their knowledge with enthusiasm. Just as fascinating for Capello the fledgling coach, however, was the part of his course that focused on psychology. By the time he left Coverciano, Fabio would be able to hold his own and even defeat anyone who wished to play mind games with him.

In 1984 Capello allegedly came under fire from a fellow coach, Luigi 'Gigi' Radice, who had won the *Scudetto* for Torino in the previous decade. The story goes that Radice asked Capello why he was fielding the son of a former football great in AC Milan's youth team for a match in Turin. The suggestion was that the lad had got in on the strength of his name alone, since his father had led Milan to the European Cup in 1963. Fabio's response was, 'Let's talk about this in a few years, because the boy is out of this world.'

They would soon see who was right because the lad broke into AC Milan's first team a few months later, aged 16-and-a-half. He was called Paolo Maldini, and his father was Cesare, who would go on to coach Italy. Gigi Radice must have felt embarrassed as Capello's judgement was further vindicated over a number of decades. Paolo Maldini became one of the greatest defenders the world has ever seen, and was still playing at the highest level aged 40, by which time Fabio was England manager.

Capello was a fine and objective judge of a player, even when it came to his own two boys, Pierfilippo and Edoardo. They both enjoyed the game, and might even have earned a living from it at some lower level; but Fabio knew they were not Maldinis in the making, and didn't have their father's class on the ball either. He explained later, 'They both tried football but they didn't have much aptitude, so I told them it was better for them to study.' It may have sounded harsh, but Fabio wasn't about to fill his children with false hope. He told it like it was when he saw and assessed any player, whether the boy was the son of Maldini or Capello. AC Milan liked his style and knew he could spot great footballing talent or a lack of it.

Despite the doubts of the occasional rival, increasingly Capello's judgement was being trusted in the formulation of Milan's policy during this, Nils Liedholm's latest spell managing the club, which was to last between 1984 and 1987. Fabio's opinion was also being sought with regard to the transfer market; so much so, in fact, that during his first press conference as England manager in 2008 he was able to look back and say, 'When I was a scout I brought Ray Wilkins and Mark Hateley to AC Milan.'

It was 1984 when the two England internationals made the bold move to Italy. Hateley had been scoring more than a goal a game for Portsmouth, while Wilkins was a Manchester United star who commanded a fee of £1.5 million for his transfer to the San Siro – a huge sum at the time. I was living in Milan the following year and saw Hateley score and Wilkins star in a Serie A match at the famous old stadium. Talking to Hateley afterwards, however, it was clear he was feeling the weight of expectation among the *Rossoneri* (Red-and-Blacks) fans. As it turned out, he only managed 17 goals in 66 appearances between 1984 and 1987, a respectable total but not enough to make him a true idol.

Wilkins stayed at Milan for the same period of time and his midfield subtlety was appreciated more in Italy than it had been in England, where he was nicknamed 'The Crab' for moving the ball sideways too often. The English didn't understand the slower rhythms of Italian build-up play, which nevertheless drained opponents before the swift, killer pass carved open a defence. How Capello would have loved a Ray Wilkins in his England line-up, someone who could retain possession with the best of them until he saw the right opening.

However, for all their attributes, Wilkins and Hateley weren't part of a particularly successful Milan side, and one Coppa Italia was all they won. No one held that against Fabio, who had worked his way up to become Liedholm's number two by 1986. Times were changing; new blood was required to take the club to another level, and not just on the playing side.

Hateley said of Capello, 'This man will not suffer fools. Not only is he a good tactician, he is a good psychologist.' Fabio was waiting for the chance to show everyone what he could do.

That chance came when he was made AC Milan's caretaker-boss towards the end of the 1986–87 season, Liedholm having been pushed upstairs. The club's new president, Silvio Berlusconi, gave Capello his first taste of big-time coaching partly because his confidence brought back memories of an old favourite. 'Something about Capello reminded me of Nereo Rocco,' revealed Berlusconi later. He was referring to an AC Milan coach with a rather sunnier demeanour, who started one of the *Rossoneri's* most glorious eras, winning the Italian league and then the European Cup – with his captain Cesare Maldini in 1963.

History would prove Berlusconi to be a good judge of football coaches, for Fabio Capello's reign, helped in no small way by Paolo Maldini's brilliance, would eventually outshine even Nereo Rocco's. But for now the target was merely to achieve qualification for the UEFA Cup, and time was running out for a faltering Milan team. Baresi, who was already captain by then, remembered, 'Capello showed no sign of nerves, even in that first brief spell in 1987, because there were guys like me in the dressing room whom he knew and had even played with. So there was already an open line of communication; he was coaching people he knew in some cases. But he still had to show that he had the character to stimulate the players positively as a coach, and he did it. He only had two months, perhaps even less, but he showed he could do something at that level, even if he wasn't quite the finished article and maybe not quite ready to take the job full-time at that point.'

The new relationship he forged with Baresi in those initial weeks, as coach and captain, would prove vital in the long run, however. Baresi said, 'I think Fabio has been involved with all his captains in the same way, with accuracy and reliability. He treats his captains with respect, but he is the boss and has the final word on all decisions.'

Capello had five games in which to prove himself and make a lasting impact. This, he later told me, was one of the toughest moments of his life in football, because he took over AC Milan at a time when the team was in some difficulty. He only had time for players who did exactly what he wanted. Later he revealed with a smile that he made an extraordinary statement of intent during this short period in charge. He took off an Italy international striker called Giuseppe Galderisi after just 20 minutes, because the player – who later became a coach too – hadn't been doing as he was told. Fabio used the example to demonstrate how he masked any early nerves he had with steely action. It worked too, because, sure enough, he succeeded in taking AC Milan into Europe. They beat Sampdoria 1-0 in a tense qualification play-off game. Capello was a success.

Fabio might even have dared to imagine that he would lead his team in that European adventure, but he was soon brought back down to earth. He had just been the caretaker, and Berlusconi brought in Arrigo Sacchi as Liedholm's long-term replacement. Reluctantly Capello left AC Milan, though wisely he didn't sever his ties with Berlusconi, meaning that he would always have hope of returning to the game he loved later. The president rewarded Fabio for his short-term achievement by handing him a role in his Fininvest business empire, and more specifically one of his media companies called Polisportiva Mediolanum. There, Capello learned how to negotiate television rights and market sports as diverse as basketball, ice hockey, rugby and volleyball. He was in a new world outside football and was once reported to have admitted that there was no guaranteed way back, explaining, 'Many things wouldn't have happened without Berlusconi. I had coached the youngsters, I had been an assistant, but at a certain point I decided to finish there. I wouldn't have been a coach. I would have transformed myself into a business manager.'

Later, Capello assured me that he had never truly left the game, not in his heart anyway, because he had never really wanted to leave AC Milan in the first place. Fabio certainly continued to keep his eye on football because it had been his life for as long as he could remember. In 1988 he visited the European Championships where he saw England meekly bow down to the might of Holland. *'Dove e la rabbia?* – Where is the rage?' he demanded of my colleague, Brian Glanville. 'I can't see any reaction in this team.' Capello still couldn't believe that an England team could simply lie down and accept their fate in this way. 'There wasn't the rage you expect from an England team that is losing,' he added. That is why the Capello of 2008 was such an admirer of Wayne Rooney. He might lose his temper too often, but at least he had a temper to lose. Capello knew it was an indicator of his raw passion for the game.

In the late 1980s, however, the blood and thunder of big-time football was starting to pass Capello by. He remained a spectator to the brilliance of AC Milan's Dutch trio Marco van Basten, Ruud Gullit and Frank Rijkaard. And along with the rest of the world, he watched in awe and probably not without a little envy as Sacchi took football by storm. Milan won the *Scudetto* in 1988, and followed up with glorious European Cup triumphs in 1989 and 1990. The European Super Cup, then contested between the European Cup holders and the European Cup Winners' Cup holders, was added to the trophy cabinet in 1989 and 1990 with wins over Barcelona and Sampdoria respectively. The Intercontinental Cup, decided in a single game when Europe's champion club played the best team from South America in Tokyo, Japan, was another great challenge – and Sacchi didn't fall short. His Milan side beat Colombia's Atletico Nacional after extra time in 1989 and Olimpia Asuncion of Paraguay in 1990. Now it was official. AC Milan were the best in the world, they had proved it twice – and Arrigo had won everything there was to win at club level.

Although some accounts have tried to place Capello at Sacchi's side during this golden period, learning from the master, Sacchi insisted later, 'Capello was never my assistant.' Fabio would answer the call to coach as and when he was asked, at any level within the club. But he was also learning from other masters. He visited Leo Beenhakker at Real Madrid during the latter's spell as coach there between 1986 and 1989, and took careful note of how the wily old Dutchman did things at Europe's most glamorous club. All the time Capello was increasing his knowledge of coaching while he waited for his own opportunity to shine on the big stage.

During the 1990-91 season, Capello visited Sven Goran Eriksson at Benfica to study the Swede's coaching techniques there. He learned from Eriksson, just as he learned from everyone he watched, though he didn't want to be more specific when I asked him what he had taken on board from the man who would manage England before him. The trip to Benfica was one of many around Europe as he increased his knowledge, preparing for the challenges to come.

In 1991 Fabio also went to see the former Colombia coach, Francisco Maturana, to watch how he was working his magic at a Spanish club called Real Valladolid. In truth, however, the most successful coach of those educational years was right there on his own doorstep at AC Milan.

The Sacchi era was a truly glorious one, as the Dutch magicians produced some of the most scintillating football of their entire careers. Who in their right mind would try to follow that? The success didn't automatically make Sacchi popular with his superstar players though, and he remembered one clash with van Basten in particular. Sacchi explained, 'Van Basten had been making public declarations in the newspapers, telling me I should be doing it this way or that way. So I took him aside one day and said, "Marco, since you know so much about football, you can come and sit on the bench with me for the next game and tell me all about it."'

It has been suggested that Sacchi made it clear he wanted van Basten out if he was going to stay, and that his 'him or me' ultimatum backfired. Silvio Berlusconi, the AC Milan president, decided in favour of the Dutchman, so it was Sacchi who moved on instead. Arrigo, on the other hand, insisted, 'That was a lie. Sure, I had a few arguments with van Basten, but that wasn't the deciding factor. Indeed, recently I spoke to Marco and he told me that it was only when he became a coach himself that he realised how much trouble he had caused me. I consoled him by telling him not to worry, because he had solved more than a few problems as well during our time together. The truth is I thought I had won everything I could win and I had wanted to stop with Milan for a while, extending my contract each time by one year only. Berlusconi was worried that I would go to another club and kept paying me until November 1991, by which time I was ready to take over the Italy national team.'

Sacchi departed confident that he had brought out the best in the stars still at the club, and suspecting they didn't have much more to offer. Even Arrigo could have been forgiven for thinking that his was an impossible act to follow. He later admitted, 'I do not take pleasure from saying this, but when I left AC Milan for the first time I thought they were a great side near to their sunset boulevard, reaching the end of an unrepeatable cycle of success. Obviously I was wrong.'

The man who would prove him wrong was Fabio Capello. It wasn't as though he had been knocking on the Milan president's door, insisting that he could be the next Sacchi. As Fabio recalled, 'It was Berlusconi who recalled me, who remembered my experiences and made me practically begin a career again.' Not that Fabio was complaining, because he had never wanted to leave Milan in the first place. Now he heard the words he had always wanted to hear. Berlusconi told Capello that he believed very strongly in him, and that he felt Fabio could become a great coach. What Berlusconi wanted to know was whether Fabio had the same belief in himself and the necessary desire to make it happen. The younger man didn't hesitate in answering that he felt he had what it took on all counts and was keen to prove it. The deal was done.

Some have tried to claim that there was a feeling of resentment in the Milan dressing room when Capello was plucked from the world of business in the summer of 1991 and thrown back into full-time, top-flight football after a four-year absence at the cutting edge. But AC Milan's club captain of the day, Franco Baresi, rejected that theory, and painted a picture of respectful familiarity rather than resentment. He explained, 'It is true that Sacchi wasn't easy to follow, because we had won everything with him and we had done it playing some spectacular football. We already knew a lot of things defensively and we knew how to be champions. But that just meant that Capello walked into a good environment. He knew a lot of us already because players such as Paolo Maldini, Mauro Tassotti, Roberto Donadoni and Filippo Galli had worked with him at the club before.'

That didn't breed complacency. Baresi added, 'There was a feeling that a change wouldn't be a bad thing at that time. We were an intelligent group of players and we wanted to win even more trophies. We weren't going to start living in the past, so we were receptive to our new coach. Capello had been all over Europe studying coaching methods, he had something fresh to offer.'

He also had something fresh to offer Alberto Cerruti, the Milan journalist who had so incensed him back in 1979 – a firm handshake. Neither man bore a grudge for that evening towards the end of Fabio's playing career when tempers had flaired. In fact, they both began to realise that in the other they had something of an ally. If Capello could achieve such a bond of trust with his players, he would be home and dry.

The Dutch superstars knew they were dealing with a winner,

even if Fabio wasn't yet highly experienced as a big-time coach. Baresi explained, 'Capello had been a great player too in his day, so he knew how to behave with champions. I remember once van Basten had said to Sacchi, "Why do you treat me like the others? I'm not like the others." He would never have said that to Capello.'

But there was another important reason why the AC Milan squad responded positively to Capello so quickly. And Baresi's revelation shatters the myth that England's manager is nothing but a rigid, oppressive tactician who works his players half to death at the expense of individual skill. He said, 'Sacchi's football had been extremely aggressive and demanding, because he had introduced "pressing". That was so tiring! It was all very rigid from an organisational point of view.'

'Pressing' involved Milan players exerting maximum pressure on their opponents all over the field, in order to win back the ball. When combined with the movement off the ball that was necessary when Milan had possession, it had made for an exhausting 90 minutes, many times over.

At first the Capello regime almost seemed fun by comparison. Baresi explained, 'There was less pressing under Capello, the football was less aggressive and not quite so rigid. Naturally we retained a keen sense of organisation, but we took our all-round game forward. Capello gave the front players more freedom, more chance for self-expression and what we call *fantasia* (flair).'

It is ironic, therefore, that Sacchi's brand of football is universally hailed as the purest form of sporting art and entertainment, while Capello's teams are criticised for a philosophy which puts winning before football, the result before the beauty of the game.

Listening to Baresi, one begins to realise that there is no beauty in football without hard work, and Sacchi's aesthetically pleasing vision was only created through the sweat and tears of his players. While Capello's defensive game didn't require quite as much frantic chasing, each player had clear responsibilities when Milan didn't have the ball. Like Sacchi, Capello also favoured hard work, and players had to act in the best interests of the team at all times. No selfishness or laziness would be tolerated under any circumstances.

Paolo Maldini explained that life under Fabio never felt like a holiday, and he seemed to disagree slightly with Baresi over just how rigid Fabio could be. 'Capello was very strict and rigid, but he perfected the mechanisms of Sacchi and he prompted the leap in quality. Capello brought out the man in me.'

The solid platform created at the back allowed room for flair going forward. There was nothing dull about Capello's AC Milan team and the 'boring' label since given to his former manager bemused Frank Rijkaard. 'I can't understand where that idea comes from,' he said. 'Capello is an excellent coach and I'm sure England will do very well under him.'

Joe Jordan, the fearsome Scottish striker who returned to the club at this time to study the latest coaching techniques, found Capello anything but boring. He said, 'I shall never forget watching Capello work with some of the greatest players the game has ever seen, Franco Baresi, Paolo Maldini, Ruud Gullit, Marco van Basten, Frank Rijkaard. He commanded such respect.'

Capello's boss, Silvio Berlusconi, offered him an uncomplicated piece of advice though: 'Try to smile a bit more.' Fabio is understood to have replied, 'I smile when I relax doing my own thing, but when I am at work there is no need to deliver anything except results.'

To achieve those results, Fabio stayed with Sacchi's 4-4-2 formation, but introduced 20-year-old midfielder Demetrio Albertini ahead of Carlo Ancelotti, who would go on to become another of the club's great coaches. Capello kept faith with Daniele Massaro, a Milan player who had served in various positions during the previous five years. There have been claims that it was Capello who, with a single stroke of genius, turned a mediocre Massaro from a midfielder into a striker. It is not true. First of all, Massaro wasn't mediocre. He was good enough to be included in Enzo Bearzot's 1982 World Cup-winning squad, even if he didn't play. As for Massaro's change of position, the player told me, 'I have Arrigo Sacchi to thank for turning me into a striker. Capello just kept faith with me in that position and I have him to thank for that.' Under Capello, Massaro clicked beautifully with van Basten, feeding his appetite at every opportunity, so that by the end of the

1991–92 season the prolific Dutchman had netted 25 goals among the mean defences of Serie A. Such a tally hadn't been reached for some 26 years. Capello's team scored 74 goals in just 34 games, and the 21 they conceded at the back were an acceptable price to pay. Opposing teams began to fear that, no matter how many times they scored, Milan would score more. No wonder Capello's men were still unbeaten as the season neared its end.

On one occasion in Sardinia, Milan were a goal behind to Cagliari at half-time. When they came back out for the second half and van Basten glanced across at his coach, Capello put three fingers up in the air. Van Basten promptly scored a hat-trick to order and Milan won 3-1. The story went that Capello had told the Dutchman he didn't just want an equaliser but three goals from his star striker in the second 45 minutes alone. When I asked Fabio about the incident, he denied that he had told van Basten any such thing. Indeed it didn't sound like Fabio to be so presumptuous. The story showed how much confidence Milan transmitted at the time. And what that afternoon on Sardinia does tell us is that van Basten positively thrived under Capello while he was still fit enough to play; and the player had a similarly powerful impact on his coach's career too.

But the aura of invincibility could have been destroyed in the final match when Milan, already champions, fell 2-1 behind against UEFA Cup hopefuls, the Italian team Foggia. Capello didn't seem to worry for a second. He simply ordered his troops into overdrive and they won by an amazing scoreline of 8-2. Van Basten only scored two that day, but he made many more. It was the ideal climax to an historic Serie A season. Since they hadn't lost a single match on their way to the *Scudetto*, Capello's first Milan team became known as the *Invincibili* (the Unbeatables). Even many years later, Baresi recalled, 'We were solid but we had real quality and that gave us great happiness. We never grew bored by the results, we just wanted more of the same, and it was a joy to be captain of an unbeatable team.' Marco van Basten, the biggest star of that spectacular show, stated memorably, 'Perfection in football does not exist, but this season we came pretty close.'

CHAPTER 9
SO NEAR YET SO FAR

FABIO CAPELLO GOT ON JUST FINE WITH MARCO VAN BASTEN and Frank Rijkaard, but with a third Dutchman it was another story. Ruud Gullit was one of the earliest victims of a management policy known as 'rotation'. AC Milan's success had attracted no shortage of talented footballers wanting to jump on the bandwagon. In addition to the Dutch trio, there were now Dejan Savicevic, Zvonimir Boban and Jean-Pierre Papin to please. An Italian winger called Gianluigi Lentini, who had cost Berlusconi a world record £13 million, thought he warranted a starting place. In total Silvio Berlusconi had spent £34 million during the summer of 1992. It was impossible for everyone to play at the same time, not least because UEFA only allowed three foreigners in each team. Inevitably there was unrest in the ranks when egos were ignored.

On the eve of a European Cup tie against Gothenburg in November 1992, Capello sympathised with his stars. 'It's very difficult for all these great players. At most clubs, there's a squad of 15 or 16. Here we have a squad of 24. They have to change their mentality, just like I've had to change mine. This is a different way of doing the job. It means they have to be prepared to work hard even when they aren't in the team. Work, work, work. That's the only way. It's not easy for them.'

It wasn't easy for the sidelined Gullit as he watched van Basten score all four of Milan's goals against the Swedes, two of them from Papin's passes. Capello purred, 'I never give a player ten out of ten but van Basten can have nine-and-a-half.'

That wasn't even a unique occurrence, because in that same month, Milan went to the Stadio San Paolo in Naples and managed to thrash Napoli 5-1, largely thanks to another four van Basten goals. Few should have been surprised, because 'San Marco' had started the 1992–93 season at a furious pace. In fact, after the first five Serie A matches alone, van Basten had already scored eight goals.

Those who believe that Capello's teams cannot entertain because they concentrate mainly on defence should have been in Pescara, on the east coast of Italy, for the most dramatic game the Adriatic had ever seen, one that set the tone for Milan's early-season fireworks. Fabio's men were behind inside a minute and were being beaten 4-2 after little more than half an hour. Then van Basten opened the instep of his right boot to give his team hope. Minutes later he showed such exquisite control that the ball seemed tied to his feet as he equalised. Magnificent Marco completed his hat-trick by conjuring the winner in the 72nd minute, a delicate chip that showed the versatility of a true master.

In early October he scored twice against a Fiorentina team featuring a young Gabriel Batistuta. In Florence the home team were again outgunned as Capello's men won 7-3 away from home. Fabio, boring? They had to be joking. He let his front players express themselves and they thanked him in spectacular style, van Basten in particular.

It was this sort of form that earned van Basten his third European Footballer of the Year award in 1992, as well as the FIFA World Player of the Year award. It seemed nothing could stop him, except of course his own body. He had undergone operations on a troublesome ankle before. He broke down again in a low-key match against Ancona and in December 1992 he travelled to St Moritz for yet another operation. The Milan medical staff believed that van Basten was running the risk of doing himself serious harm by going under the knife so often, because this was the fourth time he had trusted his future to the surgeons. Capello certainly wasn't encouraging van Basten to choose the operating table. He feared such a choice would ruin the player's career in the long run.

Meanwhile Gullit's torment in that 1992–93 season was psychological. No longer the centre of attention, it hadn't taken long for his frustration to surface. In that same month of December 1992, Ruud boarded the AC Milan team bus for a Serie A match against Udinese, having assumed that he would be a substitute at the very least. Capello sent an assistant to tell him in front of all his teammates that he wasn't involved. Worse still for the Dutchman, he was told to get off the coach. Anyone not directly involved in the match was not to hang around the central group.

Gullit later admitted that he was so angered by Capello's put-down that he 'considered hitting him.' Fabio would later put the whole incident down to a misunderstanding, and blame an unnamed member of his backroom staff for not telling Gullit that he wasn't in the squad. The Dutchman didn't see the bust-up as a misunderstanding, rather as a snub. He retaliated with a public outburst motivated by wounded pride. 'I must sort out my future immediately, as I will not stay with Milan any longer than necessary.' This went even further than Capello's own outburst during his early days as a Juventus player.

Gullit's team-mate at the time, Boban, recently said of Capello, 'Sometimes he wants to create conflict inside the dressing room because that way he can get more from his players. When you fight with Capello it is very difficult to understand if it is because he is angry or just that he wants you to react. The next day he comes to you and you are friends again. He provokes your reaction because he always wants to create a big tension in the group.'

But Fabio and Ruud didn't kiss and make up, not yet anyway. If Gullit was under any illusions about his predicament, reality hit home again when his public humiliation was repeated. He was allegedly snubbed on the team bus again, this time in the build-up to a big game with Juventus. When he protested, Capello is reported to have suppressed the perceived insolence with a simple, 'Take it or leave it.' Gullit admitted later, 'I hated Fabio Capello's guts. But he was right. He had to do it (rotate the squad) and I ended up respecting him.'

Papin, the Frenchman, had complained often about playing second fiddle to van Basten. He too paid the price with even fewer appearances. Meanwhile Dejan Savicevic had joined AC Milan from Red Star Belgrade in the summer of 1992, having earned joint runner-up spot in the European Footballer of the Year voting before he left Yugoslavia. He thought that achievement warranted slightly more than the occasional cameo in Capello's line-up. But the man who was nicknamed '*Il Genio*' – 'The Genius' – by Milan president Silvio Berlusconi only managed 10 appearances that season, scoring four goals. Savicevic recalled, 'In my first year I fought with Capello more than any other player did. I fought with him because I wanted to play. He made his own selection choices but I didn't agree with him. I fought with Capello but I also learned a lot because I had come from a different type of football. Now I had to come to terms with Italian football and the very organised 4-4-2 system, which Capello liked to play.'

With hindsight Gullit explained, 'To play for him, you need to be very well drilled and disciplined. You certainly don't fool around with him. You have to go his way or you will get in trouble. He screams at you. You don't see him laughing much. He is very moody. But he is also straightforward and knows what he wants. He was a great coach for Milan.'

Even great coaches have to lose some time. Faustino Asprilla, the Parma star who later moved to Newcastle, finally ended Milan's amazing unbeaten run in the league on 21 March 1993. It was the first time the club had lost in Serie A since 19 May 1991. The run had lasted for 58 Serie A games, including an entire season unbeaten in the league. Fabio later claimed that his individual unbeaten run as a manager – presumably including non-league matches – had actually stretched to 59. What really mattered was that Capello's Milan were already well on the way to retaining that Italian title.

Ruud Gullit would have felt much happier about it all had he not been dropped for so many of those matches. Most painfully of all, he was left on the sidelines in favour of his less fit compatriot, the recently recovered van Basten, for the Champions League final against Marseille in May 1993. (The Champions League replaced the old European Cup format in 1992.) 'San Marco' had returned in April and scored what would prove to be his last goal – an imperious header against Ancona. There was still discomfort in his troublesome ankle, and even van Basten warned that he would be no more than 75 per cent fit for the final. He had sat out AC Milan's last league match against Roma to try to buy himself some more recovery time; but he would be taking a terrible gamble with his career by making himself available for the big game against Marseille. The urge to play, however, was irresistible; he had sat on the sidelines long enough. Van Basten told me in August 2008, 'You cannot say Capello put pressure on me to play because we both wanted me to play.'

We will never know if Ruud Gullit could have done any better. Teams could only field three foreigners in those days, and Fabio clearly thought he could win without Gullit. After all, AC Milan were on a roll in Europe; they had become the first team since the Champions League was formed to win all six matches on their way to the final, seeing off FC Porto, PSV Eindhoven and Gothenburg home and away.

The showpiece itself was played in Munich in front of 64,000 fans, and Milan were strong favourites to defeat the French. Marseille explored ways to even up the odds in the build-up to the final. Later it was alleged that Marseille president, Bernard Tapie, had bribed a French team called US Valenciennes to lose a title-clinching Division One game. That way the bigger French club could concentrate on their preparations for the European decider against Capello's men. Marseille were later stripped of the French title.

At the time, Capello couldn't worry about what might be happening behind the scenes in the opposing camp, because he had enough unrest in his own squad. There was Gullit, furious about having been dropped; and there was Rijkaard, who wanted to go back to Holland. Arrigo Sacchi later saluted Rijkaard's decision and explained, 'He had family problems and decided he wanted to play back at home with Ajax the following season, even though Milan had offered him an enormous amount to stay. He did it for love, even though he would earn 10 times less by making the move.'

Capello had chosen Daniele Massaro as van Basten's strike-partner, but the decision was later criticised. Perhaps the enormity of the occasion got to the Italian marksman. It was said that van Basten created chances for Massaro, who squandered one particularly promising opportunity to score with his head. Looking back, Massaro pointed out that others shared the blame for the wastefulness, even his more illustrious strike-partner. 'I had a few chances; I missed one and gave another to van Basten, who shot straight at the goalkeeper. We weren't that great on the night.'

The way Capello remembers it, van Basten was able to move sufficiently freely to work his way into a scoring position on three occasions, only to be denied by Fabien Barthez in the Marseille goal. Fabio saw that pattern as more than enough justification for putting van Basten in the team when he was less than fully fit.

But goals were what really counted, and Basile Boli had headed Marseille into the lead just before half-time. Marcel Desailly then played like a man inspired to protect that slender advantage. When the Marseille defence was breached on one occasion, van Basten disappointingly lost control. There were other opportunities, but Barthez still seemed to have luck on his side. Van Basten, who had been heavily marked all night, took a particularly heavy knock on his ankle from the goalscorer, Boli.

Capello had introduced Papin with half an hour remaining, though too late as it turned out to do any serious damage to his compatriots. No one on the Milan side seemed to enjoy playing against Desailly, who had grace and balance to go with his power and aggression. But a brave van Basten never stopped trying to get the better of the Marseille defence, until Fabio finally put him out of his misery.

One of the biggest stars in the game's history limped off five minutes from the end, a sad figure and a shadow of the prolific striker that he had been at the start of the season. Like all great players, however, he had never lost his belief that he could make a difference, not even in those closing stages. Looking back, he told me, 'There was still only one goal in it, and I still felt I could do something for the team.'

Though the *Rossoneri* tried to keep alive Capello's dream to win a European trophy at last, it was over all too soon. Fabio had lost a final by the only goal as a player, and now it had happened to him as a coach. A lesser man might have begun to think that he was jinxed, destined never to lay his hands on the top prize in club football. Being in the final was never a consolation when you lost. Capello once explained, 'They say the important thing is taking part but that doesn't exist in my book. That's all right for the Olympics, when you have already achieved something by getting there. But when you have a winning card in your hand you have to win.'

The critics were no more forgiving after seeing such a glorious opportunity for silverware go begging, and partially blamed Capello's choice of strikers for what had happened. Fabio didn't pay too much attention. He hadn't lost faith in Massaro. Neither had he been blind to Desailly's disruptive brilliance. Out of defeat came the makings of an idea for his 1993–94 team. But for Marco van Basten the big push for glory in Munich proved terminal. Long and hard as he would try to recapture his fitness over the following months and even years, he would never play for Milan, or indeed anyone else, again. Van Basten never blamed Capello for the premature end to a sparkling career. He told me many years later in Amsterdam, 'I never harboured any feelings that he should not have played me in that final, quite the contrary, because I was only disappointed that he substituted me with five minutes to go!'

By the time the squad gathered for the new season, Fabio's other Dutch striker had also been removed from the equation, at least temporarily. A disgruntled Ruud Gullit had left for Sampdoria, so Daniele Massaro and Dejan Savicevic had the chance to combine up front more than might otherwise have been the case. Even so, when he wasn't included, the volatile Savicevic argued with Capello just like before.

'I played with Daniele quite a lot in attack but I still wasn't playing enough in the first half of that second season at Milan,' recalled Savicevic. 'I would say that the arguments with Capello continued for about 18 months, starting pretty much from the time of my arrival at the club. He is a man who can fight with you and then forgive you once it is all out in the open, but I'm not saying he did that with everyone.'

Massaro was often mystified by his own exclusion, though he controlled his emotions better than many. He revealed, 'Plenty of us had these frustrations about wanting to play more, that was natural, and I felt the same way. Capello would bring me into the side, I would score, and then the next game I was back on the bench. But the players knew the manager had his job to do, and I just kept working patiently and in the end I found my space in the team.'

So did Marcel Desailly, who arrived from Marseilles in November 1993. The £4.5 million transfer fee undoubtably helped Marseille president Bernard Tapie through the crisis caused by the corruption scandal. Tapie had more than money worries, however, because he was jailed as a result of the scandal he had caused. Meanwhile Berlusconi's 'generosity' was appreciated even more by Capello, who had seen in Desailly a little bit of someone that he had always rated highly – himself.

Desailly never forgot his first training session with AC Milan. Intriguingly Fabio had decided that Desailly would operate as a defensive midfielder, protecting the back four rather than remain at the heart of the rearguard itself. So it was with a very careful eye that Capello examined his new purchase in training on that first morning. Marcel remembered, 'I never felt such pressure as in my first practice session at Milan. I could feel Capello's eyes following my every move; he didn't stop. I knew that I had to show exactly what I could do. But it wasn't just that first training session, because you have to show him in every training session that you are the man who is going to be his first choice.'

Desailly responded to the pressure and put up with the occasional explosion of temper too, because he knew that Capello was turning him into a better footballer. He added, 'I would say that I've hardly ever come across a coach who knew me so well. If ever he shouted at me it was in private, man to man.' Ironically, a public dressing down might have spared Desailly the response of his team-mates, who decided that he was becoming the 'teacher's pet.' Desailly explained, 'My colleagues used to joke that I was his favourite, and I think that maybe he saw in me a bit of what he had been as a player. When he played, he was a tough midfielder, aware that he didn't have the technique of an artist. But he can be quite superstitious. He gave me the number eight shirt, and I inherited it from Rijkaard. Each match, just as we were lining up to go out on the field, he gave me a little tap on the back, to stress the number on my back.'

It was the same number that Capello had worn on his own back for Italy at Wembley that night back in 1973, when he had scored the only goal of the game. And when Desailly didn't play like a number eight in the Capello mould, he soon knew about it. Marcel revealed, 'Capello will show you your mistakes next day; he will shout at you and he will be very hard on you.' That was rarely necessary though, because in Desailly's case Capello could inspire without doing much at all. 'He was the chief. Just a look, or his presence on the bench, would drive me on.' When those eruptions did come, Desailly at least knew that he was not alone. Capello would lose his temper even during training if he didn't like what he saw. Desailly recalled, 'When the football we were playing wasn't hard enough for his taste, he would shout "stop" and kick the ball away, before finally screaming, "I want guys with guts!" His strength is to know how to keep his players under pressure. Even if your name was Maldini or (Alessandro) Costacurta, you were constantly pushed to your limits.'

Massaro thrived in this environment. 'I scored some important goals because a lot of our games ended 1-0 or 2-1 thanks to my winners. I scored 11 goals in the 1993–94 season, which I had never done before in Serie A.' Amazingly, that made Massaro AC Milan's top scorer. They had only scored a total of 36 goals in 34 games, hardly overwhelming; but Desailly had helped to create an extra line of defence, and Milan had only conceded a miserly 15. If that doesn't sound very exciting, then the Milan derby certainly was. Massaro recalled, 'We were playing our city rivals Inter, who equalised in the 86th minute to make it 1-1. I scored the winner in the 91st minute to make it 2-1. We had done it.'

Pretty soon fabulous Fabio had secured a hat-trick of Italian league titles, even before he could consider himself an experienced coach. Now he was out to claim the biggest club prize of all.

CHAPTER 10
SHOWING BALLS

No one gave Fabio Capello's side much of a prayer for the 1994 Champions League final, even if they had just won the title in Italy. Waiting for AC Milan in Athens were the so-called 'Dream Team' – Barcelona, coached by the confident and sophisticated Johan Cruyff. Meanwhile Milan were in such disarray that they couldn't even win a casual warm-up match in Tuscany. Self-belief was in the balance.

Paolo Maldini recalled, 'I remember the build-up to the final in Athens. Without (Franco) Baresi and (Alessandro) Costacurta, we played a friendly in Florence and lost 0-2. Instead of shouting in the dressing room, Capello said calmly, "I have realised that we are going to win the Champions League."' If a depleted Milan wouldn't believe in themselves Fabio would supply the belief for them. As it turned out, the opposing coach for the final did the rest.

Cruyff had reason to be self-assured, because his strike-force was comprised of the seemingly irresistible duo of Hristo Stoichkov, the fiery and powerful Bulgarian, and Romario of Brazil. Cruyff pointed to that fact that Barcelona had scored more than twice as many goals as Milan at the last group stage. Although Milan had scored three in their semi-final to humble Monaco, that didn't seem to impress the Dutchman. Capello's old rival from their playing days casually predicted that Barcelona would tear Milan apart.

Dejan Savicevic, the Milan 'Genius' who would have such a vital role to play in the outcome of the final, recalled, 'We heard about all Cruyff's pre-match interviews, his quips and his taunts. Cruyff fired us up more than Capello did.' Massaro agrees. 'Cruyff helped us to get fired up for that final. We knew what he had said and we knew what he had done. We heard that Barcelona had already had their pictures taken with the cup, and they had already organised a big party to celebrate winning the final. But we knew that cups were won with acts and not words. We also knew we were going into the match with a big handicap, because Barcelona were the strongest team in Europe and we didn't have two of our very best defenders, Baresi and Costacurta. But because of the way Cruyff had behaved, Capello only needed to prepare us tactically. We trained well the week before the match, no one talked much, we just worked hard and Capello didn't say anything. He was intelligent enough to realise that we already knew what was resting on the match.'

Arrigo Sacchi, Capello's predecessor, recalled monitoring Capello's behaviour from afar with profound admiration. 'Fabio didn't lose his cool and chose not to respond to the provocations. He prepared for the game as always with great attention to detail but perhaps with even more evil – in the sporting sense, of course!'

But Capello was saving his best line until last. Zvonimir Boban, the fiery Croatian, will always remember what Capello said just before he sent his team out. It may represent the shortest team talk of all time, but it harnessed the resentment everyone was feeling towards Cruyff for the way he had seemingly dismissed Milan as serious opponents.

Boban explained, 'The routine during the build-up to a match was always the same with Capello. He would tell us how to play and he would tell us how the opposition play. On the morning of a match he would talk to each player about his individual role in the match. There wasn't some big speech before kick-off, it was always more controlled and analytical. But this time the circumstances were a bit different, because we had heard that Cruyff had told his Barcelona players something along the lines of "don't even think about not winning by four or five goals against this Milan."

So Capello said to us, "If you have balls, if you are men, you cannot lose this match." I will always remember that.'

The tactical preparation had already been done. It has been written that Fabio played a 4-1-4-1 formation, with Massaro spearheading the attack and Desailly in front of the defence.

That is an oversimplification. After giving the matter some thought in 2008, Capello defined his formation that night as 4-2-3-1, with Demetrio Albertini and Marcel Desailly the rocks of defensive midfield, and Massaro indeed playing as lone striker. But Daniele wasn't alone for long; Dejan Savicevic was always ready to burst though from midfield, supported by Zvonimir Boban and Roberto Donadoni. That's why in 2008 Capello first remembered his fluid formation from 14 years earlier as a 4-2-4; it was a more accurate description of what really happened.

During Euro 2008, Donadoni, who had become Italy's national coach, described Fabio like this: 'Capello is a great coach; he was the one who introduced me to the world of tactics. Personally, I always try to establish a relationship with each player. Capello, meanwhile, is a tough guy. I think he would have made a good prison guard.' However, the players were about to show the sort of freedom in attack that prisoners only dream about. Capello had been used to relying on a simple 4-4-2, but his back four was missing its usual lynchpins. An excess of bookings earlier in the tournament had eliminated Baresi, the inspirational captain, and Costacurta, the elegant central defender. So Capello switched Paolo Maldini from his customary berth at left-back into the heart of defence, to be partnered by Filippo Galli. Mauro Tassotti and young Christian Panucci were the full-backs. It looked a little makeshift, particularly given the destructive might of Romario and Stoichkov. But with key midfielders detailed to help out in times of trouble, the feeling was that it might just work. Marcel Desailly could protect the defence generally, while Demetrio Albertini could break off and mark the highly dangerous Josep Guardiola.

Milan needed all the help they could get because, as Savicevic acknowledged, 'Barcelona were the favourites. They had Stoichkov, Romario, Ronald Koeman and Michael Laudrup available to them.' Yet Savicevic was confident and graceful from the start, and his sudden volley from an exquisite first touch almost surprised Barcelona's goalkeeper, Andoni Zubizarreta. The early exchanges created the sort of end-to-end football that made it difficult to predict who would gain the upper hand, because Stoichkov and Romario also went close for Barca. The very fact that Capello's men were competing on equal terms seemed to shock Cruyff's men, but it was soon to get worse.

In the 22nd minute Zvonimir Boban released Savicevic, who pirouetted to foil the bestial strength of Barcelona defender Miguel Angel Nadal. Soon he had made an incision right through the favourites' defence and Barcelona's goalkeeper, Zubizarreta, was forced to commit himself by diving at the Montenegrin's feet. Somehow the left-footed Savicevic managed to serve up a high and curling right-footed cross to the far post, where Daniele Massaro was waiting. It wasn't an easy chance, requiring composure and perfect technique from the most awkward of angles.

Massaro recalled, 'I was beyond the face of the goal, sliding in with my left foot, when I knew my strongest foot was my right. I was at quite an angle but I managed to catch it well.' The striker who had flopped in the previous final struck a technically tricky volley like a dream. First blood for the underdogs. There was pandemonium among the *Rossoneri* supporters and even on AC Milan's bench, but Fabio Capello betrayed no emotion. Although he stood up with his colleagues he simply looked down at his shoes, hands in pockets, refusing to smile. Perhaps he suspected a fierce backlash, and wanted to convey to his players that the job wasn't even half done. After so many heartbreaks in Europe during his many years in professional football, Fabio wasn't about to celebrate prematurely.

But what followed just before half-time was the sort of move that a manager hardly dares to imagine he will see from his team, and it would take all Capello's willpower to control his delight. A 13-pass combination, begun by goalkeeper Sebastiano Rossi and involving every Milan player apart from Desailly, reached the Barcelona by-line. Massaro recalled, 'Donadoni gave me a pass, but again it was difficult because it came back quite deep, I was almost on the diagonal of the penalty area, and I could see that Zubizarreta was positioned well in his goal. There was just one angle I could aim for from that distance, and I focused on it.' The striker's left foot connected with a vengeance from around 15 metres, and Zubizarreta never stood a chance.

Even Massaro couldn't believe it. 'We were 2-0 up in the Champions League final and I had scored both goals with my left foot when I was right-footed.' Was Capello, with his perceptive training techniques, behind the unusual strength in that supposedly weaker foot? Only indirectly, as Massaro made clear. 'Capello had a big staff and it was Italo Galbiati, who worked so hard with me in those last years of my career. You would practise dribbling and trapping the ball, then going again, and we would have to do this and play little matches in which you had to use your weaker foot. If you were left-footed you had to do all this with your right, and if you were right-footed you had to touch the ball only with your left. This must have helped me on the night.'

But it was the team combination that thrilled the experts. 'That has to go down as one of the best European Cup goals ever,' enthused the ex-Arsenal and Juventus star, Liam Brady, the BBC's summariser on the night. Capello's hard work and relentless drive could be said to have reached its full, thrilling potential in that single, extraordinary move. But still he didn't smile, even when another member of Milan's backroom staff tried to climb on his back in celebration. Instead he used the break in play to demand even more from his side. He got it too.

As though the team-driven wonder-goal were not enough to remember this final by, an even more spectacular strike arrived just after the interval – a piece of individual genius. Savicevic, the man-of-the-match, brought down a high swirling ball with his studs, which led an adversary to appeal for dangerous play. Referee Philip Don from England was used to seeing far worse back home and allowed the game to continue. In the following split seconds Savicevic had to judge the bounce of the ball, as it continued to spin, and make a decision on the run. What he came up with was an improvised, dipping lob on the half volley, which arched beyond Zubizarreta from a ridiculous angle and brought the crowd to its feet.

'That was one of the best goals of my career,' admitted Savicevic understandably. 'And if people say it was one of the best ever in the Champions League it is because it was such an important goal. The range was about 25 yards, because I was on the edge of the area at such an angle. It really was an unforgettable night.'

The goal killed off any lingering hopes Cruyff may have had and took the world's breath away. As Savicevic was mobbed by his team-mates, fellow club officials engulfed Capello again. Through the crowd, it was just possible to see that the coach had allowed himself to smile. But the rout wasn't over. Twelve minutes later Barcelona were still recovering from a raid that had seen Donadoni hit the post when Desailly charged at them. Marcel later revealed that Capello's philosophy could be summed up in the following words: 'First of all don't forget to defend our position and after that I will give you the freedom to express yourself.' Well, Desailly had defended his team's position admirably all match, and now it was time for the self-expression. The Frenchman timed his run to perfection and caught Barcelona's defenders static and square. His finish was a beauty, as he opened up his body and used his instep to curl the fourth beyond Zubizarreta.

Sacchi remembered watching Capello's reaction with interest. 'What struck me most was how much Fabio rejoiced, particularly for Desailly's goal. Fabio had transformed Desailly from being a great centre back to a fabulous midfielder and his personal gamble had won. I had never seen Capello – always so controlled, almost frowning – rejoice so blatantly, and with all the determination of which he is capable. At that moment I understood: Capello had to swallow many bitter mouthfuls, but in the end he had been right.'

There was half an hour or more left on the clock, but the contest was as good as over. When the final whistle blew in Athens, the scoreline was still 4-0 and Fabio raised his arms in triumph. If there was a touch of self-congratulation by then, it was totally deserved. As a player he had faced crushing disappointment against Gornik Zabrze, Leeds, Cruyff's Ajax and many more. Now, at last, it was Fabio's turn to be happy. He had picked the right team in difficult circumstances and his defence had held firm. The spirit in a volatile squad had grown; maintained and fed somehow by Capello's brutal honesty. The unity that resulted was as extraordinary as the margin of victory over the mighty Barcelona. Capello had stuffed Cruyff's pre-match taunts right back down his throat.

Savicevic recalled, 'Capello celebrated openly because he was so happy he had beaten a great rival, a great Barcelona. As a Juventus player, Capello's Juventus had played against Cruyff's Ajax, so the rivalry went back a long way.'

In a previous European Cup final, Capello and his Juve team-mates had been outclassed. Now Cruyff knew what that felt like, and the focus was on the two of them, even more than it had been when they were both part of an XI. In 2008 I asked Fabio if he had really delivered that immortal line, 'If you have *coglioni*, you cannot lose.' His eyes lit up as he confirmed the key address.

Capello once said, 'I never watch matches I played in, never. I only look ahead. In my house there are no pictures of me with trophies or cups. Memories do not exist for me. Those sorts of things are closed away inside boxes.' But he remembered the '*coglioni* challenge' all right. And if that night in Athens is closed away in a box or bottled somewhere, let him unleash its magical essence on England one day, just when they need it; let him show the players the sheer joy of turning the tables on the favourites when it really matters. Some would say he already has.

Boban, for one, recalled being pleased to see Capello react with so much joy. 'You have to show your emotions,' he explained. 'He could be very Germanic and he didn't like to leave anything to chance; he was very professional; his mentality is like this, he is hard. But he showed his emotions too after the game, as we all have to sometimes. Everyone did their own thing to celebrate that night. Some went to the disco; I stayed up all night talking to my family. I haven't forgotten it.'

Massaro has equally fond memories. 'We were too fired up and focused to celebrate until the end, and only then did we let ourselves go. Even then what we had done seemed impossible to us, but it was true. Capello became human and let his emotions go a little after the game. We went back to the hotel and celebrated with our families and then some went out and celebrated some more.'

Barcelona's pre-planned celebrations had gone flat, partially thanks to Cruyff's approach to a final that he had seemed to regard as a foregone conclusion. It was Capello who was quaffing the champagne instead and rightly so; he had achieved something enduring, and he knew it. Never again would he live in the shadow of his Milan predecessor, Arrigo Sacchi.

There was, however, one knock-on effect from the Sacchi era even then. And 14 years later, it was still one of Fabio Capello's abiding memories of the experience. When the AC Milan team flew home the day after their glorious victory in 1994, there was no sign of the thousands of supporters they might have expected to be waiting to welcome them home at the airport. Instead, Capello recalled, there were just 200 fans to hail the conquering heroes – a number which reflected just how used to European supremacy the Milan followers had become by then.

In the midst of such consistent success, perhaps the club's boss, Silvio Berlusconi had most reason to feel pleased with himself. He had taken a gamble by throwing Fabio Capello back into the big time in 1991. No one could really have been sure that Fabio had what it took to win the most sought-after prize in club football. Now Capello had moved from master-midfielder to magnificent manager.

Milan's Champions League triumph against Barcelona became Capello's calling card as coach, just as his match-winning goal against England at Wembley had been his calling card as a player. In Athens Capello had destroyed once and for all the myth that his teams only won by slow strangulation. If anyone chose to accuse him in future years of failing to allow his players the chance to express themselves, he could always point to Athens, where flare and individuality danced in perfect partnership with team ethic and tactical balance.

CHAPTER 11
IGNORING FABIO

On 1 December 1994 Fabio Capello's European champions played in Tokyo for the Intercontinental Club Championship, a single prestigious match against the best team from South America for the right to be called the greatest club in the world. In this particular year, Milan's opposition was a relatively unknown team, Velez Sarsfield of Argentina. It was billed as David v Goliath, with Capello's men the runaway favourites. No wonder Fabio nominated Jose Luis Chilavert, the Velez goalkeeper, as his man-of-the-match, looking back. It was a fair reflection of the amount of pressure AC Milan exerted and ultimately squandered. To everyone's surprise it was Velez who won 2-0, thanks to a poorly taken penalty from Roberto Trotta and a brilliant interception strike from Omar 'The Turk' Asad. The blows came seven minutes apart in the second half, underpinned by a common denominator.

Milan defender Alessandro 'Billy' Costacurta made the costly errors that led to both goals, was dismissed towards the end of his personal nightmare, and felt so desolate in the dressing room afterwards that he was unable to exchange any meaningful words with his coach. Capello doesn't remember saying anything to Costacurta either, because he was still too busy trying to work out how on earth his team had managed to lose such a big game.

Many years later, Costacurta still blamed himself so much for the defeat that he still wanted to apologise to Capello. He explained, 'It was my worst match. I gave away the penalty, my ill-judged backpass towards Sebastiano Rossi handed them the second, and then I got sent off (with five minutes left). I only rarely made mistakes in my career (and) in that big match I made them all in glorious Technicolor. By making those disastrous mistakes against Velez I stopped Capello from becoming a champion of the world.'

Fortunately for Capello, his team didn't have to wait long for the chance to add to their trophy cabinet. At the start of February 1995, Milan did battle with George Graham's Arsenal for the European Super Cup. The Italian giants had squandered their attempt to claim this trophy the previous year in a surprising defeat to Parma; and it was against Parma that Arsenal had triumphed in the European Cup Winners' Cup in May 1994, Alan Smith's goal the only one of a hard-fought final.

On the face of it, Milan weren't quite as fearsome as they had been. Going into the two-match European Super Cup showdown with Arsenal, their Serie A record was a distinctly average Played 17, Won 7, Drawn 7, Lost 3. But momentum was growing at last, and Capello's men hadn't lost for 10 games. Savicevic had scored four goals in one match as Milan triumphed 5-3 at Bari. They couldn't expect to run up that sort of tally against the rock-solid Arsenal back five of David Seaman, Lee Dixon, Steve Bould, Tony Adams and Nigel Winterburn, especially since the first leg was in North London. But Capello arrived oozing confidence as he strolled down the touchline before the match in a stylish long coat and scarf, with polished shoes.

He had reason to believe that his own defence, comprising Sebastiano Rossi in goal, Mauro Tassotti and Paolo Maldini at full-back, and the quality of Franco Baresi and Alessandro Costacurta between them, could hold its own. So it proved, as Ian Wright and John Hartson were denied. Not even the emotional introduction of Paul Merson, returning from a drugs ban as a 74th-minute substitute, could inspire the Londoners to victory in front of their own crowd of 38,044. Marcel Desailly intercepted many of Arsenal's threatening raids and it soon became obvious that this first clash would end in stalemate.

David Seaman did have to make a scrambled save from a stumbling Marco Simone, while at the other end Arsenal's assured defence made sure that Capello's last-gasp introduction of Paolo Di Canio didn't cause any nasty surprises. By the time the final whistle blew, Paul Merson was the only winner, applauding the Highbury crowd that still loved him for all his faults. 'He showed a lovely touch and used the ball well,' said Graham supportively, though in truth the Milanese had never been unduly troubled.

The destination of the Super Cup would have to be decided a week later at the San Siro. Disappointingly, only 23,953 turned up at Milan's cathedral to football, and Zvonimir Boban recalled, 'We didn't even play like it was a great game.'

Arsenal's star striker Ian Wright sensed that the cup was still there for the taking and put the ball in the net after some brilliant individual skill, but the goal was disallowed.

'Personally I didn't see anything wrong with it,' admitted Boban years later. Neither did Ian Wright, who put his hands together, almost pleading in prayer, smiling incredulously at the decision. It made no difference.

It might have been easier for the Gunners that night if Boban hadn't suddenly decided to defy Capello's orders and take tactical matters into his own hands. Boban revealed that the feud had been bubbling between the Croatian and Capello for some the time. 'I was unhappy playing on the right of midfield, I told him I wasn't much use there; but he was convinced that I could do it and told me the problem was all in my head. After 20 minutes at the San Siro against Arsenal I was already playing one of the worst games of my life so I decided to change position off my own bat and drop in just behind the spearhead of the strike-force. The Italians call it "*mezza-punta*" I made that decision, not Capello.'

Suddenly Milan came alive, and four minutes before the break they found a way through. Daniele Massaro recalled, 'I passed to Boban and he ran half the length of the pitch and scored.' It was probably just as well for Boban that he did, because he had to face the wrath of Capello at half-time. Zvonimir recalled, 'Capello told me "You are incorrect and unprofessional to have changed position like that, but now you have done it you can stay there." He was like that. He didn't get bitter, he was prepared to change things and he had a way of doing it without losing authority.'

Midway through the second half an acrobatic Massaro added a decisive second. 'I was really pleased with that one because I jumped higher than an Arsenal defender who was about 30 centimetres (1 ft) taller than me, Tony Adams I think. It was a really nice header.'

Boban buzzed around irresistibly to ensure that the momentum remained firmly with Capello's men. David Seaman had to make some spectacular saves just to keep the scoreline respectable, as Fabio's team roared their way to glory. Even Arsenal's tough defence struggled to cope with the mesmerising movement that Boban had inspired in the strike-force. The goalscorers interchanged with the gifted Savicevic, leaving Arsenal stretched and unsure of which way to turn. Boban said later, 'We thought it was normal to win against a club like Arsenal without a problem, we were on another planet to be honest.'

Perhaps that sort of overconfidence had been their downfall in Tokyo. On this occasion, however, they had fulfilled their destiny. Capello may not have become World Club Champion that winter, but he was certainly undisputed coaching king of Europe. When it was all over, the club could celebrate again in style, just as they had done the previous May in Athens. The European Super Cup wasn't the biggest trophy in football, either in size or standing; but it had been important to build upon the previous season's achievements, and seize a tangible reward for the hard work Capello continued to demand. Once again, Fabio wore a smile as wide as the gulf between the two teams.

George Graham claimed his side had shown Capello's men too much respect, time and space. 'If you do that, outstanding players will destroy you,' he complained. Ironically, Boban's lack of respect for Capello's formation had unlocked Arsenal. The Croatian was lucky it had, because the success of his improvised switch helped him to get away with his moment of insubordination. Fabio later confirmed the reason for their fall-out that night. It was one of many between coach and player.

Boban revealed, 'We fought a lot, Capello and I, but because it all came out in each other's faces, and it didn't stay inside us, we could work together. He doesn't do rancour.' There didn't seem much point in bearing a grudge that night after yet another English club's defence had been dismantled by sophisticated interplay from fast, clever continental strikers.

Massaro laughed when reminded of the tension that night between Boban and Capello, and said, 'When you win, even having a row can be good fun!' Paolo Maldini later told me the problem with Arsenal's defence under Graham, even though it seemed so impenetrable back home. He said, 'We played Arsenal and they defended well. But they play in a line and the two central defenders in an English side aren't usually very fast. So when you come against very quick and clever strikers, like those you get around the world at the top clubs, it becomes very difficult.'

One day Capello would have to confront that traditional English weakness, and decide for himself how far the English game had moved on. But back in 1995, as Graham trudged away from the San Siro to steel himself for his dismissal, Capello turned his attention to the business end of the Champions League. A 2-0 first leg win over Benfica at the San Siro and a second-leg shut-out in Portugal ensured a semi-final against Paris Saint Germain, who succumbed by the same scoreline in Italy and hadn't done enough at home. Once again Capello's men had made it through to European football's biggest occasion. To reach his third Champions League final in as many years was an extraordinary achievement for a man still relatively new to big-time management. It confirmed Capello's place in coaching history, even though a fourth-placed finish in Serie A meant they had to win the show-piece to be in the Champions League again the following season.

But AC Milan knew they would have to be at their very best again to defeat their opponents, Ajax of Amsterdam. The young Dutch team had convincingly beaten Capello's men, 2-0 both at home and away, during the opening group stage of the tournament. Marco Simone had enjoyed a fine season for the *Rossoneri*, scoring 17 goals back home. But Fabio suspected that he would need Dejan Savicevic to be at his most magically inventive if Milan were to prevail in Europe. Dejan had problems though. He explained later, 'I was injured two weeks before the final, a strained thigh muscle, but I thought I had recovered. Then, the day before the final, it went again.'

When Capello cast his mind back to that final, he still saw that Savicevic breakdown as critical to subsequent events. The home-grown Dutch already had the psychological advantage, thanks to their previous victories over Milan and their unbeaten record all through that Champions League campaign.

Ajax were casually brilliant. There was Patrick Kluivert, as graceful and as deadly as any striker in the business at the time, though he was little more than a boy. Then there were the frighteningly efficient De Boer brothers, Ronald and Frank, complimented by the sizzling pace of Marc Overmars on the wing. In addition to that talent there was Clarence Seedorf, who had only just turned 19 but was already on the way to becoming a midfield phenomenon alongside Edgar Davids. For experience, Ajax even had Capello's former talisman, Frank Rijkaard, who had returned to Holland in 1993. The captain, Danny Blind, was a determined little character too. Ajax had everything and they had just destroyed Bayern Munich 5-2 in the second leg of the other semi-final, to confirm their free-flowing unpredictability. Seedorf recalled later, 'Yeah, it was an incredible team – a great mix between youth and experience, and everything just clicked. It was perfect and we had a great season in 1994–95.'

Up against it when the match kicked off, Capello used all his tactical know-how to shackle the Ajax threat for most of that final. Bobby Charlton gave the man-of-the-match award to Marcel Desailly for his commanding performance. Daniele Massaro came close to firing what might have been a first-half winner with a stunning turn and shot which flashed past the post. Marco Simone was equally unlucky. But five minutes from time, Kluivert, who had only been sent on as a late substitute by Ajax manager Louis Van Gaal, put the Italians to the sword. Daniele Massaro said later, 'We didn't deserve that ending, because we had done really well on a difficult night. But then came that episode – the goal. The ball came into the area and then came the big mistake. Kluivert got hold of the ball and put it in the net and that was it.'

The 'episode' was a quite staggering collective loss of concentration, probably brought on by fatigue. No fewer than four Milan players failed to spot a gaping hole in their defence as Rijkaard, the Milan old-boy, threaded the simplest of passes into Kluivert's path. In the end Boban and Baresi just failed to prevent Kluivert from stabbing his shot weakly into Milan's net; but in truth it was a team mistake, and even the towering Desailly had inexplicably gone missing at the wrong time. It was a mistake so glaring and elementary that Capello buried his head in his hands.

Boban had no complaints. 'Ajax deserved to win, they had beaten us twice in the competition already, they were full of desire and we were already a little towards the end of our cycle with Capello by then. The hole in the defence was maybe one of the consequences of all that.'

The European Cup went to Ajax for the first time in 22 years – the first time, in fact, since the night Capello had finished on the losing side as a Juventus player.

As a result of their defeat Milan had failed to qualify for the following season's Champions League. Fabio didn't have long to prove that such an unwelcome backward step was just a temporary blip in his coaching career. Otherwise the knives would be out for the man from Pieris.

CHAPTER 12
CAPELLO'S TEARS

ON 18 AUGUST 1995, AC MILAN PLAYED JUVENTUS IN THE traditional curtain raiser between the two clubs for the Luigi Berlusconi Cup, named after Silvio's father. The match took place at the San Siro in front of 85,000 people, but the game was a meaningless sideshow. The occasion was remembered principally for two historic moments: Marco van Basten retired and Fabio Capello cried.

In a smart suede jacket, van Basten managed to jog around the stadium for a lap of honour to salute the sea of red and black that had risen as one to applaud him. It was an emotional moment, but 'San Marco' seemed to maintain his composure for the most part. As he received a warm handshake from the world's most famous referee, the bald-headed Pierluigi Collina, the Dutchman conducted himself like a man who knew his battle was finally over. He had been fighting for two years in order to salvage something of his career. Barely 28 when he had played that European Cup final against Marseille in Munich, 1993, he had never made it back to the big time. Although he had already written his name in the history books as one of the all-time greats, they say a striker peaks at 28 and remains at his most deadly until 30. Therefore van Basten had missed what should have been his greatest years.

In the dugout at the San Siro, Fabio Capello, notorious hard man, could no longer bring himself to stand and applaud because he was too overcome with emotion. This wasn't a question of a few tears clouding his eyes, because Fabio never did anything by halves. Here was a man crying his eyes out, his face contorted, his diaphragm jerking, a man covering his face and shrinking into his seat in a futile attempt to hide his loss of control. What had happened to van Basten touched Capello deeply, not least because Fabio had suffered from a persistent injury during his playing career too. His knee problem could have curtailed his career in much the same way as Marco's ankle, and he understood how a life in football could depend on a twist of fate.

Fabio Capello insisted to me that there were no feelings of guilt attached to his sense of anguish over the loss of one of the greatest players he had ever coached. We must believe him; and we must also give due consideration to Capello's own theory that poor van Basten inadvertently shortened his own career by opting for operations that were not favoured by Milan's medical specialists. But that didn't diminish the sympathy Fabio felt for his player, which overflowed into that uncharacteristic outpouring of sporting grief. Capello said later, 'The emotion is strong. It's not easy to stop. It is impossible sometimes. I had the same emotion two or three times.'

You would have thought that 'San Marco' ought to have been the one in floods of tears. Looking back at that day and Fabio's extraordinary reaction, van Basten was still visibly moved by the memory, even in August 2008. He took a moment away from his new duties as Ajax coach in Amsterdam and confided, 'That was a very special moment for me too, that farewell and the fact that Capello cried. We had a very good relationship, he and I, and it was a bit painful for both of us that we only had a year-and-a-half working together in real terms. I had to stop playing after that, and it certainly wasn't his fault. In fact he was very sensitive to my injury problem because he had suffered problems during his own playing career with his knee. There is always a good feeling whenever I see Fabio, though I don't get to do that so much these days, especially now that he is in England.'

A few months earlier, as coach of Holland prior to Euro 2008, van Basten had returned to the Milanello training ground and said of his time at Milan: 'I had the chance to work with great players and great coaches. This experience enriched me greatly and has allowed me to share what I learned with other players.'

So only great memories, mutual respect and fondness would endure between Capello and van Basten once the Dutchman had left the stage and Fabio was left to prepare in earnest for the start of the 1995–96 season. Nostalgic or not, Capello already had fresh strike power for the new campaign in the shape of another magician, Roberto Baggio, nicknamed the 'Divine Ponytail'. When he wasn't injured Baggio's inspired performances for Juventus had helped to win them the previous season's *Scudetto*. Heavy pressure from the all-powerful Milan president, Silvio Berlusconi, had ensured the signature of the most precious player in Italian football. Meanwhile George Weah, FIFA World Player of the Year and European Player of the Year had arrived too, from Paris Saint Germain. With Savicevic still in the mix, one of the most talented strike forces the world had ever seen was about to be unleashed on Serie A, as Capello went all out to take his Italian league title back. With Marco Simone breathing down their necks, the new front line would not be short of motivation.

The Weah-Baggio injection meant that Capello was spoilt for choice in terms of manpower and formations. Arrigo Sacchi once observed, 'I believe that Capello has always been a fan of the British style of football, especially the 4-4-2 system.' He could play 4-4-2 if he wanted, or even put Baggio and Savicevic behind Weah at the same time.

But in midfield, chances were limited for a young Milan player called Patrick Vieira. Perhaps that was something that Capello came to regret later, though he would always argue that the Frenchman was a victim of his age and the strength of his rivals. He explained, 'Vieira was young, and his path was always blocked by Desailly and Albertini back then. But you could already see that he had quality, otherwise I wouldn't have considered him as Rijkaard's heir.'

Vieira's recollections of what could have been a frustrating period of his career are surprisingly positive, perhaps because Fabio was prepared to mention him in the same breath as the legendary

Dutchman. He confirmed, 'Capello was always able to find the right words to motivate me. Back then, there were many other talented players and there wasn't room for me, but he made me believe in myself.' But it seemed that Arsène Wenger, newly arrived as manager of Arsenal, believed in Vieira even more, and I was soon able to break the story of the French player's transfer to the Gunners. And ironically it was to be another world-class French midfielder, a footballer far more gifted than Vieira, who was to prove Fabio's undoing in Europe that season – Zinedine Zidane.

It was never going to be easy for Capello to inspire the usual enthusiasm among the players for their annual European adventure because in 1995–96 that meant entering the UEFA Cup, which was, after all, an inferior competition to the Champions League. It was hard to escape the feeling that the season was going to be more about regaining the Serie A title.

Even so, everything appeared to be going according to plan in the UEFA Cup when they reached the quarter-final and saw off FC Girondins de Bordeaux with a comfortable 2-0 first-leg win at home. As they travelled to France they could have been forgiven for thinking they had one foot in the semis. But they hadn't realised quite how devastating Zidane could be if allowed to open his box of tricks. He wasn't exactly a household name in those days, but he soon would be. Zidane didn't score in the second leg on 20 March 1996, but he directed the orchestra in stunning style.

Didier Tholot put Bordeaux ahead in the 15th minute and the second-half assassin was Christophe Dugarry. Like Zidane, Dugarry would achieve worldwide fame as part of France's triumphant World Cup team two years later. But he made his mark with two goals in eight minutes against a Capello team still regarded at the time as one of the best in Europe. The AP news agency described it as 'the upset of the European soccer season.' Given Capello's record in the three previous seasons, it was probably was.

Although Milan were still sitting pretty at the top of Serie A, the humiliating defeat in Bordeaux probably had lasting repercussions for Capello. From much earlier in the season, the name of another coach, Oscar Washington Tabarez, had been doing the rounds in Milan. Meanwhile the AC Milan vice-president, Adriano Galliani, had offered Capello a new, three-year deal which was no more than a one-year contract extension. Fabio's future would in real terms only be guaranteed if he won Serie A or the Champions League at the end of the following season; but Capello wasn't too thrilled with the offer, and observed, 'A club which obliges you to accept clauses has no faith in you. It's a question of faith.'

Berlusconi, the man who had set Capello on the road to managerial stardom, was either silent on the rumours that AC Milan had lost faith in Capello and were looking elsewhere, or he was insufficiently dismissive of them. It was as though Fabio was being provoked, although Berlusconi was never overtly critical of him. The AC Milan president, who went on to become president of Italy too, must have known what he was doing.

On one occasion Berlusconi had said of Capello, 'Unfortunately he has one small fault. It is that dialogue forms no part of his approach. He is not on the field.'

Marco Simone, who had been injured and felt he wasn't playing enough once fit, said something similar, though his choice of words to describe Capello was rather more inflammatory. He was alleged to have claimed, 'Capello is a bit like God. He does not give equal opportunity to all.' Simone played even less after that.

Perhaps Berlusconi felt that a man who had lived by the sword should die by the sword, for there doesn't appear to have been much meaningful dialogue with Capello over the coach's future. Not that the uncertainty seemed to have any kind of adverse effect on Milan's form as they stormed to their 15th Serie A title in style. One look at the line-up was probably sufficient to strike fear into the opposition: Sebastiano Rossi, Christian Panucci, Alessandro Costacurta, Franco Baresi, Paolo Maldini; Roberto Donadoni, Demetrio Albertini, Marcel Desailly, Zvonimir Boban; George Weah, Roberto Baggio. Capello's critics might argue that with a team of potential world-beaters at his disposal, it would have been a crime had he failed to land his fourth title in five seasons. By the time the race for the *Scudetto* was over, Fabio's team had surged eight points clear of Juventus and that was impressive by anyone's standards. George Weah scored 11 goals but the team managed 60 in all, showing how many match-winners that side contained.

Strangely though, Capello still wasn't hearing the right noises from above, and began to realise that a highly successful chapter in his life was drawing to a natural close. If Milan were poised to offer Tabarez a contract behind his back, it was time to look for a new challenge. Real Madrid were interested in securing his services and a challenge abroad was just what he felt he needed. That didn't make it any easier to say goodbye to the San Siro though. Fabio ended the season as he had begun it – in tears.

Later, when he was England manager, he defended the right of a man to cry, following John Terry's tears at the 2008 Champions League final in Moscow. Capello revealed, 'Yes I cried in Milan. It was a private situation on the pitch, after the last game.' Five incredible years had brought the most extraordinary peaks and troughs, and now the adventure was almost over. He strolled out onto the San Siro turf, like a playwright walking the stage where some of the world's best actors had brought to life his ingenious works. Fabio felt the emotion behind all those triumphs surge back through him, and pretty soon the tears were rolling down his cheeks again.

It was ironic in a way that a man could be so passionate about his work and yet seemingly so determined to leave it behind him once he arrived home. When I had caught up with Capello in Milanello early in that 1995–96 season, he had emphasised how he refused to allow football to consume him completely. He had told me, 'I don't have footballing friends. I pick my friends so that I am able to avoid talking about football when I am not at work. My friends are artists, opera singers; people from that sort of world.'

So here was a man who was moved to tears by football and what it could do to people, including himself; and yet he sought a higher intellectual plain away from the game, and sometimes seemed to want to give the impression that football was little more than a job to him. This is what makes Capello such a complex character, his passions apparently torn between the refined world of art and the base blood and thunder of a football stage. He could be debating the merits of a beautiful painting one minute, and perhaps find himself involved in an ugly showdown with one of his players the next.

Indeed there was one more difficult moment to test Fabio's powers of self-control before that rollercoaster 1995-96 season with AC Milan was over. Despite realising that his time was up, Capello took the club on an end-of-season tour to China. And it wasn't long before the private nostalgia he had felt at the San Siro had given way to public anger, directed at a brilliant but highly volatile player called Paolo Di Canio.

Capello had signed Di Canio from Napoli two years earlier, after he scored this author's all-time favourite goal in the Stadio San Paolo, turning Milan's legendary defence inside out twice before finding the net from a ridiculous angle. But Di Canio's chances in Milan's first team had been few and far between since then, and he understandably saw this tour of China as an important chance to show what he could do. So he let it be known that he expected to play a lead role in the tour games.

Di Canio was one of three strikers in a game against a China XI in Beijing, and at half-time AC Milan were only a goal ahead. Capello decided it was time to protect the lead and Di Canio was the player sacrificed.

'What the f**k are you doing?' Paolo is alleged to have asked his boss as he was substituted. Capello apparently tried to reason with his player initially, answering, 'Paolo, you've got to understand that we have to maintain a certain tactical equilibrium.' Di Canio asked Capello why he was so obsessed with winning a friendly; but the coach was so infuriated by Di Canio's continued insubordination that he told the player to get out of his sight. At this point they squared up to each other and the insults flew. One was allegedly accused of being sick in the head, the other of being a dick-head. We may never know for sure which man compared the other's face to a penis as the insults intensified, because Capello wasn't keen to dwell on the exchange when asked about it. Di Canio, he claimed, had problems with some of his team-mates, not just his coach. The player was transferred to Glasgow Celtic soon afterwards, while Capello accepted the challenge to coach Real Madrid. It was the end of an era at AC Milan.

Capello looked back on that extraordinary period of his life and pointed out, 'I won a Champions League and I reached the final three times. That is a positive record that would have been better with more good fortune.' Should Capello have won more of those Champions League finals at Milan, given the players he had? 'It was the best team I have ever coached,' he acknowledged before coming to England. 'If you go 59 matches without defeat, an all-time record in Italy, it means that you have in your hands a beauty of a team, no? And the three best players I have ever coached came from that team too: Maldini, Baresi, van Basten. They were three giants, unreachable in terms of their level of play in their roles.'

CHAPTER 13
STABBED IN THE BACK
IN MADRID AND MILAN

IF FABIO CAPELLO WAS UNDER ANY ILLUSIONS ABOUT HOW demanding the Madrid public might be, he was given an indication when he visited the bull-fighting arenas. 'I went willingly,' he later admitted, 'I have friends who train bulls and friends who are matadors, and it is a fascinating world, with its own rules, a world where at times you can hear men who are risking their lives being whistled by the crowd.'

He was intoxicated by the city and enthused, 'Madrid is extraordinary, the city to live in when it comes to Europe. There may not be all that many museums, but as for the ones they have – what museums they are! The Black Paintings of Goya, what beauty! [Francisco Goya's famous 'Saturn Devouring his Son' was one of 14 so-called 'Black Paintings' with dark themes including war and witchcraft.] There is a marvellous clear light, even in the city, a light which comes from being near the mountains. The people are open and where they are different to Italians is that they are very nationalistic. Italians are more regional, with a precise idea about their own area or city but only a vague idea when it comes to their nation as a whole.'

Capello may have been a fan of the Spanish people, but that didn't mean he was used to their nocturnal lifestyle. His son Pierfilippo once pointed out, 'My father is convinced that everyone reasons like he does. For example, when we were young he couldn't understand why we would want to get in at 3am, because when he was young he was always in bed by 9.30.' It wasn't that Capello had tried to control his sons with strict curfews as they turned from boys to men. But once they had been given ample opportunity to have a beer and a chat with their friends, it seemed to Fabio entirely logical that they would want to return home, even though it was still only 10 or 11 o'clock at night.

So it wasn't hard to imagine the culture shock he must have felt during that first spell with Real Madrid in Spain, because people there often didn't begin their evening meal until 11pm. Fabio had little choice but to adapt accordingly and learn to enjoy the Spanish way of life. He slowly came to understand his sons' way of thinking better too, if only through necessity.

Capello didn't actually speak much Spanish when he first arrived there, though it didn't seem to matter. The language is not so very different from Italian and besides, not all his players were Spanish anyway. Capello brought in Clarence Seedorf, the youngster who had inspired Ajax to beat Fabio's Milan three times on the way to Champions League glory in 1995. Seedorf recalled, 'In Spain in his first month his Spanish was not that good but he made it very clear what he wanted. His body language is well known.'

His rulebook was soon well known too. The Real Madrid players were handed letters with the headings, 'Coach's rules I and II.' There would be a midnight curfew when the team was away from home, lateness would not be tolerated and fish would be the cornerstone of the new diet. There were to be no hangers-on or mobile phones in the dressing room, and players were to wear club suits of blue with white shirts. Capello later denied that he ever gave the female staff at Real Madrid a dress code, as was often written, so that their curvaceous bodies didn't present too much of a distraction for the players. Fabio insisted there was no need to do so; firstly because there were very few female staff at Real Madrid at the time, and secondly because those who did come into daily contact with the players did not dress provocatively. You could see how such myths about his legendary attention to discipline could have been born though, because if there had been a problem, you can bet he would have dealt with it firmly.

Capello was tough and demanding from the start, partly because the chief threat to Real Madrid's title hopes was a Barcelona side featuring the greatest young player in the world at the time, Ronaldo of Brazil. Bobby Robson, the former England manager, had the pleasure of bringing Ronaldo to Barcelona from their former club, PSV Eindhoven. He reckoned that Ronaldo could be even better than Pele.

Fabio didn't have Ronaldo, but he did have three goal-getters who would prove worthy rivals. There was Davor Suker, the brilliant Croatian striker who had first made such a big impact at Euro '96 in England. Then there was Predrag Mijatovic, a strong-willed Montenegrin, who would work as Capello's sporting director at Real Madrid 10 years later. Mijatovic described Capello's impact as 'a painful but necessary medicine', which summed up Fabio's work rather well. And finally there was the player who would become the biggest legend of the trio, a 19-year-old Spaniard called Raul, whose raw hunger Capello would later compare to that of England's Wayne Rooney.

Raul loved scoring goals; Capello wanted the teenager to score them, even if it meant cutting in from the left of a three-pronged attack. If only all football ideas were so simple to grasp. Raul recalled, 'It was a difficult time for the club but the most important thing is that you understand very quickly exactly what the coach wants you to do – and that is what he did.'

Given added confidence by Capello, Raul would still be scoring goals for Real Madrid more than 10 years later, breaking marksmanship records in the Champions League. By then a key Capello signing, Roberto Carlos from Inter Milan, would also have written his name in Real Madrid history.

It's curious that the England manager, supposedly so famous for boring, defensive football, created incomparable platforms for arguably the most attacking full-back ever, and the most prolific striker European football has seen so far. Not that Roberto Carlos sounded appreciative when he later told England what to expect from Capello. 'There will be no spectacle, it will be 1-0, 1-0, 1-0 ... But the team will be there, correctly set up and balanced on the pitch. And always winning.'

Fabio later claimed that the teams he coached to success were always a reflection of his own character. He had trouble imposing that character on Clarence Seedorf, even though the 20-year-old was thrilled to be at Real Madrid after a year at a much smaller club, Sampdoria. He recalled, 'Coming to Madrid, at that point the biggest club in the world, was a dream come true, because Madrid were one of the clubs I followed when I was a kid, so it was very special to sign with them.' But Seedorf, like Capello, was already a Champions League winner and was confident enough to voice his opinions, even when his boss hadn't asked for them. Similarly he would ask questions even when Capello didn't want to answer them. Every time Fabio gave Clarence an order, the former Ajax star would reply, 'OK, but why?' Eventually Capello lost patience and warned Seedorf, 'Just leave the "why" to me! That's what they pay me for!'

Capello confided to a Dutch journalist that season, 'Whenever I say anything, Seedorf always argues with me about it. Are all Dutchmen like that?' The antagonism between coach and player could have resulted in a destructive rift. Instead it became a highly creative tension, one later appreciated by Seedorf. For example Clarence thought he knew how to shoot, but Capello reminded him that there were many different ways, with various parts of the foot, and that they all had to be practised consistently. Seedorf later explained, 'One of Capello's major qualities is to get the best out of his players, to make sure everyone is committed to the team's goals. He is a tough guy, very straight, very dedicated. He was one of the best coaches I ever had in my career. He is very, very specific in what he wants from every player. Sometimes he really pushes you to the limits and that, of course, has proven effective.'

It didn't always prove entertaining though, because Capello wasn't prepared to risk throwing away games by allowing his skilful stars a completely free rein. The irony was that Capello was still playing three up front, a tactic he might have thought would win him more praise from the purists, as well as a medal in man-management for finding a way for his strikers to operate together. Arrigo Sacchi, often a critic of Capello's time in Spain, acknowledged, 'I remember the first time he managed Real Madrid, they played with an offensive "Big Three" of Mijatovic,

Suker and Raul. Believe me when I say to you, that was easier said than done!'

There was nothing wrong with the balance of the side, which improved further still in mid-winter. Capello bought Christian Panucci, the elegant right-back, from Milan to Madrid. Argentina's Fernando Redondo was still a strong and stabilising force in midfield, while a young Guti added lighter brushstrokes to the canvass.

Stars such as these helped Fabio to win more often than not. In fact he lost just three matches all season. But he was working for a president, Lorenzo Sanz, who would probably have been happy to sustain more defeats if only victory was more pleasing on the eye when it came. This was Real Madrid. The fans expected magic and entertainment.

By the end of the season, Capello's men would amass 85 goals at an average of more than two a game, a feast that might have pointed to sufficient entertainment on a weekly basis. But Barcelona ended up with 102 goals in the league alone; and their dazzling football early in the season quickly unsettled the Real Madrid hierarchy, who didn't like to see their deadliest rivals outshine or upstage them.

In England we tend to say that the table doesn't lie, but in Spain that year it almost seemed as though the table didn't matter. Sanz began to express his disapproval, and operated in a way that Capello felt showed a lack of true respect. Fabio said later, 'Every conversation we had, even between just the two of us, I found in the papers the next day. And the same thing happened with other bosses.'

Later Capello revealed that he had come close to quitting mid-season. Even though he worked on, he also let it be known that working in Spain was 10 times harder than working in Italy. Every time rumours surfaced that Don Fabio was about to resign, Real Madrid's fans would take a look at the league table and remind themselves that scintillating style wasn't everything. They shared their president's love for the spectacle; but they wanted to beat this sparkling Barcelona team to the title and for that reason the majority wanted Capello to stay.

Back in Milan, Silvio Berlusconi heard that his former coach was unsettled and wondered whether it might be possible to win him back. Oscar Tabarez had been a huge disappointment and his replacement one year later, the legendary Sacchi, had failed to recapture the magic of old. AC Milan were going to win a big fat nothing that season. 'The situation is not as dramatic as they say,' Berlusconi claimed at the time with a wry smile, though deep down he knew it was. 'All we need are the results and a bit of luck. Perhaps a trip to Lourdes would sort it all out.'

But if Saints couldn't solve his problems, Silvio reckoned he knew who could. He thought about Capello, his natural-born winner, and wondered if he could bring back the glory days. But Capello had other ideas, because there were also overtures from Lazio.

For the time being, however, Don Fabio chose to focus on La Liga even as he was complaining that it was 'impossible to find a harmony of dialogue with Lorenzo Sanz and his collaborators.'

As his return to Milan became more widely predicted, Capello denied that he was about to move back into his old house there, and tried to concentrate on putting his rival Bobby Robson back in the shade. By late April, Real Madrid were leading La Liga by eight points, with Barcelona trailing in their wake. There were only seven games left when Capello was provoked into making an announcement on his future by events beyond his control. He heard that Sanz was already courting Tenerife's coach, the German Jupp Heynckes.

In truth Capello would probably have left anyway, because behind the scenes Lazio were getting serious about bringing him back to Rome. Besides, he couldn't face the prospect of another season working with Sanz. So he announced that he would resign at the end of the season. Real Madrid fans hurled abuse at Capello when they realised he was leaving, not least because of the awkward timing of his announcement. They knew that Barcelona could still catch Real Madrid and feared that such instability might yet hand the title to Bobby Robson and Ronaldo. Capello insisted that his group would stay strong. 'Real Madrid players are professionals and we are staying together until the end,' he assured those prepared to listen. Then, referring to himself in the third person, he added, 'Capello's problem is his own, not the team's.'

But despite Fabio's reassurances, the players may have felt more resentful or unsettled than he had imagined, for Barcelona began to gain ground as predicted. In the end, however, Capello's professionalism held sway and his team held their nerve to edge out Robson's Barcelona by two points. It was a phenomenal achievement in Don Fabio's very first year in Spain. But the legacy he left in Madrid was even more impressive, as time would show.

Behind the scenes there was more drama on the managerial merry-go-round. Lazio president Sergio Cragnotti had travelled to a Madrid hotel to meet Capello and try to seal a deal for the 1997-98 season. He left apparently thinking that he had all but secured Capello's agreement to join Roma's rivals, even if Fabio hadn't actually signed a contract. Sergio's son, Massimo Cragnotti was Lazio's managing director at the time and recalled, 'We thought he was coming, he said he wanted to join us and we were only lacking his signature on a piece of paper. We even got down to talking about which players he would want us to buy for the following season – the whole project.'

Fabio's version of events is rather different, because when asked in 2008 about this contact, he insisted that he had been miles away from any firm agreement with Lazio. Whatever the strength of Lazio's overtures, they came to nothing because Silvio Berlusconi stepped in. The man who had given Capello his start in football management struck a chord with some 11th-hour persuasion. He told Capello how badly he was needed at his old club, and left Fabio in no doubt that it was time to return the favour for being given his big chance in coaching. The man from Pieris eventually bowed to Berlusconi's will.

Capello later confirmed, 'There was interest from Lazio, then Mr Berlusconi called me and out of recognition for a past debt I accepted his offer. I made the biggest mistake of my career. Never go back where you have already been.'

Those who wrongly thought he had agreed to return to AC Milan months earlier were able to claim that they had been right all along. Lazio were left stunned by the news. 'We were surprised to hear that Capello had changed his mind,' alleged Massimo Cragnotti. 'But we weren't frustrated because we understood that what he had done was more about the sense of duty he felt towards Berlusconi. Besides, we managed to secure Sven Goran Eriksson in Capello's place. He started winning us trophies almost straight away.'

Football, as they always say, is a funny old game. Had Capello gone to Lazio instead of back to AC Milan, Eriksson would obviously not have enjoyed the success he did with Lazio. Eriksson's record elsewhere may not have been sufficient to catch the eye of the Football Association, and Sven may never have become England coach. Would Capello have become Kevin Keegan's successor instead? Perhaps England may never have gone down the controversial route of employing a foreign coach at all.

By mid-June 1997, Fabio Capello had been announced as AC Milan's next manager, effective from 1 July. Many of the old familiar faces would still be there waiting for him. Paolo Maldini, Alessandro Costacurta, Demetrio Albertini, Zvonimir Boban and a few more prepared for Capello's return. Amazingly, Boban told me that it appeared the hard man of football had gone soft in Spain. He said, 'The physical preparation was not right. We were used to stronger training and more. But I think at Real Madrid everything had been done to another rhythm, "*alla Spaniola*", and Capello had come back quite relaxed in terms of his preparation of the squad. We didn't prepare as we should have done and pretty soon things became as though they were out of Capello's hands. He didn't understand what was wrong and that was one of his errors. But in my view AC Milan had never had a great spirit in the group; it had always relied on preparation and professionalism as its main strength, and that year there was less of it in evidence. '

The training regime may have seemed more relaxed to players in their prime but Franco Baresi, the club's masterful sweeper, must have known the writing was still on the wall for him at the age of 37. He doesn't have pleasant memories of that season. 'For Capello 1997–98 was not a very good time, we had lost some of the "feeling" there had been before. But I was the one who realised that it was time for me to stop playing; I took that decision myself, he didn't need to do it for me.'

Italians use that English word 'feeling' to describe a special rapport or affection. If Baresi says it had gone, you can be pretty sure the other AC Milan veterans felt the same way. Paolo Maldini was made captain after Baresi's retirement. But Boban didn't think the future legend was quite ready to have the same impact as the leader who was hanging up his boots. Zvonimir explained, 'Paolo was young, he wasn't a natural captain or a born leader, although he became a great captain later in his career. The first years were difficult as he sought his bearings as a captain; he wasn't yet what he would become as a leader.'

The players in the dressing room didn't seem to demonstrate the same desire to do well for Fabio as they had before. His return to the scene felt like a backward step for all concerned. 'I have never been a fan of reheated soup, it is never good,' said Boban. 'And you cannot just go back into a place and turn the light back on.'

Money clearly wasn't the solution either, because Berlusconi had injected plenty of cash over the summer in order to try to improve the situation. Patrick Kluivert, the brilliant young Ajax striker whose winner had cost Milan the 1995 Champions League title, joined the squad. But he failed to impress the club's elegant defender, Alessandro Costacurta. 'Kluivert and (fellow Dutchman and new signing) Winston Bogarde thought they were professors of the game already but they weren't.' George Weah was still at Milan, but struggling to hit previous heights. The Brazilian ace Leonardo added a dash of magic, but was joined by so many new arrivals that the group lost its previous identity. Christian Ziege, Andreas Andersson, Jesper Blomqvist, Ibrahim Ba, Giampiero Maini, Massimo Taibi, Steinar Nilsen, Maurizio Ganz and Filippo Maniero all came in either before or during this troubled season. No wonder the squad failed to gel. There was tension between some of the longstanding Milan players and the upstart new-boys. Capello recalled later, 'I got there having left Real Madrid and I had a team I hadn't built. Things weren't quite right there.'

In October Capello's frustration showed when he earned himself a one-match ban for allegedly shouting disrespectful comments at the end of Milan's match against Lecce. He was also fined around £2,000, though he regarded the charge as unjust. The man who could virtually do no wrong during his first era at Milan seemed less happy in his work this time around.

Christian Ziege still has positive memories of Capello that year though, and he rejected the notion that a boring brand of football was responsible for the unrest. He argued, 'Capello likes his players to understand their defensive positions but when his team attack he wants them to have their own ideas as well. I definitely would not agree with anyone who says that Capello's teams are not allowed to express themselves. When I was at Milan we had George Weah, Leonardo and Zvonimir Boban – they were creative players who could really make a difference.'

They didn't that season though, and Ziege seems to have been in a minority in his praise of the boss. Some of the self-expression wasn't confined to the pitch. There were bust-ups behind the scenes, which left lingering scars. Dejan Savicevic, who hardly played any more and was on his way out by then, revealed this much: 'Fabio Capello was often the sort of man you could have a big argument with and then make up the next day and it would all be forgotten. We were like that, him and me, but in other cases it didn't happen that way. I'm not going to name names, but I'm not sure that Capello's relationships with some of the Italian players in his last year at AC Milan were ever fully repaired.'

One of the problems Capello had was with Edgar Davids, a brilliant Dutchman who had joined AC Milan from Ajax in 1996. His gigantic ego didn't endear him to his boss or, for that matter, many of the other players. Costacurta once said, 'Davids was the most disappointing player to come to the club in my opinion, because he was the one who adapted least to our dressing room.' Compromise didn't appear to feature in Davids' vocabulary any more than it did in Capello's. The working collaboration only lasted a matter of months and even they were spoiled by the player's injury problems. Capello didn't think Davids was ready to make his mark as he struggled for fitness, and the midfielder grew increasingly upset and frustrated by his lack of progress at the club. The temperamental Edgar was sold to Juventus in January 1998, and to rub salt in Capello's wounds he was superb for his new club almost from the moment he arrived there.

Fabio Capello denies any suggestion that he lost the dressing room, and despite examples of internal discord there is evidence of players trying to give their all for him. One report from March 1998 claimed: 'George Weah fought hard to mark Fabio Capello's 200th match on the AC Milan bench with victory at Brescia. On the stroke of half-time, he equalised Dario Hubner's 41st-minute penalty for Brescia, pouncing on a loose ball after Giovanni Cervone failed to hold Patrick Kluivert's shot. Seven minutes after the break, Weah raced 40 metres with the ball at his feet before adding Milan's second. But the Liberian had reckoned without Girolamo Bizzarro, whose first Serie A goal levelled the scores in the 70th.'

So even when Weah did have the sort of day that brought back memories of his very best work as a predator, AC Milan's previously impenetrable defence couldn't close a game out. There were plenty of draws, but that wasn't the biggest problem. Capello also lost far more matches than he was used to. Indeed the statistics for that 1997–98 season make grim reading by Milan standards. They finished 10th but lost 12 games and won only 11. To be defeated by their rivals more often than they won was unheard of in Berlusconi's club.

A 4-1 defeat at Juventus at the end of March was especially humiliating, not least because Capello was sent off for protesting at the end of the game. He observed at the time, 'Apart from protesting I was sent off because I said that the ball had been out of play (before one of the Juventus goals). To be sent off for that seems excessive, especially since their linesman raised his flag and then pulled it down again.'

But the wheels were clearly falling off Fabio's chariot. And if Capello harboured any hopes of remaining in his position, they evaporated at the Stadio Olimpico on 3 May 1998, where Roma thumped AC Milan 5-0. It was almost too much for *Rossoneri* fans to bear. There was to be no consolation prize in the Italian Cup final either, because the slender 1-0 advantage gained over Lazio in the San Siro was overturned back in the Italian capital, where AC Milan were brushed aside 3-1.

Fabio later complained, 'Lazio were awarded a penalty for a foul that was two metres outside the area and that killed us.' Capello had been beaten in a showpiece by the side he had considered joining as coach the previous summer. The *Rossoneri* supporters didn't see the irony, they were just angry. Fans demonstrated towards the end of the season and there were unpleasant scenes. 'Yes, it was all a bit exaggerated, perhaps,' admitted Silvio Berlusconi after one such demonstration turned nasty. 'But as a fan I wanted to protest myself.'

In that moment Capello must have known he was about to be shown the door. And not for the first time in the previous couple of years he must have felt a little like the matador who has lost favour with the crowd and is jeered despite his stubborn bravery. At least Capello wasn't risking his life during all the hostility. Even so it was his reputation on the line and the protests must have hurt his pride – especially when he saw what his former charges at Real Madrid were doing.

In stark contrast to the uncharacteristic failure Capello tasted in Milan, he must have noticed that the stars he had gathered in Madrid were now taking European football by storm. Fabio had laid the foundations for the glitzy football his impatient Spanish employers had always wanted. Real Madrid even won the Champions League by beating Juventus 1-0 in the final. Fabio's successor Jupp Heynckes wasn't given very much credit for what had happened by his employers because he was sacked soon afterwards. With Real's hot seat vacant yet again, Capello was linked with a return. But Capello wasn't going back to Madrid, not for a good few years anyway. He wasn't staying in Milan either, because Berlusconi had sacked him the day before the Champions League final.

'I went, they booted me out,' was how Capello later summed up his miserable last season at AC Milan. Paolo Maldini recalled, 'It is true that the parting of the ways with Capello was not one of the best, a bit on the cold side. But you can't cancel out everything that happened in all our years together.' Looking back, Fabio remembered, 'They sacked me and the following year, with the team that I had built for them, they won the league, ha ha ha! Now that was my team! Ha ha!' It was an ironic remark because the 1997–98 Milan team had never truly felt like his.

But Capello would find himself in charge of other Italian teams in time. And when he returned to Serie A, he would be trying to get the better of the people who had shown him the door. That was the sort of challenge Capello would relish.

CHAPTER 14
ENGLAND AND THE CONSOLATION

IT WAS NO FUN BEING SACKED BY A CLUB HE HAD PREVIOUSLY inspired to great things, but Fabio's fate did at least allow him to spend some precious time with his beloved Laura. 'I sat on a beach and thought about football,' is what Capello is alleged to have told a reporter. Given his capacity to enjoy so much more than football, the remark was probably laced with heavy irony. Yet he was always likely to be back in the game in some shape or form before very long. He worked at big matches for Italian television and earned rave reviews as a superbly knowledgeable and incisive expert sum-mariser, even on far-flung assignments to tournaments such as the Copa America – the South American equivalent of the 'Euros'. But football management was what he did best, and when another season began without him, he let it be known that his batteries were fully recharged and he was ready for action.

The offer came to return to one of his great loves – Rome. This time it wasn't Lazio but their rivals AS Roma, the first big club he had played for as a young man. Capello knew this would be no easy assignment. Roma weren't used to winning like the big clubs up north; in fact they hadn't won the *Scudetto* for 17 years. But the expectations would still be high once Capello arrived.

Even the Eternal City was changing though. Tourists overran his beloved Trastevere, which in the days of 'La Dolce Vita' had been what Capello called 'a real place'. The city that had hosted his political awakening, the birth of his first son, his coming of age in so many ways, had moved on. American fast-food restaurants blotted the beauty spots; the quintessentially Italian feel to the city had been compromised. Rome was still football mad though. He had been 23 when he had won Roma the cup; now he was about to turn 53, and the pressure was on to win the club something else.

The invitation had come because in May 1999 Franco Sensi, the elderly Roma president, had decided to dispense with the services of a coach he liked on a personal level, the gritty Czech, Zdenek Zeman. Two years under Zeman, ex-coach of Roman rivals Lazio, had brought little concrete success. Even so the fans loved his free-flowing, high-scoring style of football, and worried that Capello would remove some of that entertainment value. 'Life changes,' said Sensi, who would eventually die after a long illness, less than a month before Fabio faced his first World Cup qualifiers with England in 2008. 'Capello is a winner and I believe in him. There will be more acquisitions. Capello is up for the challenge, he wanted a big stage again and that's what Roma is. Now we are going to fight for the *Scudetto*. With Capello, a new era begins.'

The past wasn't entirely wiped away, because Vincenzo Montella had arrived, a player whose purchase had been arranged by Zeman. Capello seemed to prefer Marco Delvecchio, who appeared more willing to backtrack than Montella. 'The defence of this team starts with Delvecchio,' said Capello firmly. Montella would sometimes find himself on the bench, but he remained determined to prove Capello wrong.

Meanwhile Franco Baldini had come on board the fast-moving Roma freight train too. Baldini had been an agent before Fabio's arrival, acting as the Roma president's consultant in the transfer market. Capello was happy for Franco to become the club's sporting director, and knew that his natural charm and sharp negotiating skills would come in useful. It was no surprise when a rapport between the two men quickly developed.

Although the jigsaw pieces for an assault on the title were beginning to fall into place, there were still a few missing. The most important was the acquisition of a world-class striker. Capello and

Baldini – England's future double act – began to focus on a player who would eventually become a sensation in England. He was a Dutchman and his name was Ruud van Nistelrooy.

In 1998–99, his first season with PSV Eindhoven under Bobby Robson, van Nistelrooy had scored 31 goals. That alerted not just Roma but Manchester United to Europe's most prolific new goal-getter. Capello knew he had to move fast, especially when PSV manager Robson returned to England. Following a friendly between Holland and Brazil in early October, Fabio and Baldini had a meeting with van Nistelrooy and his agent Rodger Linse. They seemed to agree on the way to proceed, the idea being that van Nistelrooy would do one last season at PSV before joining the Italians. 'I had van Nistelrooy,' Capello would later say, 'then he was taken away from me.'

What took van Nistelrooy away from Capello – as much as Alex Ferguson, who had just led Manchester United to Champions League glory – was a serious injury. In his second season at PSV van Nistelrooy had already scored 29 goals by March when he was sidelined with a knee problem. Roma began to shrink away from the proposed deal because they felt they could not risk big money on a player who had any kind of question mark against his long-term fitness. Sure enough, van Nistelrooy broke down completely before finally signing for Manchester United, where he would go on to become one of Europe's great strikers. Meanwhile Capello needed a quicker solution to sharpen his attack, because Lazio, the 'enemy' in Rome, were fast taking over.

Even in February, Fabio's frustrations had boiled over when he felt that refereeing decisions cost his Roma side victory at Perugia. Capello was sent off, but insisted, 'I didn't offend anyone, I just wanted the ref to take note of the damage he had done us by inventing a corner that cost us two important points. I protested in a civil way, while the referee urged me to leave with an outstretched hand, as you generally do to toddlers.'

Fabio could only watch enviously from sixth place as Roma's hated rivals Lazio won the 1999–2000 *Scudetto*, led by Sven Goran Eriksson. Roma's best chance of glory that season had disappeared in Yorkshire, Harry Kewell's winning goal for Leeds United proving

Model pupil. Although he seems smaller and skinnier than many of his contemporaries, the young Fabio (in the centre of the front row) already looks confident. He did well at school in his home village of Pieris, where his father Guerrino was a teacher.

Fabio's father. No wonder the photo looks well worn – pictures were almost all Fabio's mother Evelina had to remember her husband Guerrino by during the final years of World War II. When the odd letter did reach her from Nazi concentration camps, it emerged that Guerrino was in danger of starving to death.

Labour of love. Fabio's dad was the driving force behind the building of a new football ground in Pieris; and when Guerrino wasn't coaching or playing he even tended to the grass.

Punching above their weight. In 1941 Capello senior hadn't yet become caught up in the war. So he was able to play a leading role in taking tiny AC Pieris to Serie C, the third tier of Italian football. It was a remarkable achievement.

Home sweet home. In one of six small apartments in this faded building, Fabio grew up in cramped conditions. Amazingly his mother Evelina was still living there in 2008, because she didn't want to move away from lifelong friends.

Team Capello! The 1956–57 season saw Guerrino Capello (far right) coach a junior AC Pieris team that included his son, Fabio (front row, far left). Still smaller than his team-mates, Fabio nevertheless held his own.

Bumpy ride! Fabio Capello is thrown into the air by his Real Madrid players after winning La Liga in 2007. Eleven days later, while on holiday in Tibet, he was sacked.

Sir Trevor Brooking and Franco Baldini. When the FA were negotiating with Fabio Capello's advisors, Baldini's appointment was allegedly the sticking point. The FA seemed to want Fabio to work closely with Brooking; but Capello got his way and secured Baldini's services.

Juventus colleagues and pals. CEO Antonio Giraudo (left), Coach Capello and General Manager Luciano Moggi (right). Giraudo and Moggi were both banned from football for five years after Italian football's 2006 scandal.

Pierfilippo Capello. Fabio's son is quite happy to brave the media spotlight when he feels the need to defend his father publicly, as he did when the England manager was accused of 'reticence' in an Italian court in 2008.

A picture of elegance. Laura's exquisite fashion sense stole the show at the prestigious Laureus Sports Awards in St Petersburg, Russia, on 18 February 2008. Fabio cut a dashing figure too. The event was attended by the Russia President Vladimir Putin and movie star Dennis Hopper, among many others.

Tatoos and tactics. Capello dropped David Beckham for his first game in charge of England, leaving 'Goldenballs' on a tantalising 99 caps. But Fabio soon recalled Beckham and turned him into one of the most capped England players of all time.

Theo's 'trio'. Walcott calmly completes his hat-trick against Croatia in Zagreb. David Beckham had told Walcott to be more selfish in front of goal; and the Arsenal star took the advice on board with spectacular results. This 4-1 win had England football fans falling in love with the team all over again.

Wayne's World. Rooney scored five goals in three games for England in the autumn of 2008, including this beauty against Kazakhstan. The Capello camp had some tricky moments with Rooney before he began his goal spree, but soon the Manchester United star was praising Capello for improving his game.

Gerrard joy! Stevie G celebrates in Belarus after 'passing' the ball into the net from more than 30 yards out. It was the opener in a 3-1 win that put Fabio's England firmly on course for the World Cup in South Africa, 2010.

fatal for Capello's UEFA Cup campaign. At least there had been a new kind of joy in the Capello family; Fabio became a grandfather for the first time at the start of February 2000, his son Edoardo having fathered a baby boy. Fabio loved the new feeling and would continue to be a proud grandfather as the family slowly grew and his descendants became more numerous.

But for Roma fans it was a miserable start to the new millennium, as their hated Lazio counterparts painted the city sky-blue. They looked to Fabio to find them a superstar who might turn the tables. Montella had top-scored for Roma in Serie A with 18 goals, and he had forged a good understanding with the local hero, Francesco Totti. But Capello wanted even more goalpower.

Although Roma hadn't made the decisive breakthrough yet in Serie A, there was enough about the club, including huge financial power, to convince important players that they could become winners if they joined. Capello's ambition, Sensi's money and Baldini's charm began to work their magic in June with the arrival of Walter Samuel, nicknamed 'The Wall'. The big Argentinian would strike fear into opposing front men and prevent needless goals being conceded at the back.

But Capello still felt he needed that world-class striker who might make a difference when it came to the crunch. The answer to the problem was waiting up the road in Fiorentina, where another Argentinian had already taken Italy by storm. Gabriel Batistuta wanted to win something too, but he couldn't see it happening at Fiorentina.

Manchester United and Inter Milan had been keen to secure the player's signature. Together Sensi and Baldini treated Batistuta like a king, but it was Capello who convinced 'Batigol', as the Argentinian was nicknamed, that there was an excellent chance of silverware if they teamed up. The deal was done for a cool $35 million, an outrageous sum for any player, let alone a 31-year-old. Batistuta was asked to justify the price tag, and he was brutally honest. 'I can only say that someone who wanted to invest in the future wouldn't take Batistuta. Those who want to win immedi-ately sign Batistuta. Roma has already changed its mentality under Capello; they had a good team. Sensi will make other purchases and

I think that with me as well the club can win the title. I want to win the *Scudetto*. Capello has always had good results. I talked to Capello.' The superstar didn't mind Fabio's reputation for being harsh with his players. 'I don't need some specialist in man-management,' he argued. 'I've always been pretty easy to handle.'

So the scene was set for a memorable 2000–01 season. Then Roma fell apart almost before the campaign had begun. Playing Atalanta in the Italian Cup, they drew 1-1 at home and got thumped 4-2 in Bergamo on September 22. After the defeat, Capello blamed his team, but amazingly Totti hit back publicly on behalf of the players. 'It is everybody's fault,' insisted Totti. 'Capello's fault and the team's, not just ours. It is not a serious or pleasant argument to blame the players alone, even if we are the ones who go out onto the field in the end. The responsibility must be shared, 50 per cent by the players, 50 per cent by the coach. The only one above blame is the president, Sensi. Now we need character. Anyone who doesn't have it shouldn't play for Roma.'

With the danger of a rift forming between Capello and his squad, the situation grew even worse. All hell broke loose back at Roma's training ground, Trigoria, when the players returned. Once again Fabio was reminded what can happen when a coach fails to please the paying public. Supporters chanted, 'No balls, no heart, you have heaped dishonour on Roma,' in a general frenzied protest at what had happened.

Then Capello was targeted for some of the most vicious verbal abuse. 'Go back to Milan,' they yelled at him. 'Capello, Berlusconi's servant!' they hissed, blaming the man who had employed him too. 'Sensi, out!' was one of the more printable chants.

Franco Baldini, now Capello's number two with England, bravely walked out to the seething masses to attempt a dialogue with them, but it was no use. Totti also spoke to the irate fans outside the gates. He said, 'You are right to be angry, but we ask you to leave us alone because that is the only way we can work our way out of this situation.' He asked the club to open the gates, so that physical and psychological barriers between players and fans could be reduced. The club felt that the atmosphere was too volatile to risk it.

At the end of training Capello, Totti and Batistuta agreed to talk to a five-man delegation of hard-core fans' leaders, who were allowed into the training complex for the meeting. There was no satisfactory resolution to the ill-feeling, which had already manifested itself in the form of senseless violence. Vincenzo Montella was allegedly still inside his Jaguar and trying to leave Trigoria when his beloved vehicle was virtually destroyed by supporters. Cars belonging to Cafu, Antonio Zago, Paolo Poggi, Sergei Gurenko and Marcos Assuncao also sustained substantial damage as they tried and failed to escape the wrath of protestors. In sharp contrast Batistuta, Gianni Guigou, Abel Balbo and the local hero Totti were applauded by fans outside the training ground, exonerated from blame for what had happened.

Capello managed to drive away from work in one piece, though the atmosphere was still ugly as he did so. Looking back on that chaos at Trigoria, Fabio looked me in the eye and insisted that he hadn't been afraid for a moment; that fear is not an emotion he entertains. More than feeling afraid, he was angry at the fans for their behaviour. No result on a football field could ever justify that sort of violence, he believed. The fans saw it differently, because there hadn't just been one poor result, more of an accumulation until they could take no more. Fabio himself had always tried to let the results do the talking for him, but they made grim reading. Since March 2001, Capello had won just 11 of 29 official matches, morale was poor and the club was in crisis.

The riot at Trigoria could have been the last straw, Fabio's justification for moving on. The following weekend Kevin Keegan quit as England coach after a 1-0 defeat to Germany at Wembley. It was 7 October 2000, and the search quickly began for his successor. The FA's chief executive was a Scotsman, Adam Crozier, who decided to think outside the box of English contenders for the coveted position. At the time it seemed unthinkable that England, one of the leading football nations, could be managed by a foreigner.

Undaunted, Crozier began to look at two strong candidates in the city of Rome alone. The first was the Serie A title-holder, Sven Goran Eriksson, who spoke English already. The second was the man who had won everything at club level during the 1990s, Fabio

Capello. His results had been indifferent of late but his track record was the most impressive.

I was asked to write a feature for the *Mail on Sunday* highlighting the Eriksson v Capello dilemma: Capello the tough guy, Eriksson the more subtle man-manager, both winners. I even spoke to Eriksson by phone, and told the paper that he was the one sending out the most positive signals about taking the job, difficult though it would be for him to make a commitment mid-season.

Roma seemed more protective of their coach, Capello, who wasn't making quite such encouraging public statements about becoming Keegan's successor. But that didn't mean that Capello didn't privately want the job. There were negotiations behind the scenes, firm contact. If you talk to Capello now about those cloak-and-dagger days you realise that he was ready to begin his adventure in London even then. He was fascinated by the thought of the challenge with England, and I believe he would have accepted a firm offer from England if an agreement could have been reached with Roma. A source at the club told me, 'I think England contacted Capello two or three times in 2000. He was pleased that they were considering him.' Capello was more than pleased. He was tempted to jump ship. He thought he was close to getting the England job, so close that he was ready to pack his bags.

As it turned out, the dream remained just out of Capello's reach. Roma knew their coach was being courted. But they didn't think it was the right time to do a deal, because Capello had unfinished business with them. The club sensed they could still win the Italian title and they had invested a lot of money in Capello's signings. Even if England had been prepared to wait until the end of the season before formally announcing Capello as their next permanent coach, Roma still knew Fabio would be distracted – especially if the news leaked out.

Capello waited to see if the green light would come. But Eriksson was the man of the moment; he was the champion of Italy and the man who might have the least trouble fitting into the English scene, given his northern European roots and superior command of the English language.

Capello later revealed, 'I was asked to go for the England job before they chose Eriksson. I did so, but then they didn't choose me. I came very close but then it all came to nothing. You'll have to ask the people who were at the FA at the time why; I wouldn't like to say. I really wanted the job, but the president of the FA said he wanted a Nordic type who spoke English. I spoke a bit of English and you can learn, but I don't think that was the problem.' England's Chief Exuecutive, Adam Crozier, refused to elaborate on his decision in 2008, politely turning his back on football history by explaining that, 'I don't now give interviews on football.'

Towards the end of October, it became clear that the FA had not only chosen Eriksson, but had already begun serious negotiations. By 29 October, with the deal almost done, Eriksson was asking himself whether he would be doing the right thing by leaving Lazio come the end of the season. By extraordinary coincidence, Eriksson and Capello worked together that day at the Stadio Olimpico in Rome. As part of the Catholic Church's Jubilee celebrations, a match had been organised between an Italy national side run by Giovanni Trapattoni and a Serie A 'Rest of the World' side jointly run by Capello and Eriksson. According to Fabio, Sven took the opportunity to confide in him that day. In theory, Capello could have put further doubts in Eriksson's mind, and in so doing perhaps improve his own chances of landing his dream job. Instead, he behaved like a perfect gentleman.

'I met Eriksson at the Olimpico for the sporting event for the *"Giubileo"*,' revealed Capello. 'And he was having doubts about the offer of the England post. I told him: "Sven, go, it is a national team and above all a good team." The results showed him to be right, and in a sense me to be right too.'

It was an unselfish gesture from Capello, and one that was particularly fitting on a day when he was lucky enough to be part of another, more moving meeting – with Pope John Paul II. As a devout Catholic, this was a moment Fabio would always hold dear; and even in 2008 he recalled what profound and very strong emotions he experienced as he came face to face with the charismatic head of the Catholic Church. He wasn't the only football figure to meet the Pope that day, since both Eriksson and

Baldini were among the dignitaries who waited in line. John Paul II, a keen football fan and former player in Poland, might also have privately admired some of those who waited to kiss his hand, for their sporting prowess was well known even in the Vatican. For Fabio, this magical moment wasn't the first time he had been fortunate enough to meet a Pope. During his playing days he had also met Paul VI and Blessed John XXIII. But it was a day he would always treasure.

Capello's meeting with Eriksson was therefore rather less significant, though the consequences may have been considerable from a professional viewpoint. For Eriksson's decision to go ahead and manage England, encouraged that day by Capello, caused a knock-on effect, and all but removed a serious rival to Roma's title ambitions. Although Capello may not have suspected it at the time of his chat with the Swede, the balance of power in the Italian capital was about to change very suddenly. From the moment Eriksson was unveiled as England's future manager – just two days later, but with the intention of taking up the position at the end of the season – Lazio fell apart.

Soon after Eriksson left Italy, Capello launched a scathing attack on the Swede's Lazio side and claimed it should be stripped of the title it had won the previous year. Capello told Italian journalists, 'Last year Lazio and Inter fielded irregular players, penalising the teams that had abided by the rules. The right thing to do would be to rewrite the standings and penalise the clubs who were in the wrong. And it should be done immediately, not two years after the events. Last season Juan Sebastian Veron played as a European player for Lazio but now he is back to playing as a non-EU player. I cannot see for the life of me how if somebody cheated he can get away with it. Those who made the mistakes must pay for them. It is right that whoever has got it wrong should pay, and also by losing points in the standings.'

Lazio, who were now being coached by Capello's old friend, Dino Zoff, blamed a 3.55 per cent fall in the club's share prices on Capello's remarks and threatened to take legal action. Capello didn't seem to care that his own club, Roma, were also being investigated at the time as part of football's false passports scandal.

Eriksson was reported to have called Fabio's outburst 'mad', but the pair made up in time for Fabio secretly to seek Sven's help and advice on England matters in 2008.

When he wasn't stoking the fires of Roma's rivalry with Lazio back in January 2001, Capello was strengthening his club's performances on the field. His domestic season had begun to improve the moment his team began to dance to the tune of Emerson, a powerful Brazilian midfielder who seemed able to protect a defence and run a game at the same time. Fabio once called him 'the greatest midfielder in the world', while Emerson returned the compliment by claiming, 'Capello is the most important coach in my career.' His addition to the Roma squad was key.

Coach Capello proved again that he was more than capable of seeing beyond a rigid 4-4-2 formation when he had the players to suit another scheme. He opted for an ambitious 3-4-1-2, with Emerson protecting the defence and wing-backs Cafu and Vincent Candela given the chance to pour forward. Batistuta could lead the attack with either Delvecchio or Montella at his side; meanwhile Totti was handed the freedom he loved behind the front two.

Roma were moving up the table to challenge for the *Scudetto*, but received a nasty jolt when they hosted Liverpool in the UEFA Cup fourth round in February. They were undone in Rome by two goals from Michael Owen. In the second leg Capello's men kept Liverpool's strike-force relatively quiet and even won 1-0 at Anfield. It wasn't enough, though, and a furious Fabio maintained that overall victory could still have been his had the referee not apparently reversed a penalty decision in front of the Kop.

Capello commented, 'He (the ref) pointed twice to the spot and then changed his mind. I don't know why. I have never seen anything like that before.' It would have been an extraordinary feat to overturn the Liverpool lead in their own back yard, and he had come so close. But for all his frustration Capello had still been dazzled by the magic of Anfield, and he would later talk about Liverpool's historic home in the context of his huge respect for the atmosphere inside the great English stadia.

In 2001, Fabio's focus on Serie A now became absolute. The team was increasingly united in its belief that something special was about to happen. But at the end of April they threw away another potential derby win against local rivals Lazio, who scored two late goals to steal a 2-2 draw against their title rivals. 'There are regrets about tonight', admitted Capello, 'we could almost have sealed the title if we had won.'

He needed a good result the following week, the first Sunday in May, when Roma travelled to arch rivals Juventus. Even a draw would steady the nerves and keep the Turin club at a six-point disadvantage. But Fabio's men fell two goals behind, and looked to be about to see their lead at the top cut to a precarious three points. That was when Capello sent on Hidetoshi Nakata, a star in Japan but less adored in Italy, and took off the fans' favourite, Totti. The decision was not greeted with enthusiasm among the travelling Roma fans. Fabio still remembers how they booed him. Yet Nakata emerged as the late hero when he scored one and made another in the last eleven minutes. The grateful recipient of the equalising chance was the long-suffering team-mate Vincenzo Montella, who had warmed the bench for longer than he would have liked that season. Between them they had saved a precious point. And although Lazio closed the gap to five points that day, Juventus were down to third place in the table, and Roma were on the verge of the league triumph they had been waiting for since 1983. Above all, Capello's decision-making had been vindicated. 'It is the group that wins,' he explained afterwards, as if to emphasise that trophies are not won by eleven men alone. But he never did receive an apology from the Roma fans for their reaction when he had replaced Totti with Nakata. And despite the success of that brave comeback, it failed to convince some key players that they should always suppress their own disappointment when they didn't make the starting line-up, for the sake of the group.

In the penultimate game of the season, Montella was left on the bench in his hometown, Napoli, which only increased his frustration. Since he was second in the Roma goalscoring charts only to Batistuta, Montella quietly seethed all match. Roma struggled to scrape a 2-2 draw; and their second goal by Totti appeared to have been engineered with the help of two deliberate handballs. But the match was most memorable for Montella's reaction to Capello's order to prepare for action with only eight minutes left on the clock.

Montella regarded this decision as the final, humiliating insult in front of friends and family, so he vented his fury. He kicked a plastic bottle at Capello, showed him a middle finger and seemed to bad-mouth his manager too. After the match Capello said, 'This is not about me or Montella. This is about Roma and certain games need certain choices. The team is bigger than any individual.' Two days later Montella apologised, both privately and publicly. He said, 'I admit my reaction was a bit excessive and not very polite and I regret this.'

Remarkably, Capello not only accepted the apology but even decided to start Montella on the final, decisive day of the title race. Cynics would say he was protecting himself from the backlash that would surely have come had he excluded a fans' favourite and Roma squandered their chance of glory. But those who know Capello best insist that he only ever makes decisions for the good of the team. Montella was by now like a coiled spring, ready to release all his frustration in the last 90 minutes of the season at home to Parma. Capello could see it in his eyes. Montella was in.

Failure was still a possibility on that final match day of 17 June, the day before Fabio's 55th birthday, because Juventus had closed the gap at the top to two points. If Roma drew against Parma and Juventus beat Atalanta at home, the title would have to be decided by a play-off between the two clubs. But defeat for Roma and victory for Juventus would send the title up to Turin. Meanwhile Capello's friend Dino Zoff had made such an amazing job of rediscovering Lazio's momentum that Roma's city rivals were still in with an outside chance of forcing a play-off decider if other results went their way.

Capello warned his players to forget all the permutations because the destiny of the *Scudetto* was in their hands. If they won, no one could stop them; but there was still no breakthrough in the Stadio Olimpico when news filtered through that Juventus had scored an early goal against Atalanta. Now the pressure was very definitely on Roma. In the 18th minute, Capello watched his attacking full-back Vincent Candela cross from the left. Time froze as Francesco Totti, the hero of the *Curva Sud* (the end where the hard-core Roma fans were gathered), prepared to strike from 12 yards. He made no mistake and those supporters were suddenly in ecstasy, knowing their favourite had just damaged Juventus' chances of glory as much as he had enhanced Roma's. But the afternoon wasn't over yet, and fate could still potentially turn against Capello in an instant.

Just before half-time Gabriel Batistuta broke from the halfway line and shot from eight yards, only to see his effort brilliantly saved by Gianluigi Buffon, arguably the greatest keeper in the world by then. Who should be following in to tuck away the rebound but Vincenzo Montella, whose feud with Capello had been the talk of the newspapers. The party began; the Olimpico went wild. Twelve minutes from full time Batistuta turned the normally superb Fabio Cannavaro inside out before slotting his side's third. The Roma fans were still celebrating when Marco Di Vaio pulled one back for Parma, a goal which changed nothing.

The fans knew Roma had done it at last, and couldn't contain themselves. They invaded the pitch well before the final whistle with one objective in mind – to strip the players they worshipped of their kit. Souvenirs on such an historic day suddenly meant more than anything, including their players' embarrassment and the distinct possibility that Roma might in turn be stripped of their title due to crowd trouble.

Capello remained fully clothed, an indication perhaps of the sort of message he could send a would-be assailant with just one glare. But Fabio was consumed by an unfamiliar feeling. Later he explained, 'I remember the great fear I felt when the fans invaded the pitch before the end of the match. I was afraid of losing the title we had already won, because of that stupidity.' Capello has never publicly admitted to fear in his life, except with regard to this one occasion. As he told me later, it would only have taken one fan to pull out a knife or throw a punch in all the chaos and Roma would have lost the game – the certain punishment for crowd trouble and the abandonment of the match.

In scenes of great drama, Capello and Franco Baldini went onto the pitch, shouting, 'Idiots, get off, you'll cost us the title.' Their force of will helped to end the chaos and clear the field in the nick of time. Play was eventually restarted for long enough to bring about the final whistle, the one for which only Capello and his staff had been prepared to wait. At last Fabio could breathe a sigh of relief. Roma were champions after 18 years, and it was only the third *Scudetto* they had ever won. Fabio would say later, 'This was my most difficult title because Roma were not used to winning.'

It didn't matter that Lazio had lost 2-1 at Lecce or even that Juventus had beaten Atalanta by the same scoreline. Capello's men had come a long way since they had been treated to that violent reception from their own fans at their training ground back in September. The potential threat of physical assault the previous autumn hadn't frightened Capello at all; but the threat of having all his work undone in the final seconds of the season had been terrifying.

Now everyone could celebrate and look back on their achievement. Batistuta had finished the season on 20 goals, Totti had weighed in with 13, while Montella had also managed a creditable 13 strikes in 28 games, many of which he hadn't even started. A party was quickly organised for 19 June, two days after the triumph, and 1.8 million fans flocked towards Rome's Circo Massimo, a wonderful natural arena that had been used for big events since ancient times. Players and officials from the club arrived to lead those celebrations at a marvellous impromptu party that lasted most of the night. But there was one conspicuous absentee – Fabio Capello. He had taken a plane on his birthday, 18 June, to Vietnam in the Far East with his wife Laura, for a well-earned break and a private celebration of his own.

Six years later party-pooper Capello was still being asked to explain what he had done. 'It wasn't scheduled,' he explained, referring to the Circo Massimo knees-up. 'That party wasn't an official club event, I was already on holiday.'

Had it not been for Sven, Fabio might already have been sitting in his office at the Football Association. Instead he had the perfect consolation – the *Scudetto*. Nevertheless, England was a dream he still couldn't get out of his mind.

CHAPTER 15
FABIO CAPELLO –
MAN UTD MANAGER-
IN-WAITING

FABIO CAPELLO HAD NEVER MADE A SECRET OF THE FACT THAT
he would love to manage Manchester United if he couldn't manage
England. As early as December 2000, Sir Alex Ferguson had begun
to talk about retiring in the near future. 'I will certainly not be team
manager,' he explained. 'I think I've picked the right moment to
retire, but equally so I would love to stay on in any capacity which
does not interfere with the football.' On 17 January 2001,
Ferguson had confirmed, 'I'm definitely going. I won't be making
comebacks like singers do.'

The very next month, on 25 February, Fabio Capello had shown
that he was on the ball with regard to movements at Old Trafford
by throwing his hat into the ring as the Scotsman's potential
successor. The thrill of the Italian title race clearly hadn't precluded
a thought or two about what he might like to do next.

'Yes, I would like to manage Manchester United. I like England,'
he explained. 'I like the spirit of English football and I would like to
work in English football. I am a professional, I have to take every
chance I can and it is possible I will work abroad again. At the
moment I have signed for Roma for two years but who knows in
football? Maybe in another year it will be time to move on.'

Manchester United may already have put out feelers because Capello later admitted: 'When Alex Ferguson said he was leaving, they made contact.'

The formal announcement of Fergie's intended departure came on 18 May 2001, when it became clear that he would leave at the end of the following, 2001–02 season. He had hoped to play some kind of diplomatic role for United worldwide, but admitted the following day, 19 May, 'that's gone now.'

Manchester United appeared to favour a clean break, so that the legendary Scotsman would not be viewed as an intimidating presence lurking in the shadows when his successor took over. Of course Sir Alex had no intention of cramping the new man's style or having any kind of adverse effect on the next era. But United might reasonably have felt that any teething troubles experienced by Fergie's successor might prove trickier to handle if Sir Alex, the icon, was still in the club's employment. So in the summer of 2001, United and Sir Alex seemed to have reached the point of no return with regard to what would happen at the end of his last season.

My understanding is that during the summer and autumn of 2001, there was very strong contact between Manchester United and Fabio Capello. After a face-to-face meeting with Martin Edwards, the Manchester United chairman, Capello almost felt ready to pack his bags, believing the job to be his once Fergie stepped down. He knew he was a hot property, and in August he had added the Italian Super Cup, the equivalent of England's Community Shield, to Roma's trophy cabinet with a 3-0 victory over Fiorentina. Fabio saw no reason to deter his admirers while he was riding this crest of a wave. Instead he openly encouraged them, and there can be little doubt that some of his remarks were deliberately designed to prepare the ground for his proposed move to Old Trafford.

Even when it was claimed he was only on a shortlist alongside his old rival Sven Goran Eriksson and the highly-rated German, Ottmar Hitzfeld, Capello remained quietly confident and very positive when the subject of Manchester United was raised. This was partly because he had been led to believe that he was United's first choice, whatever smoke screens might be raised in public. On

28 October 2001, he said tactfully, 'If I'm taken into consideration for the job then I'll be pleased. All coaches aspire to great clubs and Manchester United are a great club, maybe along with Real Madrid they are the greatest club in the world. I must say that having worked in Spain and a great deal in Italy, to close my career in England and learn to speak English well would be good. An Italian or Spanish manager only thinks in technical terms. In England a manager has to think about purchases and the balancing of books. In England there can be no excuses.'

Ironically Capello appeared to be searching for excuses the very next day, when challenged on those pro-United remarks back in Italy. 'I said that I would be honoured to be headhunted by Manchester United and that is different to saying I would go and coach them,' he argued. 'Having your name linked with what, alongside Real Madrid, is one of the two biggest clubs in the world, it is an honour.'

Most people had read between the lines, however, and suspected that something was happening behind the scenes. Capello's boss, the Roma president, Franco Sensi, sounded understandably disgruntled over his employee's reaction to being linked with Old Trafford. He said, 'It seems to contradict what Capello said earlier about wanting to stay two more years with Roma. How can he then say "Manchester I am here"? Anyway, the most important thing is that Capello is our coach and he will respect the contract he signed with us; I am sure of this.'

Capello and Roma found some unity and settled down to the 2001–02 season. There was no reason for Fabio to feel distracted, since he knew that Ferguson intended to do one more season with United before stepping aside. Apart from the face-to-face meeting with the English club's chairman, Martin Edwards, there had been telephone contact with United's chief executive, Peter Kenyon. All indications continued to point towards a new adventure for Capello at Old Trafford in good time for the 2002–03 campaign.

Although Roma's Champions League form was indifferent that autumn, Serie A was still proving to be a happy hunting ground, and by midwinter Fabio had reinforced his reputation as one of the very best managers around. In Manchester, however, Ferguson appeared to be having second thoughts about retiring. On 30 December 2001, he said, 'The way I feel just now I don't think I'll change my mind about going at the end of the season. But you never know what might happen.'

Manchester United weren't waiting around to find out what might happen. On 3 January 2002, a United spokesman said, 'As always planned, we are about to embark on our search for a new manager. Nothing has changed.' And there were signs that Capello almost felt like the manager-in-waiting, because he felt confident enough to speak publicly again about his attraction to the Old Trafford post the very next month. 'To have a new experience abroad would be stimulating,' said Capello on 3 February 2002. 'I can't hide the fact that interest from this type of club is pleasing.'

Perhaps Fergie read Fabio's remarks and saw the writing on the wall, but he certainly seemed to make up his mind quickly about his future. Suddenly he wanted to stay at United after all. Later, Sir Alex would suggest that United had lined up Sven Goran Eriksson to succeed him, though significantly this was strenuously denied by the club. And it was Eriksson's old Roman rival, Fabio, who had been talking as though he were about to come to England, where Eriksson was already national coach. My understanding is that the reason he was talking in such terms is that he had been assured the job was virtually his. But such plans were about to be torn to shreds.

Just two days after Capello's public remarks, on 5 February 2002, a United statement read, 'The Board has entered into discussions with Sir Alex and his advisors on a new contract.'

Capello was stunned that the gateway to Manchester had been closed, though he knew better than most that anything can happen in football. Just over a year later, the outgoing United chairman, Martin Edwards admitted, 'We were very close to appointing someone else, probably no more than three or four days. That was when Alex made the decision to change his mind. It was just in time.'

Was it conceivable that United had lined up both Capello and Eriksson, their final choice about to be made between the two? Capello considers that unlikely, because he had the strong impression at the time that there was no other candidate. As far as he was concerned, a new adventure in England awaited. All that remained was the formality of ironing out the details and putting pen to paper. Suddenly, however, Fabio had been cut from the Old Trafford equation and left to focus on the Serie A title race again, his English dream in tatters. There wasn't much time to feel sorry for himself either, because Capello's immediate attention was quickly focused upon fresh controversy in Italy.

By February 2002, it looked as though the *Scudetto* would end up as a battle between Roma and Juventus. That was when the Turin club went to the Italian capital for a crunch clash that everyone suspected would have a significant bearing on the destination of the trophy. Accusations were made that night which would echo down the years; they would raise themes that would eventually have strong repercussions for Capello. Even when he became England manager, those themes would not go away.

Juventus defender Mark Iuliano was booked in the 39th minute and then brought down Cafu, Roma's attacking full-back, just before half-time. The referee, Graziano Cesari had little choice but to show a second yellow card and then, inevitably, a red. But the Juventus player's dismissal left two of the club's directors, Luciano Moggi and Antonio Giraudo, seething. They followed the players and referee down the tunnel at half-time to make their feelings clear, and caught up with Cesari in the corridor.

Moggi claimed later, 'Giraudo and I just pointed out to the referee that (Walter) Samuel (the Roma defender) should also have been booked but instead seemed protected by a sort of immunity.' But a Roma official, Antonio Tempestilli, who was on his way to the home side's dressing room, noticed this trio in conversation and decided to intervene. Tempestilli, who was Roma's team manager – a general administrative role far less important than that of coach in Italian football – recalled, 'Giraudo was letting fly a verbal volley at the referee in an arrogant tone of voice. I intervened to protect the interests of my team.'

A furious row broke out and the insults flew thick and fast until the protagonists appeared to be on the point of exchanging blows. The referee responded by 'sending off' Tempestilli, who was therefore unable to return to the dugout for the second half. 'The referee had to send me off and no one else – because I was accredited for this area, and Giraudo wasn't,' observed Tempestilli acidically. 'When all was said and done these people (Giraudo and Moggi) shouldn't even have been where they were. In the second place Mr Giraudo was complaining about fouls committed by Samuel and not those committed by Iuliano.'

Capello agreed the next day after that 'only the directors accompanying the team itself' can go to the referee. Therefore Tempestilli was right; Moggi and Giraudo should not have been in the dressing room area. Yet Capello's account suggested that the Juventus directors had gone even further. Fabio claimed, 'I saw Moggi and Giraudo in the dressing room of the referee, Cesari. Tempestilli went too. Then I don't know what happened.'

Juventus produced a slick defence of their directors' conduct in Rome. In the aftermath of the half-time bust-up at the Stadio Olimpico that night, a Juventus spokesman claimed, 'Cesari, the referee, pointed out to Tempestilli that a peaceful dialogue was taking place, and not to present himself at the dugout for the second half. Then he asked Giraudo to follow him into his dressing room, to finish off his clarifications, in the presence of the Roma official assigned to the referee, Mr Benedetti.'

The Italian news agency ANSA, described events like this: 'Giraudo talked with Cesari as they all walked along the tunnel towards the dressing room, provoking the intervention of Tempestilli; at this time the row broke out between the three. Arriving at the dressing room, the referee called Giraudo and Benedetti into his dressing room together.'

But Massimo Moratti, president of title rivals Inter Milan, believed these accounts missed the point, because they seemed to assume Giraudo's right to be in the vicinity. He explained, 'I have read and heard that this would be a normal thing, which happens frequently. But it isn't the case. Not only is it not normal, it is absolutely forbidden by the regulations.'

Juventus later claimed that they had been invited by the to use the corridor to the dressing rooms for security reasons. But it is unclear how confronting the referee about his decisions during the biggest match of the season improved the security of either Giraudo or Moggi. Tempestilli insisted, 'I told them it wasn't on to complain all the time, especially in circumstances when there was no reason to do so.'

It is unclear what subconscious effect, if any, the intervention of Giraudo and Moggi had had on the referee's handling of the second half, but the match ended in a 0-0 draw, an excellent result for the visitors given that they only had 10 men for that second period.

A few weeks later the Italian newspaper *Corriere dello Sport* asked Fabio if Giraudo had been exercising his power by going to the referee during the Roma-Juve game. Capello replied, 'I would say so.' Asked if he would do such a thing, Fabio responded, 'It is a question of character and respect. I really don't think I would do it. If there are rules to respect, I respect them.' The follow-up question came swiftly: 'But this exercising of power, does it have an influence on the practical side of the championship?' Capello answered equivocally. 'Championships are also won by exercising power. But in the end what counts above all is who goes out on the field.'

Capello used the same interview to criticise the conduct of the Moggi father and son publicly. It would create a sensation within Italian football and come back to haunt Fabio once he was England manager. The comments were dynamite and *Corriere dello Sport* splashed them on its front page on 7 March 2002 under the headline 'Capello Cyclone.'

Capello had been asked to comment on the way Luciano Moggi (as Juventus director) had been dealing with his son Alessandro Moggi – a football agent and leading light in an Italian agency called GEA World – with regard to the potential transfer of Italy international Alessandro Nesta from Lazio to Juventus. Capello had replied, 'It doesn't show the maximum of correctness. I don't just refer to the Moggis, but all these sons who are agents and deal with their fathers. I have a son who did the exam to qualify as a FIFA agent. I told him not to do that job while I am in football. He will have to limit himself to the profession of lawyer. That is my way of thinking, but obviously it is only mine.'

When prompted, Capello had told *Corriere dello Sport*, 'Now there is this case of GEA, which is beginning to work almost in a regime that is a monopoly. They handle six club coaches and about a hundred players. It is a clear conflict of interests. There could be repercussions and practical effects. But I don't have to think about it. Is there a governing body of football or not? I expect our directors to deal with these things, not a simple trainer like me. There is a president of our federation (the Italian FA), Carraro. And there is a league president, (Adriano) Galliani.'

The rivalry between Juventus and Roma continued to simmer bitterly. Meanwhile on the domestic front Capello was already preparing for a match that meant more to fans there than any other – the Rome derby. On 10 March 2002, Capello's Roma destroyed Lazio 5-1 and Vincenzo Montella scored four of them. Fabio was ecstatic and immodest. 'We were perfect. I saw it in training during the week. Totti, Montella, Cafu – when they play like this it is difficult for anyone.' The problem for Montella was that he still felt he hadn't been allowed to play often enough under Capello. But Fabio insisted, 'Vincenzo knows I have always had respect for him.'

Capello, who was given nine out of ten in the Italian newspapers for his tactical masterstrokes, including leaving Batistuta on the bench in order to rest him for Champions League action, had achieved god-like status in the Italian capital. It seemed that everyone dreamed of having fabulous Fabio as their coach, and he milked the rumours for all they were worth. 'Barcelona?' he mused. 'I don't exclude anything except AC Milan – I will never go back there.'

For the first time since 1994, perhaps, Capello was truly riding the crest of the managerial wave. Then that wave crashed and Capello was sent tumbling. A careless 1-1 draw at home to Galatasaray meant that Roma needed a result at Gerard Houllier's Liverpool in their final match to progress to the Champions League quarter-finals. They didn't get it. Jari Litmanen's first-half penalty and a header from Emile Heskey after the break were the killer blows. Barcelona's away win at Galatasaray meant that they progressed instead of Roma. Yet again Capello had failed to make an impact in the biggest competition of all, one in which he hadn't prevailed for eight years by then, despite coaching a series of top clubs and expensive teams.

Capello's young sensation, the 28-million-Euro Antonio Cassano, had been left to warm the bench at Anfield. That year the relationship between coach and player, once described by Cassano as 'like father and son', became so fractious, due to Cassano's unpredictable nature, that Capello coined the phrase 'Cassanata', meaning any kind of behaviour that had a negative effect on team spirit. 'Anarchy is always just around the corner with Cassano,' Fabio once famously said. The troublesome Cassano's boots couldn't do the talking for him, because limited appearances restricted him to just five goals all season.

But the wheels hadn't fallen off Capello's chariot entirely, and there was still the domestic front left to fight on. He decided that it would be a good idea to sign a new contract with Roma after all, and he did so in April 2002. It was a two-year extension (he already had a year left to run) which in theory at least would keep him at the club until 2005. Roma told the stock market in Milan that Capello would be paid £2.37 million per season, not a bad price for his loyalty.

With an unusual sense of melodrama, Capello added that he would retire from club football when he had served out that extra time in the Italian capital. 'This is my last decision. I have decided to end my coaching career. The decision to renew came to a head because we believe in the project and in the team. We have already laid important foundations and now we must look to win and be convincing. The decision to extend my contract was made by the club, not by me and it's important that Sensi has taken this decision. It's a strong signal, an act of respect towards me and what I have done until now. Another three years is enough. I will not coach another club team.'

Capello seemed to have given up on his dream to succeed Sir Alex Ferguson. But that didn't mean he wasn't still dreaming of England. Before very long he revealed his final professional ambition. 'I am not interested in the Italian national team,' he said. 'I prefer to have a new experience, outside of Italy. Between Italy and abroad, I choose England; for the language, the mentality. I believe I can do it. It is a dream of mine, something I have harboured for a long time.' Capello was already convinced that one day his time would come.

Before it did, there was the serious business of defending Roma's Serie A title. But a 3-1 defeat at the hands of Inter on March 24, with a brace from Alvaro Recoba and a brilliant header from Christian Vieri, knocked Capello's men out of their stride. Inter were now favourites for the title, Juventus were coming back strong, and Roma needed to avoid any banana skins to stay in the hunt. But when Capello's team stepped out to play lowly Venezia in the first week of April, the players seemed to lack the belief that they still had a genuine chance of glory. Catastrophically, they fell 2-0 behind before they really knew what had hit them. Roma striker Marco Delvecchio recalled, 'They were playing like it was the World Cup final, we couldn't understand where they got that stimulation from.' Although Roma eventually managed a draw, it was the sort of result that later caused Francesco Totti to accuse Capello of throwing away two titles. It was Capello's job to send his players out fully motivated and geared up for one result only – victory. Now he knew that even victory on the final day might not be enough.

Before the last, decisive matches kicked off around the country, Inter were ahead on 69 points, Juventus had 68 and Roma 67. Capello forecast that all three teams would win. He was wrong. Inter imploded 4-2 at Lazio, and the controversial Cassano's winner for Roma at Torino might have been enough to claim a second successive title. Instead Juventus managed to win at Udinese and pipped Capello by one point. Victory at Venezia, it now emerged, would have earned Roma a second successive crown.

No wonder Capello was starting to think of England. His halo in Rome was slipping. Indeed Roma's Champions League campaign started so unimpressively in 2002–03 that Capello was forced to admit, 'In Europe we have a psychological block. It is something we must overcome.' Capello's own frustration at such an indifferent start to the season seemed to be getting to him, because he was sent off by referee Paolo Dondarini in a Serie A match at Brescia for allegedly protesting too much over one of his decisions. It wasn't the last time he would see a red card that season.

Roma and Capello rallied with a magnificent victory in the Bernabeu against a Real Madrid team featuring three World Footballers of the Year, Luis Figo, Ronaldo and Zinedine Zidane.

Francesco Totti scored the winning goal in the 27th minute to reinforce Capello's reputation in Spain, and the *Giallosrossi* (Yellow-and-Reds) were soon through to the next group stage. There, however, Capello came up against the same old story – big problems against an English team. This time it was Arsenal who shook Roma's confidence with a 3-1 victory in the Stadio Olimpico, Thierry Henry erasing the significance of Cassano's opener with a stunning hat-trick. Then Ajax of Amsterdam edged out the Italians 2-1, to give Capello plenty to think about over the 2002 Christmas break.

His mood was not improved in the New Year when he was sent from the touchline yet again, this time against Atalanta in Bergamo. For an arch-disciplinarian, this was not a good example to be setting, though the sending off seemed harsh and Capello could have been forgiven for thinking that there was a conspiracy against him. He had already seen his own key midfielder, Emerson, sent off inside 21 minutes for two bookable offences. So when Fabio saw an opponent infringe blatantly, he motioned to referee Alfredo Trentalange to book the offender. In Capello's own words, it happened like this. 'I got up and with a hand gesture I asked for the booking of an Atalanta player, but I didn't open my mouth. The referee came to me and told me to go to the changing rooms.'

Capello was reported to have sworn on his grandchild's life that he had not spoken out of turn, or indeed at all, to provoke the red card. Such an extreme punishment scarcely seemed warranted. Roma lost the game 2-1.

When Fabio's team were beaten 1-0 at home by Valencia in their next Champions League match, the situation became desperate. Roma hit back with a fabulous 3-0 victory in Spain but badly needed a win in their penultimate fixture at Highbury. That night in north London was memorable for Capello's anger at the way Martin Keown had collapsed clutching his face after apparently being caught by one of Francesco Totti's elbows in the first half. Fabio thought that it was Keown's reaction that had resulted in captain Totti receiving a red card. It virtually killed off Roma's chances of progressing in the tournament, because the match ended in a 1-1 draw.

Fabio seemed to lose control in the post-match press conference as he allowed his emotions to get the better of him for once. Of the key incident Capello said, 'Totti literally just leaned on the other player. He didn't elbow him; he just touched the side of his face with his hand. The defender was a fantastic actor. Keown just did what he wanted and he meant to get Totti sent off. This time you (English) have failed in showing good sportsmanship. You are always trying to teach everyone lessons about being good sportsmen but this time you have failed. You are always saying that we Italians are always throwing ourselves on the ground and you have swapped sides in a way.'

Fabio's outburst at Highbury, applauded by members of the Italian media, provided a welcome diversion from the reality that he had failed again in Europe. Humiliatingly, Capello's team finished bottom with just five points from six games in a group featuring no clubs that could be regarded at the time as European giants. Fabio had won just one of those six matches. To rub salt into his wounds, the Champions League final that year was contested by two other Italian clubs, Juventus and AC Milan, the latter winning a penalty shoot-out at Old Trafford.

In April 2003, with domestic success already beyond them, Roma travelled to Turin's Stadio delle Alpi, where perhaps inevitably Capello was asked if he would ever consider joining Juventus. He replied categorically, 'It is not a team which interests me. I value the club, but mine is a personal argument. I say certain things, perhaps, because of my age, too, because anyone would want to go there, for what the job allows you to do. But not me. And then the Juventus team is already well coached.'

So Capello had effectively nailed his colours to Roma's mast, though the final Serie A standings didn't make comfortable reading for anyone connected with the club. They had finished an embarrassing 23 points behind Juventus back in eighth place. It felt like they weren't even in the same league any more, but there was one chance left to salvage some pride.

CHAPTER 16
JOINING THE ENEMY

FABIO HAD LED ROMA TO THE ITALIAN CUP FINAL AND GIVEN the club's passionate supporters hopes of ending that frustrating 2002–03 campaign on a high. The battle for the trophy would be a two-legged affair against AC Milan, so the bonus on offer was the chance for Capello to give his old club a bloody nose.

When Totti struck first blood for Roma in the 28th minute at the Stadio Olimpico, it looked as though such hopes might be realised, and the home side went into the interval feeling confident. When they came back out of the dressing rooms, however, Capello watched his team demolished by the club that had sacked him. Serginho scored two, Massimo Ambrosini added another and Andriy Shevchenko, still so prolific in those days, rounded off the rout a minute from time. The Roma fans were furious and Capello mania had been replaced by disdain. Between that first match and the return at the San Siro on 31 May, some Roma fans went away and made banners calling for Capello's head. Even the club's president, Franco Sensi, criticised Fabio in the aftermath of the defeat. 'Capello didn't realise what was happening in the second half, he claimed. 'Emerson was injured and others were just not up to it. In the first 10 minutes Milan did all the damage. This is a serious error for a coach of his undoubted level.'

Unaware perhaps of the strength of negative feeling that was beginning to build against him, Fabio gave a seemingly flippant reply when asked about his hopes for the future. 'I want Sensi to buy David Beckham,' he said.

At the time Barcelona, Real Madrid, AC Milan and Inter Milan were all said to be interested in securing the England captain's signature. But Capello was never sufficiently serious about Beckham to sit down with his sporting director, Franco Baldini, to discuss the Manchester United star. Indeed Fabio's long-term ambitions didn't even lie with Roma once those ugly banners were unfurled in the visiting supporters' section at the San Siro. The sight of them among Roma's own fans cut deep into his soul and from that moment he began plotting his revenge. Fabio said later, 'There was something about Roma which stuck in my throat in that penultimate year. The banners unfurled at the San Siro for the return match of the Italian Cup final against Milan. "Resign", "Capello Go", and things like that. I didn't think I deserved them.'

It was a rare admission from the tough guy of football that he could be hurt, or at the very least angered, by the protests of ordinary fans. Capello certainly didn't react immediately, because he stayed another year, and some would say that he only used those banners as an excuse for his later conduct. But he explained it like this. 'Yes, I stayed to do as well as I could and take the team as far as I could, but always with that dispute lodged in my head.'

For the record, the second leg ended 2-2 and therefore Milan took the Italian Cup 6-3 on aggregate. Francesco Totti had set the away fans dreaming by putting his side two goals ahead, but Rivaldo and Filippo Inzaghi put the destination of the trophy beyond doubt.

Capello had talks with Roma president Franco Sensi and secured an agreement that he could leave if the right offer came in. Fabio was still dreaming of succeeding Eriksson with England, and revealed, 'I'd like a new experience outside Italy. Made to choose between the national teams of Italy and England, I'd go for England. I adore London. I like the language and I like the people. I also like the England fans. It's just a dream for now, but one day I will go to England. It'd be a challenge, but I've always loved challenges and near-impossible missions.'

He would prove as good as his word, although at the time he had a 'mission impossible' closer to home – to win back the Roma fans and put the club back on top of Serie A. Perhaps Capello felt like he had nothing to lose, but his Roma side of 2003–04 played with a refreshing lack of inhibition, especially in their opponents' half. The irrepressible Totti scored 20 goals that season after Capello pushed him further forward than ever before.

Cassano, also given his freedom up front, was beginning to look worth his massive price tag. Not surprisingly, the calls for Capello's head receded, though he hadn't forgotten them.

Cassano's performances for Roma began to attract the attention of the national team and he scored on his international debut for Italy against Poland in November 2003. Unfortunately his new status seemed to go to his ever-volatile head. Cassano fell out with Capello only days after that landmark game, when the coach tried to bring him back down to earth by omitting him from a practice match. The feud would rumble on, but Roma's momentum remained irresistible. In Serie A they notched up seven consecutive victories leading up to Christmas. Roma battered Juventus 4-0 and Inter 4-1 to stake their claim as serious title contenders once again. The drubbing they gave Juve helped Luciano Moggi, Antonio Giraudo and the other Juventus directors to conclude that perhaps it was better to put Capello where he could do them good not harm – in their own camp.

In an interview published on Christmas Eve, Capello talked as though his seduction by Juventus might already have begun. Asked whether he would work with Moggi, the man he had criticised so publicly in times gone by, he replied, 'Why not? Every so often we tease one another, but we have an excellent relationship. We have known each other for more than 30 years: I played in the Juventus team, he was (the general manager) Italo Allodi's man for the junior sector.' Perhaps sensing that he had given a green light to Juventus, Capello cleverly indicated that he had only been imagining Moggi coming the other way, because he added, 'Roma, however, has great directors already: Baldini, Prade . . .' In fact he was paving the way, either consciously or subconsciously, for what would eventually happen.

Halfway through the season Serie A appeared to be shaping up for a two-horse race for the title. Only AC Milan seemed capable of keeping up with Fabio's Roma as the race began to hot up. The clubs met on 6 January 2004, at Rome's Stadio Olimpico, for a showdown that many people saw as a decisive battle for the Scudetto. Andriy Shevchenko, who never seemed to leave his shooting boots at home in those days, struck Milan's first blow in the 24th minute. Cassano duly replied on the stroke of half-time to help justify Capello's patience with his unpredictable nature. But it was Milan coach Carlo Ancelotti, Capello's former player, who found the most inspiring words during the interval. Shevchenko netted his second midway through the second half and it proved to be the winner.

Roma never quite achieved the same momentum in the second half of the season. Cassano's feud with Fabio flared up again. Capello decided to go public about what was going on behind the scenes. 'My next argument with him (Cassano) is only just around the corner. The last time we had words he shouted at me and ran away like a rabbit.' But Totti felt as aggrieved as the youngster when he discovered that Capello was telling his team-mates not to take their captain as their role model. Capello later admitted, 'I told Daniele De Rossi not to follow Totti's example, but to follow Emerson's lead if he wanted to achieve results.'

Some would argue that Capello's ability to alienate his captain and key striker when the title was still there for the taking was counter-productive. At this point, Capello was asked again about the possibility of joining Juventus, who weren't quite the force they had been the previous season. On 7 February 2004, Capello responded, 'Me, go to Juventus? I would never go to Juve, even though I consider them to be among the top five clubs in the world. The fact that I'm not going to Juventus does not mean that they haven't been seeking me. I respect the club, but I'm just not interested in going there. These are lifestyle choices.'

It sounded as though Moggi had made an approach, even if Fabio had so far rejected his advances. The problem for Capello was that, as the season dragged on, he felt he had given Roma just about as much as he could. Later he explained, 'I had finished my cycle at Rome and therefore I went. I couldn't go home without feeling for the team any more as I wanted to. I don't believe I betrayed Roma. After a number of years a coach just can't stimulate players like before, because they know him too well, they know things by memory; so I decided to go after the fifth year. That was because I saw that there was less motivation inside the dressing room. Then if there aren't leaders in the dressing room who are going to help you then it is also difficult to give fresh stimulus.'

Hampered by personality clashes for which Capello must take his share of responsibility, Roma lost momentum dramatically and finished a frustrating second in the league, 11 points behind AC Milan. The men from the San Siro had lost just two matches all season; and although Roma had only been defeated five times, they ended the campaign well off the pace. Totti, the captain, looked back on the season as a second title opportunity wasted in three years. The statistics supported his argument. Roma had outscored the champions by 68 goals to 65 and their goal difference was superior to Milan's at 49 to 41. Something was wrong with the way they had defended. Ironically, given Capello's reputation for dour, safety-first football, it appeared that his team had been punished on this occasion for taking precisely the opposite approach. Totti blamed Capello for the fact that Roma had missed out again. 'Ask Capello why we threw away two championships. He lost two titles,' argued Roma's much-loved hero later that year. In time Marco Delvecchio also suggested that the team 'should have won more than one *Scudetto*.'

Not that Fabio wanted to stay around the Italian capital to debate the matter. To continue at Roma the following season, he had realised, would be unfair on everyone now that he had lost his appetite for the task. Franco knew that Fabio was restless, and believed Roma's best chance of keeping their coach lay in an apparent lack of takers among Italy's biggest clubs. He persuaded Capello to attend a lunch at Trigoria, Roma's training ground, to welcome a highly-rated new Roma signing, the French defender, Philippe Mexes.

A few months later, Mexes revealed some of the details behind that event, which seemed to tarnish those final days of Capello's reign. Mexes felt that it was right and proper to establish a trusting relationship with his boss from the start. At what he regarded as an important meeting with the man he thought was his new coach, the Frenchman wanted to satisfy himself that Capello saw his future at Roma too.

Mexes later told French newspaper *L'Equipe*, 'The day that I arrived in Rome, I had lunch with Capello at Trigoria. He said that the fact that he was sitting there having the discussion with me suggested that he would stay with Roma. The next day, he signed for Juventus.' Totti backed up this claim by saying, 'He managed to mess Mexes around. The day before leaving he explained to Mexes all (Roma's) plans, right here at the training ground. This is Capello.'

The accusations are harsh, because it wasn't Capello who had organised the lunch, rather his assistant, Baldini. Fabio had in fact been put in an awkward position, where he felt some obligation to go through the motions on behalf of the club he was about to leave. (He actually switched clubs two days later not one). Baldini has since explained the circumstances to Mexes, and taken much of the responsibility for what happened at the lunch. However, it has to be said that such confusion wouldn't have arisen had Capello been more open about his precise intentions. For his part, Fabio would argue that he was quite open with Baldini that very afternoon, not long after the lunch with Mexes.

Capello did let Franco in on his move, that much is beyond question. The problem, from Baldini's point of view, was that Fabio did so in a manner that Franco took to be bordering on the frivolous. 'You'll never guess who wants me to work for them,' said Capello at Roma's Trigoria training ground. 'Juventus!'

Baldini knew that Inter Milan had been interested, and had been bracing himself at one stage for the possibility that Capello might leave Roma to join them. However, that previous interest from Inter had failed to result in anything concrete, and it seemed there was nothing tempting on the table to precipitate Fabio's departure. Certainly the idea of Fabio going to Juventus, after he and Baldini had both spoken out so strongly against the way the northern club went about its business, just seemed too ridiculous to warrant further discussion.

'I don't believe it,' Franco smiled.

'It's true!' Capello is understood to have insisted cheerily. He explained how a highly respected Italian sports journalist called Giorgio Tosatti of the newspaper *Corriere della Sera* had acted as intermediary for the approach, initially testing the water over how Capello might feel about a serious meeting with the Juventus directors, Antonio Giraudo and Luciano Moggi.

'Fancy that!' added Capello with a smile that seemed to convey his amazement that the 'enemy' would dare to court him.

'Yes, fancy that,' echoed Baldini, laughing along with what he thought was tantamount to a joke.

Baldini thought no more of it at the time, though he would have reason to remember the exchange soon enough. Capello, meanwhile, felt he had shared his secret with his close colleague in plain terms – and if Franco hadn't been listening properly, that was his problem.

Two days later, reportedly driving his Roma company car, Capello turned up in Turin. At 7.30am Baldini, still in Rome, received a phone call from an Italian television reporter asking him what he thought about a story that had appeared in the Italian press that day. It announced with some confidence that Capello was moving to Juventus. Hardly daring to ask the question, Baldini wanted to know which paper and reporter had broken the story. The answer was Giorgio Tosatti of *Corriere della Sera*. Now he understood everything. Capello had been trying to tell Franco that he was on his way. He had been preparing the ground.

Fabio had decided to do the one thing he had always insisted would never happen – return to the club known as *Vecchia Signora*. It wasn't just Capello's defection that infuriated Francesco Totti. The coach had arranged a gruelling pre-season tour of the USA for the Roma squad; but two of Capello's favourites were soon going to be joining him in Turin instead. The €28 million transfer to Juventus of the influential Brazilian midfielder, Emerson, who followed young Jonathan Zebina, compounded the fury of Fabio's critics.

In Rome there was the sort of uproar that Capello must have foreseen, and Totti allegedly called him 'a traitor'. The Roma captain was seething for a long time afterwards, and was withering in his criticism when invited to compare Don Fabio with his successor as coach in the Italian capital, Luciano Spalletti. Totti said, 'Spalletti, compared to Capello, is a real person. You see how he behaves with the group of players; he doesn't make any distinction between Totti, Montella and the others. Capello, on the other hand, behaved in a different way with certain important players. Never again will I play under Capello.' He was as scathing about Emerson as Capello. 'I'll only give him the obligatory handshake when I play against him, I won't go further because there is rancour ... What a disappointment.'

Capello insisted that his actions reflected his honest acceptance that he had come to the end of the Roman road. Even so, many thought he should have kept his Roma boss Franco Sensi, who had financial problems and wasn't a well man, better informed of his intentions. As Sensi would later argue, he had always agreed that Capello could leave Roma when he wanted to do so; but at the same time Sensi felt it was reasonable for Roma to be given suitable notification so they could make other plans.

Capello complimented his former boss in the aftermath of his controversial move. He said, 'I have always given the president, Sensi, credit for having built, with me and the staff, a great team that did great things for four years. And it is always important for a club to remain on the up and keep hitting the heights.'

But if he had so much respect for Sensi, why didn't he inform him properly of his decision? Capello argued that he had tried to bid the president farewell. 'It wasn't my fault,' he said. 'I called Rosella (Franco's daughter) to say goodbye and asked to be passed to the president. She responded that he was unable to come to the telephone. The only people who call me a traitor are those who don't know certain situations and factors that I hold dear, ones I have explained before: good behaviour travels along on a wave of respect for all the people with whom I work or have worked. In summary, I don't believe I have betrayed Roma.'

So why the secrecy? The answer, in all likelihood, was that Fabio knew perfectly well what uproar his chosen destination would cause with his employers and the Roma supporters in the Italian capital. He didn't want any obstacles in his way until he was already travelling safely away from the Italian capital.

Whatever the explanation, Capello had decided that he would never again make a decision out of some misguided sense of moral obligation. Look what had happened when he had gone back to Milan to please others. Now he would please himself. But there still remained the manner of his departure, the way he appeared to have taken flight by night. 'I didn't take flight, I didn't escape,' he insisted. So why hadn't he organised a press conference or said goodbye to the fans? Didn't he regret that? Capello thought for a couple of seconds. 'No, no regrets,' he replied. But Roma fans regretted the manner of his departure rather more, and Capello would require protection every time he visited the Italian capital in the aftermath of his decision.

Capello admitted 18 months later, 'I really loved Rome, its sunsets and the history that breathed out of its every corner. My trusted dentist is there and when I go I have to inform the Special Branch first. I certainly can't just walk along the street alone or go and get myself a coffee in a bar.' The days of Capello being able to explore Rome in a carefree way, as he had done in the magical 1960s, were over for a while, though by 2008 he was insisting that he had been feeling perfectly safe again on visits to Rome for some time. He denied that he had ever needed a personal bodyguard there, as had been widely reported.

Meanwhile in the immediate aftermath of Capello's switch to Juventus, Franco Baldini was utterly dismayed – he didn't think Fabio had adequately forewarned him of his sudden departure. The sense of hurt remained until he gave a controversial interview on an Italian television show, *Parla Con Me*, 'Talk with me'. In that interview he criticised Juventus, GEA World – the powerful sports agency co-run by Luciano Moggi's son Alessandro – and all the unfairness that was becoming the norm in Italian football. Baldini was appalled that Capello had joined the very club they had both criticised for practices they believed to be incorrect.

Of his relationship with Capello, Baldini pointed out, 'It was a really important friendship, not just for theatre and pictures ... we thought in the same way on many things, referees, doping, GEA ... better still it was he who opened my eyes on many things. Now we

each other, so little that I still haven't had the
sk him why he went to Juventus.'
e-opener' had allegedly come when Baldini aired a
y of his while having a conversation with Capello at
Roma. ~~~ believed that when smaller clubs complained about
the controversial decisions of some referees in favour of bigger
clubs, it was just an excuse for their own inadequacies and openly
dismissed conspiracy theories of suspicious favouritism among
referees towards the big clubs, claiming they were a myth. But
Capello is understood to have turned to Baldini and said, 'No,
Franco, it's really true, it really does happen.'

Meanwhile Luciano Moggi and his fellow directors had decided
to invite Baldini to a meeting to offer him the job of sporting
director at Juventus. Baldini attended that meeting out of courtesy
and curiosity, to hear what Juventus would say. But he couldn't
accept the job, because it went against everything he believed in
about fair play in football.

Shortly afterwards, Baldini left Roma, partly because of his
objection to the direction in which he perceived Roma to be
moving under Rosella Sensi, who had taken over from her ailing
father Franco as the club's chief. It seemed to Baldini that she
favoured a closer alliance with the big northern clubs. Baldini had
no wish to see the big clubs getting bigger and the small clubs
getting smaller. Besides, he couldn't see how Roma would ever be
granted true equality alongside the northern giants when it came to
any major administrative or television deals. Franco wanted no part
of any proposed alliance, and went off to work in television instead.

Capello's friendship with Baldini seemed irreparable; they
hadn't talked for months. Meanwhile a time bomb was ticking in
Turin, even as Capello began his two-year reign there.

CHAPTER 17
WINNING WORTHLESSLY

SEEMINGLY OBLIVIOUS TO THE SENSE OF BETRAYAL AND outrage that he had he had left behind him, Fabio Capello continued to build for a bright future with Juventus. Fabio Cannavaro arrived to reinforce the defence at a cost of €10 million from Inter. But existing Juventus squad members were warned that they too could expect more defensive responsibilities, no matter where they played. Pavel Nedved was used to a free offensive role in the Juventus midfield, and might have thought he had already learned everything he was going to. But Capello added an extra dimension to his game, so that Nedved contributed more when his team didn't have the ball: 'Without a doubt he has strengthened our defence,' the Czech star would later say. 'Compared to when Marcello Lippi was in charge, I have to defend much more. Now I'm a true midfielder.'

Already Capello was stamping his authority on the club he had served so well as a player. Thirty-four years earlier, as we have seen, he had risked his career to attack the self-indulgence of certain Juventus players and their lack of team ethic. Now he was in the position to ensure that the latest stars in the black-and-white stripes worked together, with hard work and organisation the key to success. As for passion, no one at the club doubted it would play a big part in this of all years, especially on the European stage.

The 2004–05 Champions League campaign would be poignant for Juventus, because the climax of the competition would mark the twentieth anniversary of the Heysel disaster, when marauding Liverpool supporters caused panic and the crushing to death of 39 Italian fans at the 1985 European Cup final in Brussels. In order to pay a fitting on-field tribute to those who had lost their lives in Belgium, Capello's Juventus would have to negotiate some tricky opponents early in the tournament and avoid the humiliation of an early exit.

In August 2004 Juventus entered the tournament at the third qualifying round stage, and only managed a 2-2 draw with a little-known Swedish side called Djurgarden in their first-leg match in Turin. Suddenly the sort of high-profile contests that Juventus had hoped for during the latter stages of the competition the following year appeared to be in considerable jeopardy. All eyes were on the return match against Djurgarden in Sweden as observers sensed the possibility of an upset. When it really mattered, however, Juventus won 4-1 and went through to the Champions League group stage. There they were due to play Ajax of Amsterdam, so it was particularly convenient for Capello's European hopes that the Dutch threat had been weakened just in time. By the end of August, Ajax's star striker, Zlatan Ibrahimovic, had joined Fabio's Juventus for a fee of €19 million. The skilful Swede would show himself to be useful not just for his own deadly marksmanship, but also in creating more chances for his strike-partner, David Trezeguet.

Between September and December 2004 Juve won their Champions League group emphatically with five victories, a draw and no defeats. During that time they twice did 'the double' over opponents, with home and away wins not just over the impotent Ajax but also over the dangerous Bayern Munich. People had already begun to talk about Juventus as serious contenders for the European crown, and if they were right Capello would claim his first Champions League for eleven years.

Their first test at knockout stage would have made a worthy final in itself, because the opposition was the mighty Real Madrid, Capello's old club. Spanish defender Ivan Helguera's solitary goal won Real the opening clash in the Bernabeu; but David Trezeguet sent the tie into extra time at the Stadio delle Alpi with a vital strike 15 minutes from the end. A Uruguayan called Marcelo Zalayeta handed Juventus a famous victory just when everyone had begun to think about a penalty shoot-out. Juventus were now favourites for the Champions League.

As fate would have it, waiting for Capello's men in the quarter-final were none other than Liverpool. Juventus hadn't met the Reds in competitive football since that horrific night in Belgium 20 earlier. Plenty of public relations work went into the build-up to the first match at Anfield in order to ensure that the tinderbox atmosphere didn't lead to fresh trouble. The trauma was still understandably fresh in the minds of many, and it was clear that the survivors had never stopped suffering but the emphasis was on forgiveness where it existed – and it did, in abundance. On the night of the game on Merseyside, some very fitting commem-orative touches paved the way, and the players were left to play football without any incident.

Gianluigi Buffon, arguably the world's greatest goalkeeper, had only been beaten twice all tournament; but that didn't stop big Sami Hyypia from sending a thunderous left-footed volley past him after just ten minutes. Capello must have been a worried man when the skilful Luis Garcia sent another volley beyond Buffon from 25 metres. However, the goal that blasted the tie wide open came when Zambrotta's cross found Cannavaro's head in the 63rd minute. Juve fans would have left Anfield in even more optimistic mood had Mauro Camoranesi's attempted equaliser not swerved just wide in the closing stages. But the way it finished, Juventus required just a single goal on home turf to go through.

Perhaps Capello's Juventus had forgotten just how capable Liverpool were of transforming themselves, on big European nights away from home, into a defensive team of superb tactical organisation and know-how. No matter how great the pressure in Turin for the return match, the Reds appeared determined to hold firm. Then a pivotal moment left Liverpool hopes hanging by a thread for a few dramatic seconds. Cannavaro met Del Piero's free kick 12 minutes from time, but his header struck Dudek's post and no one was able to take advantage. Juve's best chance had gone, Liverpool were through and would go on to win the Champions League.

In a familiar career pattern, Capello was left to reinforce his reputation as a superb manager in the domestic leagues. He did so by leading Juventus to the Serie A title, 2004–05. The *Vecchia Signora* had left AC Milan trailing by seven points, an emphatic dominance if ever there was one. Ibrahimovic was Juventus top-scorer with 16 Serie A goals, though perhaps it was a reflection of Capello's increasingly cautious style that no fewer than six players from other teams scored more goals than the champions' chief marksman.

If some of the football had been less than spectacular, Capello's latest *Scudetto* triumph had caught the eye of the king-makers in England. Fabio was still being linked with Manchester United, as everyone assumed that Sir Alex Ferguson would retire some time soon. The following winter, with Juventus well on the way to defending their Italian title, Capello was asked about the rumours that simply wouldn't go away.

'To be coach of Manchester United would be a dream come true,' Fabio admitted, 'but I have not had any offers from the directors of Manchester United. There are rumours linking me to Real Madrid and Manchester United but at the moment I want to end my project with Juventus and see them through to the summer. But I would never discard a chance to work in England if the circumstances were right. The Premiership is very attractive and I would love to prove that I can work in England as well as in Italy and Spain.'

Meanwhile it appeared that the power brokers at Old Trafford had rivals in London. The Football Association was still looking at Capello as a future England manager, and behind the scenes there were discreet enquiries about his ability to extricate himself from his existing obligations in Turin. The 2006 World Cup was just around the corner, and the FA's new chief executive, Brian Barwick, had already made it clear to Sven Goran Eriksson that his services would no longer be required after that tournament. Once again, Capello was a serious contender for the England hot-seat.

Though the Football Association let it be known that they were interested in Fabio, this time the contact was more tentative than it had been in 2000, and proved inconclusive. Meanwhile Juventus desperately wanted Capello to stay.

For a man in so much demand, however, Fabio found life a little precarious during his next assault on the Champions League. It was March 2006, and not even the quarter-final stage of the tournament, when Juventus were only two or three minutes from being dumped out of the competition in humiliating style on home soil, by the mediocre Werder Bremen. With seconds left on the clock in the Stadio delle Alpi, it was almost time for Fabio to prepare his excuses for more European failure. He could look back to the first match and the lapses in concentration that had cost Juventus near-certain progress. The underdogs had ruined Capello's night in Germany when two late goals had given Bremen a 3-2 first leg win.

That slender advantage had looked easily reversible in Italy until Johan Micoud, the first-leg match-winner in injury time, had struck first blood. With his team therefore 4-2 down on aggregate, Fabio had read his players the riot act at half-time and sent them out early for the restart. They had responded well, though without actually making the breakthrough they needed; so Capello had introduced his attacking substitutes, Alessandro Del Piero and Adrian Mutu. The pressure had begun to tell at last, and Trezeguet had scored after combining with Nedved. The Werder Bremen goalkeeper, Tim Wiese, had seemed to misread the Frenchman's shot completely.

Now Juventus only needed one more goal to go through, but the clock was against them. It looked as though yet another of Fabio's European dreams would turn to dust. Then, in the 88th minute, an extraordinary piece of goalkeeping changed everything. Catching the ball, Wiese suddenly and quite unnecessarily executed a forward roll and accidentally threw the ball to the retreating Emerson's feet. Having committed that catastrophic error, he failed to close down the Brazilian midfielder, who simply booted the ball into the net to settle the issue. Juventus marched happily on to a date with Arsenal in the quarter-finals. It was as simple as that.

For Patrick Vieira, the Gunners' icon who had been Capello's big capture at €20 million the previous summer, that incredibly lucky escape from elimination, combined with the reward of a tie against his old club, must have seemed like destiny. Fabio had landed the Frenchman, who had been allowed to leave his Milan squad back in 1996 for just $5 million, to bolster his midfield and give Juventus fresh physical strength. But there was no happy North London homecoming for Vieira as Capello's men went two goals behind at Highbury in the quarter-final first leg later that month. Cesc Fabrigas and Thierry Henry, the man who had sunk Capello's Roma in the same competition a few years earlier, were the executioners. Juventus slowly lost momentum without the suspended Nedved that night, and eventually they lost their discipline too. By the end of the game, Arsenal's opponents didn't resemble a Capello team at all. In fact they didn't particularly resemble any kind of football team, because Fabio only had nine men left on the field. Mauro Camoranesi and Jonathan Zebina were both sent off for second bookable offences in the final three minutes. This was hardly Fabio Capello's finest hour.

'We should have defended better and when we started losing players we had no chance,' he said afterwards. But within days he had warned Arsenal that the second leg would be very different. 'We will start to attack in the tunnel while we are entering the field.'

Meanwhile the experienced Juve defender Lilian Thuram, a 1998 World Cup winner with France, should have known better when he claimed before the game, 'Man for man, the Juventus team is superior to Arsenal's, and it would not be a surprise if we scored three or even four goals.' Therefore it was particularly embarrassing for Capello, Thuram and company when Juventus went out of the Champions League with more of a whimper than a bang. A goalless draw in Turin was more than enough to send the Gunners through.

Two Champions League campaigns with Juventus, two disappointing exits at the hands of English clubs, against whom Capello's men had been expected to do far better. A grouchy

Fabio went through the motions at his post-match press conference. There was a stale, dissatisfied atmosphere about the Stadio delle Alpi that night. It was a soulless place, and you sensed that all was not well at the club, even though Juve's Italian rivals seemed to have so much trouble matching them on a weekly basis in Serie A.

Life at Juventus had become more intense during Capello's two seasons than some of the players were used to. 'It would be nice if he lightened up once in a while,' said the goalkeeper, Gigi Buffon. Fabio Cannvaro went a little further: 'When you see the boss he is almost frightening and he isn't keen on certain attitudes. If training is at 11 that means 11 and arriving at five past is a lack of respect.' Another star player, the long-serving Alessandro Del Piero, viewed what he perceived as Capello's kill-joy attitude and rigid tactical demands with distaste, and he was further infuriated by Fabio's seemingly relentless habit of substituting him. Del Piero's subsequent verdict on Capello's failure to inspire Juventus in Europe went like this: 'Considering the men we had, we went out of the Champions League too soon; but, considering the way he made us work, it was what we deserved.'

Yet the gruelling physical demands of Capello's regime didn't seem to do any harm to Juve's hopes of winning the *Scudetto* again. By 14 May 2006, it had become clear that one more victory, against Reggina of Calabria, would secure Capello's men their second successive title. Unfortunately for Juventus, much more had become clear early that May – for the Italian football scandal known as *Calciopoli* had come to light.

The central allegation in the scandal was that the results of some matches might have been tainted by the undue pressure placed both on referees themselves, and those who chose them for specific matches. A culture of favouritism seemed to revolve around Luciano Moggi, the Juventus General Manager. Moggi later sought to portray himself as a victim in the scandal, though he admitted to having been influenced by Italo Allodi, his old boss in times gone by, if only because of Allodi's extraordinary ability to 'network'. Moggi once revealed, 'I knew Allodi and knowing him carried me along to learning important things that were then useful for arriving in decisive places. But I have never had a guardian angel or sought one. Let's say I was a niaive person who grew ... When I arrived at a certain height people started to shoot at me from all directions, because obviously they were scared ... that I would grow more.'

In fact Moggi's critics were so numerous and vociferous because he appeared to be trying to remove competitive fairness from parts of Italian football and, on occasion, games in European football too. Moggi continues to deny that he ever tried to do such a thing. Old allegiances had existed in the Italian game since before his day, Moggi argued – it was the way of the world. In Allodi's day, mutual understandings required one club virtually to gift a match to another club if that second club needed the result more. At a later date, the favour would be returned. Luciano once told Italian newspaper *La Repubblica*, 'Allodi's system was very simple. It was the system of *ascendenza* (ancestry or influence) among football clubs. That's how it was in his time and I inherited it.' When asked to explain the meaning of the word *ascendenza*' in this case, Moggi added, 'The system of unspoken rules. An example. If Team A had nothing more to claim from a championship and they met Team B, which was fighting for survival, they left the match to them. They would play the game putting some youth or reserve side out on the pitch, or in any case send out a line-up that wasn't competitive. There was no need for agreements.'

The interviewer asked, 'This was in Allodi's world, and in Moggi's?' It was the key question. Moggi replied, 'Each person weaved the thread he had, trying not to have it cut with scissors. Look at my relationship with (Adriano) Galliani (vice-president of AC Milan and President of the Italian League). Now they say we were *pappa e ciccia* (an Italian experession that means a friendship tied by an agreement). In reality he looked at me through the key-hole and I looked at him through a half-closed window. The fact is that I only had to protect a great group and a great club from swine. This was my constant worry, apart from creating a great team.'

However, the primary concern, the protection of football itself, had been sacrificed along the way; and it was only a matter of time before Moggi found himself in trouble. The authorites stumbled across the scandal after first launching judicial investigations into separate allegations – that drugs had been administered to Juventus players during the previous decade, and that illegal betting had taken place within the game.

In 1998 the respected Cezch coach Zdenek Zeman had claimed that Italian football should 'get out of the pharmacy' and pointed the finger at Juventus. After 281 different drugs were found at the Juventus training ground, the club doctor, Riccardo Agricola, was sentenced to twenty-two months in prison in November 2004, though he never served a day. Agricola was cleared on appeal in December 2005 after it emerged that there was no proof the drugs, allegedly administered between 1994 and 1998, had been performance-enhancing. Antonio Giraudo, the Juventus director who had also been dragged into the storm by the time of the appeal, was similarly acquitted.

Fabio Capello tried to stay out of the controversy. He explained: 'In my career as a player and as a manager I have seen how things are done, but it doesn't seem right to me to denounce them now.' The investigations into what the Italians called 'doping' turned up no enduring evidence of systematic abuse and the betting scandal allegations were equally impossible to substantiate. But the Italian authorities began to focus increasingly on the activities of GEA World, co-run by Luciano's son Alessandro. Capello, while at Roma, had already pointed to the conflict of interest involving the Juventus General Manager, Luciano Moggi, and his son, Alessandro back in 2002.

It appears that the Italian authorities had become increasingly more worried about GEA World and the Moggis over time. The tapping of telephone lines seemed to raise questions about Luciano Moggi's apparent ability to influence just about every aspect of Italian football, so that *Calciopoli* was soon known as *Moggiopoli* too. Both names were a play on the word *Tangentopoli*, roughly translated as 'Bribesville', a tag given to the largely corrupt Italian political system of the 1980s and early 1990s.

When the telephone 'interceptions' were first made public

early in that May of 2006, they sent shockwaves through football. On 8 May Franco Carraro, President of the Italian FA, resigned. On 11 May the Juventus board resigned, leaving the club in turmoil for Capello's key, title-deciding match against Reggina three days later. But the tapes were so damning that Luciano Moggi and Antonio Giraudo, the Juventus CEO, appeared to have little choice but to resign as shares in the club started to tumble.

One tape, for example, captured Moggi and Giraudo discussing Swedish striker Zlatan Ibrahimovic, whom they had wanted to sign with the minimum fuss from Ajax of Amsterdam back in the summer of 2004. The implication contained in the following exchange from August 2004 seemed to be that Giraudo and Moggi had told Ibrahimovic not to do anything too outstanding on the field of play, in case it created a tug-of-war between the clubs, or increased the transfer fee. Apparently ignoring those instructions, Ibrahimovic had just scored a hat-trick for Ajax.

MOGGI: What the hell, but I specifically told him to play badly.

GIRAUDO: I told him! We had agreed that he would play badly, go see the manager after the game, tell him that he would never play for them again and demand that he be sold to us.'

After only scraping a draw with Djurgarden in the first leg of their 2004 Champions League qualifying match in Turin, the transcripts showed that Luciano Moggi had been furious with the way the match had been officiated. He had called the Italian and UEFA referees' official, Pierluigi 'Gigi' Pairetto, to complain that a Juventus 'goal' had been disallowed.

MOGGI: Gigi, what fuck of a referee did you send us?

PAIRETTO: (Herbert) Frandel? He's number one, he's a top guy.

MOGGI: Yes, whatever, but Miccoli's goal was valid.

PAIRETTO: No.

MOGGI: It's valid, it's valid.

PAIRETTO: No, it was right in front (of the ref).

MOGGI: What are you talking about ... it wasn't in front ... the entire game was an absolute disaster.

PAIRETTO: But you know he (Frandel) is one of the best guys.

MOGGI: Well I tell you, he can really fuck off. I have to make the return match in Stockholm secure, no?

PAIRETTO: For fuck's sake ... mamma mia ... this (one) really has to be a proper game.

MOGGI: No, we are going to win ... but with another (referee) like (Frandel) it's going to be a bit difficult no? You follow me?

Moggi then tells Pairetto whom to appoint as referee for a series of domestic games, including one against AC Milan.

MOGGI: And (against Milan) it has to be Pieri.

PAIRETTO: We haven't done that yet.

MOGGI: OK, we'll see to that later.

As it happened, when Juventus played Milan on 28 August 2004 the referee was Pieri and Juventus won 1-0. But Moggi wasn't always given his own way in the selection of referees for Juventus matches. The following, separate transcript shows how Moggi had assumed that a Portuguese official called Lucilio Cardoso was going to referee the second leg of the Champions League qualifer against Djurgarden in that August of 2004. Instead he had been told that Graham Poll of England had been chosen instead. On 24 August Moggi had called Pairetto, clearly furious.

MOGGI: So it's Cardozo, eh?

PAIRETTO: Eh?

MOGGI: It's Poll, Graham.

PAIRETTO: What?

MOGGI: Poll, Graham.

PAIRETTO: Well something has happened at the last moment, he was sick or something.

MOGGI: Find out.

PAIRETTO: Yes I'll look into it right away.

Juventus won the second leg against the Swedes 4-1 as we have seen, though there is no suggestion that Poll was involved in any wrong-doing. Indeed his reputation for unimpeachable fairness is precisely what seems to have unsettled Moggi, who had realised that he would have no say in the big game.

These tapes asked questions about the validity of Juve's previous two seasons, and the questions simply weren't going to go away. It was against the backdrop of these bombshell revelations in May 2006 that Fabio Capello had to prepare for the final, decisive match of his Serie A season against Reggina in Bari. Events from almost two years earlier had returned to haunt Juventus and off-the-field distractions were unprecedented. As the chaos raged all around him, Capello held firm and told his players to show their worth on the field. It wasn't a pleasant situation, but the controversy ought to give the team all the more reason to want to perform to their best ability. They did just that in the hot frenzy of the southern Italian stadium, and clinched a 2-0 victory to seal their second successive *Scudetto*.

In his moment of triumph, Capello treated the Italian football scandal with great scepticism. 'Let's wait, and perhaps we will be laughing about this soon … I am and will remain a friend to Moggi. It has become a sport to attack Moggi and Juventus.' As for his own Juventus team and their back-to-back titles, Capello argued, 'For seventy-six matches we have always come off the field with our heads held high. Today we come off the field with our heads held even higher … My future is certainly at Juventus.' He even told everyone he looked forward to seeing them on 15 July, when Juve's pre-season training would begin.

But once the telephone transcripts were fully digested, the backlash against Moggi and Juventus grew in momentum. It was clear to everyone that Moggi viewed referees with contempt. Indeed, Luciano had shown such little respect for a referee called Gianluca Paparesta – whose poor decisions had contributed to a 2-1 defeat of Juventus in Reggio Calabria the previous season – that he had devised a shocking story about having locked the poor official in his own dressing room after the game.

Moggi had called a friend, Silvana Garufi to let off steam after the relevant match.

MOGGI: No, look … one thing … two goals disallowed … a penalty … scandalous.

GARUFI: Yes, yes, I saw it, I saw it … a scandal though.

MOGGI: I shut the referee in the changing room and took the keys away to the airport with me.

GARUFI: Yeah right!

MOGGI: No, no, it's true, it's true.

GARUFI: Ah ... so?

MOGGI: I locked him in and took away the key. Now they'll open it. They'll break the door down.'

Witness statements later cast doubt on the story. Nevertheless, Moggi's sense of outrage was equally clear when he later complained to his fellow director Antonio Giraudo, 'We have never asked anything of him (Paparesta) in particular, but he didn't even give us what we were due!'

When I later tried to talk to the England manager about the scandal, Fabio quickly distanced himself from what had happened, partly by claiming that he hadn't featured on any of the interceptions. That wasn't quite correct, although Capello certainly hadn't been heard to say anything that might incriminate him.

In the following conversation, Capello is heard telling Moggi that GEA was about to be subjected to a full-scale investigation by the Itailan Antitrust Authority (the authority to prevent monopolies or conflicts of interest in the Italian business world).

CAPELLO: I'm at home. I just wanted to tell you one thing ... Quick, quick, quick. Listen.

MOGGI: Tell me

CAPELLO: My son called me from Milan, no?

MOGGI: Uhm

CAPELLO: That they've told him ... For sure, eh ... that the Antitrust is looking for the telephone numbers of all the players who have had any dealings with your son ... to question them.

MOGGI: Wi-with all the players

CAPELLO: That have had dealings with your son ... No? With your son's agency to question them.

MOGGI: Uh, eh ... All in all, I don't believe..

CAPELLO: No, no, I ...

MOGGI: No! No! No! No! Great, great!

CAPELLO: OK ...

MOGGI: OK! Listen, I'm in the office ... If you have a spare minute ...

Later Capello said, 'I wasn't aware of the opening of an

investigation by the Antitrust of GEA. My son, who is a lawyer, told me about this inquiry and I advised Moggi of this.'

Pierfilippo Capello confirmed this to me. He had heard from a contact that the Italian Antitrust Authority wanted to investigate because they had been told that GEA was becoming too powerful in the transfer market. But by the summer of 2006 Capello was aware of the content of the tapes just like everyone else, and he might have wondered whether his friendship with Moggi would have an adverse effect on his own career. If Fabio did consider this at any stage, it didn't make any difference to his decision.

I have been told by someone very close to Capello that he continued to support Moggi because few others would do so after the scandal broke. It seems that Fabio watched so many who had previously hung on Moggi's every word suddenly disappear; Capello decided that he was not prepared to be such a man. Capello had known Luciano Moggi for more than 30 years, from when he played for Juventus and Moggi was Italo Allodi's man for the junior sector of the club. So he would continue to take Moggi's calls, he would exchange greetings with Moggi at Christmas; once a friend, always a friend.

A sporting tribunal subsequently banned Luciano Moggi and Antonio Giraudo from any involvement with the game for five years. The club they had run was hit hard too. Not only were Juventus relegated to Serie B; they were also deducted nine points for the start of the following season. AC Milan, Fiorentina, Lazio and Reggina had also been found guilty of wrong-doing by the tribunal but to the dismay of some Juventus followers, the other guilty clubs all escaped the trap-door to Italian football's second tier by the time the appeals were over. These teams were deducted 8, 15, 3 and 11 points respectively for their next Serie A campaigns.

When Juventus were stripped of the two titles they had won in 2004–05 and 2005–06, most people still thought justice had been done, however. Not Fabio Capello: 'In the year of the second title that they took away from us, there wasn't any interception. However, if the law says that Moggi and the others made some error then it is right that they pay, but they remain friends.' Sara

Faillaci of *Vanity Fair* found it hard to reconcile Capello's criticism of Moggi back in 2002 with their friendship. She reminded Fabio, 'Nevertheless it was actually you, when you were coach of Roma, who accused Moggi of an excessive power in football's transfer market.' Capello replied, 'I wasn't just speaking about Juventus but also Milan and Inter. When I coached Juventus, on the other hand, I didn't have anything to do with the transfer market directly.'

On 18 June 2006 Fabio Capello celebrated a landmark birthday with his family. His sister Bianca well remembers what he said and she revealed. 'We had a big party for Fabio's 60th. I remember him saying there was only one thing left for him to do in football – and that was to manage England. It was one of those dreams that you keep in your bottom drawer.' England would have to wait a little longer, however, though Fabio's reign at Juventus was only weeks from coming to an end. Capello's immediate future lay elsewhere, though he was determined to leave the disgraced Itailan club with his head held high. He would continue to insist that Juventus had deserved their success with him, and said of that final season, 'We won the title on the field and on the field only. The Juventus I coached was a stupendous team, it didn't need external support.'

Stupendous or not, Capello resigned on 4 July 2006, as it became clear that there would be no reprieve from relegation. Not everyone was sorry to see Fabio leave Turin. Soon after his departure, Alessandro Del Piero, Juve's senior player, said, 'The relationship with Capello wasn't satisfactory from many points of view. If he had remained I would have gone abroad.' The world-class Juventus goalkeeper, Gigi Buffon, appeared no more nostalgic when he claimed, 'Capello was a dictator. What he said was the way to go. He had little dialogue with his players.'

Unfortunately, Fabio's friend Luciano Moggi had entered into far too many dialogues with various figures within the game, and the consequences had been far-reaching. Whatever Capello achieved at Juventus – and he did build a decent team – has since been wiped from the history books. Passionate defenders of football will probably feel reassured by the fact that Juve were stripped of their domestic honours. 'A win is a win,' or so the sporting cliché goes, but where there is no level playing field, it's not such a high accolade.

CHAPTER 18
DISSING BECKHAM

FOR MONTHS THERE HAD BEEN RUMOURS THAT FABIO WAS being courted by Real Madrid, who reportedly wanted Capello to return to the club he had coached to the La Liga title 10 years earlier. The Spanish giants had taken on a new look at the very top that summer. A member of Capello's Real Madrid squad of 1996–97, Predrag Mijatovic, had become sporting director, headhunted by a new president, a 55-year-old lawyer called Ramon Calderon. So the breakdown in Capello's relationship with Lorenzo Sanz could be forgotten.

However, it wasn't just Calderon and Mijatovic who had met Capello behind the scenes earlier that summer, as Juventus awaited their fate and the Real Madrid presidential elections drew near. A third man, as charming and as witty as ever, had played a part in trying to persuade Fabio to return to Spain. That man was none other than Capello's old friend and colleague, Franco Baldini. England's future management double-act were about to find themselves working together again.

Baldini had been working in Italian television since leaving AS Roma in March 2005. Like so much about their relationship, the reunion between Franco and Capello had been dramatic; it was even televised. Baldini had been working on a show for Sky Sports Italia as an expert in the transfer market. In October 2005 he was handed the inevitable assignment – travel to Turin and interview your old Roma colleague, Fabio Capello at Juventus. Baldini accepted, even though he hadn't seen Capello since Fabio's sudden departure from Rome. There was every possibility that the atmosphere would be tense.

When he began the interview, Franco kept the tone professional, but it was only a matter of time before the pair revisited the circumstances behind Capello's departure from Roma.

'I left because of a banner from a year earlier,' Capello told his future England assistant, remembering the demonstration among hard-core Roma fans at the San Siro. Then he launched his bombshell by adding, 'You already knew everything about my departure, because I told you.'

'I didn't see it that way at the time but if you say so,' replied an embarassed Baldini, who was aware that he was being made to look a little foolish on film. Mercilessly, Capello continued to insist that he had told Baldini just how close Juventus were to employing him. He seemed to be enjoying this clash much more than the interviewer. And although Franco knew in his own mind that their final exchanges as Roma employees hadn't been so straightforward, he wanted to save himself from a further on-screen mauling. Therefore he acknowledged that he had realised during those crucial days that Fabio would soon be on the move if he had his way. Wishing to restore some harmony to proceedings, Franco didn't pursue the matter further; and although they disagreed on the finer details, Fabio emerged as the clear winner of this particular argument on points. What mattered, in hindsight, was that their differences had been aired – quite literally. It didn't seem so important any more that their accounts varied; Capello and Baldini had broken the ice, and they could begin to mend their relationship.

They began to speak every so often on the phone, and in time found a way to enjoy complete mutual trust again. Fabio knew that Baldini was the sort of person who would always speak out if he felt something was fundamentally wrong. Perhaps that is why he seemed to accept the potentially damaging interview that his former sporting director had done on the Italian television programme *Parla Con Me*, in which Baldini had claimed that it was

Capello himself who had opened his eyes to issues such as GEA World, doping and referees. Capello still respected Baldini's integrity, and Franco knew how well they worked together. To remain apart would be a waste in professional terms.

Having been approached by Real Madrid's new leadership-in-waiting, Baldini had therefore been prepared to join Calderon and Mijatovic earlier that summer in a secret visit to Capello's holilday home on the island of Pantelleria, near Sicily, to discuss the coach's future. Fabio had been receptive to Real Madrid's offer, though he had waited to see what would happen to Juventus before making any official decision. Now that Juve were doomed to relegation, his next step became clearer. In the first week of July, the Spanish giants duly announced what was already common knowledge – Capello was to be their new coach. For Fabio, it was almost like coming home.

When he returned to the familiar, spectacular stage of Real Madrid in 2006, there were still players waiting there from his first reign in 1996-97. The likes of Raul, Roberto Carlos and Guti had turned from impressionable young men to veterans of big-time football. More signings would join the old stagers.

On 3 July 2006 Calderon said, 'I want to represent all the fans and excite them by putting together the best possible team. We will start this very afternoon with Fabio Capello in charge as I promised. He will arrive this evening and start working with Mijatovic to construct the new team that will be capable of winning a trophy next season.'

Capello would reunite David Beckham, who had joined Real from Manchester United in 2003, with his old team-mate Ruud van Nistelrooy, the player Fabio had so wanted to sign while at Roma. Another English-based star, Jose Antonio Reyes, would be brought home from Arsenal. Fabio, it was predicted, would have learned from his last Real Madrid experience; so this time perhaps he would be able to win over the thrill-seeking Bernabeu crowd more quickly. While he did that, he could even feed his old passion for bullfighting – 'one part risk, one part ballet' as he saw it. What could possibly go wrong? Surely Don Fabio knew too much to be gored by club politics in the Spanish capital this time?

Fabio Cannavaro, who had just lifted the World Cup for Italy at 33, bore no ill feeling towards Capello either for the loss of the two titles they had won together at Juventus. Like Capello, Cannavaro believed that those titles had been won fair and square on the field of play. As far as Cannavaro was concerned, the responsibility for the club's humiliation lay with Luciano Moggi and his unnecessary meddling off the pitch. Asked if he was angry with Moggi, Cannavaro replied, 'Yes, actually. I'm disappointed that having won two titles, I've nothing in my hands for it.' He hoped it would be third time lucky and the Spanish experience would see the two Fabios celebrating something that history would continue to recognise. Emerson wanted to be part of Capello's latest adventure too. So Cannavaro and Emerson both left Juve for Madrid at a combined cost of €20 million.

Capello seemed to be relishing the change of air too, when he told Madrid reporters, 'Spanish football is more evolved on a technical level, and you have added a dash of South American football which makes it a great spectacle. In Madrid and in all Spain they love goals, flare and enjoyment. If they win they throw beautiful parties; if they lose they don't have it in for you, as in Italy where one defeat is subjected to a thousand trials. Italian football is more controversial, there is more foul play and less flare; it is less attractive and less enjoyable. And the people on the terraces often yawn.'

When it was pointed out to Capello that AC Milan and the Italy national team still faired very well against the rest of Europe, he acknowledged, 'It's true, because our football is solid, practical and cynical like no other. And the Spanish are always ready to criticise us because they can't bear our victories; they are envious. But you still have to recognise that in Spain the people at the matches enjoy themselves more, boredom doesn't exist.'

Plenty of people would have it in for Capello before the end of the season, precisely because they felt he had reintroduced boredom to Spanish football. For others it was a price worth paying. The Madridistas may have liked entertainment but they also wanted to win something. Soon after he arrived, Cannavaro revealed, 'It's pretty clear from the atmosphere that people here want something fast. They walk around downtown and they come up to you and say, "Win something important".'

There was ruthlessness in the air from Capello's first big meeting with his bosses. Later Capello revealed that, in his first meeting with Ramon and his technical staff, the club had made it clear they wanted Raul sent out on loan. Capello argued Raul's case and was allowed to prevail – this time. Defying Calderon from the start may not have been the most diplomatic path for Capello to choose, but he never had claimed to be the world's greatest diplomat. Just ask former Everton hero Thomas Gravesen, who later said to journalists, 'Capello is selfish and arrogant. He arrived in Madrid and told me in a very arrogant manner – without having seen me play – that he had other ideas for the team. He never gave me a chance. He is not a nice guy. He doesn't even know my name.' But Capello seemed just as angry with Gravesen for falling out with his team-mates and allegedly arguing with Robinho. Fabio had said, 'His behaviour? I don't like it. He wants everyone to do what he wants, and I have told him so.'

During his first months the Real Madrid fans were disappointed by the Italian's apparent lack of progress. Cannavaro and Emerson looked out of sorts, and Mahamadou Diarra, the Malian midfielder, scarcely looked worth the €26 million euros he had cost from Lyon. Capello seemed to take out his frustrations on the remaining 'Galacticos' or superstars, Ronaldo and David Beckham, in ruthless style.

The sad thing for Ronaldo was that Fabio instantly recognised that the Brazilian was the greatest striker he had ever worked with, better even than Marco van Basten. Fabio told me that he had never seen such a dream combination in one player alone – faultless technique matched with searing pace. Van Basten rivalled Ronaldo for technique and all-round know-how, but he couldn't have lived with him for speed, even when the Dutchman was fully fit. Ronaldo simply had everything, and then he gave himself more . . . especially around the midriff.

According to Ronaldo, however, he was kept in the dark about just how angry Capello was over his growing waistline. 'I know it sounds unbelievable but we didn't actually have a problem,' said the player later. 'We just didn't speak; he didn't tell me the problem, I don't know why, it is kind of sad.' He only had to look in the mirror. Increasingly, Ronaldo found himself on the sidelines. 'I can't be happy because what makes me happy – playing football – is missing from my life,' explained the Brazilian known in Spain at the time as '*El Gordo*' – or 'Fatty'. He added, 'The worst thing is not to have the trust of the coach, and to not know how to regain it.' A diet would have been a start.

David Beckham was also suffering increasing degrees of isolation as time went on. The season had started promisingly for the Englishman, when Capello gave him a spot on the right of midfield ahead of the Brazilian Cicinho. 'Goldenballs' had scored in the third game of the season. But on 13 September 2006 in the Champions League, at Gerard Houllier's Lyon, Beckham had a stinker along with the rest of the team. Real were lucky to lose only 2-0. Beckham was taken off in the 54th minute, an indication that he still wasn't dancing to Capello's tune, even after a stern half-time team-talk.

At the end of that fiasco Capello launched into all his players. Cannavaro revealed, 'He certainly raised his voice. He wasn't happy. There were some strong words. When that happens, you can say some things that might come out the wrong way. But I should think even the players who don't know him well now understand the message.'

The message was that Capello does not like his team to come second in any department. 'Lyon did a lot more technically and physically, they were better,' Capello had to confess after the match. David Beckham was made a scapegoat and left on the bench regularly from that point.

For the English icon, the timing couldn't have been worse, because he had been left out of Steve McClaren's first England squad on 11 August, and everyone thought his international career was over. Now he had to absorb another crushing blow, and he didn't understand why.

A source close to the Capello camp told me that his exclusion wasn't down to injuries, or any particular physical problem. It was because he gave the impression of not wanting to put his foot in when it came to really tough tackles. In old-fashioned football parlance, Capello wasn't convinced that Beckham really wanted to get stuck in. Fabio's camp may have been mistaken, but they began to develop the suspicion that the former England captain was prepared to commit his body to challenges that he knew he could win, whereas he was more hesitant when the chances of bringing the ball out of the tackle were 50-50 or worse. It seemed that Beckham didn't want to risk hurting himself, though naturally the player would argue that he always gave everything to the Real Madrid cause.

By late October, after he had played no more than a meaningless cameo as a late substitute against Barcelona, he felt the need to speak out publicly. The 2-0 victory over the Catalans would have far-reaching consequences come the end of the season, but Beckham wasn't to know that at the time. He said, 'Every day I feel sad and very frustrated as a footballer because I am not playing for my country or for my club. Two more years on the bench would be very difficult. At the moment it is very difficult for me not playing. I am not even thinking about retiring. When my heart and legs give in then that will be the time, but that is not the case now.'

Capello seemed unmoved, even irritated. He responded a few days later. 'Each player has to respect my job because I take decisions based on what is best for the team. You have to show respect for the club, coach and team-mates.'

Antonio Cassano, the brilliant forward who had fallen out with Capello so many times at Roma and had signed for Real Madrid in January 2006, didn't seem to get the message. He had a huge dressing-room bust-up with Capello after being left out of a match at Gimnastic de Tarragona. One of the more printable things Cassano yelled was, 'Have you no shame? I gave everything for you at Roma and this is how you repay me, with a place on the bench?' The club website confirmed his suspension as a result of that outburst on 30 October.

By November Ronaldo was hardly ever starting matches for Real Madrid. Capello made it clear how much more work one of the world's greatest players still needed to do. 'He's lost a lot of weight but he still needs to lose more to become the player that everyone knows,' said the coach. Ronaldo hit back, 'I don't have a problem with what he says. What bothers me even more is how the press interpret things … I think it's ridiculous that we're still talking about this. You are great when you score, and fat when you don't.'

As for Beckham in mid-November, it must have felt like he was barely noticed when he was in Madrid, but condemned when he wasn't. Capello had ignored the Englishman for weeks, but when Becks flew to Rome to attend Tom Cruise's wedding to Katie Holmes, the Italian was livid. He ordered his player to return within 24 hours, which meant that Victoria Beckham had to attend the ceremony and party without her husband. Since Beckham was injured anyway and doing what training he could alone, the added torture of being forced to watch his team-mates play Racing Santander from the sidelines was as much as he could bear. 'It is always difficult watching games where I'm not playing,' he admitted. 'Actually watching in the stands is frustrating and difficult for me.'

Capello remained unsympathetic. As far as he was concerned Beckham was a disappointment. By the beginning of December, 'Becks' had started only four of Real Madrid's 16 games. When he did play, the results were unimpressive, because the team had lost two and won only one of those matches.

Fabio was fed up with the so-called *Galacticos*. If Ronaldo still had a sizeable belly, another player had a mouth to match. At Christmas, Cassano, already on what amounted to a final warning, further jeopardised his inclusion from Capello's plans by delivering a remarkably accurate impersonation of Fabio on the touchline, straight-backed and gesticulating, complete with vocals. Unfortunately the 'show' was caught on camera, and Capello simply had to watch television to become aware of what had been done, albeit in fun, behind his back. Whether or not the impersonation was accurate – and privately even the Capello camp admits that it was – the player was clearly a loose cannon. It wasn't the latest show of disrespect that sealed his fate, rather those which had gone before. But it was easy to understand the younger man's take on the breakdown of his relationship with Capello, as he looked back on the moment when he had to accept yet another club fine and the humiliation of being cast into the wilderness.

Cassano admitted, 'We had already fought so many times. We had fought two months earlier, and that impersonation was what made the vase overflow, so to speak.'

It may have been the wrong gesture at the wrong time, but a little more fun within the squad wouldn't have gone amiss according to Beckham. He explained, 'I have friends – Ronaldo, Roberto Carlos, Michel Salgado – but we don't go out enough. At Manchester United we players used to go out to dinner every fortnight, including times when Sir Alex Ferguson and all the coaches came along too. In the three years I have been here we have done that four times.'

In all that time Beckham had won nothing of importance. He would be out of contract at the end of the season, and began to wonder whether it would be right to sign the extension that was offered by the Spanish club. By mid-January 2007, Real Madrid president Ramon Calderon was claiming, 'Beckham's representatives have toyed with us for the last two months.'

Already there were overtures from the Major Soccer League in the USA. AC Milan, Capello's old club, came calling too, offering Beckham a new life in Italy, a country both David and Victoria Beckham loved. The choice was between the prospect of more Champions League football in Europe, the sort of football adventure he already knew, or something completely different in the USA. The football might not be of the highest quality in America, but what did that matter now that England manager Steve McClaren had frozen him out of the international scene?

He could try to negotiate a future at Real Madrid, but the club was in a certain amount of turmoil. A 3-0 defeat at home to Recreativo Huelva in the last game of 2006 had sent Real Madrid into the winter break in the worst possible shape. Then Capello began 2007 by losing embarrassingly again, to a Deportivo La Coruna side that hadn't won for the last nine league matches. That made it three defeats in four matches, virtually unheard of at such a huge club.

An emergency meeting was called at the Valdebebas training ground. Real Madrid president Calderon and his sporting director Mijatovic were on one side, coach Capello and Baldini on the other. After the meeting Mijatovic claimed, 'We have detected all of the problems and we are able to solve them.'

In reality, the meeting had been rather less smooth and systematic. Capello and Baldini told Calderon and Mijatovic that success would take time, because they were still in the process of changing the entire culture at the club. The 'big' players had previously been allowed to behave exactly as they wanted, some of them in a less than professional manner. Fabio and Franco warned that it might only be towards the end of the season that Calderon would start to see the fruits of Capello's labour; and it might not be until the following season, after more Capello signings had arrived, that Real Madrid would be restored to its former greatness. To Calderon, it all sounded like delaying tactics. He wanted to see improvements straight away, so that he didn't have to take any more heat from the Madrid fans and media.

Against that sort of fractious backdrop, it was hardly surprising that Beckham chose to pursue his dreams in California, where he felt he could have the biggest initial impact and make the biggest difference in the long run. On 11 January 2007 he signed a $250 million five-year deal to join LA Galaxy at the end of the season. That worked out to about £25 million a year, an amazing salary even by Beckham's standards. But he insisted it wasn't about money and said, 'There are so many great sports in America. There are so many kids that play baseball, American football, basketball. But soccer is huge all around the world apart from America, so that's where I want to make a difference with the kids.'

'David Beckham is a global sports icon who will transcend the sport of soccer in America,' said Major League Soccer commissioner Don Garber. But a source close to the Capello camp told me how the deal was almost the last nail in Beckham's Spanish coffin. If David hadn't wanted to put his foot in before – which was the way the management had perceived it, though not necessarily the reality – what was he going to be like now? They feared that Beckham could not possibly give Real Madrid his full commitment after signing such a big contract with Galaxy.

Capello came out with a statement as soon as he heard about the deal. Without bothering to talk to Beckham first, Fabio told the world's media, 'Let's make this clear – a player that has such an important contract with another club can't play for us. He will not play. He will train with us but he is not going to play. It's the club's decision. When a player has a contract with a different club he can't have the same desire to play. We don't have any choice. We won't count on him because he has committed himself to another club. Is it better for him to go now? That's a matter for Beckham. It doesn't depend on me if he goes now, it depends on him. Let's see what he has to say, but he will not play for us.'

Beckham's representative, Simon Oliveira, issued a statement saying that Beckham was 'surprised at the quotes from Capello' and by Real's decision but determined to 'continue to give his full commitment in a professional manner,' to the club.

Meanwhile Real Madrid president Ramon Calderon practically accused Beckham's camp of double-dealing. 'Whenever his representatives met Predrag Mijatovic they never informed him or the club that he had agreed a contract with another club. They never told us that Beckham had made his decision, that he had bought a house in Los Angeles. I don't feel that it's right and I certainly don't like it. I can understand Capello's decision to leave Beckham out of the team. The player has his mind somewhere else.'

Calderon called Beckham 'a half-baked actor', and even dared to say that no one else had wanted him – a claim for which he quickly had to apologise publicly. Much later Capello suggested that he, as coach, had been 'supporting' the president by leaving Beckham out in the cold. At the time of Beckham's announcement, however, Capello and Calderon were both sufficiently angry to want the same thing – the Englishman's exile from the main squad.

Fabio made Beckham train with bad-boy Cassano, in isolation from the rest of the squad, as if his conduct warranted outcast status. But Real Madrid and Capello didn't seem to understand Beckham at all. Having done a day's PR work to fit in with LA Galaxy's announcement of the mega-deal, the player was, again, totally focused on Real Madrid. He aimed to prove Capello wrong.

Meanwhile Fabio faced a backlash in the magnificent Bernabeu stadium during the next home match, against Real Zaragoza. Even though his team won 1-0, he was subjected to constant baiting by the crowd. Fabio had once talked about how noble bullfighters are sometimes heckled by the crowd at the very moment they are risking their lives. In the Bernabeu that night, Capello must have felt more like the bull than the bullfighter. The Madrid public let him know what they thought of the turgid football now being served up on a weekly basis. Some of the abuse was up-close and personal.

In the end it appears Capello could take no more and he cracked, turning round to give the fans a one-fingered salute on the final whistle. Defending his actions later, he explained, 'Since the first day I arrived there have been two people who have continually offended me and today it went too far. They are the same ones that were here 10 years ago because I recognise their voices. The gesture was towards those two but, as coach of Real Madrid, I apologise.' Apparently Capello had been outraged that his tormentors had brought a sign to the match saying, 'Ronaldo stay, Capello get lost.'

At any rate, Capello stayed and Ronaldo got lost. The Brazilian World Cup winner was dispatched to AC Milan for €7.5 million just before the transfer window closed. He was reported to have taken a wage cut from €6 million to €4 million, although the compensation for the financial hardship was that he could apparently cash in the €11 millions' worth of annual image rights he had been sharing with Real Madrid. There was another bonus about life with AC Milan, where he liked the shirts and the effect their vertical red and black stripes had on his shape. 'It was the white shirt at Madrid that made me look fat,' he once said, in one of world football's more hilarious moments. 'It is not weight but Body Mass Index that counts, and mine has always been fine. Also, a person's ideal weight is the one that makes them feel most well.'

The player Capello regarded as the most talented he had ever worked with was gone. Now it looked as though he had lost the support of the board and the crowd too. At least he hadn't entirely lost the dressing room. That month he admitted, 'Not all the dressing room is with me, but a great part. I've closed training to the press and public because the team need maximum possible concentration. Until now we've been lucky; despite everything we're still close to the top.' It was true, because Barcelona and Seville, above Real in the table, had not shown the consistency to open up an irreversible gap.

But on the question of David Beckham, Capello refused to change his rigid stance. 'Beckham does nothing for me,' he said at one press conference. 'He has been here three years and the results have not been good ... I am convinced of my decisions. For example he played against Deportivo and we lost.' Who could possibly have thought that a year later Capello would be the one to breathe new life into Beckham's international career. Back in Madrid, Becks doubted he would ever play for Capello again at club level, let alone for his country.

CHAPTER 19
LOVING BECKHAM

FABIO CAPELLO'S TREATMENT OF DAVID BECKHAM WAS starting to overshadow everything else that was happening at Real Madrid. On Wednesday 7 February 2007, Beckham admitted, 'It is very hard for me because I would like to help the team. I'm desperate to play again . . . I don't know if I will but I've got to keep on training. I want to leave this club on a high.'

Behind the scenes Beckham's team-mates, including Ruud van Nistelrooy, Raul, Iker Casillas and Guti, all argued for his reinstatement. Capello listened but was adamant the decision would be his and his alone. He watched Beckham carefully, studying his demeanour. Then he thought he detected a change in the English player, and more fire in his belly. It seemed that the superstar was prepared to get stuck in after all, even in little training matches. So it became obvious to Capello that Beckham was ready to risk himself and give everything to Real Madrid after all.

Beckham, of course, would argue that he had always been prepared to do this, and Capello and his backroom staff had only just noticed it. At any rate, Fabio later admitted, 'Clever people are capable of rectifying their mistakes, and recognising when they have said or done something wrong.' At the end of the season, when the drama was all over, Capello would further confess, 'A major fault of mine was not to recognise Beckham's potential.'

Some tried to claim that president Calderon had forced Capello to put Beckham back in the side in a bid to win over the fans again. Capello's supporters rejected the suggestion that Fabio changed his mind because of pressure from above at Real Madrid. They insisted that Capello doesn't respond to pressure from anyone or anything. At the time, Fabio explained, 'The only thing that influenced me has been Beckham's work and attitude. We doubted he could train with the same enthusiasm after signing that contract, but he has been training perfectly.'

Looking back on this strange saga, Beckham recalled, 'When Capello said I would never play for Madrid again, I convinced him the same way I've always come back from things – by being professional. However, he didn't come to me and say: "Sorry David, I was wrong." Without doubt he's a strong-minded person, who is respected throughout football.'

But Beckham didn't care too much about the lack of an apology because he suddenly heard that, after 37 days in the wilderness, he had been picked for Real Madrid's match at Real Sociedad on 10 February. To celebrate, he scored a superb goal from a free kick and Capello's men eventually won 2-1.

Van Nistelrooy said after the game, 'You cannot write Beckham off. We're all pleased for him and happy to have him back. When you go for a month without playing it isn't easy to be at your best but he always trains so hard and has a very positive attitude. That's why you can always bet on him. It was a great day for him.' Madrid's top daily sports paper, *Marca* ran a front-page headline, which translated to, 'Capello, you owe him one.'

The Italian coach may not have thought so when Beckham was sent off in stoppage time in a match against Real Betis on 17 February – the game preceding the important Champions League first leg against Bayern Munich in the first knock-out phase of the competition. The domestic affair had been Beckham's 150th game in a Real Madrid shirt. It had ended 0-0, even though Beckham had set up a golden chance for Ruud van Nistelrooy, who had hit the bar. Despite being dismissed for the eighth time in his career, on this occasion due to a careless tackle, Beckham had been applauded on his way back to the Bernabeu dressing room. That was more than could be said for Capello. He and Calderon were shown the dreaded white handkerchiefs by the Madrid crowd, the local sign of disapproval for just one win in four games.

'I think the referee was too hasty in sending Beckham off,' said Capello loyally afterwards. Calderon was less concerned about Beckham's sending off than the hostility of the crowd to his own regime, and he blamed Capello. Another bust-up quickly followed, and there were strong rumours that Capello was being pushed to the point of resignation only days before the biggest game of the season (against Bayern). Coach and president drew back from the brink just in time so that the club could focus on their biggest challenge of the year.

Real Madrid needed a hero if they were to avoid humiliation at the hands of the Germans, and Beckham duly obliged. He became the architect of all three Madrid goals in a thrilling 3-2 victory over Bayern Munich in their Champions League first leg. The Bernabeu crowd chanted 'Beckham! Beckham!' – something that hadn't happened since his early days in Spain. Van Nistelrooy and Raul were in frightening form up front, but Capello wasn't slow to give the Englishman his credit too. 'Beckham played very well, he was very important. When he has been in the side he has always played at a high level. He created two tonight and scored one the other night and I recognise that.'

All was well again between Beckham and Capello. But the problems between Fabio and the squad were not entirely behind him. He had fallen out with so many players that it had almost become a theme of the season up to that point. Guti, the Real Madrid stalwart who had played for Capello 10 years earlier, thought he should have been given more chances to feature in starting XI. But Capello wasn't entirely convinced by his attitude. Once, for example, Fabio realised that Guti was late for training. When the midfielder arrived a few minutes behind schedule and rushed into the dressing room to get changed, Capello ordered his players to stand in the centre circle. When Guti emerged, presumably hoping to join the squad unnoticed, he was confronted by the sight and sound of all his colleagues giving him a sarcastic round of applause for belatedly turning up to work. There was an edge to this kind of humour, and it was only a matter of time before the tension came to a head. In February, having bruised an ankle in training, Guti had begun to walk towards the dressing room. Capello told him to come back because training hadn't finished. Guti made it clear that he was injured and didn't care whether training was finished or not. Fabio then reminded his player who was in charge and ordered him to come back – otherwise he would be in big trouble. Guti is alleged to have ended the exchange by suggesting that Capello was the one in big trouble, before heading for the dressing room as planned.

Even the players, it seemed, already had the impression that Capello's days at Real Madrid were numbered. Unfortunately for Capello, it looked as though Guti had a point that month, particularly after Bayern Munich ended Fabio's latest European dream. The Germans scored after just 10 seconds in the return Champions League match, and went on to beat Real Madrid 2-1. That meant Bayern and not Capello's team progressed to the quarter-finals. For a club that had conquered Europe nine times, it may have seemed as though Capello, with just one Champions League triumph under his belt from 13 years earlier, could not deliver the biggest prize. Real Madrid president Calderon began to sharpen the axe, and Capello knew he had it coming.

With an extraordinary lack of subtlety, Real Madrid added weight to the rumours that they were lining up the German coach Bernd Schuster as Capello's replacement. They asked Franco Baldini, Capello's number two, if he would be prepared to work with Schuster at some time in the future. Baldini told his bosses to wait and see how the season developed with Capello, trying to buy his compatriot more time. Naturally Baldini loyally informed Fabio of what had happened.

One of the difficulties of being a top manager is that even when you know that your fate has virtually been decided, you still have to keep up appearances in front of the world's media. Capello was understandably short with his interrogators when asked repeatedly about his future in early March 2007. 'Look, you have asked me that question about 50 times already and my answer is always the same – that's the president's call, OK?'

Fabio was still highly motivated and tried to focus on the big domestic tear-up with Barcelona in the game known as '*El Classico*'. But the Madrid journalists were enjoying their sport and asked Capello whether life in their city was now becoming torture for him. 'I'm working as a coach, it's not hell,' he hit back. 'It's a job I like and that I've done for many years. So far I've done my job with enthusiasm.'

The rest of Madrid shared that enthusiasm when Capello's men went 3-2 up in the Nou Camp. There were only seconds to go when Lionel Messi conjured an equaliser for Barcelona. That kept the Catalans in the driving seat in the big race for the title. Instead of giving up, however, Capello harnessed the siege mentality that was developing in the dressing room in the face of all the criticism. Suddenly it was Fabio's team against the world.

That feeling was only reinforced when Arrigo Sacchi, who had worked at Real Madrid as director of football but had left before Capello's arrival, hit out at his fellow Italian towards the end of March. 'I don't think he is the ideal coach for Real,' said Sacchi. 'Capello's football has little poetry or harmony. It is based principally upon taking advantage of opponents' errors, on counter-attacks. I still think Real can win La Liga this season though, because it is a mediocre competition. How is it possible to be just five points off the pace with seven defeats?'

A knee injury had interrupted Beckham's best period under Capello so far, and he was back on the sidelines for more than a month. But the irrepressible Englishman returned to make a difference yet again. Indeed, in the 10 league games that Beckham played after being brought back from exile, Real Madrid never lost. Emerson and Diarra would click in midfield before the season was over too, silencing their critics at last. Ruud van Nistelrooy embarked on a typical goalscoring spree that netted him 25 by the end of the season. Raul, the man the Real bosses had wanted to farm out at the start of the season, chipped in with vital scores as well.

Capello achieved all this with precious little support for his future building plans behind the scenes. Later he claimed that he had been denied the chance to buy the Romania captain and ace defender, Cristian Chivu. 'We had a 6 million euro bid for Chivu in April, Baldini had it all sorted, but it wasn't possible to close the deal because they (the Real Madrid board) told us, "We don't love players who come from the Italian league".' Real Madrid president Calderon had his own take on this attempted activity in the transfer market. 'All season long, people had said we were too defensive, and Capello goes and asks me to buy a defender! A defender? How dare he? The new, exciting Real Madrid cannot go around buying defenders.'

When Franco Baldini targeted Pato, the latest sensational young striker to come out of Brazil, the proposed deal was knocked back.

Capello explained, 'Baldini went to Brazil and saw Pato. He called Mijatovic and said, "I've seen a lad here, he's an extraordinary player." With a bit of luck we could have got him for €2 million. But Madrid said, "No, too young." Now he is playing for AC Milan and worth €20 million. The strange thing is that they only gave me €30 million to make signings. We made a miracle in building the squad we did. You can't form a winning team in July, it is necessary to make signings in May.'

While support from Fabio's bosses dwindled, support from the dressing room strengthened – and Beckham played a leading role in creating a new unity. Capello wasn't slow to pay tribute to the man who had taken everything on the chin and shown the Italian forgiveness, loyalty and total professionalism. After a mid-May win over Recreativo, Capello said, 'Yet again the Englishman was the decisive player. He was a titan and he gave us a festival of measured passing. At times it seemed he would win the game on his own.'

That month of May saw Beckham's farewell ceremonies begin. He had a small get-together with some of his closer friends from the squad in a restaurant he particularly liked just outside Madrid. David was presented with an engraved silver tray to thank him for the memories. Grateful as he was, there was only one piece of silverware he really wanted by then. 'I want the league title before I go,' he announced. 'And I'm sure we can get it now.'

Despite sometimes feeling that he had one hand tied behind his back, Capello shared that same belief. Fabio and Beckham were driving Real Madrid along with a fierce, defiant momentum, determined to go out on a high.

By 17 June 2007, with a little help from their colleagues, they had put Real Madrid on the verge of one of the unlikeliest La Liga comebacks of all time, and their first title since 2003. If Real Madrid beat Mallorca at the Bernabeu in the final match, David Beckham could leave Spain as a winner at last. It would be the icing on the cake because Steve McClaren had even recalled Becks to the England team. The problem was, Beckham had picked up an ankle injury on England duty a few days before, and wouldn't be one hundred per cent fit on the decisive day.

The men in white were in deep trouble when they fell behind in the 17th minute to a goal by Fernando Varela. They were under increasing pressure as news filtered through that Barcelona were doing well enough to take over at the top. Carlos Puyol set Barcelona on the road to a 5-1 win at already-relegated Gimnastic Tarragona, and for over an hour it looked as though the title had slipped from Capello's grasp.

Beckham sent a shot curling against the Mallorca crossbar, his last big contribution in a Madrid shirt, before that nagging ankle rendered him too ineffectual to continue. Capello sent on his ace substitute, Jose Antonio Reyes, for the limping Englishman; and Reyes equalised within a minute of Capello's masterstroke midway through the second half. When Mahamadou Diarra scored a second and Reyes added a spectacular clincher seven minutes from time, the Bernabeu could really start to celebrate. Although they had amassed 76 points like Barcelona, it was Real who had a better head-to-head record against the Catalans that season by virtue of that 2-0 win gained the previous autumn. Madrid's party was long and loud and it began right there in the stadium.

Somehow Capello and Beckham had emerged victorious at the end of their strange year together, and they were both in the mood to release some tension. There were extraordinary scenes, with Beckham leaping high towards the dugout, and Capello thrown into the air out on the pitch by his victorious team. The 'bumps' were an unexpected climax to what had, at times, been a miserable season; but that demonstration of loyalty and affection for Capello, still in his suit, tie and glasses, was a clear signal from the Madrid players that they felt he was the man to thank for turning the club around.

The date of La Liga victory, 17 June, was precisely the same as Capello's *Scudetto* triumph in Rome six years earlier. While the celebrations continued in the stadium beyond midnight, Fabio realised that he had another reason to celebrate. It was now 18 June, and his 61st birthday had arrived in style.

Beckham was equally ecstatic. He had pulled off a glorious finale against all the odds. 'I couldn't have dreamt it any better,' said the former England captain. 'It's been about winning the title for the last six months, and we've deserved it tonight. It's been an incredible experience, but all I remember now is the good things. Winning this tonight now puts to bed everything else.'

Guti was of the same mind when he reflected later, 'Fabio is a strict coach; the strictest I've ever known. But he is a good character, respects the players and gets them to work for him. He always guarantees results with his approach.'

The latest fruits of that labour had Madrid in raptures. Around 1.2 million fans converged on the Cibeles fountain, where they always celebrated their titles, and this 30th triumph felt extra special under the circumstances. Raul, whose future at the club had been protected by Capello, draped the Spanish flag and Real Madrid scarf over the central monument, watched by his coach. Fabio had missed the big party to celebrate Roma's title triumph, but he wasn't about to miss this one. He and Franco stayed at the Cibeles fountain along with their players, enjoying the reception they received from the delirious Real Madrid fans into the early hours, then savoured victory in a favourite restaurant until four o'clock in the morning.

Capello was understandably strident when asked about his future at the club. 'Calderon signed me to win and we won. I think I did my duty. Calderon knows that I have two years left on my contract and that I am going to respect them. But if he has to pay me off, I want to make it clear that it will have to be for every last cent. The president is free to decide what he wants. Has he chosen Schuster? That is something for him to answer. I'm off for a long holiday in China and Tibet, and then I'll stop off in Pantelleria (his home near the island of Sicily); so I've got a lot of time to reflect, to decide my future.'

Before he left on his travels, he couldn't resist a couple of withering counterblows to an attack by his old adversary, Arrigo Sacchi. Fabio's fellow Italian had said, 'I'm not surprised by Real's victory, it is a very uncertain championship, also quite mediocre on a technical level, and I believe that in mediocrity Capello nearly always wins. Compliments to him, however . . .'

Capello hit back with venom and said, 'With that big mouth Sacchi can say what he wants. He failed at Atletico (Madrid) as a coach and then as sporting director at Real. If the criticism came from Giovanni Trapattoni, who after his triumphs in Italy went and won abroad as well in Germany, Portugal and Austria, I promise I would accept it. But from Sacchi no; from that pulpit I won't stomach preaching.' Four days later Capello added a touch of humour to his remarks about Sacchi. 'His comments for me are a compliment because he knows the reality in Madrid well. They threw him out of Atletico and Real, and obviously he hasn't yet come round from the two blows he took.'

Sacchi couldn't resist continuing the war of words to set the record straight. 'Capello is confused because I wasn't sacked by Real, I resigned. What's more, they wanted me to stay so much that they wanted to make me coach. I'm stunned by his comments; I said in a normal championship he nearly always wins, it didn't seem like something so offensive that it would justify these lies.' Later Sacchi told me, 'I think Fabio was already feeling stressed at the time, because the Spanish media had been critical of his coaching at Real Madrid.'

Eleven days after winning the title, with Capello and his wife Laura in Tibet, he was sacked. The news brought a genuine reaction from the Englishman whose heart he had all but broken earlier in the year. 'I was sorry about what happened to Capello in the end,' insisted David Beckham, and you believed him. What neither man knew was that they hadn't seen the last of each other.

Back in Spain, few tears were shed over Capello's fate. 'We've laid the foundations, but we need to find a more enthusiastic way of playing,' said Ramon Calderon, paying no attention to the extraordinary foundations Capello had laid before leaving 10 years earlier. The team he had created in 1996–97 had promptly turned into one of the most exciting of all time the following season, though Calderon clearly thought there was little chance of history repeating itself if Capello stayed.

Predrag Mijatovic, Capello's former player from his first period at the club, seemed particularly lacking in generosity of spirit when he explained the reasons for Capello's departure. 'It was a difficult decision but a unanimous one based on an exhaustive report I made to the board. We don't think Capello is the right person to lead Madrid into the future given what we want this club to achieve. Now we have time to think over who will be the next head coach.' It was a strange remark considering that most observers thought Bernd Schuster had been earmarked in February, and virtually confirmed by mid-March.

Experiences such as this one reminded Capello how football had given him such a leathery skin, if he didn't have one already by the time he had left the poverty of Pieris. Television work beckoned back in Italy, and it would prove a breeze by comparison, though he found the Italian air a little stale. And his comparison of Spain and Italy was about to create a huge storm.

'In Madrid I breathed a sparkling atmosphere,' Fabio said, forgetting the two gentlemen who had constantly abused him from behind the dugout in the Bernabeu. 'I breathed the air of a country in Europe making the greatest progress. When I returned to Italy it seemed I had taken two steps back. Spain summed up? Latin warmth and creativity regulated by a rigorous order; the order which comes from Franco.'

When it was pointed out to Capello that General Franco was a dictator, he is alleged to have replied that everyone leaves something good behind them. In Franco's case, Capello claimed, 'he left a legacy of order. In Spain everything works well, there is education, cleanliness, respect. We should follow their example.'

There was an outcry back in Spain when they heard that Capello had apparently been endorsing Franco, even though in reality Fabio had only touched upon one aspect of the dictator's era. The newspaper *El Pais* reported, 'Capello has committed a deplorable act in support of fascism.' Another Spanish paper, *Sport* suggested, 'Either Capello is very ignorant or he has a view of social order which is quite dangerous.'

A Spanish Euro MP, Raul Romeva, lodged a motion in the European Parliament seeking its view on Capello's comments. Unusually for Fabio, he seemed to distance himself from his remarks. 'I just wanted to say that Spain is better than Italy in some respects and provide a political context. I would never dream of praising dictatorships. My father conceived me after having been imprisoned in Nazi concentration camps.'

It wasn't an ideal piece of public relations, not when Fabio was about to be considered for the England job. And even much later, Capello was still arguing privately that it is simplistic in the extreme to insist that General Franco, or for that matter Mussolini, never did anything good. It is too easy, in his view, to condemn their every action on the grounds that they were dictators. He believes it is braver and more honest to admit that, however monstrous many of their actions, they were also capable of doing positive things too, just like any other human being.

If he was playing with fire by airing such views, Capello didn't seem to care. For their part, England's Football Association was prepared to overlook most manageable controversies in pursuit of that elusive second World Cup, especially if it suited them to do so. Indeed, Fabio's name was now being linked so strongly with the England job that he felt compelled to speak publicly about the prospect. 'England?' Capello said on RAI, Italian state television. 'It would be a challenge, a beautiful test. I'm the right age.'

Now he was talking the FA's language. Chief Executive Brian Barwick wanted a big name, one that wouldn't reject him or make him look foolish, as Luiz Felipe Scolari had done while still coach of Portugal in 2006, before Steve McClaren's appointment.

'I don't know why Scolari said no (to England) but I say to him thank you, thank you,' Capello later commented – a clear indication that he thought Big Phil would have succeeded where McClaren failed.

When McClaren had succeeded Eriksson, Capello had wondered whether his chance to coach England had gone once and for all. 'It was a dream I thought I couldn't realise,' he admitted.

But the door had opened again because of bad results. The former Middlebrough manager had done his best but failed to qualify for Euro 2008, and Soho Square had felt a change was needed. Barwick then appeared to suffer another snub post-McClaren, in late 2007, at the hands of Jose Mourinho. First the former Chelsea boss had appeared to want the England job, then it emerged that he didn't want the post at all. Had the FA refused to meet Mourinho's demands? Whichever party had ultimately turned the other down, it had begun to appear as though Barwick's reign at the FA might be defined by rejection. Perhaps another big name, someone who definitely wanted the job, would help to restore Barwick's credibility, and Fabio seemed to fit the bill. In fact the Capello option suddenly looked very attractive indeed, whether he recognised some favourable aspects to General Franco's legacy or not.

CHAPTER 20
ENGLAND, FRANCO AND FAMILY

THE FA WAS MORE THAN WILLING TO CONSIDER THE possibility that Fabio Capello's impressive record of domestic titles would translate into international glory. They didn't focus on his record of failure in the Champions League over the previous decade or more, because everyone said he was a born winner. In fact he hadn't won the Champions League since 1994; but he still had what he loved to call that 'winning mentality'. The FA was fascinated, particularly Barwick, who wanted to meet the managerial legend face to face. A date was set – 12 December 2007.

Barwick headed up the welcoming committee, an FA delegation including Sir Trevor Brooking, the organisation's Director of Football Development, Simon Johnson, Director of Corporate Affairs, and Adrian Bevington, Head of Communications. They met Capello secretly at Wembley Stadium after the Italian and his advisors, including his son Pierfilippo, had landed secretly at City of London airport. Barwick's enthusiasm, even before the meeting got under way, was understandable. Managers of quality who were actually willing to accept the poisoned chalice and become England manager were few and far between, and among them Fabio Capello appeared to represent the best bet for success.

For his part, Fabio was so keen to impress his prospective new employers that he had prepared a formal presentation. 'If you are interested in me,' he said confidently, 'let me show you how I work.' He showed the FA men 10 slides on an overhead projector to illustrate his *modus operandi*. They conveyed key bullet points, outlining his philosophy and how he likes to organise his team, his staff, the scouts and the overall structure of his operation. He didn't talk about the specific identities of the men he wanted in his backroom team. 'If you tell me how you work,' he added wisely, 'I can adapt this model to your needs.'

But Capello was bold enough to set out in no uncertain terms what he had in mind for the England players too, right down to the way they should be feeling and behaving while representing their country. Fabio said that he would expect them to show spirit yet respect, to be on time and always dress as England players while on international duty. Above all, he said, they should be proud of wearing the Three Lions on their shirt.

When it came to training, Fabio offered a telling example of how he liked to work. Having set a five-a-side match in motion, for example, he wouldn't stay in the thick of it, because he had staff who could handle that part of training and report back to him. What Fabio would be more interested in observing, especially in the early stages of his reign, was how the players who were not involved in the match were reacting. Would they switch off, would they laugh and joke as though they didn't care what was happening among colleagues on the pitch, or would they realise that it was necessary to operate as a squad at all times, and maintain their focus?

Having held the attention of the FA men admirably and then answered their questions, Capello didn't want to hang around for more detailed talk of a possible contract. He would leave that side of negotiations to his son Pierfilippo and his other lawyer, a Spaniard called Diego Rodriguez. It was clear he was ready to leave, so Brian Barwick said, 'We have listened carefully to you, and we need to discuss this with our board, but if everything goes ahead and we reach agreement, we would be happy if you would be our coach.'

Fabio said, 'I'll be proud if you want me as coach,' and with that he left the room. He wasn't obsessed with how much money the FA were prepared to pay, he would only hear later about their generous offer of more than £6 million per year. What was important to him was that all had gone well, and both sides seemed delighted. But the deal wasn't done yet, and there was still an opportunity for Soho Square to make a mess of it.

It might be said that diplomatic relations had not always been Fabio Capello's priority. His assistant, Franco Baldini, on the other hand, had probably missed his true calling as an Italian ambassador or peace envoy in the world's most challenging trouble spots. One of Franco's main strengths was that he would know how to ask the FA or Premier League managers for whatever Fabio needed. People naturally warmed to him, and that was one reason why Capello trusted Franco so much. Fabio didn't allow many people to get close to him, but when he did he would give them the keys to his house, such was his faith in that individual. But it wasn't just a question of personality; Baldini had also shown himself to be a shrewd judge of a footballer and he knew all Capello's likes and dislikes on and off the field. If Capello got the job, Franco could watch Premier League matches and know what Capello was looking for as he began to build a team. In fact, Franco understood exactly what Fabio required on all fronts, so it should have come as no surprise to anyone who knew the pair that Capello would want to bring Baldini to England with him, if he was going to accept the post of national manager.

The Football Association didn't see this step as quite so logical. They understood why Fabio would want to use his own technical specialists on the training ground. But Baldini didn't seem to fit into this or any other category. He had worked with Capello at Roma and Real Madrid, they knew, mainly in the transfer market. But there were no transfers in international football, so why was Baldini going to be necessary? The FA already felt they had good managers in their various departments, so wherever Baldini came in, it appeared that he would tread on somebody's toes. They conveyed their concerns to the Capello camp; but Fabio simply sent back the answer that Franco was important to the way he worked. Baldini would help to get things done Capello's way, he would not be trying to usurp anyone else's role. He insisted that everyone would soon see why Baldini was useful, if they just allowed him the chance to show them.

Yet in the 24 hours after Fabio had successfully sold himself to his prospective new employers and returned home to Italy, Baldini's appointment gradually became a sticking point in negotiations between the Capello camp and the Football Association. Stories were even recycled in the press highlighting an old allegation about Baldini's alleged role in the procuring of a 'fake' passport for Inter Milan's Uruguayan star, Alvaro Recoba, at the end of the 1990s. Had he been asked about this case, Franco would have been only too happy to explain.

Baldini had been contacted by Gabriele 'Lele' Oriali, Inter's Technical Director at the time, to see if he knew someone who could arrange a legitimate EU passport for Recoba. Among other clubs AS Roma, where Baldini had just arrived as sporting director, seemed to be discovering enough relatives of European origin for some of their South American players to stake a claim for European passports. This was an effective way of getting past the restrictions operating in Italian football at the time on the numbers of non-EU players allowed in each team.

Franco didn't know the ins and outs of how this worked but had previously used an agent in Argentina called Barend Krausz as a talent-spotter, and thought he might understand more about the passport process. He gave Krausz's number to Oriali, and that is where Baldini's problems began. Krausz allegedly helped to organise the 'issuing' of what was claimed to be Recoba's 'fake' passport for $80,000, though Kraus always maintained his innocence in the affair. Indeed when the authorities questioned Oriali, he explained that he thought Krausz must be a man of integrity because another man of integrity, Franco Baldini, had recommended him. Nevertheless, before he knew it, Baldini was dragged into a scandal he hadn't seen coming. There were even suggestions by prosecutors acting on behalf of Italy's sporting authorities that Baldini should face a ban for his involvement, but those moves were dismissed. So much time had elapsed before the question arose of any formal proceedings against Baldini that he was automatically cleared. This wasn't enough for Franco. He demanded that he be judged anyway, so that he could clear his name officially. Sure enough, the judge at a preliminary hearing dismissed the case against Baldini at once, confirming that it was 'entirely without substance'.

If England's FA was ever worried about any of this as they considered Baldini's suitability for appointment as Capello's number two, it certainly didn't form the central pillar in their argument. The FA's main reason for hesitating over Franco, it would appear, was because ideally they wanted an Englishman to work closely with Capello. That way, at least Barwick and his buddies would have some ammunition against those who were ready to criticise English football's governing body for appointing another Jonny Foreigner like Sven Goran Eriksson.

The Englishman favoured by the FA power-brokers was their own man, Sir Trevor Brooking. The idea was that Brooking would oversee Capello's reign in a directorial role and be his point of reference for any problems that he might have. He would be Fabio's confidant, and their relationship would ensure that close communication between the Italian coach and his new employers was maintained. However, Capello's camp politely pointed out that Fabio already had a confidant, someone he trusted completely and was used to working with extremely closely. That man, of course, was Franco Baldini. Fabio didn't want someone looking over his shoulder, he was used to being the boss and he wanted to call the shots.

Within the FA there was allegedly concern that if they relented on Baldini, his role as some kind of 'sporting director' would clash with Brooking. It is difficult to see how any such confusion could have arisen, since Brooking dealt primarily with kids and the future, while Baldini was going to deal with senior England players and the present. Franco was going to mediate with their clubs and, if necessary, Capello's bosses at the FA too. But that seemed part of the problem, as the FA saw it. They didn't want anyone coming between them and their new star coach. They appeared to prefer direct, undiluted contact with the man they were about to pay so much. Wouldn't Fabio be bringing enough non-English staff with him already, at no small cost? Capello's proposed backroom staff would include his long-term assistant on the training ground, Italo

Galbiati, his goalkeeping coach, Franco Tancredi and his fitness coach, Massimo Neri. To pay them and Baldini adequately, the FA would need to release another £1.4 million per year in addition to the reported £6.4 million per year that they planned to pay Capello.

Fabio didn't mind finding a spot on his backroom team for an Englishman too. In fact he was soon to explain that he regarded such a man (it proved to be Stuart Pearce) as essential. 'I always asked for an English coach to be integrated into the staff, just like I have done at every place I have worked. I think it is vital to have someone who understands the national football and the language,' he insisted.

But it was Baldini he really wanted at his side, so his representatives – including his lawyer son Pierfillipo – continued to fight hard for Franco's inclusion in the deal. Without a tactful assistant at his shoulder, it was likely to prove rather more difficult for a tough character like Fabio to make friends and influence people to quite the same degree. Slowly but surely it appeared that the FA board's resistance to Baldini was softening, though it hadn't been brushed aside entirely.

As time stood still, Baldini didn't want to see his employment or otherwise with England become a make-or-break factor in the Capello deal. He told the media during an uncertain 24 hours, 'I understand the FA has, in principle, said yes to me doing this job. If I don't, I think Capello will still be England coach but maybe he will be less comfortable.'

Fabio's message to the FA remained simple and consistent: I need Baldini and you will see why. He knows how I work, he delivers what I want. He knows what I can and cannot do. But he will not step on anyone's toes; he will not come between me and anyone at the FA. He will not be taking anyone's job or eating into anyone's role. He will fit in well and he will be a great help to us all.

While the deal remained in doubt, Capello stayed at his house in Lugano, Switzerland, waiting for removal men to bring some of his furniture and art treasures from the home he had recently vacated in Madrid. At the same time he waited for the English FA to agree to his preferred choice of assistant, or General Manager as he would eventually be called. Meanwhile England fans waited with increasing anxiety as Fabio began to tell radio reporters that he wasn't England manager yet, and that we would have to wait and see whether he would be. England's future and Fabio's hung in the balance.

For too long, Fabio's flirtation with England had been a story of so near yet so far. Capello had hoped the FA would give him the England job in 2000, while he was at Roma. But just when he thought he was about to be offered firm terms, Sven Goran Eriksson had pipped him at the post. And seven years later Fabio seemed to think he was about to be denied again, just when the position was within his grasp. He explained later, 'This time there was the same sensation.'

There was something comical about the FA's apparent failure to understand that Baldini could potentially make life run so much more smoothly for all concerned. They almost seemed to be pretending there would be no need for a skilful go-between should Fabio face stiff opposition to any of his measures or requests.

In the end, however, Barwick and his board relented on the issue of Baldini, having accepted Fabio's assurances. Capello had already made it clear that he would also recruit an English assistant at the earliest opportunity. What Capello didn't say was that the Englishman he chose, Stuart Pearce, would have only a minimal influence over the match-by-match progress of the England team. But so far there was no strict definition of what the Englishman's role would be; they could come to that later.

The main thing was that Fabio was ready to put pen to paper, which he did right there in Lugano using a fax machine. Once the signed contract was back in the hands of the FA lawyers, Capello's appointment could be announced. No one was happier than Fabio, whose longstanding ambition had been fulfilled at last. 'It is a dream come true and I hope I don't wake up, or else I wake up happy, knowing I've achieved something,' he said breathlessly. 'I have wanted this job for a long time.'

Part of him had admired English football ever since the days of the great Stanley Matthews. And when Fabio was a boy, his father Guerrino had sung the praises of 'football's mother country'. Now England had offered him the perfect way to end a life in football;

the chance to go out in a blaze of glory by winning the World Cup. Dino Zoff, who had known Capello for more than 35 years and had coached Italy at major tournaments, commented, 'Fabio gets the best out of everyone and if players don't show guts he will find other players. With Capello you can start dreaming of winning something again.' Even the former AC Milan and Italy coach Arrigo Sacchi, who had publicly fallen out with Capello only months earlier, admitted, 'If the England players are capable of winning something, Capello is the one who will bring it out in them.'

Players who had helped Capello win his only truly significant European trophy, that Champions League title back in 1994, were still prepared to sing his praises too. Former AC Milan midfield magician Dejan Savicevic said, 'Capello gets the best out of his players, and that is why he will get the best out of England, who have great players such as Wayne Rooney, Steven Gerrard, Frank Lampard and John Terry.' Milan's star striker that year, Daniele Massaro, was also optimistic on England's behalf. 'He has always succeeded, including at Roma, which was difficult, because he is a winner by nature. The England players only have to make sure they understand what he needs of them, because that is important.'

Sacchi did sound one note of caution, though: 'We all know Capello's strengths; he is a winner. In time you will get to know his weaknesses too.' Fabio didn't intend to show any. He would start watching games immediately, go in search of England's dream team, and embark on a labour of love. 'English football is more physical, but at the same time there is more going on,' he explained. 'The stadiums are always full; families can go in the stands wearing the shirt of the team that is close to their heart. There is real support, but when the game is over they are calm.'

Back home in Italy, there seemed to be mixed support for Capello's decision from his own family. Fabio's sister Bianca was certainly making all the right noises about his appointment as England coach. 'If our father was alive today, there would be such an explosion of joy,' she said emotionally. But Guerrino Capello's widow, Evelina Tortul, was less joyful when she heard what was happening. In Capello's home village of Pieris, on a plain between the spectacular Dolomites and the Adriatic Sea, Fabio's 87-year-old mother admitted, 'I am not very happy about this. The newspapers and television are going to be on his back all the time now and talk badly about everything he does, whether it is good or bad. It is not what I would have wanted, but I hope it goes well for him. He has not been here since September, but I hope he will visit before he goes to England. When he goes I suppose we will see him even less.'

He hadn't called her for two days. 'It is very unusual because he normally calls me every day. He must be very busy, but he has not said anything to me about the England job. I am hearing everything from television.'

You had the impression that Evelina wanted to be closer to her boy than his job had allowed. 'The mamma is always the mamma, you know. I would have wanted him to stay in Italy, and to have trained an Italian club. Also a bit of rest would have done him some good. But he is a big boy now and he's old enough to make his own decisions.'

Fabio's wife might be feeling less than enthusiastic about the upheaval too, Evelina warned. 'I don't think my daughter-in-law Laura is going to be jumping for joy over this. She wanted him to stay in Italy, too. He has been everywhere, and it was time for him to spend some more time at home. This will be the third time she has had to move house this year, to Spain, and then back to Italy and now to England.'

The consolation prize for Laura, in time, would be a 120m (400ft) square luxury home on the border between Chelsea and Belgravia in West London, just a 10-minute walk from Harrods and every other fancy shop in Sloane Square, the King's Road or Knightsbridge. She and Fabio would be able to choose from an extraordinary variety of West End shows whenever they liked, a volume and variety of artistic entertainment not seen anywhere else in the world. Before long, Capello would be able to say, 'In London we often go to concerts and the theatre, our passion.'

That was not to be confused with nights during which they might be caught in the spotlight. A close family friend revealed of Laura, 'She is a very private person. She does everything she can, not to get caught up in the celebrity circuit. In all the decades they have been married, he has rarely been out of the public eye and she has never given an interview.' A rare photograph of the pair together at a glamorous event came just a few weeks into Fabio's England reign, at the prestigious Laureus Sports Awards in St Petersburg, Russia. Even in their 39th year of marriage, they still looked relaxed and in tune with one another.

But Fabio's mother knew how hard he worked and she feared that such opportunities for relaxation might be limited. Fabio probably knew what his mother's attitude would be, because later he revealed, 'I go back to Pieris, where I spent my childhood, to see my mamma. Every time she says, "But when are you going to stop working?"' Meanwhile Evelina revealed, 'I like football and I try to talk to Fabio about it, but he says, "Mamma, please, can we talk about something else other than football? That is all I hear at work."' Between them they painted a touching scene of the loving relationship between mother and son. But work was going to take up most of Fabio's time for the forseeable future. Capello was England's golden boy now.

At the press conference to unveil Capello on 17 December 2007 (he was due to start work on 7 January 2008), Barwick was clearly basking in the glory of having appointed a big name. He insisted the appointment had been unanimous, which by then it was, and rejected the notion that the appointment had been pushed through at the cost of the 'root and branch' review he had promised.

He maintained, 'I always said there would be no time frame. I've been accused of dithering so I can't win at this. I said I'd do it at the pace it takes. There was a momentum last week I felt it was worth capitalising on. I was able to get the FA board together on a telephone conference call. We had two telephone conferences and I have to say the vote for Fabio on that telephone conference call was unanimous . . . We know we owe the fans and we believe Fabio Capello is the man to restore our pride.'

It was strange to talk about national pride being restored by a man who wasn't English, but Barwick was ready for that. He added, 'I think it should always be the ambition of the FA, when possible, to recruit an England manager from within our own country. On this occasion we felt it was important to get the right man whatever the nationality.'

So Fabio's mother would have to get used to seeing him even less than usual, though she wouldn't stop talking about him in warm and sometimes even controversial terms. When Evelina was asked a few months later what Fabio was like as a child, she replied that he had been a *mammone* – a mummy's boy. She didn't see anything wrong with saying it, because she insisted it was true. But inevitably the English media picked up on this, and by the time the story got back to other members of Capello's family in Italy it had been blown out of all proportion.

Fabio's sister, Bianca, explained why nothing could be further from the truth. 'It is not true that Fabio is a mummy's boy; he is very independent like the rest of us in the family. How can he be regarded as a mummy's boy, when he only goes to see his mother, a woman pushing 88, once or twice a year? Maybe it could be three times a year, I don't know, but I'm not criticising him for that. He is still a loyal son who will be there if his mother needs him. Besides, I don't see our mother much more than Fabio does, and I only live an hour or two away. She has her neighbours, we speak by phone and she knows we will be there when she wants us to be there. What I'm trying to explain is this: from the outside we could be perceived as cold to each other, and it is true that we are northern in our ways, but we love each other all the same. We are a family but we are also individuals; we do our own thing and we are not fixated with each other. I'm not fixated with my own children either; they go their own way. We are gypsies in our family, in the sense that we value our freedom.'

Fabio valued his freedom too; the freedom to work abroad, this time in England, to try to win the World Cup and cap a spectacular career.

CHAPTER 21
NO FALSE GIFT
FOR BECKHAM

FABIO CAPELLO'S ENGLAND REIGN DIDN'T GET OFF TO AN ideal start from a PR perspective. An investigation into Capello's tax affairs in Italy in January 2008 was one potential source of embarrassment. Fabio's son and lawyer, Pierfilippo, admitted, 'When the news broke he was really displeased and angry, though not so much because of the investigation itself. These investigations seem to happen to so many well-known people in Italy; he knew he wasn't the first and wouldn't be the last. No, the reason he was so displeased and angry was that one of the first public stories connected to him after taking over as England manager was a negative one. He felt that he had somehow connected the FA to this tax issue and he knew how historic and important the FA was in England.'

Italian tax inspectors were trying to decide whether Capello might owe them more than an explanation for the millions of euros that had been deposited in an offshore account in Guernsey under the Capello Family Trust. Capello's camp insisted that every penny of Fabio's earnings had been declared in the right way, and that he didn't owe any more than he was already paying the authorities, honestly and openly. The taxman was focusing on a company called Sport 3000, also controlled by the Capello Family Trust and based in Luxembourg, another tax haven.

In January 2008, only weeks after his appointment as England manager, Capello had emphasised, 'With my advisors, I have always endeavoured to conduct my financial business with integrity. I have assured the FA that my finances are in order and that I am not aware of any matters which would be of concern.' At the time the FA echoed, 'We have spoken to Fabio and his advisors. They have explained the facts. They have also given their assurances that Fabio's tax payments are in order.' The FA added that none of his salary was being paid into the Family Trust, that this was a private matter for Fabio and they were quite satisfied that all was well.

Capello's lawyer–son Pierfilippo said in January, 'They (the Italian tax authorities) have made a big thing about it because he is England manager ... and there is absolutely no question he has done anything wrong.' In early April Vincenzo Pacileo and Marco Gianoglio, the Turin prosecutors leading one branch of the investigation, told *La Stampa*, the Turin newspaper, that they were summoning 15 people for questioning. These included Laura, Pierfilippo and Edoardo Capello. Suddenly Fabio's wife and sons had been caught up in the investigation too.

Pierfilippo explained that Laura had taken the news without blaming her husband for the embarrassment the investigation was causing. He explained, 'My mother was just sorry when she saw how angry Fabio was. She told him, "I have known you for 40 years and you never did anything wrong, so if anyone did anything, I know it wasn't you." She has never been interested in money. She is interested in Fabio's life and career, of course, and her sons and grandchildren.' So Laura showed the understanding her husband needed at that difficult time and the family stuck together.

It was Capello who bore the brunt of the adverse headlines, though. Some newspaper stories talked about the threat of a six-year jail term if Fabio was prosecuted and found guilty. It hardly seemed appropriate to be talking about a punishment before any wrongdoing had been identified, particularly when so many people in Italy have their tax affairs investigated. The presumption of innocence unless proven otherwise, so fundamental in English law, seemed to have gone out of the window.

In September 2008 Pierfilippo told me, 'In Italian financial law, every transaction needs a concrete reason for having been made. If you cannot provide a concrete reason, it is up to you to prove your innocence rather than for the authorities to prove your guilt. But the bank which acts as trustee to the Capello Family Trust in Guernsey is also used by many highly respected public figures, and that shows what a serious organisation it is.'

Yet the Italian tax authorities still seemed interested in certain aspects of the paper trails that preceded some deposits into the Capello Family Trust. Pierfilippo explained, 'One issue is taxes paid by my father when he was the coach of Roma. Before that, when he was coach of Real Madrid in 1996, he realised that his name and image was going to be known worldwide. So he thought he would use his name as a brand to make some money. Therefore he registered "Fabio Capello" and "Don Fabio" as brands. Later, when Fabio was at Roma, Sport 3000, who had bought the trademarks by then, made an agreement with Roma to sell perfumes under the brand "Fabio Capello" and there were also plans to sell ties, scarves and pashmnas, all these items to be of the highest quality. But soon Roma found themselves in a tough financial situation and they weren't able to pay all the money for the merchandise to Sport 3000. So in the end, after about two years, Roma and the company reached an out-of-court settlement for the money owed. And the merchandise didn't go on sale partly because of the fact that fashion changes, and the prices would have been too low at the outlets who were interested by then, which were not as up market as had originally been planned.'

The Italian authorities were keen to investigate whether the 'Fabio Capello' and 'Don Fabio' brands, together with the business arrangement entered into with Roma, could have been used as vehicles to avoid paying tax, though Pierfilippo insisted that his family had all the documentary and material proof necessary to show that the ventures had been genuine. Fabio Capello was mortified by the entire controversy. He said, 'If there was one thing that I've always said to my consultants it was that I didn't want to end up on the front page because of tax problems. But it has happened. I am very convinced that everything has been done in the correct way, I am calm.'

A separate investigation was launched into transactions surrounding shares Capello had bought in a toy company called Giochi Preziosi, run by the president of Genoa football club, Enrico Preziosi. After several years Fabio decided to sell those shares, and they went through a variety of companies before ending up back with the Preziosi side of the business. It wasn't Fabio who profited directly from the sale of the shares, rather companies with which he was linked, and again Pierfilippo insisted that the paperwork for each transaction was correct. The problem was that the authorities saw the complicated paper trail another way, and believed that Capello could be liable to pay Capital Gains Tax, however complicated and indirect the movement of shares and money. Furthermore, they began to examine what the motive for the movement of the assets through so many different companies was. The Capello family argued that it was part of Fabio's restructuring of his business affairs, so that he could create a sizeable and lasting nest-egg for his family whatever happened in his football career from that point on. The authorities were sceptical and seemed to be considering whether or not all the complex procedures could amount to tax avoidance. Again, Pierfilippo was adamant that Fabio's intentions were honourable and there was no wrong-doing behind the movement of the money. If any mistake had been made, it wasn't made by Capello. If anyone had failed to give sufficient attention to the question of Capital Gains Tax, it was certainly not the England manager, who paid other people to handle his affairs in the right way. Besides, they still doubted that he owed Capital Gains Tax for the Giochi Preziosi deal. Since the business transactions had in themselves been above board each step of the way, the Capello family didn't see a problem and believed the authorities would ultimately clear them.

At the time of writing, no charges had been levelled at Capello or his family, and Fabio continued to express the belief that, although the investigation was ongoing, all would be well in the end. England and the FA naturally hoped that there would be no distractions as they sought World Cup qualification. With the strong support of his family, it seemed unlikely that Fabio would be thrown off course by the tax investigation.

Against a backdrop of complicated financial and legal wrangling, one might have thought that Capello's challenges with regard to English football would have seemed straightforward by comparison. After all, England fans wouldn't really care if Capello was in some kind of trouble with the taxman, as long as he was ensuring the right numbers on the international scoresheets. And if the tax story had been something of a PR own goal, it would only take a few popular choices on the football field to put Fabio firmly onside with the English public. However, Capello never had been one to pander to public opinion, or for that matter to England's biggest stars.

In the opening weeks of the Italian's reign in England, it was claimed that senior players such as the former captain David Beckham and the most recent captain John Terry hadn't even been contacted by the new international manager. In Terry's case in particular, regular England observers had expected such a basic courtesy to be extended.

When Capello and Terry did bump into each other in the stands at Goodison Park one evening, there was only a handshake and a few polite words – nothing that amounted to relationship building, or a meaningful conversation. Terry was injured at the time, and though he was probably reassured to know that Capello was taking some sort of interest in his progress, it didn't exactly amount to unequivocal support with regard to the Chelsea man's England future. In fact a source close to the new regime at the time told me that neither Capello nor Baldini would be dropping in for a detailed chat with Terry any time soon, even if one of them were to visit Stamford Bridge for a match. There would be no need, or so the argument went, because Big John wasn't going to be ready to play against Switzerland in the opening match of Capello's reign on February 6. When he was fit he would be evaluated for England. If he was looking good enough he would be put in the squad. Then Capello would talk to him.

Fabio's treatment of Beckham was similar when he first arrived. Reports claimed he had not called England's superstar, the man who had helped him win La Liga with Real Madrid as recently as the summer of 2007, to check with the player directly on his fitness. Beckham was stuck on 99 caps and was desperate to reach his century. Capello left him none the wiser as to whether he might achieve his personal goal. Typically, media-savvy Beckham had already said all the right things about their previous stint together. 'There were ups and downs with me and the manager at Real Madrid,' he echoed, referring to the way he was played, dropped and then reinstated by Capello in Spain. 'But he had the belief in me to put me back in the team. It gave me an amazing end to my time there and I was sad when he got the sack as I believe he had turned the club and the players around and given the fans what they deserved, a trophy.'

There were glimmers of hope in Fabio's initial remarks about the England player he knew best. 'I had a contrasting relationship with David Beckham at Real Madrid but in the end he demonstrated what a great man and great player he is. Also he is the kind of person, I believe, when he sets himself something he will achieve it, so you never know, but obviously I will have to make choices. I believe David's behaviour is important.'

Reading between the lines, the message seemed to be that if Beckham worked hard, kept his head down and showed the right attitude, then the door was open for him to reach that wonderful milestone. But there was still no personal contact. And it was hard to see how this attitude was going to make England's senior players warm to Capello. As Fabio said later in the year though, 'I'm not trying to get the England players to be my friends; I'm trying to get them to play their very best for England.' He didn't want Terry and Beckham to feel comfortable. He wanted to keep them guessing and to keep them working.

The majority of the English public and even the media seemed to feel that Beckham should be given what he deserved, a special night at Wembley in recognition of all his efforts in an England shirt over the years. The first match of the Capello era was only going to be a friendly against Switzerland, so on the face of it there didn't seem to be a very strong argument for excluding him.

Even various sources in the Capello camp were making noises about honouring Beckham's international career by giving him the captain's armband again for that historic evening. I was told the recommendation had been made to Capello. John Terry, who could have been forgiven for assuming that the armband was still his to hand over (since everyone else thought so too), spoke publicly to endorse the idea of making Beckham captain for the night. The only slight problem was that Beckham's latest club, LA Galaxy, weren't playing any football at the time because their season hadn't started. Therefore Beckham wasn't match-fit; and even when America's Major Soccer League (MSL) did start, it wouldn't be as demanding as any in Europe.

So now David had made a few phone calls and hatched a cunning plan – to train with Arsenal. The idea was for David to get himself super-fit in order to justify his inclusion in that England squad for Switzerland. Arsène Wenger and his Arsenal players welcomed the ex-Manchester United star and some even said he was looking sharp. The PR machine was rolling in Beckham's favour again.

Capello was due to visit Arsenal's training ground at London Colney in his very first week as England manager. Sources close to the Italian had indicated that he would take the opportunity to sit down for a one-on-one chat with Beckham that day, to assess his hunger and commitment to the cause. The stage was set. Tickets for Switzerland were selling like hot cakes, 70,000 snapped up a full month before the match. The FA couldn't have been happier. They were turning a meaningless friendly into a cash bonanza, a dramatic occasion full of sentiment and hero-worship, an evening that would be remembered forever. All the fans wanted to be there when Beckham made history. What else was there to look forward to, when England hadn't qualified for Euro 2008?

It would be a wonderful way to send Beckham's tired old legs out to pasture; and Capello would be applauded for having a heart after all. More importantly, Fabio could move forward towards the competitive future with the nagging Beckham dilemma off his back once and for all. Becks had made it clear that he would always be available to his country if England needed him. But no one outside David's immediate circle of family and friends would really care if Beckham was ever picked again, because one hundred was a nice round number, and even the player himself, you imagined, would be satisfied with that. Joining the One Hundred Club would represent a powerful symbol of excellence.

It seemed that all he had to do was avoid pulling a muscle or calling Capello names. Then suddenly the momentum stopped. Capello had been to see Arsenal as arranged, but the one-on-one with Beckham hadn't happened. Now the noises from around the Capello camp were far more equivocal. They talked of the need to study Beckham's fitness data before any personal contact between player and manager; they played down the issue of the England captaincy for the Switzerland match entirely.

This didn't sound good for Beckham at all, and suddenly you suspected he was going to be bounced out of the picture. At the very least there was some backtracking and fence-sitting going on. After making further enquiries, I established that the results of fitness tests on Beckham had been less than outstanding. Even so, there was time for Beckham to get ready. There had to be, didn't there? The tickets had been sold. The FA wouldn't be happy if the star of the show was left at home when it came to the big night. Sources indicated that Fabio was aware of the situation. But the FA was not applying any pressure – they appreciated that the decision was down to Capello and no one else.

So Beckham was left in the lurch and we were left waiting too. Unfortunately, it was a spectacularly bad idea for Beckham to go globetrotting just days before the final decision was due to be made, even though his entourage pointed out that these trips had been planned well in advance. But with his international career on the line, couldn't they have been postponed? He turned up in Sierra Leone as an ambassador for UNICEF and then on a beach in Natal on the northeastern tip of Brazil. There he played keepy-uppy for the cameras while promoting the site of his latest proposed soccer school. If his physical condition had failed to convince Capello so far, this was not going to help his cause.

A few days earlier, a newspaper report alleged that Capello had dined with some Italian journalists and told them that Beckham wouldn't be picked for the England squad against Switzerland because he wasn't fit enough. Capello denied saying any such thing.

In Brazil, Beckham was blissfully unaware that any doubts were being raised about his fitness. 'I feel great,' he told *The Times* of London. 'Arsène Wenger came up to me and said, "Fitness-wise you are looking good and looking sharp." Arsenal are one of the fittest teams in the Premiership. The England manager has been kept in the loop of what I have been doing. That is what he wanted.'

Beckham prepared to fly back to England for the squad announcement, and said before leaving South America, 'It is good to have that anxiety, wanting to know whether you're in. It would mean the world. Getting picked for your country is always special. The one hundredth game makes it extra special. Hopefully it will happen. Hopefully I've worked hard enough to get myself fit, but we'll have to see.'

When I spoke to a source close to the Capello camp the day before the official announcement, the voice on the other end of the phone was reluctant to break any definitive news. So I asked whether it was more a case of 'Beckham-yes' or 'Beckham-no' at that moment in time. There was an ominous pause. Then I heard it was more likely to be no.

What about the idea of giving Beckham his one hundredth cap and then saying goodbye, I wondered? That had always seemed to be the simplest way of dealing with the situation and many others were of the same opinion. Fabio Capello, however, was not of the same opinion. In fact, he regarded Beckham too highly to do that to him. If Capello gave Beckham his one hundredth cap in this match, I was told it would be nothing more than a false gift because he wasn't match-fit. Fabio had more respect for Beckham than to give him a cap he didn't deserve. It would be something artificial and that wouldn't be fair to Beckham or the other players. Sure, the FA would like to see Beckham play but they would accept Fabio's decision.

Capello's verdict was such a bombshell that when I gave this news to a best-selling national paper, they didn't run with it, choosing instead to sit on the fence as though it simply couldn't be true. But there was another amazing revelation from the same source about Fabio's first-choice goalkeeper. Robert Green and Scott Carson were being touted at the time so I put these names forward and asked which Fabio favoured. The reply came in the form of a name that had been ridiculed and forgotten by many international football followers – David James. Yes, David 'Calamity' James, the 37-year-old, who hadn't played for England since May 2005. This seemed astonishing, although admittedly James had been looking leaner and sharper of late than he had for some time. However, later Capello vented his frustration at having to recall James, but put it down to the lack of choice he had, due to the make-up of the Premiership. He said, 'Only 38 per cent of the players are English. The drawing pool is constricted. I've had to recall a 38-year-old goalkeeper.'

Well, James was in his 38th year anyway, so that wasn't where his argument fell down. But unfortunately for Capello, he had been quoted only the previous September, saying: 'All this talk about foreigners being in the way of the success of national sides is just nonsense. Everyone is free to think what he chooses and I am not going to impose my opinion on anyone but that's what I think.'

Had he changed his mind so soon? Possibly, because he had adjusted his position yet again by midsummer, even though the percentage of homegrown players had dropped further still. Veering back towards his original opinion, he said, 'I know only 35 per cent of Premier League players are English, but if enough of that 35 per cent is at a high level then you can succeed. And I am confident they are.' A confusing business, managing England.

Back in the build-up to the Switzerland match the squad was announced. Sure enough, Beckham was out and James was in. So most of the talk was about Beckham and the end of his England career. The epitaphs were rolled out thick and fast. Later that day, when the fuss had died down, I spoke to a source near the Capello camp again. Was it true? Had Beckham's last chance really gone? I was assured again that it hadn't. Although Capello didn't want to give Beckham this artificial gift against Switzerland, he would gladly give him that one hundredth cap with a genuine call-up if he earned it properly at some time in the future. Once Beckham was playing competitive football again, Capello would take another look.

Fabio apparently failed to convince the former England captain that his hopes were still alive, because David seemed so upset at his exclusion that he failed to show at a charity dinner and apparently left the country as quickly as he could. Should there have been room for sentiment on this one occasion? Some said yes, others said no. The man who mattered, Fabio Capello, didn't make decisions based on sentiment.

So the question of who would lead England for Capello's first match was suddenly open. I found out it would be Steven Gerrard, though Rio Ferdinand would be a candidate for the future as Capello intended to audition a few skippers. Meanwhile the fascinating prospect of Wayne Rooney as future England captain had been debated in the papers. The hot-head, whose lack of self-control had so hurt England in the past, was now being touted as a future leader. I asked a source in the Capello camp whether the responsibility could help him to mature. The concern expressed at the other end of the phone related to what might happen if Rooney lost his head in a big game when he was captain. One for the future, maybe.

We left it at that, and I gave the same newspaper as before my little scoop about Gerrard as captain for the Switzerland match. This time they believed me and splashed the story on the back page. Most people would have predicted that Gerrard would be named captain in the absence of John Terry; but no England player could feel entirely secure about his future when the squad gathered at the five-star Grove hotel in Hertfordshire for their first pre-match get-together. Beckham and Terry had already discovered that Capello was not going to try to make any individual feel special. Those two hadn't even made it to the hotel. And there was a reason why Capello didn't encourage any extra focus on one player alone.

'You should never bet too much on a single person,' Capello explained once. 'You need to be able to improvise. Your important player, the one you have bet everything on, could be off the pitch at any given moment.'

That sounded particularly promising, because if Sven Goran Eriksson had made one big mistake it was to give the impression that he was trusting England's success to the mental and physical fitness of Wayne Rooney, at a time when the youngster simply wasn't ready for the burden. Capello heard all about Eriksson's experiences, and what might be learned, from the horse's mouth. Fabio talked to Sven in Liverpool and Baldini talked to Tord Grip, Sven's assistant, in Manchester.

Had they known this at the time, the English media would probably have placed a negative slant on this secret contact. It would have been all too easy to suggest that the FA were paying £6 million a year to a second foreigner, who was taking advice from the first. Capello's regime could mistakenly have been portrayed as little more than an extension of the old, failed England regime of Eriksson and Grip. But the media didn't pick up on the clues contained in public declarations by both men. Eriksson said, 'I have known Fabio Capello for many years. I was his opponent in Serie A for 10 years. He is a very good man and manager. Capello is one of the best managers you can find.' Meanwhile Capello mentioned, 'At the moment I am working towards understanding what needs to be done, also gathering information on where I can work in order to avoid making the same mistakes that were made before.'

That was no slight on Eriksson's reign; it just underlined the fact that the secret collaboration between the two regimes was only natural and logical. Eriksson and Capello had both been coaches in Rome at the start of the new millennium, and Fabio had even urged the Swede to take the England job when he was wavering, as we have seen. Back in the 1980s Capello had visited Eriksson at Benfica to study his coaching methods. Now Capello was interested in learning from Eriksson again. Later Fabio told me that he learned plenty from consulting Eriksson about his experience as England manager.

Meanwhile the managers' assistants knew each other even better. Tord Grip had been Franco Baldini's coach at a small Italian club called AC Campobasso back in 1986. Two of football's nice guys, they struck up a rapport right away and they had remained friends down the years. Now Grip provided Baldini with detailed profiles of each individual England player. The focus was not so much on each player's qualities as a footballer, which Capello and Baldini would be able to gauge by watching them repeatedly. No, the Capello regime wanted to know more about each character, what made them tick, what their strengths were and what might prove to be an Achilles' heel.

In the case of the brilliant and perplexing Wayne Rooney, however, there wasn't just a fiery temperament, vulnerability to injury and a Liverpudlian accent that foreigners found almost incomprehensible. Eriksson and Tord had tried to turn Rooney into an out-and-out striker, and eventually they had concluded that it simply couldn't be done. The more the Swedes had told Rooney to restrict the amount of turf he covered in each international – in the hope that England's star man could relax and save his energy for some ruthless finishes in front of goal – the more Wayne had struggled to comply. Reluctantly, Eriksson and Grip had decided there was nothing for it but to leave Rooney to play his natural game, dropping deeper to get more involved when he felt like it. The price they paid was to wave goodbye to the dream of developing a potentially world-beating striker. But it seemed at the time that Rooney just couldn't be a striker in the traditional sense, so perhaps the dream had never been realistic in the first place. Grip warned Baldini of the struggle Capello might face if he too had planned to turn Rooney into a prolific marksman.

Baldini and his boss Capello took all the advice on board; but that didn't stop them from succumbing to the urge to see for themselves if anything else could be done to harness Wayne Rooney's ability in a way that might hurt the opposition most – in front of goal. Capello respected Eriksson, but in every top coach there is something that says he can do better than the last man or in this case the one before that. The problem for Capello, as he prepared for his first match in charge, was that if he gave up trying to turn Rooney into a star striker, who else was going to become that star striker? At the time, the new England management didn't seem to have a great deal of faith in Michael Owen's potential to return to the devastating player he had once been. So they still saw Rooney as the answer.

Fabio and Franco didn't bother to consult Steve McClaren, their immediate predecessor. Perhaps his experience had been too short and painful, maybe they didn't think they could learn much from the so-called 'Wally with a Brolly'; but I was told that the overwhelming reason for the collaboration with Sven and Tord was that Capello and Baldini knew them so very well. It was different with Mc Claren. When they occasionally bumped into the man with the cheesy grin in football stadiums during 2008, one England regime would always acknowledge the other, and convey best wishes for the future. McClaren, like Eriksson, knew what a phenomenally difficult task Capello faced. Generously, he wished Fabio well.

For now, Fabio had at least taken the first, important steps towards establishing his own authority over England's players. He had knocked all sense of self-importance out of the biggest names in the England squad. The next stage was to build the confidence of the players back up again, stamping his own character on the team, so that he could try to turn his players into world-beaters. It would be a long, hard road. For Fabio it had felt a bit like that already.

'My life has been FA, hotel, matches,' Capello admitted rather wearily after the opening month of his reign. Given that earlier in his managerial career he had also once admitted that he hated hotels, and needed a real home to go to, this must have been a tricky time for him personally. Now he would start to find out if the trials and tribulations of life in England were worthwhile. At last, the time for action had arrived.

CHAPTER 22
LIVING THE DREAM, LEARNING THE LESSON

SOME OF THE PLAYERS SAID IT FELT LIKE GOING BACK TO school. Like his father Guerrino, Fabio Capello intended to be a strict schoolmaster. But he didn't want to generate fear; because it was the fear of failure – or so he believed – that had caused so many of England's problems in the past. Instead his aim was to inspire through a strong, clear sense of purpose, to present his iron will and ensure that his confidence and hunger for success was infectious.

'If being serious means being tough, then I am seriously tough,' he said. 'Let's not forget that in the dressing room, when I am dealing with an entire squad, it is one against 25, so everything you do will be judged and discussed by 25 people. But relationships need respect. I do not want respect out of fear, but because of my personality.'

Capello was interested in the personalities of the England players too. I had been told that the behaviour of each player, when they were in the England camp and when they were away from it, would be evaluated. If each man's contribution when he joined up with the squad was greater than what he threatened to take away through any self-indulgent behaviour elsewhere, then fine. Adverse headlines from nights out on the town might be tolerated up to a point; but the moment such behaviour started taking more away from the England team as a group than any offending player was able to give, that would be the end for him.

Capello insisted he wasn't a dictator, just a firm boss. In many team matters, he intended to seek the views of the players and use that insight. 'I make the decisions – after I've heard the opinion of the squad. Above all I ask for sincerity from my players. I do not want to be surrounded by "yes men" and when we come together I often go around the room twice so that I get clear and frank replies.'

On the issue of the England captaincy, however, he simply wanted to observe the way the players reacted to each leader he auditioned, rather than asking them to vote for a captain. The answer to the captaincy issue, he reasoned, would make itself clear in this way over a period of time. Apart from the man named captain, not many England players were prepared to put their head on the chopping block by being too forthright too early. They would all get to know each other soon enough, and they would not find Capello unsympathetic if they had genuine problems. He considered it his duty to respond to those carefully, because to do otherwise could alienate a player forever.

'I consider myself balanced and attentive,' he had declared before, 'especially when it comes to the personal side of things. That's the most delicate part, and everyone has the memory of an elephant. They are ready to recall things that were said and done six months before.'

On the other hand he had also vowed 'never' to be a footballer's friend. 'If you become a footballer's friend,' he explained, 'the others are immediately jealous and then start to think someone is playing just because he is a friend.' Well he had certainly shown the England players that he was not going to be David Beckham's friend just because Becks had helped him win La Liga. At least that was the way it seemed at the time of the Switzerland match.

What Fabio really wanted to know from his players was the answer to an age-old question: why couldn't they give their country what they gave their clubs? Why had England underperformed for so long, culminating in failure to qualify for Euro 2008?

'I'm going to try to understand what happened by talking to the players and I believe that wearing the England shirt should be a matter of pride and I want to see all players play for England like they do for their clubs.'

Capello, who had conducted all his press conferences so far in Italian, had vowed at his unveiling in December, 'I'm convinced that, in one month, when the national squad will meet for the first time under me, I will be able to speak the language. I believe that it is very important to be able to communicate with the players.'

If he did speak to his players in English during that first get-together he must have done so with difficulty. Even in May 2008, when he began to conduct media interviews in English, he wasn't easily understood. But back in the winter, linguistic fluency didn't seem to matter, judging by the awe-struck reaction of temporary captain Steven Gerrard. The Liverpool star said, 'He has an aura when he walks into a room and those are the type of managers you want to play for.' Body language spoke louder than words; and there were advantages to the distance created by the language barrier, as well as the obvious drawbacks.

McClaren had tried to create 'Club England', an atmosphere in which the players could feel part of something intimate, relax and be themselves. You could understand his objective; but the end result was a group of players who were not pushing themselves hard enough and lacked the discipline to do so. Although he never consulted McClaren in the way he had spoken to Eriksson and Grip, Fabio agreed that England should feel like a club, in fact later he said so: 'We need to play like a club. We are a very important football nation and we have to play to win.' But Capello's club was to have the strictest of house rules.

Capello wasn't going to allow any kind of indiscipline to ruin his regime while the players were gathered as an England squad. The rules meant no PlayStations or mobile phones at inappropriate moments, no 'flip-flops' or wild clothes, no junk food, no cliques and usually no golf before the match. Everyone was to eat together and leave the table together, look smart, call each other by a respectful name – which meant their real name – and do everything to generate the right kind of team spirit.

'We need to have rules because we only have three days together and we need to establish a way of working together. Things like eating together, getting up from the table together and being punctual; it is all about respect for each other. I don't know why anyone would want to break those rules,' Capello said.

Once they had got over the shock, a lot of the England players didn't seem to mind. Some of the more senior figures may have thought Capello was a bit of a dinosaur by insisting upon the sort of behaviour they thought had gone out with their grandfathers, but they knew there was no point arguing and they accepted the changes. Strangely the younger players were even more enthusiastic, seeming to appreciate the firm guidelines and boundaries that had been set, when instead you might have expected them to rebel first.

David Bentley said later, 'I loved the whole set-up under Mr Capello and I had no problems with the rules he imposed. If I'm given an inch, I'll take a mile. I know what I'm like and, to an extent, it's human nature. All players are like that. Young, rich footballers need reining in and have to be controlled. Deep down, we all know it.'

The new regime kept everyone on their toes; it was stimulating. Even Prime Minister Gordon Brown saw fit to comment on the England football team's new regime. 'Mr Capello looks as if he has made a really good start with off-the-field-discipline,' Brown gushed. 'I think a good manager will insist people's eyes are on the ball, that they are not distracted by electronic games or whatever and they are actually contributing. Look, we pay a lot of money if we go to a football match, the public pay for their tickets, they deserve to know the footballers are making the right preparations for the match. I don't think it is good for young kids to see players both committing offences but also arguing so much with the referee. The discipline of football has got to be, when the referee does make his decision, people accept it. If the message went out that the captain is the one who is talked to by the referee and held responsible, he would get the players into line.'

The permanent England captain was still a mystery, and would remain so for months. In fact, until the last possible moment before travelling to Wembley for England's first match under Capello, just about everything was a mystery. David James revealed, 'No one knew the side other than Steven Gerrard until 10 minutes before we left on the bus ... Mr Capello had a flipchart and lifted a sheet up to reveal the one with the team on it. I was waiting for the crowd to cheer.'

Despite his privileged position, Gerrard hadn't exactly indicated that he wished to make the captaincy his on a permanent basis. In a pre-match interview, he had claimed that the absent Terry 'was still our leader.' But Capello was looking for genuine challengers to Terry's previous leadership. So, in the absence of a truly commanding figure in his squad, it was becoming increasingly clear that Capello himself would be the centre of attention on the night of the Switzerland match.

Fabio studied the faces of his England players in the Wembley dressing room before the match. They were tense. Once, when talking about the Rome derby between Lazio and Roma, he had given a wonderful description of a coach's lot. 'A coach has to plan the match; he has to choose the formation,' he had said. 'He has to scrutinise the souls of his players and perceive their fears, anxieties and nervousness. He mustn't make a wrong move. A player only thinks of himself. He trains during the week, keeps in shape, minds his diet and goes out on the field. If the team loses but he has played a good game, he leaves the scene of the match with his head held high. For a coach there is no way out: his derby is defined by the result. You can have done everything perfectly: but if your players don't put the ball in the net and your opponents score with a long shot, you are an idiot.'

A friendly between England and Switzerland certainly wasn't a derby-day scenario, yet Capello could still detect fear among his players. What he may not have realised initially was that he might have been generating some of it unintentionally.

Stuart Pearce, who had spent 11 years playing under one of the most fearsome managers of them all, Brian Clough at Nottingham Forest, explained later, 'You've only got to spend 10 minutes in Fabio's company to realise that he is a serious performer and he gains immediate respect for that. I find him very similar to Brian Clough. I worked with Brian and he scared the life out of me. You were on your toes all the time. I get the same impression working with this fella. He doesn't want to talk for hours about this and that rubbish. He just wants to get on with the job. You could feel the respect in the dressing room before the Switzerland match. You could sense he had the players on their toes. To be honest, I think that can only be good for the English game. I think we need to get a little bit serious about what we're doing after not qualifying for Euro 2008.'

The Switzerland match wasn't a qualifier of any kind; but Capello knew he would still be blamed if England lost, even though the nature of the performance would matter far more to him than the result on this occasion. Perhaps that was part of the reason why he didn't want any great fanfare to mark his first match in charge. As he walked down the Wembley tunnel dressed in a smart navy blue coat, light blue shirt and dark blue tie, he remained well behind his players as they marched out for action. There was no ready smile or salute for the 85,000 England fans, many of whom had bought tickets to salute a legend but were now intrigued to see whether they were to witness the coming of a new Messiah.

Capello looked serious, as though he meant business. He wanted his team to create his rapport with the fans through the quality of their football. At least the waiting would soon be over and we would see what magic Fabio had been able to weave in such a short space of time. This Wembley crowd would want something to remember the evening by, some special moment as compensation for having been denied David Beckham and the history that would have come with his inclusion. All eyes were on Capello, who ushered Stuart Pearce to his seat near the touchline before taking his own.

The Swiss had brought 2,200 supporters to the home of football and their spirits were high as they began their preparations to host Euro 2008. They made their presence felt during their national anthem, and then it was the turn of 'God Save the Queen'. We watched to see whether Capello would sing too but he just stood there. To his right, England physio Gary Lewin sang proudly. To Capello's left, Stuart Pearce looked as though he would burst as he did the same. Still there was nothing coming from the mouth of the new England manager, though he did at least applaud when the anthem was over. Sven Goran Eriksson had never sung the national anthem either, so this was nothing new.

It is easy to sound like a Little Englander if you dare to express the view that there is something fundamentally wrong with an international football team led by someone from another country. But Gareth Southgate, an intelligent man and former England player, believes the use of a foreign coach in international football simply defeats the object of the exercise. FIFA chief Sepp Blatter had been against Capello's appointment too.

Blatter said, 'I would say it is a little surprising that the mother-land of football has ignored a sacrosanct law or belief that the national team manager should be from the same country as the players. I have never seen Italy, Germany, Brazil or Argentina with a coach from another country. In fact most of the best teams have a coach from their own country.'

Not everyone was against Capello. Five supporters at Wembley that Wednesday night carried bold red letters on black back-grounds. The letters, of course, were F, A, B, I and O. The hero worship had started, albeit a little early. But everyone wanted to wipe away the memory of the recent past and the defeat to Croatia under McClaren on 21 November 2007 that had ended England's involvement in Euro 2008 before it had even begun. Capello seemed to feel the same way, because he started with only three England players from the team that had lost the key match. The captain, Gerrard, Joe Cole and Gareth Barry were the survivors from that sporting disaster. It was as though Capello was telling us that he didn't have much time for losers.

The starting 11 featured a surprise name in defence – Matthew Upson. Like James, he hadn't played for his country for years, and seemed forever plagued by injuries. But this was a new start for everybody. Indeed there were only two important concessions to the past. There was a minute's silence for the Busby Babes who had died in the Munich Air Disaster 50 years earlier. Then there were the historic undertones to the England strip on Capello's first big night. The players wore red shirts, white shorts and red socks, just as Bobby Moore and the boys of 1966 had done on that sunny Wembley afternoon when England had won the World Cup.

After three minutes Fabio was already out on the touchline trying to sort out the mess that was starting to unfold on the pitch.

Gerrard was caught in possession on the edge of his own penalty area and Tranquillo Barnetta tested David James. But there were bigger problems.

Joe Cole and David Bentley were positioned so far away from Rooney that the 4-5-1 formation remained just that, and there was precious little cohesion. The midfielders weren't bursting past the front man as Capello had hoped, while Rooney squandered the pair of half chances that did come his way. This wasn't the sort of purposeful start for which Capello had hoped. He folded his arms and looked mildly dissatisfied with his new charges. The vast Wembley crowd didn't look too pleased either. The man wearing David Beckham's shirt was always going to be an obvious scapegoat.

As Bentley looped in a lame cross from the right, the scene of so many exquisite deliveries from the past master, England's faithful suddenly vented their fury. 'One David Beckham, there's only one David Beckham . . .' There was an edge to the tone, a hint of early rebellion in the air, and it felt as though Capello's honeymoon period was over already.

The first half seemed to be stuttering to a close in the same disjointed way it had begun. An unsmiling Capello let out a cough in the cold night air, his folded arms looking more and more defensive. He wanted England to pass the ball; short passes that would find their target. Finally his players began to respond with a patient build-up. Some impatient supporters booed as though bored, because this wasn't the English way. And if this was to be Capello's way, it seemed for a moment as though he wouldn't last much longer than Steve McClaren.

Then, with merciful timing, Jermaine Jenas scored with a tap-in and all at once a crisis of faith had been averted. The football was pretty ugly to watch but Capello the winner was at least ahead, as was his habit, when the players disappeared down the tunnel for their barely-earned break.

At half-time Capello told his men that they were not doing what he had told them to do. He wasn't angry, he knew they were trying to achieve the objectives he had set them, but there was much more work to be done. With body language and gestures as much as words, he began to impose his own character and desire to win on his team. He made no changes but players knew the clock was ticking. All Fabio wanted to see was the sort of spirit and confidence they showed for their clubs, allied to an ability to keep possession. Was that too much to ask?

The England that began the second half played with a new fizz and sense of enjoyment, at least for a while. The man being paid £6 million or more to turn around England's fortunes had just begun to earn his vast salary. Rooney missed a sitter in the 48th minute, superbly set up by the defiant Bentley. Suddenly the Manchester United star began to show why he had been heralded as England's greatest talent for years: a brilliant chip towards goal came down just too late, and a fierce volley was deflected.

Then Capello's substitutions brought an end to the momentum. Jenas was taken off to give Shaun Wright-Phillips a run-out, and Joe Cole's evening was over as Peter Crouch was introduced to spearhead the attack. Rooney drifted towards Cole's former berth as Capello began to experiment. But within a minute of those substitutions, Switzerland were level.

Eren Derdiyok had come on at half-time for the visitors and Rio Ferdinand clearly hadn't identified the new threat. The Manchester United defender was caught sleeping as Derdiyok rifled his equaliser past a helpless David James. Capello threw his arms up in disgust and turned away, then quickly recovered his composure and clapped to encourage his players. They responded with fresh urgency.

Crouch's header, Rooney's flick and Gerrard's nicely weighted pass all invited Wright-Phillips to provide the killer finish. He did so with relish, and it had taken just four minutes for England to regain their lead. Clearly Rooney was playing better supporting a main striker than when Capello had asked him to be that main striker. Fabio stood on the touchline and could be heard shouting 'pass, pass, pass!' No one responded better than Bentley, and Beckham's one hundredth cap began to look a little more elusive.

Whereas the home supporters had jeered a string of England passes towards the end of the first half, they cheered a similar demonstration of how to retain position in the 78th minute.

Rooney was called off with three minutes to go, and Capello slapped hands with the striker as he strode past, his job done.

The Swiss nearly spoiled the party when James flapped at a cross and invited punishment. None came, but even then you couldn't escape the feeling that England's defence would have been torn apart by a better side. As it was, it all ended happily and Capello had his first win.

Gerrard explained afterwards, 'The manager wanted a winning mentality and we've got that. He wants us to be difficult to beat and exciting going forward. It is going to take time and we've got that too, so it is going to give us a chance to get used to each other.'

It remained to be seen whether Gerrard would get another chance as captain. While he hadn't been a failure, neither had Capello been entirely convinced that he had just seen a true international leader. Fabio's instructions hadn't been carried out to the letter, especially in the first half when England had struggled to overcome their nerves. While Gerrard wasn't blamed as such, neither was it felt he was someone to whom you could easily give precise instructions. Rightly or wrongly, the Capello camp initially regarded him as an anarchic player, running free and playing on instinct. How could he be expected to see to it that his team-mates were following the manager's strict tactical orders?

There was also England's failure to leave behind the self-doubt that had proved such a handicap over the years. Why were they still scared? Capello certainly didn't want to be the source of that fear. 'I don't eat anyone,' he said memorably after that first match. 'I don't see why they should be scared. I think at the back of their minds was the failure to qualify for Euro 2008. At the start they were very nervous; then we shook off the pressure of Wembley from our shoulders.'

He referred more than once to 'the pressure of Wembley', though the players should have been more used to that pressure than Capello. Fabio may not have looked very emotional at the end of his opening night on the big stage, but his composure was deceptive. He revealed, 'I felt great emotions, being here at Wembley to live this moment, to live with the squad and make a new start and to achieve results. It was very important to be in this extraordinary stadium with these extraordinary fans. It was a new experience and a good feeling. Now I know what it feels like to be England manager.'

And what it felt like to be England manager that night, he later revealed, was to be worried. During Euro 2008, he looked back and explained, 'I was very worried because I didn't see the spirit and the English characteristics. I saw some problems. There was no confidence and players weren't playing like they do for their clubs. That was my first impression.'

It could have gone either way, that nervous opening night against Switzerland. He had begun his reign with a win and that was something. Technically, however, he knew he was up against it. His assistant, Franco Baldini, pulled no punches when he spoke to the media afterwards. 'We need more technical skill, but unfortunately we only have the players for a few days every two months. We are trying to play with the ball more because the English culture after two or three passes is for the ball to sail through the air like a crow. We have to play with more confidence because it is easier to play when the ball is at our feet. We have to try to incorporate this in our game to give us more chances. Some things were good, some were not. England have to play like England, but maybe a little better.'

Capello's predecessor at Milan, Arrigo Sacchi, knew what Capello liked and disliked about English football. Sacchi said, 'Fabio has always been attracted by English football, by the beauty of the stadia, the perfect pitches and their close proximity to the fans. He loves the English desire to fight for every ball, playing physical and aggressive football. He does not rate, I think, the tactics often used by English teams, especially in the past, at great international tournaments like the Euros or the World Cups or in the European Cups, particularly in away games.'

Sacchi was right. Back in 1995, Fabio had told me why he thought Roy Hodgson might do reasonably well as coach at Inter Milan. 'Normally the English coaches are obsessed with their own schematic way of playing. They leave little space for flare and imagination. But Hodgson, having been in Switzerland, which borders Italy and has some Italian influences, has worked with players who have some imagination, and this personal experience can help him at Inter.'

What was Capello saying back then? That English managers had pretty much coached all the imagination out of their players, and Hodgson's saving grace was that he had escaped the country where this kind of rigid destruction habitually took place?

Those of us who talked to him back in the mid-1990s remember that when English football was English, he didn't think much of the English footballing brain. He liked the passion, the grit, the aggression, but he seemed to look down on the lack of intellectual flexibility. Of course in those days, the foreign revolution led by the arrival of Arsène Wenger at Arsenal was only a dawn on the horizon. English football offered a very different landscape in 2008 and beyond, so Capello's international players were used to being exposed to all kinds of foreign adversaries and team-mates on a regular basis. As Sacchi pointed out, 'In recent years, thanks to the "foreign legion" of managers and players in England, much has changed.'

But how much had English football really changed by the time Capello arrived in England during the 2007–08 season? Back at Milanello training ground in 1995, I had talked to Paolo Maldini about English football, and what needed to be done to improve it. As a Capello player at the time, Maldini's views probably weren't that far from Fabio's. And the fascinating thing is that some of Maldini's criticisms back in 1995 still held true in 2008.

Maldini told me then, 'In England every team plays the same way and so they get into the habit of playing against similar teams and styles. But in Italy we create devastating counterattacks after sucking teams in. I think the English try to create very little, especially from central defence, where they remain too stereotypical and flat. This is the difference between us and them. In general they try to construct little from the back. They just kick it a long way for the attackers.

'They could try using the ball a little to gain some confidence. If you pass the ball around and the opposition are running and chasing everywhere, they tire. Then you have an advantage. It is a completely different footballing concept to yours. This is the general problem that English teams have now. You have to open your minds, try different schemes of playing. You need more imagination, more technical ability – not just in midfield and attack, but at the back too. No more hopeful passes aimed in the general direction of attackers. That mentality is completely old-fashioned. You've got to think about it, because the England national team didn't even go to the World Cup last year (1994). You've got to show some curiosity in order to see how others play. It'll take time to change things in England, because even the kids play like that. So it's going to be difficult to change the mentality. The coaches must change too. You have to bring foreign coaches into your game – and I don't mean Scottish or Welsh – to change your style and improve your results.'

To an extent English football listened to this sort of argument by bringing in so many foreign coaches and players. England also took the brave step of bringing in a foreign coach to run the national team for a good number of years. Sven Goran Eriksson came, saw and might even have conquered, had he relied a little less on the volatile and injury-prone Wayne Rooney, or had the foresight to embrace the expertise of the most progressive sports psychologists when it came to penalty shoot-outs.

But old bad habits die hard, and just as England failed to qualify for the World Cup in 1994, they also failed to qualify for Euro 2008. And after Fabio Capello's first game in charge, that narrow win over Switzerland, Franco Baldini was sounding much like Paolo Maldini had 13 years earlier. There was still a widespread concern that there was insufficient emphasis on technique when our youngsters were taught the game. In a 2008 interview, Sir Trevor Brooking, the FA's Director of Football Development, claimed that English kids were given only a third of the contact time with a ball enjoyed by Dutch children. How were our youngsters supposed to be as good as the Dutch or anyone else if someone forgot to give them a ball?

At least under Capello the right structure could be put in place, and he pushed for an English version of the Italian Coverciano academy to be built at Burton. Meanwhile the FA banned serious competition for Under-8s later that year, so that skills could hold sway over results. With the right habits adopted at the very top and at grass roots level, there was hope for the future. And perhaps that was more important in the long run than winning the World Cup. But the sort of inadequacies highlighted by Baldini – and later Capello – with regard to that Switzerland opener made you wonder what the lasting legacy of the foreign coaches had been in England.

Under Eriksson England played with a little more culture than before, but seemed to lose what Fabio Capello had always valued most – that fight and aggression that had so often scared opponents of old. Once Eriksson had gone, England often seemed too confused to recapture that passion and fire in time to qualify for Euro 2008.

At club level the foreign coaches introduced more of the passing game that Maldini had pointed to in the previous decade, but the identity of English football, with its strong fighting spirit, had begun to disappear. Players such as Alan Shearer, Paul Scholes and Jamie Carragher all quit the international scene early to concentrate on prolonging their club careers. Somehow Capello had to make it a big deal for England players to represent their country again, without giving them stage fright. Increasing their sense of pride in the England shirt was never likely to prove the easiest task when he wasn't even English himself. But this was a battle Fabio simply had to win. England players may not be as technically accomplished as those from the very top countries in football; but there should never, ever be an occasion when they want victory less.

Slaven Bilic, whose Croatia side had appeared to want to qualify for Euro 2008 more than England did, said, 'People are crazy about football in Croatia. Children play it everywhere. The stars are perhaps closer to the kids and the common folk than is some larger, wealthier countries.'

Meanwhile, for all their technical excellence, Brazil and Italy only win the World Cup when their desire and sense of unity are at their peak. Fabio Capello revealed at Euro 2008, 'I spoke with Luiz Felipe Scolari (the coach who led Brazil to World Cup glory in 2002) and Marcello Lippi (who did the same for Italy in 2006) and they both told me that they had a very, very strong group, a very strong unit, which was very focused.' Capello had always liked impossible challenges. Now his challenge was to turn England into a unit equally capable of winning the World Cup. Did he have the character to succeed? He was certainly tough enough.

CHAPTER 23
BECKS OR STELLA, SIR?

DAVID BECKHAM, IN A STATE OF ANGRY BEWILDERMENT AT his exclusion from Capello's first squad against Switzerland, might have been entitled to echo Antonio Cassano and scream, 'Have you no shame? I fought for you in Madrid and this is how you repay me.' But Beckham, the sporting icon, was too clever to say that. Instead he headed for the USA, hoping against hope that he might one day be allowed to win that one hundredth cap for England.

To be fair to Capello, he had never given the impression that the door was closed. Noises from Fabio's camp suggested that a friendly match against the USA at Wembley in late May 2008 would provide the ideal platform for Beckham to reach his ton. Then something strange happened. Capello had a meeting with a group of England fans, a sort of informal, question-and-answer session. The supporters made their feelings very clear: they wanted Beckham to reach his milestone; they felt he deserved it. Whether Capello's longstanding respect for the passionate English supporter played a part, it is difficult to say. At any rate, Capello gave the fans his word that either he or his assistant, Franco Baldini, would travel all the way to Dallas on 17 March to check Beckham's fitness in a friendly match there involving LA Galaxy. If Beckham was fit enough, he would receive a call-up for a rather more prestigious friendly – against France on 26 March.

While we awaited Dallas and the possible repercussions, other England fans were given their first in-depth look at their new manager in rather strange circumstances. Indeed, all of Britain was treated to the bizarre sight of Fabio having his portrait painted by a controversial 'Brit Artist' called Stella Vine for the Sport Relief charity on BBC television. Vine had asked for Capello, and amazingly he had obliged as someone who understood and adored art. Capello might have been uncertain of his best England team, but he could name his favourite artists without thinking. The Russian expressionist Wassily Kandinsky was one, along with Kandinsky's compatriot Marc Chagall. Piero Pizzi Cannella, the Italian artist, was reported to be a personal friend of Fabio. Meanwhile the abstract work of the American, Cy Twombly so absorbed Capello that he likened the paintings to Spanish football, because you could read so much into each example.

'I'm an art lover and modest collector,' Capello told us, playing down the estimated £17 million he had invested in his collection over the years, and the estimated £7 million worth of art that was said to line the walls of his Milanese residence alone.

But back on the BBC, Fabio was showing, through his passion and knowledge, that art isn't about money, whatever the figures banded about. 'I first heard about Stella Vine when Saatchi bought her portrait of Diana. That was when people first started talking about her in Italy too. This is the first time I've ever sat for a portrait. I've seen some of her work and liked it a lot. It'll be interesting to see what she manages to get from my face. But above all I trust the excellence of the artist.'

Deep down Capello didn't enjoy the experience of posing for a portrait, it took so long and he wanted it to be over. He was too polite to convey this to the artist, however. Indeed, Vine told us, 'It is wonderful when you meet someone who really appreciates art and is really passionate about it. He has got a nice face, very understanding, and you can feel that empathy, and that he is trying to help me. He has got very pretty eyes; I imagine he must have been quite a looker in his early years. He still is of course. His eyes have a tinge of violet in them, which will be very nice to paint.'

An amused television audience saw Stella create something that didn't look much like Capello at all, a rather comical-looking man with a younger face, rosy cheeks, big wide eyes, far more open and softer in his features, and staring through preposterously thick glasses. He was dressed in a blue jacket with lines of white trim, white shirt, dark blue tie and grey trousers. Fabio was on the touchline at a match, one arm gesturing across the other so that his body was almost contorted. Fabio, who was familiar with the artist's brilliant lateral thinking, still looked baffled when he saw Vine's preliminary work, saying, 'Oh, uhmm … nice? I like. Ha, ha, ha. Yeah.' His brain seemed to be working overtime as he began to 'get it'.

Capello, a man of great culture, knows how to tune into the minds of the greats, whether his senses are trained on art or classical music. He once said, 'When (Claudio) Abbado directs the Berliner (Philharmonic Orchestra) I cry.' There was no sign that he might be moved to tears as he gazed at Stella's work, though. It may have interested him, and he continued to respect the artist, but he wasn't tempted to buy the portrait himself, and he never did bother to find out how much it sold for.

Meanwhile Baldini could have been forgiven for shedding a tear or two, because he was duly required to travel some 10,000 miles in a gruelling round trip over a couple of days in order to see if an ageing player might still have the legs to do something significant in an international arena. There was method in Capello's madness: he figured there was no point in playing Beckham in a jamboree match against the Americans – just to gift him a one hundredth cap – if he still didn't know whether he could turn it on against higher-quality opposition. Far better, Fabio reasoned, to give him a run-out against France and the likes of Franck Ribery and Nicolas Anelka, to see if he could still live with some of the best in the business. If Beckham could still shine in Paris then Capello would feel more confident that his former Real Madrid star might be useful when the serious football began – with the World Cup qualifiers in September and October 2008.

Even before Baldini flew all the way to Dallas, Beckham was insisting that he was in great shape for an England recall. 'Fitness-wise I'll be perfect,' he had promised on LA Galaxy's three-match tour of the Far East. Baldini went to see for himself, talked to the player and his manager Ruud Gullit, flew all the way back to London, and told Fabio that, in his opinion, the former England skipper was worth a recall. Capello trusted Franco's judgement as usual, and when the news became official there was the sort of fanfare that had previously been prepared for the Switzerland game at Wembley. When asked whether Beckham would definitely play, Capello confirmed with a smile, 'I'm not going to bring him all the way over and then not play him. He will start.'

So the big Parisian party was on, and Beckham invited his entire family to the Stade de France for the big occasion. There were cynics among the media who were claiming that Beckham's selection was a masterstroke in order to be rid of him once and for all come the final whistle, since he obviously wouldn't be up to the job. But this wasn't the way Capello thought. He would have had no problem leaving Beckham on 99 caps if he had genuinely wanted to ditch him.

The former captain's selection on the right of midfield didn't go down too well with Blackburn's David Bentley, who must have thought, along with his manager Mark Hughes, that he had done enough against Switzerland to warrant a starting place against the French. The explosive Theo Walcott, who was becoming more dangerous with every Arsenal game he played, might also have had reason to wonder why the very real effects of Old Father Time were not being taken into account, though he accepted the decision without complaint. Indeed there was widespread joy on Beckham's behalf.

Capello was given a problem shortly before the match against France in Paris when Frank Lampard pulled out with a stomach upset. There were those who suggested at the time that Lampard's sudden decision might have been prompted by the suspicion that he had been left out of the starting line-up. Though these mischievous rumours were doubtless untrue, they also happened to reach the Capello camp. Therefore poor Lampard, who would lose his mother a few weeks later, had some work to do later that summer in order to convince Capello that he was still truly passionate about playing for his country. But that subplot in the

Paris soirée was hardly noticed, because there were other issues to consider.

For a start, Rio Ferdinand had been made captain for the evening. Capello had stood up briefly at a team meal and said simply, 'Captain for this match is Ferdinand.' Then he had sat down again. Sitting next to Ferdinand was the man most of us had expected to be given the armband, since he was fit again and it had been his before – John Terry. The Chelsea skipper swallowed, hid the sick feeling inside and congratulated his fellow central defender. 'It was a bit embarrassing really,' admitted Ferdinand later. 'That was the first I had known about it.' But that didn't mean he wasn't grateful, or didn't want the captaincy on a permanent basis if offered it later.

The *Daily Mail* disapproved, offering the headline, 'England's boss promised us a model captain. Instead, we got this snarling drink-driver who starred in a sex video and was banned for missing a drug test.' But Ferdinand had spoken eloquently before the match, suggesting that if people couldn't be forgiven and allowed to grow up then we might as well give up. There was a quiet determination about Ferdinand, arguably England's most talented defender, and he really did seem to be growing into the role right before our eyes – a worthy contender for the captaincy John Terry had made his own under McClaren.

Also growing into his role was Stuart Pearce, the England Under-21 manager who had been made a coach in the senior England set-up too. However, for a man who had efficiently managed a Premiership club, Manchester City, the amount of responsibility he was given with England was minimal. In the build-up to the France game, Pearce happily revealed that he was acting as Capello's mouthpiece much of the time: 'Yes, I am helping to convey team talks. I think it is general points Fabio really wants to nail home and emphasise. He will ask me "Tell them this, make sure they know that." He has spoken it in English but wants to make sure they hear it from a voice through which he knows they're going to understand exactly what he means.' We could only hope that Stuart's voice achieved clearer meaning when it really mattered.

Even so, it had already been made clear to me that Pearce was not expected to initiate any important interaction with the senior England players off his own bat. Capello had no intention of creating any kind of wedge between the head coach and his players. If Pearce had observations to make, Capello expected his homegrown lieutenant to make those observations either to him or to Franco Baldini. Then the Italians would decide what – if anything – needed to be done as a result. Franco Baldini was Fabio's real assistant, the man whose judgement on players Capello trusted so well. While Baldini was there, Pearce would only have a peripheral role. Stuart wasn't so unimportant that people could dismiss him as nothing more than a 'token Englishman', though. As England Under-21 manager, his opinion would of course be heard, especially on the younger players. Pearce revealed, 'In the first chat I had with Fabio, he told me he wanted a full report on all my (Under-21) players.

Was Pearce being groomed to become England's next manager? I was told that it was possible in theory that Pearce could succeed Fabio, and down to the younger man to impress the powers that be. Whatever the future held, Pearce was in a position to act as the FA's historian for the Capello era. Even if he didn't get the England job when Capello left, Pearce was ideally placed to make a note of all the intricate details of the Capello regime. Dietary preferences, in-house rules when the squad met up, tactical approaches towards the England team and their opponents; you name it, Pearce was in prime position to soak it all up. That way the country would never again be short of expertise or thorough planning. Capello wanted to lay the foundations for England's future, and Pearce would study his methods carefully at first hand. By the time Fabio left, the man they called 'Psycho' ought to have assembled enough knowledge of his so-called 'winning mentality' to make Capello's legacy a lasting one.

Wherever the coaching staff came from, there was only one true test of whether England's managerial pecking order would remain satisfactory to the FA and the fans – what happened out on the pitch. And only one Englishman was ever going to be the star of the Parisian stage – David Beckham. He had chosen to wear flashy golden boots just in case anyone didn't already think he was the centre of attention. England had even made up a special shirt for him to play in, rather undermining Capello's ethos that no one was special in a football team, only the team itself.

Written in gold letters on Beckham's shirt was the following: 'France v England: 26.03.2008. 100th Cap.' Now all he had to do was to come up with a performance worthy of the recall and the occasion itself. Becks looked tense as he stood in the tunnel, waiting for his proud moment, and he stayed well back as Ferdinand led the team out. Seven thousand England fans had travelled over to cheer the centurion out, and there was a tear in Beckham's eye as he sang the national anthem. Capello still didn't sing, but then neither did Wayne Rooney. It was how England played that mattered, with their former captain back in the team.

Beckham chased back well, proving a satisfactory degree of fitness and commitment to the cause. In the 14th minute he had a half-chance to score a fairytale goal; but he couldn't quite connect after France keeper Gregory Coupet had parried Ashley Cole's cross. Then something strange happened; working to Capello's instructions, Beckham fell in at right back behind the advancing Wes Brown. They began to alternate on the flank, though it still wasn't creating the required penetration. There were flashes of cohesion, when England passed the ball around adequately; but France never looked threatened. Indeed, after 32 minutes of looking perfectly comfortable, the home side scored. François Clerc's pass caught John Terry sleeping on the wrong side of Nicolas Anelka, and the Chelsea striker raced clear to confront David James. The England goalkeeper clattered into Anelka so clumsily that the Frenchman was sent spiralling up into the air, and it was fortunate that he landed without doing any serious damage to himself. But no one could complain about the penalty award, and Franck Ribery calmly converted the spot-kick. Capello, arms folded, bowed his head momentarily in disappointment.

Two minutes before half-time England managed their first and only effort on target, when Rooney met Gareth Barry's cross without sufficiently threatening power or direction. Before we knew it the half-time whistle had blown, and Beckham walked off, perhaps wondering whether the final curtain had already come down on his England career. Instead Capello called time on

Rooney, Steven Gerrard, Joe Cole and John Terry for the evening. Their replacements were Peter Crouch, Michael Owen, Stewart Downing and Joleon Lescott. It didn't make much difference, even though Beckham probably had his best quarter-of-an-hour. He swung in a dangerous corner which was headed over by Crouch, delivered a fine pass for Downing which was mis-controlled, and set Owen and Crouch in motion with his last contribution of the match.

After 62 minutes and 30 seconds Beckham pulled his special shirt out of his shorts and returned the applause of the generous thousands. He looked up to his wife Victoria and the rest of his family and friends, who were clapping enthusiastically up in a hospitality box. Particularly memorable and moving, however, was the fact that the French supporters also gave the English hero a standing ovation, something that went against hundreds of years of mutual disdain. It seemed that Beckham's popularity really was universal, for the quality of his display alone could not have merited such a unique reaction from 78,500 supporters. He had completed 40 passes, sent in 10 crosses, had no shots on goal and made ... er ... two tackles. The completed passes, and this seemed crucial, had usually been from a deep position, sprayed diagonally, not the hardest angle to defend against. But without Beckham, it seemed there was even less about England's pitiful attack to trouble France. The match finished 1-0.

Capello sniffed moodily, but David Beckham clearly wasn't going to let the result spoil his night. He shook his head and smiled at an optimistic William Gallas of France and Arsenal, who asked for Beckham's historic shirt as though the Englishman would be more than happy to give away one of his most treasured possessions to the first person who asked.

He prepared his words for the media, and his key message seemed to be that this was not the end. 'I never thought I'd get to one hundred and hopefully beyond,' he said carefully. 'It is a proud moment to be mentioned up there with Sir Bobby Charlton, Bobby Moore, Billy Wright, and Peter Shilton. Fitness-wise I felt great, I felt a lot better than I actually thought I would.'

Capello's analysis of a performance which had produced just one effort on goal all match was bizarre. 'I'm very happy,' Capello insisted on the night, proving that some people can be very easily pleased indeed when the mood takes them. 'I've told my players as well, that I think we've improved compared to the Switzerland game. I saw important things. We kept possession quite well, there are still a few things we need to improve on obviously, but as it stands I'm happy. I saw a good Beckham, in good condition, he could have played more but I replaced him because I wanted to see other players as well. '

Former England manager Glenn Hoddle better represented the feelings of those who had been watching. He told Sky Sports viewers, 'There are not many positives, I would say. There was no imagination about our play, and I haven't seen an England side for a long time create so few chances. What chances did we have in 90 minutes? Probably one. I think Capello still doesn't understand the English footballer at the moment, and you can't expect him to, and that's the downside of having a foreign coach. You do need some time.'

Alan Hansen continued the theme on BBC TV. 'The French were better in possession and there lies Capello's problem, because he is trying to make England into a passing side. Now a manager can give you certain things, he can give you inspiration, belief, confidence, he can get you organised, but he can't make you into a better passing side unless you've got nine or ten outfield players that are very good technically and comfortable in possession. England just haven't got that.'

England might have had that if they had listened to the likes of Paolo Maldini, while he was playing under Capello back in 1995. But perhaps it would take another 13 years for the required philosophies to come to fruition in England. Beckham's old England team-mate Alan Shearer, who had become a BBC pundit, didn't mean to sound unkind about Beckham when he commented at the end of the France game, 'I don't know whether it is lack of match fitness or whether he can't do it any more.'

As for Beckham, he was still talking like a man who didn't even want to ask himself that question. 'I'm very stubborn, of course things change, but I want to carry on playing for my country for as long as possible, and hopefully I can. I proved my fitness, that's the thing . . .'

That night in Paris, it was hard to escape the conclusion that Capello had spent much of his time over the previous two years not playing Beckham when he should have done . . . and playing him when he shouldn't have done. Still, Don Fabio knew best. Perhaps it was worth giving him a little more time.

So the relationship between Fabio Capello and David Beckham, which had begun so stormily, both in Madrid and England, took one bizarre twist after another. In the aftermath of that disappointing France game, for example, Capello was presented with a theory – that Rooney and Gerrard couldn't play for their country as well as they did for their clubs, because they didn't have international team-mates who brought out the best in them in the same way as Cristiano Ronaldo and Fernando Torres. Fabio replied, 'I have David Beckham and Rooney can be our Torres.'

That prompted headlines such as 'Beckham is our Ronaldo', accompanied by suggestions that Capello was starting to lose the plot completely. Surely there wasn't anything else he could do to endorse Becks, the fading superstar . . . was there?

CHAPTER 24
HEADLINES AND HEADACHES

From the moment Capello took the England job, his relationship with Luciano Moggi was likely to raise questions, but Fabio stubbornly insisted that he wasn't going to be a fairweather friend.

On 31 March 2008, the dynamic between the two men came under fresh scrutiny when Moggi was one of six people placed on trial, accused of putting excessive pressure on players to agree to be handled by the football management agency, GEA World.

Capello appeared to show warmth to Moggi and another former Juventus director, Antonio Giraudo, during breaks in the proceedings. Giraudo wasn't one of the accused in this case; but he was still serving a five-year ban from football for his role in *Calciopoli*. Perhaps Fabio was just relieved to see friendly faces after being bombarded with questions he genuinely couldn't answer. Either Capello couldn't remember or he didn't know, he said repeatedly when asked to go into specifics about the inner workings of Juventus and GEA.

In court, Fabio denied involvement with the directors of GEA or being put under any kind of pressure over the management of players during his time at Juventus. He denied dealing with transfers at all. He said, 'I have never heard about players being put under pressure or of incidents relating to players' contracts. At

Roma and then at Juventus when I was boss, I only dealt with coaching decisions. I only did the shopping list, the club did the rest: I never concerned myself with the economic aspects.'

Fabio went on to insist that although he had 'heard rumours' in the past that Luciano Moggi, the General Manager of Juventus, was involved with GEA World, he'd had 'no knowledge of the exact relationship'. Capello's taped conversation with Luciano Moggi in 2004 indicated that may have known that Alessandro Moggi had a significant role within GEA World by then. But it would appear that he may have tipped off Luciano about the imminent investigation into GEA simply because he considered Luciano to be a friend, and because he had realised that the investigation could affect another member of the Moggi family, Luciano's son. There was no law against that.

When giving evidence as a witness in court in 2008, Capello also played down his comments in his 2002 interview with *Corriere dello Sport* while still coach of Roma, in which he attacked Moggi's conflict of interests and GEA's near-monopoly of the transfer market. He said they were not based on anything concrete, but were rather a tactic in support of his club at the time: 'I did that interview because I thought it was right to do something for Roma. I knew about GEA, I knew that many players were gravitating towards that company.' But all Capello knew about how GEA worked back in 2002 'was that it existed. I didn't even know who ran it ... I said it seemed strange to me, the existence of a company that acted as agent for a hundred players and some coaches, but I said it because I intended to say something in favour of Roma, the club I was coaching at the time.'

The public prosecutor Luca Palamara said of Capello's testimony in 2008: 'We ran into a brick wall of reticence. In this court whoever is called to give evidence is obliged to tell the truth, not to refer to gossip or repeatedly say "I don't know" or "I don't remember." Surprisingly Palamara warned that he would study a transcript of Capello's evidence before deciding whether proceedings should be brought against him. Capello's former colleague at Juventus, the club's CEO Antonio Giraudo, was also warned that he could face a similar charge of reticence over the evidence – or lack of it – he had given.

Meanwhile another witness, Capello's England number two, Franco Baldini cited occasions when, as sporting director of Serie A club Roma, he felt that GEA had an undue influence over players he was trying to sign. He also recalled a dinner held at Christmas 2001 by the Italian Football League. At this gathering Luciano Moggi allegedly expressed his displeasure at the difficulty his son Alessandro was having in signing up certain Roma players to GEA. Baldini claimed that Moggi said, 'You know, you've got to give us a hand. One year you work here, another year you work there and another year you don't work at all.' Baldini took this to imply that he might be frozen out of Italian football if he tried to defy the Moggi family.

Back in the courtroom in Rome in 2008, it seems that Baldini suffered yet another threat, right in front of the court as he gave further evidence. Capello was waiting outside the courtroom for his turn to give evidence, and was therefore oblivious to what was happening inside. There, as Baldini prepared to reveal more, Moggi is alleged to have made a gesture with his arm stretched in front of him and his palm facing towards the ground. It is understood that such a gesture signifies a warning in Italy that someone should be careful what they say or face the consequences. Baldini looked his tormentor in the eye, determined to show him that he was not afraid, and said, 'Luciano, you have eighteen lawyers, leave me in peace.' He immediately attracted the attention of the judge to what Moggi had done and complained that it 'could be taken as intimidation.' Baldini added, 'He was giving me the usual threatening signals he gives me and always has done.' The judge warned Moggi that he would be thrown out of court the next time he made any such gesture or showed any disrespect to the court.

Understandably the headlines back in England the next day concentrated on Capello and made grim reading for Fabio and the Football Association. The *Daily Mail* back page announced: 'Tell us the truth, Fabio.' The front page of the *Daily Telegraph* sports section read 'Capello embroiled in corruption case', while *The Times* went with 'Capello fuming over the threat of prosecution in corruption case.' *The Times* suggested that Fabio had told friends he was deeply upset and angry, feeling that he had already cooperated fully by giving his evidence to the public prosecutor at a private preliminary hearing some 18 months earlier, only to be summoned again to give evidence in public because he was a high profile international manager.

Capello's lawyers countered the public prosecutor, Palamara's suggestion that their client had been 'reticent' with a statement which read, 'We are really surprised by the public prosecutor's declaration. Mr Capello was heard as a witness in the proceedings against the GEA company and confirmed before the Court of Rome all of the declarations that he had already provided to the public prosecutor during the investigation. At the end of the hearing, Mr Capello was certain that in his capacity as witness, he had given all the information required of him to the prosecutor and the court.'

Vanity Fair's Sara Faillaci felt that the prospect of a charge was tricky enough in itself. She put it to Capello: 'During the testimony in the trial against GEA, with Moggi the main accused, the pm (prosecutor) accused you of reticence, and now there is a risk you will be charged with false testimony.' Capello responded, 'It surprised me a lot. I had already been heard by the pm during the inquiry and on the occasion of the trial I repeated the same things that I had already told him.' Indeed, Fabio is understood to have called his son Pierfilippo after appearing in court on the last day of March 2008, and told him that everything went fine. He had told the authorities everything, he assured Pierfilippo, just as he had before, behind closed doors.

'I'm convinced that it will all sort itself out soon,' Capello told *Vanity Fair*. Sara Faillaci asked: 'Isn't there a risk that the English will become irritated with all these judicial problems, also taking into account the renowned British press?' Fabio replied, 'I answer to the Football Association and with them I have clarified myself ... Since I am utterly convinced that everything was done in the correct manner, I am calm about this. Then for sure the English media concentrates on the national coach, perhaps too much, and I didn't expect this. But every paper there has at least three sports pages and perhaps there is pressure because for decades they haven't won anything.'

Despite the momentous pressure, Fabio seemed tough enough to take it all. Indeed, Capello's sister Bianca told me, 'I'm not worried at all about this trial business, he'll be all right and this will not stop him from concentrating on his work – he works so hard. He will succeed with England, it'll just take a bit of time, he can't just wave a magic wand, but he will get there.'

Everyone hoped Bianca was right. But then in May came the news that the Football Association must have been dreading. The public prosecutor, Luca Palamara, had carried out his promise to study the transcript of the Capello testimony in court, and had decided that there was enough which troubled him to take further action against the England manager. Fabio was put formerly under investigation for what the *Daily Telegraph* described as allegations of perjury. If the investigation was to uncover sufficient evidence to put Capello on trial, they wrote, and he was subsequently found guilty, he would face a maximum of six years in prison. The *Daily Telegraph*'s headline was 'Capello will face perjury charge.'

Fabio's son Pierfilippo later insisted that what Capello had been accused of was not perjury – which is basically lying in court – but reticence or withholding information. He suggested that the charge was essentially born of a simple misunderstanding – because Fabio simply couldn't remember all the details in the answers he had given the preliminary hearing some 18 months earlier. Since then he had coached Real Madrid, left that club and begun the England job. A lot had happened to make events at Juventus a distant memory. So, according to Pierfilippo, Capello had asked Palamara to read back his previous answers from the preliminary hearing, so that he could confirm to the court that the information contained therein was accurate. Only when he had heard his previous statements could he determine whether he might be able to add anything. But Palamara was having none of it, and refused to oblige Capello by reading back what he had said before. It is conceivable that Palamara wanted to see whether there would be any discrepancy between Capello's previous and latest answers, but this rigid stance hardly helped the rapport between the two men. So Capello had been forced to try to dig deep into his memory. He wasn't going to be drawn into saying anything in a court of law of which he was not sure after so much time had elapsed; but he did feel that he had answered all the questions more than adequately, in so far as was humanly possible.

I had a meeting with Fabio Capello on 20 May 2008 in Italia Mania, a little restaurant in Soho Square, London, near the FA headquarters. I wanted to ask Capello about his friendship with Moggi, and even risk Fabio's legendary temper. Franco Baldini was at the meeting too, so the Moggi issue would be a sensitive one.

I tried to put a simple argument to Capello, hoping to speak for all football fans. When we go to see a football match, especially when we have paid good money for a ticket, a long journey and perhaps even a hotel, we want to know that both teams are giving their all to win. We want to know the referee is doing everything he can to make fair decisions. We demand a level playing field. His friend Moggi, on the other hand, had appeared in the recent past to be rather more interested in destroying the level playing field. So how could Capello remain a friend to Moggi? I asked Fabio straight out, as we ate pieces of pizza without a knife and fork, hand-held in serviettes, Italian style.

Capello answered along the lines of what he had told *Vanity Fair*. Moggi was a friend of the family, he had been proven guilty of nothing in a court of law, and if he had really made a mistake then he could expect to be punished for it like anyone else. I asked Fabio to explain his relationship with Moggi further, in case there was an Italian cultural dimension to the friendship between the two men that I had failed as an Englishman to understand. Capello's response was that he felt he had dealt with the subject adequately.

I had also taken the opportunity to ask him about his former friend and neighbour, the late Italo Allodi. You will recall that attempts by intermediaries to influence the referees for Juventus matches against Derby County in the two-legged European Cup semi-final of 1973 had prompted the late Brian Clough to call for a full investigation. As a player Capello did not have the slightest inkling of what appears to have been attempted behind the scenes but reiterated that Derby would not have complained had they won the tie. It appeared that in Capello's eyes, Allodi was guilty of nothing; and Derby's protests were to be regarded as trivial.

In comparison to some of the world's cares, of course, football is a trivial matter. Capello has always been careful to keep the importance of football in perspective, while helping to make the world a better place where he feels able to do so. In addition to a significant financial contribution for the repairs that were needed a few years ago to the parish church in his home village of Pieris, he helped to support the humanitarian work of the local nuns there. Add to that Fabio's own revelation: 'I pray twice a day and I am not keen on the current abortion law. I admire Pope Benedict; as far as I'm concerned, the church needed a tug in the direction of respect for tradition.'

Clearly Fabio is not a man who takes moral issues lightly. But how did his moral code apply to football? Capello had helped to front the Football Association's Respect campaign in early 2008. In May 2008, he had said, 'As a coach abroad I was always impressed by the respect the English players had for referees, compared to the players I managed in the leagues I worked in. In recent times, in the last season, we have taken a step back. So we need to go back to respecting the referees and officials ... It is important I enforce strictness, especially at the top level. You need to bear in mind that all the top players at the highest level are watched by children and young people across the nation and influence their behaviour. So it is vitally important they set the right example to them. As for what my role is in all of this, well it is my job to sit down with the players and deal with it if there is a problem of this sort.'

In June 2008 I asked Keith Hackett, General Manager of the Professional Game Match Officials Board, what he thought about Capello's friendship with Moggi. Did he think it was compatible with the England manager's role as an FA figurehead demanding greater respect for referees? 'I don't know,' he began, 'That is for the FA to decide. They are his (Capello's) employer, not me.'

Hackett admitted that he was aware of Moggi and what had

happened in Italian football and pointed out that we shouldn't assume Capello had been influenced in any way by Luciano's behaviour. I wondered whether Fabio should at least strongly condemn the way Moggi had apparently compromised the integrity of the game in Italy. 'That's entirely down to him,' Hackett said. He wanted to make it clear that he was highly appreciative of Capello's declared intent to bring his players into line and show greater respect to referees. 'If he follows through with that,' he added significantly, 'it will help both at the professional level and grass roots level too.'

Jeff Winter, long time Premiership referee noted: 'During the week in which the FA was launching the "Respect" campaign, there was a wonderful opportunity to make an example of Ashley Cole by leaving him at home for the friendly in France. He had shown a deplorable lack of respect to a Premier League referee, Mike Riley, even turning his back while Mr Riley was talking to him. Perhaps Mr Capello and his advisors could have taken a stand then. But it didn't happen and unfortunately a lot of what the FA does is just a noise without any action to back it up . . .'

Lord Triesman, a former Foreign Office official, had oozed confidence as he set out his vision for football in the spring of 2008. During his impressive speech he said, 'There are a number of values which in our book at the FA are to do not only with the highest reaches of the game, great and excellent as that is, but have got to run right through football as a whole. Values about fairness, values about good competition ... values which emphasise a degree of respect for the laws of the game, for the players you play with and the players you play against, for the officials who look after the game, and for everybody who is involved in trying to make sure that it is the favourite sport of our country.'

As the amiable priest in Capello's home village, Don Pierpaolo Soranzi would tell us, protecting football's integrity is even more important than winning the World Cup. Making sure values run through football doesn't mean the game has to go soft or lose its edge, quite the reverse. A fair fight increases the edge and the drama; it is what we expect to see when we go to a stadium, and what some people live for. And it struck me that if Capello didn't use his high profile to harden his stance against the ever-present threat of corruption in football, then the next Italo Allodi or Luciano Moggi could be only just around the corner.

CHAPTER 25
OMINOUS PREPARATIONS

CAPELLO HAD DEMANDED PRIDE AND INTENSITY IN THE build-up to the friendly match against the USA at Wembley on 28 May 2008. He said, 'I want to see one team playing like a group with courage, and strong. It is very important for me to recover the spirit of the England team. When you play for the national team you have to play like it is a final in every game.'

Fabio showed the players a video of the Americans beating Poland in order to remove any complacency. If that wasn't enough, they knew they were competing for their places in readiness for the serious action in the autumn. Courage, strength, spirit, passion; these were the qualities he wanted to see. Play like it's a final.

Wayne Rooney took it all rather too literally when the match got underway at Wembley. His first-half challenge on Ricardo Clark could have earned a straight red card; instead he was let off without so much as a yellow. Capello told the Croxteth fireball to calm down during the interval. But in the 76th minute another rash challenge, this time on Frankie Hejduk, left the Greek referee, Kyros Vassaras, with little choice but to caution Rooney officially. He received an angry gesture from the Manchester United star for his trouble; Rooney was probably fortunate that it had only been a friendly.

Later Capello revealed that what we had seen on the pitch that night had not been the first signs of Rooney's irrational behaviour that week. Fabio explained, 'I saw the same thing from him in training. On Tuesday, in the last session, it was the same. It is normal for him and I told him that. I was worried for the other players.'

Rooney's temper was something the Capello camp had already been warned about. Few could forget the sight of Cristiano Ronaldo winking happily, as his Manchester United team-mate was shown the red card against Portugal in 2006. Fabio admitted, 'Yes I have to keep him on the pitch for 90 minutes and so I have to speak with him. I have to speak with Rooney and explain to him that he mustn't do these tackles. I won't do it now, but in time. The next time I see him (which was due to be August), I will speak to him.'

Some so-called experts had already been trying to talk Rooney up as a possible England captain, on the basis that the extra responsibility might help him to mature. The response from around the Capello camp was that, although it was an interesting theory, it would be much worse if Rooney lost his head again in a major tournament as captain. It was bad enough to have to worry about it happening when Rooney was just one of the lads.

David Beckham learned his lesson after being sent off against Argentina in the 1998 World Cup. Since then he had usually been diplomacy personified, and he had reaped incredible rewards thanks to his stability. Not only did Becks start for England against the USA in his 101st appearance for his country, but he also collected a golden cap, encased in glass, from Sir Bobby Charlton before the match. The gift was in recognition of the century he had reached in Paris, and it was more of a handful than England had been that night. 'It was so heavy,' smiled Beckham later. 'I tried to lift it and then thought to myself, "It's not going up." But it was such an honour to receive that from Sir Bobby Charlton who was my dad's hero and my hero.'

And typically it was Beckham who provided the perfect free kick delivery for John Terry to head England's first goal of the evening in the 38th minute. It was the ideal way for Terry to celebrate being awarded the England captaincy in front of more than 70,000 at Wembley that night. The goal also gave Terry temporary relief from the nightmare of his penalty miss in the Champions League final against Manchester United in Moscow just a few days earlier, a slip-up that had cost Chelsea the trophy. Capello said afterwards, 'Terry has charisma when he is with the other players; he is a natural leader. But all the players did what I told them to do. They played the English way, with intensity, and they got the ball back quickly when they lost it.'

Those comments seemed to offer a clue to which way Capello was starting to lean when it came to his permanent England captain. He had said from the start that he would be looking carefully at the reaction of the players around each captain he auditioned. Now, it seemed, he had found the reaction he had been looking for.

Meanwhile Beckham made way for David Bentley at half-time, but the replacement failed to shine. No wonder Becks was smiling so much after the game. In central midfield Gareth Barry was an impressive substitute for a tired Frank Lampard; and immediately he delivered a killer pass for Steven Gerrard to add England's second in the 59th minute. Capello applauded with a look of complete satisfaction on his face, because swift movement had undone the opposition convincingly. From that moment the USA were down and out, even though the match only ended 2-0. Afterwards, Beckham said of Capello's England regime, 'Things have been serious in training and serious for the match, but I knew how Capello works from our time together at Real Madrid, and we all know what he wants.'

But now Fabio was smiling too, in a way we hadn't seen since his arrival in England. He conducted his interviews in English, and explained why he was so happy. 'We played without fear. This was another step along the path.' Fabio was speaking English fearlessly too, and was clearly delighted to have made the breakthrough. Only eight days earlier I had suggested to him that it was time he communicated with the fans in their own language. He had seemed hesitant, even reluctant to do so when we had spoken about it. Now, in an instant, his rapport with the media looked a little more comfortable. He had entered a new phase in his adventure with England.

England were about to meet a fresh challenge too, in the shape of a friendly against Trinidad and Tobago in the Caribbean. The jaded players needed this fixture like a hole in the head, and seven England players from the Chelsea v Manchester United Champions League final were told they could stay at home. Rio Ferdinand travelled, giving us the impression that perhaps he was still the favourite for the permanent captaincy after all. But then something remarkable happened. Capello made David Beckham England's Caribbean captain. Yes, two years after Beckham had resigned that captaincy, having seen the writing on the wall, he was back wearing the skipper's armband for a 59th time.

The conspiracy theorists – and to an extent I was one of them – claimed that it was a PR stunt because England wanted the FIFA vice-president Jack Warner's vote for their World Cup 2018 bid. Warner headed CONCACAF, the football federation for North and Central America as well as the Caribbean. He was due to sit on the 24-man FIFA executive committee that would choose the host nation for World Cup 2018. Warner was the man to please, and that was part of the reason why England had agreed to play Trinidad and Tobago in the first place. Big Jack wanted a show fit for Trinidad's centenary celebrations; and it so happened he was a great Beckham fan.

'He can do for the World Cup what he did for the Olympic bid,' said Warner, though the FIFA vice-president was clearly fearful for England's World Cup 2018 chances if their campaign was left to others. 'The FA have to find the means to divert people from the belief that there is a kind of arrogance in England. Whether that is just a perceived arrogance is not important, it must be removed.' England needed to show they were listening to the man whose vote they had come to court.

The back page of the *Mail on Sunday* read: 'BECKHAM FARCE.' It summed up the mood of many of the so-called experts, and even Beckham hinted at a certain amount of bewilderment. 'It was a huge surprise,' he admitted later. 'I wasn't expecting it. When I resigned the captaincy in 2006, I never thought I would wear the captain's armband again, but it was an honour then and it is an honour now.'

The media were sceptical, but Fabio insisted, 'My work is not PR, my work is to be manager and to win, nothing more. It's possible, I think, for the FA the match is PR. For me, it's a game. It's not because of his name that Beckham is here, it's because he is fit and a very good player. The appointment is not a political move. I work for this game. The political is for the FA and they have not suggested to me that Beckham should be captain on Sunday. There was no pressure put on me. No one could do that to me. I decided as I've decided throughout my life. David was happy when I told him. There were five or six candidates to be captain. I do not know the future. It is possible Beckham will play at the 2010 World Cup. It depends if he is fit physically.'

Privately I was assured that there really hadn't been any diplomatic pressure behind the appointment of Beckham as captain for the Trinidad and Tobago match. The thinking behind the decision had been clear and simple: David was playing well, he was fit; he had more than a hundred caps to his name and a wealth of international leadership experience. It seemed only right that he should be given the chance to show what he could still do as captain. It was Fabio's decision. No one at the FA could pressure him into doing anything.

Capello's friend and old team-mate, Dino Zoff, could see why the England manager was sticking with his ageing star. He explained, 'Beckham's continued selection could be regarded as a surprise given his age, but in modern-day international football defences are so hard to beat that you need what Beckham can offer. You need a dead-ball specialist for free kicks and corners because that can make all the difference.' Capello continued the theme later that summer when he pointed out, 'Modern football is a nine-defenders-and-one-striker formation. Without flare it is impossible to score goals.'

You could score without flare against Trinidad. Jermain Defoe even did it twice without playing outstandingly well. Worryingly, despite Defoe's brace, we could only reach familiar conclusions: England, in the summer of 2008, still did not have a star striker. And what of Capello's goalkeeper dilemma? During the first half of the Caribbean match, David James came thundering out of his goal like a spooked rhino and almost broke the legs of Trinidad and Tobago striker Kenwynne Jones in a crazy attempt to reach the ball. The Capello camp was already furious that he had done something similar to give away a penalty against France. But when Fabio sent on young Joe Hart as a second-half replacement, he didn't look convincing either. Conclusion? We still didn't appear to have a world-class keeper. Gordon Banks, the greatest England goalkeeper of them all and a World Cup winner in 1966, was of the same opinion. He said, 'People ask me who my first choice would be at the moment and it is a difficult one. There are youngsters coming through but you need a lot of games behind you to start playing for England.'

The bright spot of the 3-0 victory over Trinidad and Tobago was another commanding display from Gareth Barry, who scored his first England goal, took the captain's armband for the second half and outshone Steven Gerrard in the centre of midfield. Stewart Downing also did his chances no harm by creating two goals and working well on the left. On the other side, David Beckham had started well, creating chances for Defoe and the out-of-sorts Dean Ashton. But Becks had faded as the game went on, and his set pieces were unusually poor too. David Bentley wasn't much better when he replaced Beckham for the second half, though he did play a part in Defoe's second goal.

What had Capello learned from his extended period with his players? 'That some players train better than they play,' was one of his more forthright answers. He might also have said that it still looked as though we only had half a team capable of competing with the very best. And after six months or more in the job, there weren't many other places Fabio Capello could look.

No one had ever said that managing England was easy, and Capello had been the first to acknowledge what a difficult challenge it was. He could try to turn England into a slick passing side, but privately even he had to accept that there was only so much he could do in the short time he had with his squad. Similarly, he could tell the players to live healthily, and warn Wayne Rooney not to put too much jam on his toast; but what was the point in that, when Fabio could pick up a newspaper along with the rest of us during the summer of 2008 and see photographs of Rooney smoking a cigarette on his honeymoon?

Capello was used to laying down the law, and his rules were strict. But as an England manager, his control and influence over his players was so very temporary. In the end, it was the England players themselves who had to bring about the required changes to their approach if they really wanted a greater chance of success in tournaments.

World Cup-winner Banks wasn't talking about any player in particular when he called for the sort of pride that the 'Boys of 1966' had shown, if Capello's England were ever to emulate them. Banks said, 'If they are not proud enough and not that bothered about playing for their country, we'll probably stick as we are and miss out on more tournaments. If their attitude can change, or the coach can get that attitude to change, I think they'll be OK. But it's going to be hard for us to qualify for the World Cup.'

Captain Beckham was aiming higher than mere qualification at the end of the Trinidad trip. He said, 'We want to win something. We're looking forward to getting the qualifiers started now, that's the big thing for us now.' We were all looking forward to the qualifiers. The alarming development at the time, for those expecting a brave new dawn, was that Beckham – aged 33, of LA Galaxy – might still carry England's hopes.

Perhaps such concerns would prove groundless, and it would be all right on the night. We would soon find out, because the time for talking was almost over – and so were the seemingly endless auditions for the captaincy. On his return from Trinidad, Capello announced that the fight for the armband had now come down to two candidates, though he hadn't yet decided between them. Those candidates, I learned, were Rio Ferdinand and John Terry. Ferdinand was regarded as the better player, marginally less injury-prone and more likely to be guaranteed a place in the starting line-up over the years to come. He had learned to talk a good game for the media too. For all those reasons, Ferdinand seemed to be a sensible choice as captain. But I was told that Terry had something Capello particularly admired, a force of personality and charisma that carried his team-mates along with him. It began to look as though we had come full circle, and ended up precisely where we had begun just before Capello arrived – with Terry at the helm when England stepped out on the long road to South Africa. Mercifully, we wouldn't have to try to read Capello's mind for much longer, because the captain would be announced prior to the friendly against the Czech Republic on August 20.

Meanwhile Wayne Rooney's best position was still a lingering problem and there was no obvious solution. On 13 June 2008 Capello seemed to hint that he might finally have admitted defeat in his bid to turn the Manchester United star into an out-and-out goalscorer. He described Rooney as 'a perfect second striker' (to operate behind the main man) instead of the goal machine he had hoped for at the spearhead of his attack. We thought it was the end to the saga, but within a couple of months we would find out that it wasn't.

Tactical and selection issues suddenly paled into insignificance when there was another disturbing development in the battle of wills between England General Manager Franco Baldini and Luciano Moggi, both friends of England coach Capello. On 19 June, 2008, the day after Fabio's 62nd birthday, Baldini had been about to give more evidence at the ongoing trial involving Luciano Moggi and GEA World.

Recalling what happened next, Franco alleged, 'I am tired of this situation. And now I want to tell you what happened outside the courtroom: Moggi came up to me, pointing his finger about 10 centimeters from my nose, and said, "Good day, piece of shit, be careful because like this you'll come to a sticky end." I replied, "If I were you I wouldn't aggravate your position."'

Baldini entered the courtroom and was asked by the judge exactly what a player called Davide Baiocco was supposed to have told him five years earlier. Franco alleged that Baiocco, then a player with Perugia, had told him he was being pressurised to join the GEA agency so that he could be transferred to Juventus. Baiocco's 2008 account differed, however, because he insisted that he had never told Baldini any such thing.

In the courtroom in June 2008, Franco told the judge that although he was sure about the essence of what Baiocco had said, he couldn't remember Baiocco's precise words after all the time that had elapsed. The bombshell came when Baldini bravely added that he could, however, remember the precise words relating to a far more recent alteration with Luciano Moggi, just a few minutes earlier. Franco repeated Moggi's words in court and informed the judge that a journalist from *Corriere dello Sport*, Ettore Intorcia, had heard Moggi's threat and was willing to testify.

The judge quickly decided that Moggi's alleged comments should be set aside for separate consideration, to determine whether or not further charges should be brought. It seemed that the battle of wills between Baldini and Moggi was set to intensify, and Franco was well aware of the potential consequences for him. He admitted to being concerned, as any normal human being would be; yet he was not the sort of person to back down if he knew that he was in the right. Therefore he was prepared to accept the risks that his gutsy actions carried with them, in order to try to make the world a better place for the next generation, in his own small way.

When Fabio Capello learned of what his friend Moggi was alleged to have done, it is understood that the England coach showed enough concern to ask Franco if he was all right. Baldini assured Capello that this was his own fight, not Fabio's. And so, strange as it might seem, England's 'odd couple' prepared to continue to work together as before.

First Fabio took advantage of an opportunity to break off from his seemingly endless list of England duties and return home to his native Pieris. There he would have seen his elderly mother, who had gone many months in winter and spring without seeing her boy.

Given that he regularly goes to mass, there was every chance that Fabio would have bumped into Don Pierpaolo Soranzo, his mother's priest, while he was home. Since Capello would have been trying to relax away from his professional environment, Don Paolo would have had to pick his moment carefully to remind Fabio of his own personal World Cup record, and point out that there were standards to maintain if the priest's latest congregation was to produce his second World Cup winner. The weight of expectation on Capello's shoulders was heavy enough already. The time was fast approaching when he would have to prove himself as an international manager.

With the first World Cup qualifier just around the corner, Fabio faced the press at the McDonalds Football Festival, an event held for kids at Wembley. Inevitably he was asked about the newspaper photographs of Wayne Rooney smoking on holiday. Fabio tried to play down the issue, thinking back to his own playing career. 'Many of my friends among the players smoked,' he said. 'It's part of life and, with Rooney, a part of his private life too. It really depends on whether he is smoking one, five or twenty.'

It was a clever answer, designed to take the heat out of the situation; but with so much attention paid to a healthy diet in the modern era, you can bet that he was less than impressed by Rooney's apparent lapse in self-discipline. However, it was the Manchester United star's lack of self-discipline on the field of play that had given far more cause for concern. Even in a relatively meaningless match against the USA earlier that summer, Rooney's temper had reared its ugly head.

Capello had assured the media that he would be speaking to Rooney about his temperament before the game against the Czech Republic in August, so that England fans didn't have to worry any more about the possibility of losing their best player in the biggest games. But now Fabio was treating the subject as though it were closed. 'I don't think it will be a problem,' he argued. 'Rooney is just married, he will be better now. They find a balance when they are married.' So England's salvation now lay in Coleen McLoughlin.

CHAPTER 26
SHARPENED KNIVES

THE EXPERIMENTATION WAS SUPPOSED TO BE OVER BY THE time England stepped out to face the Czech Republic in front of 70,000 fans at Wembley on 20 August 2008. This was meant to be Capello's strongest team, the one that would perform well enough to lead us all the way to South Africa in 2010. England fans looked forward to seeing the 'real deal' at last.

John Terry was named as Capello's captain, the Italian explaining that he had made his decision on the basis of the Chelsea defender's 'big personality'. Rio Ferdinand, he emphasised, was still 'important' and would be vice-captain. Terry had only been told after training the day before the match, which didn't give Ferdinand much time to get over the disappointment. And the England team to face the Czech Republic was only announced to the players just before they boarded the bus to take them to the stadium. The only certainty in the build-up to those events was the absence of Peter Crouch, because he hadn't been included in the squad at all. Croatia's manager, Slaven Bilic, had singled out Crouch as England's most significant striker when I had met him in Amsterdam a few days earlier, so he was probably delighted.

But even after everyone knew who was playing against the Czechs, a new cloud of uncertainty descended just before the match, because rumours reached the England management and some of the players that Brian Barwick, the FA chief executive who had hired Capello, was about to be axed. It was ironic, because the England squad had just done a campaign to help rid young people of knives. Barwick had been passionate about it, but he didn't seem to see the knife about to be planted between his own shoulder-blades. Capello had not been made aware of developments behind the scenes at all, and was astonished to learn on the evening of the match itself that the man who had done most to bring him to England was soon to be removed from the equation. Before the rumours could be verified, Fabio had to shut out all political developments and their potential consequences. He needed to concentrate on the game that so many fans had come to see. It was hard to quantify how much the players were distracted by the sudden instability in the England camp.

In Crouch's place, Capello had called up Emile Heskey, though even he didn't make the starting line-up. Fabio opted for Jermain Defoe, with Wayne Rooney playing behind him in a free role. The problem, when the game started, was that Rooney felt so free and came so deep at times in search of the ball that Defoe was left completely isolated up front. Some observers felt that Rooney should have been playing on the left, since there appeared to be a vacancy and he had been doing a decent job for Manchester United drifting inside from that sort of position. To everyone's surprise, however, the left-hand berth was filled by Steven Gerrard, prompting an angry outburst afterwards from Portsmouth manager Harry Redknapp, who said simply and dramatically, 'He is not a left midfielder. It is unbelievable. He has to be in the centre. We are killing Gerrard.'

Bizarrely, Capello later argued that Gerrard had not been playing on the left because he had in fact been part of a pair, with Rooney the other man, supposedly operating behind the main striker in a 4-3-2-1 formation. Perhaps our eyes had been deceiving us. But the central midfield role had certainly gone to Frank Lampard, who failed to impose himself sufficiently on the evening's events while playing alongside the unusually anonymous Gareth Barry. Out on the right, Capello was persevering with the veteran Beckham, whose inability to beat a player and reach the dead ball line meant that he resorted to swinging hopeful crosses at the Czech box from 35 or 40 yards out, regardless of the fact that there was no one of sufficient height to meet them.

In defence there was little more cheer, because Wes Brown, built more for central defence than right-back, was hopelessly wrong-footed by Czech midfielder Radek Sirl before he crossed for Milan Baros in the 22nd minute. Baros, whose best Premier League days were far behind him, nevertheless made Terry look third rate as he swiveled unchallenged and scored with relative ease, helped by a deflection off left-back Ashley Cole's foot. Even Rio Ferdinand wasn't at his best as the home side struggled to find some composure.

With England behind, news began to filter through that the FA chief executive, Barwick, would indeed be stepping down at the end of the year. Barwick had lost his power struggle with Lord Triesman, the independent FA chairman. The new structure of the organisation, with increased powers for the chief operating officer, Alex Horne, meant that Barwick was surplus to requirements. But how this development could have been made public during the match itself was almost beyond belief, even by the FA's pitiful PR standards over the years. On the pitch, Beckham's corner was met by Brown for an equaliser just before half-time, though at the time it was hard to escape the feeling that this goal might actually be bad for English football in the long run, because it strengthened the case for both players, with their glaring weaknesses, to be included in the future.

Marek Jankulovski's curling free kick deceived a clueless David James in England's goal to restore the Czech lead just three minutes after the interval, hardly a great tribute to the power of Capello's half-time team talk, or indeed the Portsmouth keeper's ability to read the flightpath from boot to net. James lost his head a little later when he came running out of his goal for no reason and found himself completely stranded, though on this occasion it didn't cost his side a goal. However, as England limped towards what looked like certain and humiliating defeat, it was the same old story – Capello didn't appear to have a top goalkeeper, he didn't seem to have a top striker (unless Michael Owen was about to explode back into the reckoning), he didn't have a right back and he didn't seem to know what to do about it.

Heskey had replaced Defoe for the second half, but didn't look dangerous. Midfielders Stewart Downing, David Bentley and Jermaine Jenas were introduced too late to make much impact. At least Fabio had put a disorientated Gerrard out of his misery and introduced Joe Cole, whose scrappy strike deep into added time papered over the widening cracks in a dreadful performance. It finished 2-2, but England fans booed and jeered Capello's team off the pitch. As preparation for the World Cup qualifiers, only a fortnight away, things couldn't have gone much worse. And Fabio suddenly looked that little bit more vulnerable now that Barwick would no longer be around to defend his appointment.

Lord Triesman sought out Capello and his assistant, Franco Baldini, five minutes after the end of the match to confirm that Barwick was on his way out. Understandably, Fabio's and Franco's heads were still full of what they had just seen out on the pitch. The FA chairman explained that he and Barwick had failed to agree on a business plan for the future, and thought it only fair to put Capello in the picture, because Fabio was about to face the television cameras for his post-match interviews.

Capello pointed out after the game, 'I am friends with Brian but I am also friends with the chairman (Lord Triesman),' as if to ward off any suggestions that his own position had been weakened. Meanwhile Fabio tried to put a positive gloss on the performance, though even he expressed concern that England looked so vulnerable to counter-attacks. As Harry Redknapp said later, 'That was one of the worst performances I have seen from an England team. How can you take positives out of that?'

Prior to the match, Capello had admitted, 'The most suprising thing about coaching England so far is that the players do not achieve the same level of performance playing for their country as they do playing for their clubs; but that it my job, to do something about that.'

So far he had failed to do anything about it, hard as he had tried. It seemed that time might even be running out on Capello, partly because he took such a savaging in the English press the next day.

'Wally without a brolly,' the *Sun* newspaper called Fabio in a new twist on his predecessor Steve McClaren's nickname. 'Wasters' they called our 'pampered stars', who they claimed had 'shamed the national game yet again.' On that same back page, they added the line that 'FA axe man who hired Capello.' The *Daily Mirror* declared, 'Same Old Shambles.' This didn't so much sound like the end of the honeymoon as the beginning of the divorce.

Even Sir Bobby Robson, the last England manager to have taken his country to a World Cup semi-final, felt compelled to deliver a withering verdict on Fabio's achievements with his adopted country up to that point. Sir Bobby, Capello's old rival in Spain, told the *Mail on Sunday*, 'Fabio is meant to lead, but the only place we've gone so far is round in circles ... The weeks of dithering about who should be England captain summed it up for me. I'm sure the intention was to give everyone a fair chance, but it made him look weak and indecisive . . .' Sir Bobby also urged Capello to 'pick vibrant wide players rather than starting with Beckham, who doesn't get forward like he used to . . .' And he finished with the following classic line on Fabio, a conclusion all the more powerful because the former England manager was not someone given to criticising others for the sake of it: 'We just need him to be Winston Churchill, not Gordon Brown.'

But you wondered whether even Sir Winston Churchill might have struggled to ensure that some of the England players did exactly as they were told. A character as forceful as Sir Alex Ferguson of Manchester United was still struggling to persuade Wayne Rooney to perform in the way he wanted. In the aftermath of the England game, Sir Alex spoke to the *News of the World* about Rooney and said, 'He shows heart, the quality of his game is there and he knows his position on the pitch. What we are seeing is someone who is expending too much energy in the wrong way. If Wayne is prepared to listen to us, we'll stop it ... Although we accept he has that selfless nature we still want him to be regarded as a goalscorer ... The fact he runs around the park, it's a mental thing. What he needs to do in terms of his own contribution is to be involved in more goals . . .'

Sven Goran Eriksson and Tord Grip had told Rooney as much

several years earlier, and Capello had told him in the spring of 2008 to 'be more selfish.' Still it hadn't made any difference, because Rooney was happy to point out in August of that year, 'I'm a team player, I am not concerned about being selfish. Everyone is talking about me scoring more goals but we (Manchester United) won the Premier League and the Champions League last season so if that happens again I'll be delighted.'

But what had England won, or even qualified for? And why couldn't Rooney see that, although football is a team game and he is a team player, the primary objective for that team is to score goals? Therefore if he was being asked to score more goals by his team managers, both at club and international level, that was what he should try to do, in exactly the way he was told. However talented he was, he needed to show that he was capable of taking precise instruction from those who could see the bigger picture.

Capello hoped Rooney would listen sooner rather than later; and many seasoned observers hoped that Fabio, in turn, would listen to widespread demands that he bring down the curtain on David Beckham's distinguished career. Prior to the opening World Cup qualifiers against Andorra and Croatia, Capello's constant reliance on the fading star from the Galaxy was starting to look a little embarrassing. Perhaps Beckham would prove his critics wrong, he had done so before. But in the mean time there were bigger problems on the horizon.

The week before England gathered to prepare for those first steps on the long road to South Africa 2010, Capello suddenly came up against the might of two of the Premier League's biggest clubs. Liverpool announced that Steven Gerrard would miss Andorra and Croatia because he needed a groin operation, which was news to Fabio. He had believed that Gerrard's niggling injury could be managed with the right amount of rest between games. If the player ended up going under knife, Capello certainly didn't think it would be in England's hour of need. However, worse was to come, because Sir Alex Ferguson promptly warned Capello that Owen Hargreaves would not be fit for international duty in September either, even though for a while he was still due to play in Manchester United's European Super Cup showdown against

Zenith St Petersburg, shortly before the England games. The tendonitis in the Hargreaves knees required rest, Sir Alex explained, just as Gerrard and Liverpool felt that England's vital games were the best moment for the player to take a break and get his groin right.

It made you wonder whether Gerrard would have been so willing to sacrifice the chance to play for England had he been given a more comfortable role against the Czech Republic a couple of weeks earlier. As it was, his decision to put his own long-term fitness first was understandable. He wasn't being given the chance to thrive in a familiar position in England's midfield, so the timing of his operation, shocking though it remained, was forgivable. As for Hargreaves, he appeared to be a pawn in the sort of power game Ferguson had seemed to relish during Sven Goran Eriksson's England reign.

The English press was not slow to pick up on the tensions that were developing. 'Angry Capello set for first battle of wills with Ferguson,' predicted the *Independent*. 'Capello on collision course with top bosses,' warned the *Daily Telegraph*, bringing Liverpool manager Rafa Benitez into the equation. 'THEY ARE SCREWIN YOU, FAB' roared the *Sun*'s back page provocatively. As preparation for the biggest test of the entire qualification phase, Croatia away on 10 September, this all appeared to be potentially disastrous. Now it seemed that Capello would require something akin to a miracle if he was to come away from Zagreb with a victory. Still, football, as we all knew, was a marvellously unpredictable sport. Only time would tell how England might perform under Capello in a truly competitive match, and whether a siege mentality might take over. Could all the problems off and on the field work in Fabio's favour when it really mattered, or would they merely serve as the precursor to more harmful blows? It was starting to look as though Fabio's reputation as an international manager – and perhaps even his long-term future – would depend upon the answer.

Capello knew the score. In the last week of August 2008, he said, 'If you win, you are the best. If you lose, you are a stupid man. If you can't take the pressure, you can't do the job.' But I was starting to hear privately that the attitude of the English media was beginning to get to Fabio. Not in any crippling sense; he just found it intensely annoying that so many reporters appeared to be just waiting for him to fail, when he had imagined that at the very least the English journalists who followed England would want him to succeed. He seemed to want to tackle the press head-on when he told them, 'The biggest problem in this country is the newspapers, not the supporters.' This was not a wise thing to say, even if many England fans thought it to be true, because he was provoking journalists further at an important time. One hack quickly offered a sarcastic reply. 'Yeah, we keep giving the ball away, don't we?'

This caused confusion because neither Capello nor his interpreter, who was still at his side just in case there was a communication breakdown, 'did' irony. 'Could you repeat the question please?' asked the interpreter. 'I said the newspapers keep giving the ball away,' repeated the journalist obligingly. 'That was a question?' The interpreter was still confused. 'No, it was a joke,' admitted the reporter. 'A joke,' repeated Fabio, although by now it almost looked as though he had never heard one. 'No, just a question,' fired back the press man mischievously. Press 1 Capello 0.

Some of the growing tension between manager and press manifested itself further when Capello was asked about David Beckham, who had recently flown to China – on the back of a poor performance for England – to be part of the Olympic ceremonial handover from Beijing to London for 2012. Goldenballs had then flown back to the USA to play a little more football, but was due to join up with England a few days later.

Capello began, 'In his last game he ran a lot and physically I think he was good, but he does travel a lot.' Then he added, 'It's interesting. When I didn't call him up for the first match there was massive uproar in the papers. Now you are saying I shouldn't call him up?'

That was precisely what many members of the press were suggesting. And it was hard to see how Capello had failed to grasp that, while most observers believed that Beckham had deserved his one 100th cap, they didn't want to see him carry on indefinitely, when it appeared that he was well past his best. Some believed that if Capello perserved with Beckham for much longer, it might even cost the Italian his job, because England would fail to find the required pace and cutting edge in attack to qualify for World Cup 2010. It was strange. The destinies of Capello and Beckham had been closely interwined for the previous two years with Real Madrid and England. And still there seemed no end to the soap opera, because Capello picked Beckham for his initial England squad to face Andorra and Croatia.

The legend everyone wanted to see picked, in order to increase our hopes of snatching a vital goal here or there, was Michael Owen, who had begun to find the net again for Newcastle. Owen and Rooney, the new dream ticket up front – that was the buzz. But Capello left Owen out because he wasn't fully fit. Not fit to start, maybe; and Jermain Defoe's superb display for Portsmouth at Everton suggested that he might have earned that right. But how could Capello leave Owen out of the equation completely? How could he not be worth so much as 15 or 20 minutes if England had drawn a blank in a big qualifier and needed ruthless experience?

Meanwhile Joleon Lescott, the Everton defender whose naïve play, I believe, had contributed to England's failure to qualify for Euro 2008, was picked. I had watched him in the flesh the day before the squad was announced, as Everton crashed 0-3 at home to Portsmouth. Lescott had not played as well as hoped. Finally, there was a newcomer to the squad, Jimmy Bullard of Fulham, a man entirely without international experience. Bullard was a chirpy character with a lovely touch, but was this really the time to try him out? The general feeling at the start of September could be summed up by one question: what the hell is going on?

If he won with these gambles, Fabio was right – he would be regarded as 'the best'. But if he lost, he was also right, because he would be regarded as 'a stupid man'. We waited for the drama to begin, and hoped it would end neither in tragedy nor farce.

But even as the England squad gathered in the build-up to the Andorra match, there was already a slightly farcical flavour to this crunch time of the year. The *Sun* splashed a story on their front page with the headline, 'ENGLAND TIL I DIET – Capello starves our footie stars.' It claimed that Fabio was forcing his players to go eight hours without eating and leaving them dizzy and nauseous as a result. Allegedly, some England stars had begun to smuggle chocolate and crisps into their room to beat the tough diet.

I was told that the reality was somewhat different – though the Italian regime didn't consider it beyond the realms of possibility that the England players were still trying to eat rubbish, since the management felt that 75 per cent (probably an exaggeration) of what they had been eating when Capello arrived had been just that – rubbish. Little by little, the new regime had tried to remove food they felt even the average man in the street ought to steer clear of – never mind athletes. The butter went walkabout; the ketchup disappeared; the mayonnaise went the same way. Even the fried chicken – apparently an England star's favourite just hours before an international – was told to cluck off. Capello and his team had tried to cure what they felt was little short of a prevailing ignorance among footballers in England of the correct diet for a top athlete. But if the England players knew what was good for them by mid-to-late 2008, they didn't always seem to care, as that summer's photograph of the cigarette in Wayne Rooney's mouth had apparently illustrated. As for the England players being starved, it just wasn't happening. I was told there was almost enough food left on the table at meal times to feed the Third World. But then again, perhaps that was because the multi-millionaires had been too busy chomping secretly on their crisps and chocolate bars, as the *Sun* had suggested.

After so many years of failure, England fans hoped for harmony between squad and manager when it mattered, the right players on the pitch – and victories. The time for talking and for getting used to each other's different cultures was over. Capello's England was about to show its true face.

CHAPTER 27
ANDORRAN ACID

THE ANDORRA MATCH WASN'T MEANT TO BE THE ACID TEST; but we all knew that England's first World Cup qualifier, to be played in Barcelona, would become seriously corrosive if England didn't take three points from it. Perhaps that was why Capello sounded a little tense on the eve of the match, as if still smarting from the recent criticism he had suffered from the likes of Portsmouth's manager, Harry Redknapp. Capello said, 'Some managers spoke about the game against the Czechs. I do not speak about club games. I'm the England manager and respect the club managers. I want them to respect me as president of the League Managers Association. Sometimes criticism is OK. Sometimes it's not OK.'

This outburst was a little surprising, given that Redknapp had already backed away from a potential conflict with Capello when the managers had come face to face at Portsmouth a few days earlier. 'Capello told me that if I can play Sylvain Distin on the left side of the Portsmouth defence, he can play Steven Gerrard on the left for England,' smiled Redknapp, as though there had been no edge to the conversation at all. Then he added, 'Look, Fabio is a great manager and if anyone can get England going again, he can.' We thought that had brought an end to the tension; apparently not.

There had also been rumblings of discontent from respected

football figures over the absence of Michael Owen from the England squad for Andorra and Croatia, especially since Capello didn't seem to have a high-scoring striker on the plane as an alternative. Owen had scored 40 goals in 89 internationals and most people thought it was madness not to put him on the bench at the very least, in case England failed to score in Barcelona against Andorra or fell behind against Croatia in Zagreb. A stubborn Fabio was adamant that he had made the right decision and said, 'I know Owen scores, but I saw his last game in the Premier League [Newcastle's defeat at Arsenal]. I checked him very well, and decided he was not fit for this game.' That explanation wasn't enough to satisfy some press men, and one piped up, 'But you played Beckham against France and he wasn't fit.'

'It was a friendly,' responded Capello, although earlier in the year he had made it perfectly clear that all his players, including Beckham, had to be fully fit if they wanted to be considered for England matches, including friendlies. 'I know what you think about Owen,' he continued, taking on his critic, 'but he has to be fit. For the next games [in October], it is possible he will be there.'

The following day, the first Saturday of September, England stepped out for action with just 17,500 spectators waiting in Barcelona's Olympic stadium. In doing so the team took its first, tentative paces on the long march towards South Africa 2010. It shouldn't have been a daunting task because their opponents were part-timers. The Andorra team boasted a council official, a gardener, an insurance salesman, a student, a tourism officer, a policeman and even a professional footballer. Ildefons Lima played for Triestina in Italy's Serie B, the club where the fearsome 'Bora' gales used to cause matches to be abandoned during Capello's childhood. By half-time in the qualifier, Capello might have had reason to wish that the Bora would hit Barcelona and cause the game against Andorra to be abandoned, because England still hadn't shown the wit to break the defence of a team ranked 186th out of 207 FIFA nations.

There had been near misses, as we might have expected with Theo Walcott picked ahead of David Beckham. Accepting a clever return pass from Wayne Rooney, Walcott had carved a dangerous path toward goal as early as the third minute, but then he hooked his shot over the bar from close range. The Arsenal star had returned the compliment for Rooney in the 16th minute with a perfect lay-off, but this time it was the Manchester United man who fired too high. These moments would have far-reaching consequences for Walcott and for England, though no one suspected it then. Instead of marvelling at Theo's speed, the fans grew anxious, and they were not alone. The longer that first half went on and the less impressive England became, the more agitated Capello grew. He gesticulated, clearly frustrated, while his team began to look ragged. Not far away from Fabio on the England bench Beckham, who had been smiling earlier, began to shake his head. It was just as well that Andorra had nothing in attack, because Joleon Lescott was partnering John Terry at the heart of defence and Glen Johnson had been selected at right back. These players were far better going forward than they were at defending, which may have been why they were picked for what was expected to be an entirely one-sided encounter. Meanwhile Ashley Cole tried to raid down Andorra's left from the other full back position, which was a relief since Stewart Downing was misfiring badly ahead of him.

England's players were wearing red shirts emblazoned with the date, '06-09-08', and the names of the nations doing battle that day. Why the kit manufacturers had been told to go to such elaborate lengths was something of a mystery, though it might have been a psychological ploy to emphasise the importance of the match, despite the lowly opposition. Those special jerseys soon threatened to become shirts of shame as dreadful passes from Terry and Downing provoked angry jeers from the 10,000 England fans present. Capello tried to clap some encouragement, but only a goal was likely to improve the increasingly dark mood in the stadium, and that goal was unlikely to come until England midfielders such as Gareth Barry and the increasingly shabby Downing began to realise something simple: there wasn't much point in sending high crosses into an area where the strikers, Jermain Defoe and Rooney, were too short to compete in the air.

When captain Terry sent another daft pass sailing straight off the pitch shortly before half time, there were loud jeers from England supporters. Why couldn't the best players in the country select a simple, sensible passing option and adopt a more patient build-up than the one they seemed so intent on trying? A wayward pass from his Chelsea colleague, Frank Lampard, provoked more booing, and Capello grimaced. The half-time whistle sparked the sort of hostile reaction that had been aimed at Steve McClaren a year earlier. The favourite old chants, 'You don't know what you're doing' and 'what a load of rubbish,' wafted around the ground in the warm night air. These were ugly scenes, and you shuddered to imagine what the final whistle might bring if England had not scored by then. Before England's players could contemplate such horrors, they had to explain to Capello why they had failed to turn their 75% share of possession into a goal. The dressing room was not a serene place, and Capello sent his team out for the second half 4 minutes early. For Defoe and Downing, the evening was already over and they were replaced by Emile Heskey and Joe Cole respectively. I had once asked the Capello camp why Joe Cole was not more strongly favoured for a place on the left of midfield, since there was no great contender for that spot. I was told that the Italian management felt Joe Cole's best work for Chelsea was on the other side of the pitch, and that they doubted he could make the same impact from the left. But Cole did his best work as a free spirit, whatever his starting position, and he was about to illustrate that.

Three minutes after the break, Lampard delivered a quality free kick, Lescott cushioned a beautiful pass with his instep, and Joe Cole popped up unmarked in the area to volley the opening goal with power and relish. Suddenly the nightmares had receded, the points looked secure, and new life had been breathed into Capello's reign. With his jacket off and his sleeves rolled up, Fabio looked satisfied at last with what he had just seen. His team was soon to hit new heights. Walcott passed to Joe Cole in the 55th minute and set in motion a move to savour. Barry threaded a neat pass to Rooney, who conjured the killer ball for Joe Cole. The little Chelsea man had never stopped moving and found his reward when he slipped England's second under the Andorra keeper, Koldo. The fact that Koldo was also Technical Director of the Andorra FA provided a further reminder of the makeshift nature of the opposition. But the moment of magic was welcome just the same, and Rooney had actually 'nutmegged' Andorra's top professional, Ildefons Lima, to give Cole his scoring pass.

England flowed more freely for a while, the fans were delighted and the overall mood in the stadium had much improved. Finally Johnson had a stage on which to show his attacking elegance. The Portsmouth man twice went close and only saw his low-drilled 'goal' in the 62nd minute disallowed because Joe Cole had drifted offside. 'God Save the Queen' rang around the stadium as the fans looked forward to more goal-scoring fun. The only hiccup came when David James and his central defence looked uncertain about how to deal with a searching Andorra free kick, though fortunately the ball veered away to safety. All looked well, but over on the touchline Capello was in a rage. He began to scream at Joe Cole and Rooney. Their crime was that they had begun to drift so deep in search of possession that Heskey sometimes looked as though he was in solitary confinement. Fabio wasn't happy. He was even less thrilled when his efforts to push Cole and Rooney further forward initially seemed to fall on deaf ears.

With 10 minutes left, David Beckham added to his ever-lengthening portfolio of England caps with a cameo appearance. The fans chanted Beckham's name and he responded with a free kick which curled straight onto the head of the advancing Terry, who didn't manage to convert it. As England failed to add to their two-goal advantage, Capello was seen puffing and gesticulating, in sharp contrast to his assistant coach, Stuart Pearce, who sat impassively beside him. A frustrated Terry rose with Andorra's number 11 – whose name, appropriately enough, was Xavier Andorra – and accidentally butted him in the back of the head, an incident doubtless unconnected to the fact that they had exchanged words a few minutes earlier. Joe Cole almost secured his hat-trick after Lescott had once again showed that he is better in attack than defence. And then, mercifully, the final whistle blew and the ordeal was over, with relieved England fans cheering wildly. Three points and a modest victory against a team 171 places below England in the rankings might not have seemed like much to shout about on the face of it; but supporters who had been through the humiliation of failing to qualify for Euro 2008 wanted results above all – and this was a result.

The hero of the hour, Joe Cole, said, 'People think it's easy in games like this but it isn't – not when the opposition have ten men behind the ball, you are playing on a sticky pitch and confidence is a bit low. This is a small step to where we want to go, but judge us after Wednesday's game against Croatia.' Cole was asked about Capello's shouting and added, 'We saw a different side to him here and you get the feeling the serious business has started.' Fabio was happy to explain why he had been yelling at Cole and Rooney: 'When we got to 2-0 we started dropping back and I wanted them to get further forward, closer to Heskey. I tried to transmit it to them but they were a bit far away.' Like Cole, Capello blamed the lack of goals on Andorra's refusal to come out and play. That prompted Andorra's coach, David Rodrigo to take a verbal swipe at Fabio after the match, as if the moral victory had been his. Rodrigo said, 'Mr Capello says he does not understand Andorra's defensive tactics. Well he can try coaching Andorra and I will try coaching England – I am sure we will beat Andorra by more than 2-0.'

The suggestion seemed to be that England's players had more potential than Capello was so far able to bring out in them. By coincidence, Steven Gerrard chose that weekend to reveal that his own talent had, in his view, been misused over the years. His absence from the England camp due to the need for a groin operation had not stopped him from venting his frustrations about being moved away from his favoured central midfield position while on international duty. He told *The Sunday Times*, 'I've paid the price for being able to do a decent job in other positions. Others don't get shunted around because they can't do it. I've played in my favourite position for England five times in 68 games. What can you do? I go into training and try to prove myself. Every manager I've worked under knows where I want to play, but they pick the formations and I play where I'm told.'

As a warm-up for the game against Croatia, the climate surrounding the Andorra match had been far from ideal. In fact, some of the criticism aimed at England had sounded decidedly acidic at times. Despite flashes of promise, the football had been pretty dire. Few people thought England had what it took to become serious contenders again in the foreseeable future. That's what made Theo Walcott's post-match analysis sound naive: 'Every single player who puts on an England shirt will be world class.' What was Theo talking about? They had barely managed to prove they were Andorra-class! But there was even more incredible optimism to come from the 19-year-old when he was gently reminded, in the nicest possible way, that England had just been terrible – with the possible exception of his good, young self and Joe Cole. 'It doesn't matter how we play as long as we get the result. If we win you can play like that ... get to the World Cup final, we'll win, it doesn't matter, it's all about getting the victory, that's the main thing.'

Get to the World Cup final? England were going to be very lucky if they made it to the tournament at all. The cauldron of Zagreb was going to be a stroll in the park if you were prepared to listen to Theo's view. 'I'm buzzing, I'm flying, I'm looking forward to it,' he chirped. 'I just can't wait for the Croatia game on Wednesday. The confidence is there.'

Poor lad, we thought, could anyone's confidence be more misplaced? It seemed a fairly safe bet that Capello wouldn't even pick Walcott for Croatia. He would start with the experience of Beckham instead. That was why Goldenballs had been on the bench in Barcelona, wasn't it? To rest his ageing limbs so that he could be trundled out for set-pieces in Zagreb; so that England could stagnate, cling to their not-so-glorious past and maybe even steal a draw or lose with honour, with the score-line at least respectable. Why else had Fabio persisted with Beckham through all those mind-numbing friendly games, if the man from the Galaxy wasn't going to feature heavily when it really mattered? So Theo could talk all he liked but he would remain a spectator for most of the game in Croatia, along with the rest of us...or that's how it seemed.

CHAPTER 28
REVENGE IS SERVED

'I PREFER TO PLAY AWAY,' SAID FABIO CAPELLO IN THE BUILD-UP to England's Croatian crunch. He hadn't seemed so keen at the start of the year, when it came to arranging the month and venue for England's first match against Croatia. The decision was made in a face-to-face meeting between Fabio and his opposite number, Slaven Bilic in Zagreb on the 14th of January.

I bumped into a relaxed Bilic at the Amsterdam Hilton in early August 2008. And although he considered it a little early in the season to be talking about September's big international, he invited me to sit down with him anyway in the hotel's outdoor, terraced restaurant. A few yards behind us, Theo Walcott was standing in the hotel lobby, already preparing himself mentally for Arsenal's game against Seville in the Amsterdam Tournament that night. Bilic wasn't there to watch Walcott, though. He was in town to check on the progress of a new recruit to the Croatia cause, an Argentina-born striker called Dario Cvitanic. Inevitably we couldn't stay off the subject of Croatia v England for long; and Bilic was happy to tell me the story of how England had ended up having to play the first match in Zagreb.

It was a deal that didn't seem to favour England, looking at it objectively from the outside. Croatia had never lost at home competitively; and they had won the vast majority of their matches

309

in Zagreb with ease. Slaven appeared to agree that he had outwitted Fabio in this key meeting, because he revealed, 'When I met Capello to discuss the fixtures it only took us five minutes to decide. He wanted the first match to be at Wembley in September, and I wanted Zagreb in October. So I gave him September and he gave me Zagreb. We are favourites at home, we are confident, we are a better team now than the one that beat England at Wembley late last year, and maybe we can open up a points gap before we have to go to Wembley again.'

So why had Capello given Bilic the luxury of Zagreb, when Croatia had never once slipped up there in a competitive football match? Slaven replied, 'He wanted September because England's players will have played Champions League games by October and they will not be so fresh. I wanted October for that same reason, but we had to compromise somewhere.' Compromise they did; but Capello had lost Wembley as the vital first venue.

Some would say that Fabio was playing a clever game, because if you regarded the crunch fixtures against Croatia like a European tie, with one match at home and one away, most managers would say they preferred the first game away and the truly decisive, second encounter on home soil. 'I'm not like that,' said Bilic. 'I always like to play at home first, because the opposition don't try as hard, knowing they still have the second match to put things right. And I don't mind playing away in the last match, because Croatia play well away.' England had learned that to their cost at Wembley the previous November, when Bilic and his team had broken English hearts and destroyed Steve McClaren's dream of qualification for Euro 2008. Their last-gasp 3-2 victory had sparked wild celebrations among the Croatia players, even though they had already qualified for Euro 2008 before that match. Now Bilic seemed to be suggesting that England might not try so hard in this first World Cup qualifier in Zagreb, because subconsciously they would be aware that they were going to get another chance to put things right at Wembley later in the qualification process.

However, Bilic was wrong. Behind the scenes, Fabio Capello had discussed England's predicament with his trusted advisor, Franco Baldini. They decided it would be foolish to set up their team to try to take a draw in Zagreb, then wait an anxious year to play the Croatians again in what might become a high-pressure, winner-takes-all showdown between the group's two best teams at Wembley. No, Fabio concluded, there was only one thing for it: England were going to go for a win straight away. Against all odds, against everything their form had told the world, Capello's men were going to attack Croatia and try to pierce their aura of invincibility in their own back yard.

It was a gamble, but perhaps understandable given what had gone before. Fabio's team had been so awful against the Czech Republic at Wembley in August that home advantage didn't seem to exist for England. Capello's decision to attack would backfire disastrously if England were left open defensively; and that war-hardened, fiercely patriotic Croatian crowd could become a twelfth man for the home side if they smelt vulnerability in the opposition. So England would attack, but not recklessly. Like most Capello sides, they would have to press hard when the opposition had the ball, in order to maintain the right balance between ambition and self-protection. The opening exchanges might determine whether England were up to this demanding job, or whether Capello was committing tactical suicide.

The Maksimir stadium was not going to be a venue for faint hearts, so when Capello said, 'I prefer to play away,' the remark naturally commanded instant headlines. What sort of bluff was this? Or perhaps it was a fair reflection of his feelings for England's spiritual home of football? Sure enough, the remark was interpreted in some sections of the media as 'I don't like Wembley.' This wasn't quite what the FA wanted to hear after spending a cool £800 million on their new stadium.

Fabio, of course, wasn't thinking about the FA. He was sending a strong, defiant message to his own players and to Slaven Bilic. Maybe the Croatian coach hadn't got the best of that deal the previous winter after all. Suddenly Capello was giving the impression that he was where he wanted to be, when he wanted to be. Defiantly, Fabio insisted that England would be ready for the challenge, even though Croatia's unbeaten run in Zagreb stretched to 37 matches.

Capello didn't try to hide the fact that England would be bold and play to win. It was a positive war-cry, feisty and potentially unnerving. And Fabio enjoyed an advantage, because few believed him. No one had seen enough quality from England during Capello's reign to have any faith that his team might be ready to overcome this, the toughest of obstacles on the road to qualification for South Africa 2010. As for Slaven Bilic, he seemed pretty confident before the match, as he had been in Amsterdam, that Croatia were the real deal. Fifth in the world and still improving, always playing to their full potential because of their unique team spirit – that was the way Bilic liked to describe his team. And he couldn't resist a little jibe about England. In Amsterdam he had told me that Capello's England would 'play the way his teams always play'. He had been reluctant to explain exactly what he meant by that remark, but you had the feeling that Bilic saw Fabio's England as predictable and cautious in character. He had talked of Fabio's habit of including a holding midfielder in most of his teams throughout his managerial career. Now he launched a new verbal volley, expressing his disbelief at how England had failed to 'click' as a team, even when all their most talented stars were fit. There was something wrong, he claimed, and few people would have disagreed with him in those hours before the big match. We waited to hear how England would line up, and feared the worst, assuming that Fabio would once again leave his team short of identity, trapped somewhere between the past and the future. Capello's love affair with David Beckham showed no sign of dying; and in the build-up to the Croatia game, Goldenballs had argued that Zagreb was a place for experience. It would have been a compelling argument if England were going to aim for a draw, as most of us thought Capello still would.

But when that team news filtered through from the bowels of the intimidating Maksimir Stadium, we were astonished to learn that the natural passage of time had finally been acknowledged, and that Walcott was in for the big one. Meanwhile there was no obvious holding midfielder of the kind Bilic had anticipated, because Frank Lampard and Gareth Barry both liked to attack, even if the Villa man might be prepared to sit back more often than his colleague.

With Walcott raiding down the right and Joe Cole cutting in from the left, England's attacking partnership of Emile Heskey and Wayne Rooney could look forward to some decent service. But there seemed to be precious little protection for the back four from the threat of Croatian attacks. And worryingly there was no one to mark the dangerous Luka Modric, the Tottenham playmaker who was widely expected to dash England's hopes. At least Rio Ferdinand was back to partner John Terry in the centre of defence, and Wes Brown was picked ahead of Glen Johnson at right back, the lesser of two evils in the eyes of many. Ashley Cole was an experienced figure at left-back, and with David James in goal you hoped that the defence would hold firm in front of him.

The Croatian fans packed the Maksimir long before kick-off, their patriotism both deafening and visual. One section showed off a national flag sporting the words 'Vukovar 1991,' a reference to the way the city proudly braved a Serbian siege for one painful month after another. Football wasn't the same as war to these people – but it provided the latest vehicle for a national pride that was more evident here than perhaps anywhere else in the world.

In the English dressing room, Fabio Capello gathered his players together and demanded that they demonstrate some national pride of their own. 'You are some of the best players in the world,' he told them. 'Now is the time to show it.' He looked them in the eyes, summoning their true character at last. It was a moment reminiscent of the famous 'Coglioni Challenge' to his AC Milan stars prior to the 1994 Champions League final. Capello had told me that when he looked into the eyes of his players he knew what they needed to hear from their boss. What Fabio saw this time around was not the fear or doubt he had sometimes seen in his England players before previous matches. This time he saw hunger and determination. This time they were ready to show how good they were.

When the team ran out, all eyes were on Theo Walcott. The fact that he was keeping out a living legend must have added to the pressure as we waited for kick-off. The television cameras settled for a moment on David Beckham, sitting on the bench with a slightly glum expression on his handsome face. When you were analysing a superstar's career, there was always a number to play with. It wasn't enough that he had already defied the odds by going well beyond the 99 caps he had been stuck on when Capello took over from Steve McClaren. Now we were told he was stuck on 99 starts for England, so a new little sideshow was born. Whether Beckham ever started for England again, we suspected, might just depend on how Walcott performed in the next hour or so. And that was why Beckham's pre-match advice to Theo – to be more selfish – was such an admirable gesture.

The opening signs for England, playing all in white, were not good, though. The crowd jeered as Wayne Rooney lost control of the ball; then it roared with delight as Modric began to run the show. Capello, his arms folded, looked tense in his dark suit. But suddenly there was hope when Lampard released Walcott down the right with a superb pass, leaving the Arsenal man in all the space he needed to do some serious damage. What would Theo do with this glorious opportunity? He clipped the ball clumsily against his standing leg, and the move died. Was he going to 'choke' under such pressure? If he was, it might quickly cost England dearly. David James spilled a corner at the other end, only for Vedran Corluka to fire into the side-netting. Lampard's range-finder began to fail too, and he booted the ball out while trying to serve Walcott again. Rooney seemed to be playing too deep for the second time in four days, and Terry was forced to make a desperate block after Joe Cole's mistake. These were not reassuring moments.

Gradually, however, the tide began to turn and England found some of the confidence that had eluded them for so many months. Heskey's physical presence up front had something to do with it, and he appeared to be pulled down in the penalty area by Josep Simunic after 23 minutes. Capello threw his arms in the air in protest; but the Slovakian referee, Lubos Michel, remained unimpressed. Still England attacked, and three minutes later Rio Ferdinand raced forward to begin a promising move by passing to Rooney. The Manchester United star's attempt to maintain the momentum was less than perfect; but it caused enough panic in the Croatian defence for Danijel Pranjic to hoof the ball straight into Robert Kovac's back. Almost miraculously, the ricochet landed at the feet of Walcott, and all of England held its breath. Joe Cole waited unmarked in the middle. However, Theo decided not to cross at all, and took Beckham's advice to be a little more selfish instead. It seemed that no one was expecting the low shot he drilled towards goal, least of all the Croatian goalkeeper Stipe Pletikosa. A split second later the ball was nestling in the far corner of Pletikosa's net, Walcott had turned away, his arms outstretched, and a baffled Joe Cole looked almost too shocked to celebrate on his team-mate's behalf. Fabio Capello hardly reacted either, not even allowing himself a smile on the touchline. He quietly mouthed 'goal', and clapped about as enthusiastically as most of us would applaud if we had just seen a player make an efficient tackle. By far the most memorable reaction came from Brian Barwick and Lord Triesman, who leapt to their feet in the posh seats and shared their unrestrained joy at England's opener. It was an extraordinary and strangely moving sight, Barwick celebrating with the man who had effectively brought the curtain down on his FA career. But it told you something about Barwick; he loved England and football in general, so much so that his passion in this thrilling moment had conquered any sense of wounded pride. And Barwick had every right to be pleased, because his own leading role in the appointment of Capello was bearing fruit at last. For the first time, it seemed that Fabio's success in club football really could translate onto the international stage.

Just a minute later Walcott almost scored again from a similar position, but Croatia's shell-shocked players quickly pulled themselves together and poured forward. James was stranded again as Mladen Petric unleashed a mighty volley, bravely blocked by Brown. England survived, but the difference in this match was that they had ways of relieving the pressure by showing invention in attack. Theo was still turning it on with drag-backs and accurate passing, and Croatia didn't seem to know how to deal with him. Simunic resorted to a fierce body-check as the boy from Berkshire raced forward again. The foul was made much worse by the fact that Walcott had already delivered a superb pass to Rooney. For his desperate measure the Croatian received a yellow card, though to a cynic it would have seemed a price worth paying, because Walcott suddenly looked down and out. A worried Capello demanded to know from his staff if an immediate change was necessary, or whether it was worth waiting to see if Theo could recover, with only five minutes left before half-time. Walcott had been lifted onto a golf buggy by now, and was driven off the pitch for swift assessment. His senses soon returned and he was allowed to keep battling. Meanwhile England fans sang 'God Save the Queen' until the half time whistle blew. Walking toward the dressing rooms, Bilic was visibly scratching his head as if still wondering what had hit his team. These were good signs for England. Capello's men had only managed one shot on target, but what did that matter when it had resulted in the only goal?

Another nail should have been hammered into the Croatian coffin just four minutes after the break, when the villainous Simunic fouled Rooney on the edge of the area. Somehow he avoided a second yellow card and the red that would automatically have followed. Lampard's free kick, hard and low, prompted a lively save from the keeper; but it wasn't the outcome England deserved. Justice was better served a few short minutes later, however, when Robert Kovac almost took Joe Cole's head off with a leading elbow. The aerial challenge seemed to leave the Chelsea star in a state of shock. He rose for a moment and walked a few paces before he felt the blood pouring past his ear from a huge gash on the side of his head. Unsurprisingly, he collapsed at that point and waited for treatment, though the way he suddenly succumbed to his injury probably made it easier for referee Michels to show Kovac what he deserved – a straight red card. Cole, still losing a lot of blood, held a tissue to his head to stem the flow as he became England's latest casualty to be placed on the golf buggy. Jermaine Jenas readied himself for action.

Jenas could replace Cole, but Croatia were still a man short and it didn't take long for cracks to show. In the 59th minute, Capello witnessed the sort of moment that all managers dream of – a fluent passing movement rounded off with a killer finish. Heskey benefited first at the sharp end, and showed superb control to set up Rooney. The man from Croxteth could have shot, but showed enough composure and awareness to thread a sweet pass to

Walcott, unmarked again on the right. Two quick touches with the outside of Theo's right boot left the ball just where he wanted it. His diagonal strike was cleaner and more powerful than the first. It proved unstoppable and England were two goals ahead. This was better than anyone outside the England camp had dared to imagine. Capello, his arms still folded, remained virtually expressionless, though there might just have been the hint of a grin to betray the fact that his dream of coaching England back to prominence was showing the first signs of coming true. As the small but merry band of travelling fans celebrated wildly, Croatian supporters fell silent. The next sounds some of them made were monkey noises aimed at the influential Heskey, who had earned himself a booking for a clumsy foul. The Croatian FA were later fined £14,920 for the racist behaviour of the ignorant minority among their following.

'You're not singing any more' yelled the England fans to rub in the fact that a first ever defeat in Zagreb looked more than likely for the hosts. And after 63 minutes, the dream became indisputable reality. Ashley Cole showed the very best of his feisty nature when he refused to let Croatia bring the ball out of defence, timing his intervention superbly. Jenas was suddenly bursting down the left, and looked up in time to pick out Rooney as he advanced into the area. The cross from Jenas was pure perfection, angled and weighted off the outside of his boot with mathematical precision. Wayne just had to find the right connection with his instep, which he managed with aplomb. Three-nil and, judging by the smile on his face, Rooney's revenge tasted sweet. His goal was no more than 'Wazza' deserved for a sparkling display which had seen him feed off Heskey and support him too, just as Capello had demanded. For his part, Rooney had shown that he didn't necessarily have to stick to the Wigan striker like glue on the front line in order to torment the opposing defence; but at the same time he had never gone too deep for too long in search of the ball. Croatia simply couldn't cope with a fully fit Rooney's relentless movement in and out of the danger areas; and you could argue that both Wayne and Fabio had been vindicated in their debate about what constituted Rooney's best position and correct energy expenditure as England went forward.

It was virtually game over and there was almost half an hour still left on the clock. With a three-goal advantage, all England had to do was knock the ball about among themselves, which they did in a manner so nonchalant that English cries of 'ole' rang around an otherwise-silent Maksimir. Ten, twenty, thirty passes were strung together before Ashley Cole flashed a shot across the Croatian goal. And I couldn't help but think back to the opening match of Capello's England career, against Switzerland at Wembley, when Fabio had urged his team to pass like that and soon deduced with horror that they were simply unable to follow such simple instructions at the time.

Had Capello transformed England in the space of ten days away together? Before that, a series of pitiful performances had left some people vowing never to watch England play football again. Had Fabio suddenly stumbled across the right formula in the nick of time, aided by more than a week without interruption? It wasn't quite that dramatic, I was told soon afterwards. The ten days away had certainly been a key factor in this extraordinary success; but the performance had been the product of many difficult months, during which Fabio had spent a few days here and another few there, trying to teach England's players a new way of thinking and playing, free from fear. Now they had listened, and they understood what it felt like to be truly confident in their ability at international level. Perhaps they wouldn't prove to be world-beaters; no one could predict the future. But it was their duty to themselves and to the talent they possessed to prove that they were better than most rivals; and in these extraordinary moments on the night of 10 September, 2008, spraying the ball around like champions, the players did just that.

In the 76th minute Croatia's humiliation should really have been complete, because Lampard danced his way through their defence with ease before rifling what we all thought was England's fourth. Absurdly, the referee penalised Heskey for the slightest and most irrelevant of contacts with a Croatian defender off the ball. Yet he didn't penalise Darijo Srna for a high kick to John Terry's head, before the same player broke clear and delivered a scoring pass to Croatian substitute Mario Mandzukic. There was little

James could do to prevent the goal, with Terry still grounded nearer the half way line. Capello raged at the referee in protest, and for a few minutes you wondered whether a glorious night was going to be ruined by an outrageous comeback. Many of the home supporters had already given up and were filling the aisles in droves as they headed for the Maksimir exits. 'We can see you sneaking out' sang the England supporters happily. But there was soon more thrilling entertainment on the pitch. The rampant Rooney showed impossible skill to bring a wild pass under instant control; and the through-ball he conjured for Walcott, almost in the same, graceful movement, was breathtaking. Now it was all down to Theo, who was clear and on a hat-trick. The problem was that he had moved onto his weaker left foot, and his eyes had shown the keeper where he was going to put his shot. Yet it made no difference, because by now Walcott could do no wrong, and he found a way past Pletikosa anyway. England's newest superstar was soon sliding along on his knees in celebration. It was the first competitive hat-trick from an England player since Michael Owen's three goals in Munich helped England to a 5-1 win over Germany in 2001. That was the night Sven Goran Eriksson had become a managerial god, at least for a while. Suddenly Capello was hitting similar heights, ironically having ignored the clamour for Owen's return. At last, it seemed, England might be on the verge of something really big, if only this confidence could endure. On the touchline, Fabio finally allowed himself to punch the air in celebration.

Up in the stands, Barwick and Triesman smiled as though they wanted each other's babies. What a weird and wonderful night this was turning into; there was no end to the fun. So it didn't matter that Walcott was substituted for Beckham with 6 minutes left on the clock, because the changing of the guard had effectively taken place already. And Beckham seemed to accept that his time had come to step aside, from the starting 11 at least, because he was laughing as Walcott came to greet him. The superstar who had told Walcott to be more selfish said something to the youngster before they passed each other. It was hard for an amateur lip-reader to make it out exactly; but the two, light-hearted words Beckham chose appeared to be 'greedy f****er.' Delivered with a warm smile, it was easy to see that Beckham's congratulations were genuine, whatever colourful form they took, and he was truly pleased for the teenager.

With his 105th cap safely in the bag, Beckham could afford to see the funny side. As for Walcott, he would probably have laughed at anything, because he was in football dreamland. He had only known he was going to play two hours before kick-off. Now the scrawny teenager was a national hero. And what about Capello? When had he decided that Walcott was going to start the big one? I was given the answer a couple of days later, and the truth was amusing. It had taken 20 minutes of the match against Andorra for Fabio to make up his mind. Theo's explosive energy in Barcelona was so impressive that he knew there and then that the boy could be a match-winner in Zagreb. And so, for all the speculation there had been about Beckham's likely return to the starting line-up in time for the Croatia Crunch, he had effectively been ruled out before the first quarter of the opening qualifier against Andorra had even been completed.

As the clock ran down in Zagreb, Joe Cole returned to the dug-out, suited and booted with a scar down the side of the head that made him look as though he had been treated to a lateral lobotomy. Somehow little Joe had convinced the doctors that he was well enough to avert an overnight stay in hospital. He didn't want to miss an evening like this, and when he shook hands with Capello he knew the job was done. England were back – battle-scarred and glorious. When the final whistle blew it was almost an act of mercy, because Wayne Rooney had been rubbing it in with a spot of ball-juggling during the dying minutes. Under these painful circumstances, Bilic was very sporting as he smiled and congratulated the England manager. Fabio knew that Slaven would go away, try to work out what happened, and see if he could come up with a way to beat England at Wembley the following year, as he had done the previous year. However, the circumstances seemed so different; this time England had drawn first blood and seized the initiative in their World Cup group; this time they had a manager the players looked up to. And Croatia's players knew that their own coach had been well and truly outwitted. I thought back to

Amsterdam. Bilic had been so pleased to be able to play England in Croatia first. He wasn't pleased any more.

Fabio knew it was still a long way to South Africa; but that didn't mean he was incapable of savouring this particular moment of triumph. Long after the final whistle, he waved at the ecstatic England fans still locked inside the stadium, and allowed himself a humble smile. Then he told reporters, 'The score is incredible but the performance was very good. The secret is that we had ten days together – I always said step by step. At last we played like we train, and this is the start. Tonight we played with a lot of confidence and we played without fear. We made a little mistake with their goal but we played with a lot of courage. As for Theo, I'm very happy for him. He is one of the most important young players in England and I hope he doesn't get injured because he is so fast and so dangerous. When I chose Theo, I chose well! I'm happy that I chose Theo but it was the whole team that played well.'

Walcott was quick to agree, saying, 'There were eleven stars out there and it shows how strong and together we are. It has been a long ten days but the football was brilliant and I'm just grateful that Mr Capello has given me an opportunity. My dad was here tonight and I'm so pleased because he would have died if he hadn't seen it.' Theo's father Don admitted, 'I had tears in my eyes. I was sitting in among all the Croatia supporters so I had to be careful, but I was so proud. I wouldn't have missed it for the world. David Beckham has been great with Theo – he's an absolute gentleman. I've had a feeling for a while that something big might be around the corner.'

Wayne Rooney had been planning something big ever since the World Cup qualifying draw was made at the end of the previous year. It had offered the prospect of making amends for 21 November, 2007, the night England's Euro 2008 qualification dreams were destroyed at Wembley. 'It was because of them and because of our own mistakes that we didn't qualify and that hurt,' Rooney explained. 'Tonight there was a bit of revenge in mind for us and it was a great performance. We were all looking forward to the game after their over-the-top celebrations at Wembley when they knocked us out. We wanted revenge. We remembered that day and victory here has softened the blow.' As for his ball-juggling, he confessed, 'I don't like to disrespect teams but their celebrations were still in the back of my mind when I did that.'

Just as AC Milan were running on anger the night they won the Champions League by scoring four goals to silence Johan Cruyff's Barcelona in Athens, 1994, so England had been fuelled by a lingering grudge in Zagreb as they put four past Slaven Bilic's Croatia in 2008. But you don't beat the fifth-best team in international football on emotion alone. And Frank Lampard described what those who worked with Capello at AC Milan had learned a long time ago. Lampard said, 'The manager has instilled a team ethic, that's where his big success has come in the past. He's worked with fantastic players, but he is very strong on the team thing and there wasn't a single player playing for himself out there. We're building as a team because we were at a low point after not qualifying for the Euros. We haven't performed for the past two years and now it's about regaining confidence. We all want to perform as part of a team, not as individuals.'

The trademark Capello message had finally hit home, loud and clear – the same message for which he had so nearly sacrificed his own playing career, when some of the Juventus superstars of 1970 had spent too much time dribbling and not enough time thinking of their teammates. For the best part of 40 years Fabio had understood that football is a team game. England's players knew it deep down too, though they hadn't always played that way. Now they had grasped the reality of what could be achieved when obvious words were backed up by collective action. And they liked that victorious feeling, which stemmed from Capello's self-professed 'winning mentality.' Many of us had doubted how much substance lay behind Capello's catch-phrase, largely because Fabio had not won a Champions League since 1994. Suddenly we realised there was still something behind the soundbite after all, and it didn't even seem so fanciful to start dreaming of World Cup glory again. Almost insanely, Theo Walcott had dared to picture England playing in a World Cup final, even after the rubbish the team had produced against lowly Andorra. But following the glory of Zagreb, England fans were prepared to entertain Theo's outrageous dream too. The only question now was this: why did

Theo want to imagine England playing badly in a World Cup final?

Fabio Capello and Franco Baldini were keeping their feet on the ground, although they did choose to drink the champagne given to them by the pilot of their Luton-bound plane, a few short hours after England's victory in Croatia. They did so not because they were euphoric; rather due to a sense that it would have been rude not to accept. And there was plenty more waiting in England to massage their egos, should such massage have been required. As they landed, the following day's papers were already being rushed out onto the streets. Of course, there was only one hero on the front and back pages, and it wasn't Capello. 'Trio Walcott' roared the *Sun*'s front page, while the *Mirror*'s back page had 'Theo the Lion.' The *Daily Mail* screamed 'Boy Wonder!' and on it went. But Fabio did receive plenty of praise inside those papers. Harry Redknapp, the Portsmouth manager who had criticised the way Capello had allegedly misused Gerrard against the Czechs, admitted inside the *Sun* that Fabio had 'breathed new life back into the Golden Generation.' Elsewhere after a few days' reflection, Piers Morgan, the *Mail on Sunday*'s star sportswriter, used his weekend column to apologise to Capello for having doubted him. 'Mi dispiace,' he wrote in grovelling Italian.

Though Fabio wasn't displeased to hear that public opinion had shifted so dramatically, the truth was that he didn't care what the papers or their experts were writing – as long as the press seemed prepared to let him do his job at last, without denting morale. Fabio had lived through the ups and downs of professional football for the best part of half a century, and he wasn't about to allow himself to be carried away by one result. The day after his latest amazing triumph, he was already thinking about the next match – against Kazakhstan on 11 October. Capello didn't want the Croatia result to become his calling card, as England's 5-1 victory over Germany in Munich had remained Sven Goran Eriksson's calling card, right up until the day of the Swede's departure from his managerial post some five years later.

Fabio wanted to do even better than Eriksson and his respectable but uninspiring World Cup quarter-final place. Capello still dreamed of taking England all the way. And if there really was a chance of making that dream come true, it was already time to look ahead. There was no room for prolonged self-congratulation because that could lead to complacency. England needed to stay focused now that they were on the right road for South Africa at last. The journey would be long and it had only just begun; it was important to maintain momentum. Even so, beyond the sound common sense and floorless managerial logic, there was no getting away from it: Fabio Capello's England had been more than good in Croatia – they were fantastic. Whatever happened next, no one could ever forget the night it all came together and English football fans fell back in love with their national team.

CHAPTER 29
LIONS FOR AFRICA

If England's rout of Croatia was about as handsome as football gets, we were soon reminded of the sport's uglier side. Just 10 days after the miracle of Croatia, Fabio Capello's assistant, Franco Baldini was back in Italy; and his feud with Capello's friend, Luciano Moggi, was in the spotlight yet again. Moggi's alleged threat to Baldini, the England General Manager, just outside a courtroom back in June, was now officially entered in the register of the Rome Magistrate Luca Palamara, who was also prosecuting in the GEA case. It meant that, on top of the original charges he faced, Moggi now had to answer for allegedly threatening Baldini, and also for allegedly slandering an Italian *Carabinieri* policeman called Attilio Auricchio. It seemed that Moggi would have plenty to occupy his time while he continued to serve out his five-year ban from football.

As for Baldini, he was soon busy again with his England duties, because there was an ideal opportunity for the Capello camp to consolidate upon their success in Croatia with an easy-looking home qualifier against Kazakhstan on 11 October. The build-up to the Kazakhstan game, however, was dominated by one question – whether or not a fit-again Michael Owen would make it back into Capello's England squad. Fate seemed to be conspiring against Owen, England's most prolific striker of modern times. Capello had decided to fly up to Newcastle to see Owen lead the Geordie line against Blackburn. But at the last moment fog meant that Fabio's flight was delayed and he cancelled the trip, realising that he wouldn't have reached St James' Park in time. You wondered whether the Italian would take the trouble to study Owen again. Doubts were further raised when Fabio subsequently warned reporters that Owen's three goals in recent matches for his club – five for the season so far – were not necessarily going to count in his favour.

In truth, Capello just didn't fancy Owen all that much, though he sent Baldini to watch Everton play Newcastle on the Sunday of the squad announcement. Unfortunately for Owen, he was not able to do anything memorable at Goodison Park, and his immediate fate was sealed. Michael was out, and David Bentley also found himself excluded from the Kazakhstan squad at the expense of Shaun Wright-Phillips. Only time would tell whether the press had jumped the gun with their Owen obituaries – as they had with their Beckham obituaries back in February – or whether this really was the end. Whatever happened, he would always be remembered for his virtuoso goal against Argentina at the 1998 World Cup in France.

Meanwhile Steven Gerrard's future also looked uncertain, despite his return to the England fold following his groin operation. The Liverpool captain's recent lament about not being able to play in his favourite, central midfield position for England, had been noted by the England management. However, Gerrard's claim that he had played in his best role just five times in 68 England appearances raised an eyebrow or two in Soho Square. Surely he had been given that platform in at least a quarter, if not a third of his internationals? The Italians who held the key to Gerrard's England future were of the opinion that his lacklustre performances for his country were more to do with confidence, or a lack of it, than positioning. After all, wasn't he pretty much the same player, wherever he was asked to start in England's midfield? Wasn't he always given the license to roam, to cut in from any wider berth as he attacked? What Capello required from Gerrard was more tactical awareness of his position when England didn't have the ball. If there was a gap to plug in England's defensive midfield line once the ball was lost, 'Stevie G' had to show he could quickly plug that gap and press up on the right opponent before the enemy poured through. So far he had been less than convincing defensively.

Yet Capello remained determined to try to find a solution to the age-old dilemma of how to play Gerrard in the same team as Frank Lampard. Unfortunately, when England played Kazakhstan in a Wembley stadium packed to its 90,000 capacity, Gerrard flopped again. He seemed unable to thrive alongside Lampard despite the presence of Gareth Barry as anchor in a three-man midfield. Ahead of them the story was no more encouraging in a frustrating first half. Fans who had flocked to marvel at Theo Walcott saw only the occasional glimmer of the brilliance that had stolen the show in Zagreb. Those of us who had watched Walcott play for Arsenal at Sunderland a week earlier knew he had gone off the boil; and the Capello camp had been warned of this temporary loss of form. Now he was struggling again; while on the other side of Emile Heskey, Wayne Rooney was also failing to strike up the same sort of rapport with the big man as he had enjoyed in Croatia. This 4-3-3, even against such lowly opposition as Kazakhstan, just wasn't working.

None of us expected the first 45 minutes of this vital World Cup qualifier to be memorable for the plucky performance of a young Kazakhstan player called Tanat Nusserbayev. He almost scored in the 21st minute for a team ranked 131 on the FIFA lists. Nusserbayev wasn't finished, because his persistence soon troubled Matthew Upson, playing in place of the injured John Terry. A tentative Upson attempted an ill-advised back pass to David James and chaos ensued. Somehow the Kazakhs squandered their latest opportunity to go ahead, but Capello's men were living dangerously. And Rio Ferdinand's captaincy in Terry's absence didn't seem to be giving England the urgency, energy or even the basic confidence that was required.

Perhaps Fabio had seen this frustration coming even before the game had begun, because he had begged the England supporters not to boo their team if the deadlock wasn't broken in the first twenty minutes. So the England fans waited until the half time whistle blew, with the score still 0-0, and then let the players and coach have it with both barrels. As the jeers rang out and Capello and his men retreated down the tunnel, the euphoria of Zagreb was already history. Forty-five minutes remained in which to avoid humiliation and secure three points. If they could be secured, those points would be every bit as important as the win earned in Croatia the previous month. But the pressure was on, and worryingly England had slipped up in this kind of situation before. They had stuttered to an embarrassing goalless draw against Macedonia in their Euro 2008 qualification campaign, and ultimately it had cost them dearly. Fabio therefore had his work cut out in the dressing room. He later admitted that he had 'not been happy with the first forty-five minutes.' Neither was anyone else, and it almost got much worse.

Gerrard was nowhere to be seen as Sabrykhan Ibrayev burst down the Kazakh's right flank and crossed for Sergey Ostapenko to set up Nusserbayev. Somehow the 20-year-old blew his big chance by firing too high and Capello's men breathed a sigh of relief. Fearful fans looked for signs of encouragement. At least the shape of the England team had become more familiar. This proved that, unlike some of his predecessors, Capello had a 'Plan B' when the initial plan went wrong. Gareth Barry had been sacrificed at half time, and Shaun Wright-Phillips sent on to create a 4-4-2 formation, with Walcott on the other flank. The players soon looked more comfortable. Wright-Phillips won a corner on the left and Lampard conjured some dead-ball class with a looping corner towards the far post. Ferdinand rose unchallenged to show that he could lead from the front after all, and headed home with aplomb. After 51 minutes and seven seconds England were finally off the hook. A delighted Fabio was able to give a double 'thumbs up'.

Kazakhstan were only a goal behind and far from subdued. Nusserbayev stung James' fingers with a blistering drive, and the spirit of the underdogs shone just as brightly as before. Luckily for England, Lampard had the chance to deliver a second telling set piece, a curling free kick after 64 minutes. Under pressure from the shaven-headed Rooney, Kuchma Alexandr headed into his own net. 'Franky' Lampard had done it again; and it was easy to forget that his own England future had seemed in doubt that spring. By autumn, however, he had been told 'You are in the moment of your life' by a senior member of Capello's management team. It was quite a turnaround, because now he had been the architect of two England goals at Wembley in an addition to his commanding display in Croatia.

Thanks to Lampard's telling deliveries, England felt able to relax. The problem for Ashley Cole was that he relaxed too much. Encouraged by Ferdinand to attempt a back-pass, Cole lazily hooked the ball straight into the path of Zhambyl Kukeyev, who rifled a stunning reply low past James to make it 2-1. Capello turned away in disgust, literally jumping with fury at Cole's carelessness. Later he made no apology for his extreme reaction to the setback. Fabio explained, 'I'm not an actor. That was the real me. I could see it was going to be a goal.'

But he couldn't have anticipated what he heard from a significant section of the crowd, the very next time the Chelsea left-back received the ball. The England fans began to boo Cole; not just once but every time he took possession for a good few minutes. Eventually the boo-boys were drowned out by fans who wanted to be more positive, and the change of mood was helped by Rooney's twisting header from Wes Brown's cross. That restored England's two-goal cushion at 3-1. However, the hostile reaction of the crowd towards Cole would dominate the headlines the next day. And almost overlooked was the fact that, after 78 minutes and 43 seconds of the match, some England history was made. In that moment Walcott was replaced by Beckham, and Goldenballs equalled Sir Bobby Charlton's record as the third-most capped player of all time with 106 appearances. Now Beckham was only two caps short of the late Bobby Moore on 108. David had come a long way since being dropped by Capello a year earlier at Real Madrid.

Fittingly, it was Beckham's 86th-minute free kick which allowed Upson to create a distraction in the Kazakhstan defence. Rooney seized the moment to notch his second and England's fourth. Capello knew the three points were safe now, and Rooney had been superb yet again. Playing in a more central role and just off Heskey in the second half, Wazza's double meant he had scored three England goals in two games. He might even have completed a hat-trick against Kazakhstan alone, had he not been substituted immediately after scoring his second. So it was Jermain Defoe who made an impact in the last minute instead, released to slot England's fifth thanks to some one-touch magic from Heskey. Kazakhstan had faded badly, clearly lacking endurance, and suddenly England's 5-1 looked like a romp. In reality it had been anything but; and the relationship between the players and fans was the hot topic for post-match debate.

A surprised Capello said, 'I don't understand why the crowd would boo Ashley, you have to help players more when they make a mistake.' Meanwhile captain Ferdinand suggested that the fans who reacted in that way 'should be ashamed of themselves.' Perhaps neither man understood quite how unpopular Ashley Cole was with some fans. The booing did seem counter-productive and excessively harsh though, coming as it did so soon after Croatia, where Cole had played his part well. In the end the fans had been well entertained, after all; and the bonus was that Croatia had only drawn against Ukraine, leaving England sitting pretty at the top of the qualification table. But England's victory had lacked something, and Steven Gerrard took some of the blame when the inquest was held. His international future seemed to hang in the balance over the next few days, as England prepared for the tricky challenge of an away qualifier in Belarus.

Captain for Capello's first match back in February, Gerrard was suddenly talking like a man trying to avoid the swing of the axe. As he reflected upon his latest failure to make a big impact in an England shirt, he said, 'I don't want a manager to give up on me for club or country – I want them to keep trying to improve me as a player. The Kazakhstan game was a bit frustrating. In the second half the manager asked me to be disciplined and try to change the play. I've had criticism that I haven't reproduced my club form for England. Sometimes I'm thinking about it too much and going out on the pitch trying too hard. Maybe I have to relax – but I've every confidence in this manager that he can improve my form.'

Then Gerrard addressed his recent claim that he had only played five times in his favourite position in 68 appearances for his country – a comment that had prompted Capello to reply publicly, 'He will play where I want him to play – always.' Gerrard was anxious to set the record straight and insisted, 'I was not complaining or having a dig. I had been asked how many times I'd been played in my favourite position for England compared to Liverpool and I gave an honest answer. It was a guess but if I'm in the starting eleven and asked to do a specific job by a manager, I will go out there and give it everything no matter where I'm asked to play.'

This was what the Capello camp wanted to hear; fewer excuses and more analysis in Gerrard's own head of what was going wrong. And because Joe Cole was still out injured, there was room for both Gerrard and Lampard to feature in England's midfield again in Belarus. Could Capello's perfect start – in terms of points at least – continue? Rio Ferdinand, who would captain the side again in Minsk, insisted that England were focused on achieving results like never before. He explained that under Sven Goran Eriksson, 'we became a bit of a circus in terms of the WAG [wives and girlfriends] situation. It seems like there was a big show around the England squad. This regime is very watertight. When Fabio came in it was very much, "I'm the boss and this is what happens."'

England would need a strong boss in Belarus. Fabio's opposite number, Bernd Stange, had always been a thorough gatherer of intelligence on the opposition. He had once been an informer for the Stasi, the notorious East German secret police. After that he had managed Iraq under Saddam Hussein's dark regime. So Stange was a formidable adversary; and Capello warned his players before the match that the first 20 minutes would be very important.

But the Belarus coach didn't seem to have prepared for the possibility that an English midfielder could seize upon the creative control of a teammate, in this case Wayne Rooney, and suddenly pass the ball into the net from 31.4 yards. That's what happened after 11 minutes, and the early hero was precisely the player whose England future appeared to be on the line – Steven Gerrard. The Liverpool captain had obeyed instructions to drift in from his starting position on the left and shoot on sight. His uncharacteristically wild celebration told the world how he felt about scoring for his country in such a big match.

It was a pity, therefore, that Gerrard still couldn't get a handle on his defensive duties. His confusion was apparently compounded by the nervousness of Wayne Bridge, deputising for hate figure Ashley Cole, who had cried off with a hamstring strain. Perhaps sensing a lack of communication between Gerrard and Bridge, Belarus completed an extraordinary 23-pass move, which allowed Igor Stasevich to pierce the left side of the English defence. He wrong-footed Bridge and teed up a simple chance for Pavel Sitko to equalise after 28 minutes. Capello clasped his hands, as if in prayer, and turned away in disgust, his mood not helped by the fact that Wes Brown had even appeared to duck as the Belarus player's cross came his way. Meanwhile Theo Walcott had let the goal-scorer run clear on the other side of the area. This defensive generosity wasn't what Capello expected of his players. But with Matthew Upson making up the back four, this just wasn't a first-choice defensive line-up, and perhaps we should have known there would be problems.

England were being out-passed, out-fought and out-thought in midfield. The interval gave Fabio a welcome chance to turn the tide. Frank Lampard hadn't imposed himself in the way we had expected, his chemistry with Gerrard remained less than encouraging, and Gareth Barry seemed strangely out of sorts in the anchor role. With Walcott and Gerrard stuck out wide, England had seemed outnumbered as Belarus charged through the middle. Once again it was time for Capello to bring out Plan B, though first Fabio simply warned his players that they weren't doing nearly enough when England didn't have the ball. Ferdinand later revealed what the Italian had told his men at half time. 'He just said push up from the back, get our midfielders onto their midfielders and keep competing. You think it's going to be rocket science because it's a foreign manager but he just keeps it simple.'

Not quite that simple. Capello gave Gerrrard a specific second-half mission – to neutralise the Belarus number two, Aleksandr Kulchy, and push forward behind Emile Heskey and Rooney when the time was right. Suddenly England had gone from a shaky 4-4-2 to a 4-3-3 shape, which suddenly looked far more purposeful than it had at Wembley a few days earlier. And even though Walcott wasn't firing on all cylinders, the beauty of the movement between Heskey and Rooney was breathtaking. Just five minutes after half time, Heskey produced explosive pace and mesmerising skill down the left to deliver a killer pass to Rooney. Wayne's timing and confidence in front of goal was a tribute to Capello's determination to add composure to his armoury, and turn Rooney into a top-notch finisher. All year it had appeared that England didn't have a striker, that they lacked a genuine goal-scorer. Now Heskey was showing that you didn't have to score goals to play up front to stunning effect; while Rooney was showing at last that you didn't have to be an out-and-out striker to score goals regularly.

So England were 2-1 ahead and back on top. And even when Peter Crouch came on for Heskey and Shaun Wright-Phillips replaced Walcott, the momentum was maintained. Gerrard showed his strength going forward yet again, and Rooney did the rest. With a brilliant dummy and more superb movement off the ball, Wayne made himself enough time and space to collect his fellow Merseysider's neat through ball. Within moments he had beaten the Belarus goalkeeper with nonchalant ease. Now England simply had to close out the game.

At 3-1, Capello yelled his favourite instruction: 'Pass, pass, pass.' England did just that, until, four minutes from time, Gerrard rounded the Belarus keeper and stared at an open goal. Unbelievably, he hit the post with a shot struck off the outside of his boot. 'For any school children who were watching,' he said with sheer class afterwards, 'I should have rolled it in with my left. You have to work on your weaker foot.' But the glaring miss hardly mattered. In the 88th minute, Rooney came off so that Beckham could win his 107th cap, thus beating Sir Bobby Charlton's total. One more appearance and Goldenballs would be equal with the late, great Bobby Moore, the only English captain to lift the World Cup. Whether Beckham could go one better than the legendary Moore to become the most capped outfielder in English history would depend on whether he could stay match fit for the 2009 qualifiers. That was why, in late 2008, there was already talk of him returning to Europe on loan, perhaps even with Capello's old club, AC Milan. Time would tell. But already in those dying seconds in Minsk, veteran Beckham's latest international cameo was part of an impossibly romantic sporting soap opera, one you couldn't help but admire and enjoy on a dramatic, human level, even if some of us didn't really think it should have happened.

Up in the stands, Brian Barwick, watching what was due to be his last competitive match as FA chief executive, chuckled heartily. Four successive wins in World Cup qualifying had never been achieved by an England manager before. Sir Alf Ramsey had achieved just such a run in qualifying for the 1972 European Championships. But now the coach Barwick had appointed, Fabio Capello, had done it in the build-up to the biggest tournament of them all. No wonder Barwick felt he was leaving England in good shape. Fabio's team were now five points clear of Ukraine and Croatia, with a vastly superior goal difference over both, after scoring 14 in four games. It felt like they had one foot in South Africa already.

Not that Capello was counting his chickens. 'No, no, no' he insisted, thumping his fist on the table for effect. 'Four wins doesn't mean anything yet. We need more victories if we are going to South Africa.' But the reporters still wanted to know what the secret had been to England's historic start to their World Cup campaign, especially after all the failure that had preceded it. 'No secret,' said Fabio modestly. 'It's just hard work, creating a group, a mentality with confidence.'

Rooney seemed to have more confidence than most, with five goals in his last three England internationals. He had always scored in fits and starts, but this time he seemed to think that something new was happening to him. 'This is the best I've ever played for England,' he said. 'Capello has added something to my game at international level. Since he took over he has helped me with my finishing. We have worked hard on it, and he has given me advice on movement and where the spaces are on the pitch. I'm already looking forward to meeting and working with him again so I can improve even more. If I can't learn off Capello, I might as well pack it in now.'

Rooney didn't say it, but it almost sounded as though Capello was having a greater impact on his game than Sir Alex Ferguson, the man Fabio had come so close to replacing at Old Trafford. At least Rooney's tribute to Capello was proof that he had begun to listen to the England manager, who could see the bigger picture tactically. It appeared that finally the Manchester United star had accepted that goal-scoring ought to be a bigger part of his game on the international stage. Rooney hadn't always been so humble in his dealings with the Capello camp. There had been some feisty exchanges behind the scenes between England's star player and the team management, especially when earlier matches hadn't gone according to plan. Sometimes it had seemed as though Rooney was stubbornly resisting attempts to shape his game to Capello's needs. Now that Wayne was thriving, however, he was complimentary – even thankful to Fabio. His goals had persuaded him stop arguing, or at least that is how it seemed. Whatever the reason, they were all on the same wavelength like never before. Rooney's Italian bosses didn't want to dwell on some of the tensions that had preceded Wayne's goal feast. They were just pleased with the breakthrough that had been made. And a modest Capello was happy to give all the credit to the player for his most prolific spell in an England shirt. Fabio said, 'Rooney is very, very important, he scores goals, he works a lot, he plays for the team; he is a fantastic player. I remember people saying "you have to wait for Rooney;" a lot of journalists criticised him. Now you have to change your opinion.'

We all hoped Fabio was right; that Rooney's work rate and emotional turbulence wouldn't prove to be his undoing in the end, as they had seemed to be in the past. At various times fatigue, indiscipline or injury had dulled his cutting edge. Wayne was still a 'second striker' rather than a true target man, and he was still covering every blade of grass on the pitch – Capello hadn't cured that exhausting habit. But perhaps Rooney's tendency to drop deep wasn't so alarming now that Capello had shown him how to time and plot his return to the danger zone.

Goalkeeper David James later revealed, 'We have even watched videos of the goals we have scored and the manager has complained about the players' runs. He has made it clear we should have done better. And it is not for the sake of moaning. It is because he has seen something and knows he can improve upon it. He is not frightened to criticise someone, which is a good thing in my book.'

Rooney seemed more ruthless than he had ever been before. If the Manchester United star could stay fit, and Fabio could tweak that troublesome midfield, perhaps England really could mount a serious assault on the World Cup. But hadn't we heard that somewhere before, during Eriksson's era? Were England becoming too dependent on Rooney again? And wouldn't Heskey be too old to play so well by the time South Africa came around? Capello appeared to have thought of all that too, because in the aftermath of the Belarus victory he announced, 'I will experiment with new players during the friendly matches to come. I might have to pick a player for a big match because someone is injured. I also have to think about the future.' Though he didn't have another qualification match to consider until April 2009, Capello was already covering all the bases. And as England completed their World Cup qualifying schedule for 2008, Fabio had plenty of reason to feel satisfied with his work. He had taken a team with precious little confidence, focus or identity, shaken them up with some sharp discipline and set them firmly on the right road for the finals. A year earlier, our national team looked to have fallen to pieces; and the first six months of the Capello era had appeared worrying too. But Fabio's results had been magnificent when it mattered, and therefore the feel-good factor had, by and large, returned. Capello had completed phase one of his World Cup mission in glorious style.

Fittingly, the England team flew back from Minsk to Luton on the same plane that had brought them back from Zagreb. They even had the same pilot, and the same generous offer of champagne. Capello and Baldini accepted the captain's offer again, as they had when they left Croatia, and this time there was a small celebration on the plane of what had been achieved so far. No one was allowed to get carried away or forget how long the difficult the road to South Africa would be; but you had to let people enjoy the moment to a certain extent when they had worked hard and done well.

There was more happiness on the horizon in Capello's family life too. Fabio's son Pierfilippo was looking forward to the birth of his first child, a baby girl who would be called Maria Laura after her two grandmothers. Another joyous occasion was keenly anticipated since Pierfilippo was due to marry his longstanding partner Tiziana in 2009. That development was likely to please Fabio and his wife Laura almost as much as the arrival of another grandchild; because in the spring of 2008 Pierfilippo had underlined to Sara Faillaci of *Vanity Fair* magazine his parents' very traditional views on marriage. He had explained, 'Neither my brother, who has two children, or I are married. We live with our partners, we are a beautiful family and we don't feel the need to get married. My father hasn't taken well to the idea. Both he and my mother are upset about it.' Pierfilippo later made it clear that his parents, Fabio and Laura, had always wanted their sons to be happy above all. Therefore the England manager and his wife would never have tried to pressure their children into marrying their partners. They had agreed to disagree on the question of marriage, and left it at that. Now Pierfilippo and his partner, Tiziana, had decided for themselves that the time was right to tie the knot. And they might just have had one eye on the England football schedule for 2009 as they selected a suitable moment for their happy day, since they wouldn't have wanted Fabio to miss their special occasion.

All in all, life looked good for Fabio Capello in the autumn of 2008. The critics in the media were off his back; and although members of the English public would always feel entitled to tell him how to do his job better, dealing with such advice had always been part of an England manager's lot. We tend to think we know better than the man in the hot seat. Deep down many of us yearned to be in Capello's shoes, picking the team. The closest I ever came was a surreal moment early in 2008, when a top member of 'Team Capello' asked me for my England starting eleven. When I laughed, he insisted it was a serious question and all ideas were welcome at that stage. You'll probably have your own team, so I won't bother to bore you with mine, though I don't mind saying that Theo Walcott was in and David Beckham wasn't. And even though the member of England's management team was probably trying to stifle a chuckle as he listened to the names and positions being 'announced' down the phone, I'm prepared to admit that the experience gave me a thrill of absurd proportions. I bet you would feel the same, given the opportunity to reveal your favourite England line-up to the men who matter. However, as I pointed out at the start of this journey though Capello's life, being in his shoes cannot always have been an easy experience, with so much expectation on his shoulders and the fans' anger ready to surface the moment something goes wrong.

It is easy for us to pick our England team, that is the fun part; but could you handle the pressure when that selection backfires? You could? Well, if you can convince the men who matter, there might just be an office waiting for you at the Football Association one day. On a multi-million-pound salary, you might get to live at a fancy London address somewhere near Sloane Square. You won't have to take the tube to work, because an FA car with tinted windows will pick you up and take you straight to Soho Square, just off Oxford Street in the heart of London's West End. All you will have to do is open the car door at the other end (you could wait for it to be opened for you, but that might be going too far!) and walk a few steps into the FA building. There you will probably want to say a warm hello to the two attractive ladies who will be waiting to greet you at reception. Then you can walk round to the lift and go up to the fourth floor. In no time at all you will step out, turn right and walk into a large, open plan working environment. But don't worry; your employers know that you require more privacy than that. You are not part of the open-plan set-up, strictly speaking, because you have your own large office with a door you can close. Colleagues can see you through the glass, and you can see them, but enough privacy exists to keep your decisions secret until you are ready to announce them to the outside world. This is your space and there is plenty of it; so step in and close the door behind you, England manager.

On the walls you see pictures of England players from all levels, not just the senior team. Superstars are not worshipped here; you will find no individual portrait of David Beckham staring down at you. But would you like to make any alterations? Depending on how good your geography is in relation to your own country, you may want to take down some of the maps on the walls. That's entirely up to you, of course. Similarly you can either have two desks in your office, as your predecessor, Mr Fabio Capello, preferred, or you can go it alone and have just one. That will make the office look even bigger, and you might just feel even more important. Fabio liked to have his trusted assistant, Franco Baldini, close to hand though, so Franco had a desk in the office too.

It is your call whether or not to keep the table in your office, though it might be advisable. It is not too big to make the place feel cramped, but pretty useful if four or five people come in for a confidential chat. They might want to take notes when you are speaking, or have somewhere to put the drinks an FA secretary will probably be kind enough to fix for them. Don't isolate yourself too much, now. It can be lonely at the top. So there you are; settling in nicely? It's a lovely dream, isn't it, to be the king (or queen!) of English football.

But don't start dreaming about succeeding Capello just yet because, at the time of writing, he had unfinished business and South Africa on his mind. What happened after that was another matter, because Capello had caused controversy in July 2008 by allegedly suggesting to an Italian newspaper that he would leave England after the World Cup. Asked if that tournament would represent his last great challenge and bring the curtain down on his coaching career, he had allegedly replied: 'This is certain.' Fabio back-tracked quickly in the days after that interview, claiming that he had misunderstood the question and that he fully intended to continue in his post through to 2012. Even so, in the aftermath of the Belarus win, the Sunday newspapers were full of stories suggesting that Fabio would quit if he won the World Cup.

Maybe he would do that if he won the trophy itself; but two separate sources very close to Capello told me that they believed he would want to stay on and see out his contract after South Africa 2010. The job, they explained, was simply too prestigious for Fabio to leave so easily after the World Cup.

First England had to get there. If Fabio's team didn't make it to the World Cup, a clause in his deal gave the Football Association the right to tear up the final two years of Capello's contract, without paying him a penny in compensation on his £6 million annual salary. It was brave of Capello to have allowed such a clause during the negotiations in late 2007. His faith in his own ability stood to cost him more than £12 million if games didn't go his way.

If England reached South Africa but the FA were not satisfied with results at the tournament, they could still terminate the remainder of Capello's contract. But they knew they would have to act quickly if they wished to wield the axe, because a clause stated that they only had a window of a very short time after the finals in which to give Capello the boot. And if they were to use that moment to show Fabio the door with a polite thank you for services rendered, the FA also knew they would have to stump up a 'penalty payment', call it compensation if you like, though my understanding was that they wouldn't need to find the full salary they had been paying Fabio in order to make a clean break. If Capello took that undisclosed sum as he walked out of the door, he wouldn't be able to work elsewhere for a certain period of time either. By taking another job in football, he would lose the money England had given him as part of the farewell.

The question was this: what would constitute underperforming at the World Cup in the FA's eyes? Would failure to reach the quarter-finals put Fabio in jeopardy? A semi-final place would surely protect his future; so it seemed conceivable that even the manner of a quarter-final defeat might tip the balance either way. There was a fine line between success and failure in any knockout tournament, which is what made the clause in Fabio's contract so extraordinary. For Capello, however, the only real measure of success would be winning the trophy itself.

Perhaps that was why Sir Bobby Charlton, an England World Cup winner from 1966, compared Capello to the man who had masterminded that solitary, historic triumph more than four decades earlier. 'Capello is direct and sure of himself. He knows what he wants. He reminds me of Sir Alf Ramsey. I don't think he will confuse players for a minute, no more than Alf did. He will let them know what he wants and he makes it clear when he is not satisfied.'

One thing seemed to satisfy Capello more than any other – winning. Fabio shared Sir Alf's disdain for potential complications or distractions; he wanted to win the World Cup and fully believed that he could achieve his goal. But if he did succeed in emulating Sir Alf, would Capello then prefer to walk away in a blaze of glory? Even though there was no 'escape clause' in Fabio's contract for any stage of his England tenure, there could be little doubt that his feelings would be respected, and an amicable solution found, if he really wanted to call it a day straight after South Africa. Quitting at the very top of world football would be neat and dramatic, though it would beg an awkward question: what would he do next? Sources close to Capello suggested that, at 64, he would be far too young and active mentally to be content with retirement. Club football might still be an option, though top jobs in club football only became available every so often. Besides, few if any would carry the kudos that went with the England job. That's why those who knew Capello best didn't think he would find it so easy to relinquish his post prematurely, and thought he might stay the course until Euro 2012 after all, if his employers wanted him to do so.

It was always tricky trying to predict the future. The focus was on World Cup 2010; beyond that, the future would take care of itself. Was glory for England in South Africa just a dream? Maybe so. But then again, victory in Croatia had felt like a dream . . . and yet it really happened. Dreaming is half the fun anyway, isn't it? That's why Capello had already achieved the first part of his mission by the end of his first year in charge, simply by giving England fans reason to start dreaming about the big one again. Confidence had made anything seem possible.

Anything that added to the growing sense of optimism was welcome. So I couldn't resist putting in a call to Don Pierpaolo Soranzo, Mamma Capello's amiable priest in Fabio's home village of Pieris, to see what he made of the story so far. It was the day after England had beaten Belarus in Minsk. 'Four successive victories in qualification?' he asked, seeking confirmation. 'I was listening to the story on the radio last night. Fabio has certainly brought a breath of fresh air to the England team.' Was Don Paolo's own dream, of having a second World Cup winner among his flock, about to come true? 'Let's hope so,' he answered breezily. 'Fabio certainly has a winning habit.' Don Paolo always made it sound as though important England victories under Capello were meant to be. Then he let me in on a little secret. 'I met Fabio in the summer,' he began. 'We spoke a little and I told him how Enzo Bearzot had been a member of my congregation when he won the World Cup for Italy in 1982. You should have seen the smile on Fabio's face when I mentioned it.'

Hadn't Fabio made this connection between his mother's priest and World Cup glory after a 44-year wait? Apparently not; so Capello had returned from his brief summer holidays with a fresh reason to feel buoyant. Even before World Cup qualification had begun, the signs had been good. Was it England's turn to end 44 years of hurt? If only the 'man upstairs' could be persuaded to see it that way . . .

'What a pity that God doesn't take sides in sport and you can't pray for England,' I said to Don Paolo, reminding him of what he had told me a few months earlier.

'The Lord watches matches from above,' Don Paolo suggested, almost reassuringly. 'And I pray that Fabio does well in his work, that he is happy.'

Make of that what you will – I certainly did. Praying for Fabio's success at work could only mean one thing. Don Paolo, the priest with the World Cup 'previous' was praying for Capello's England after all, as the Three Lions marched towards South Africa. The rest was down to the players, and a very strong-willed coach who firmly intended to lead England all the way to the Soccer City Stadium, Johannesburg, on 11 July, 2010. You could picture it already, starting with the team talk. . . .